Textiles
5,000 Years

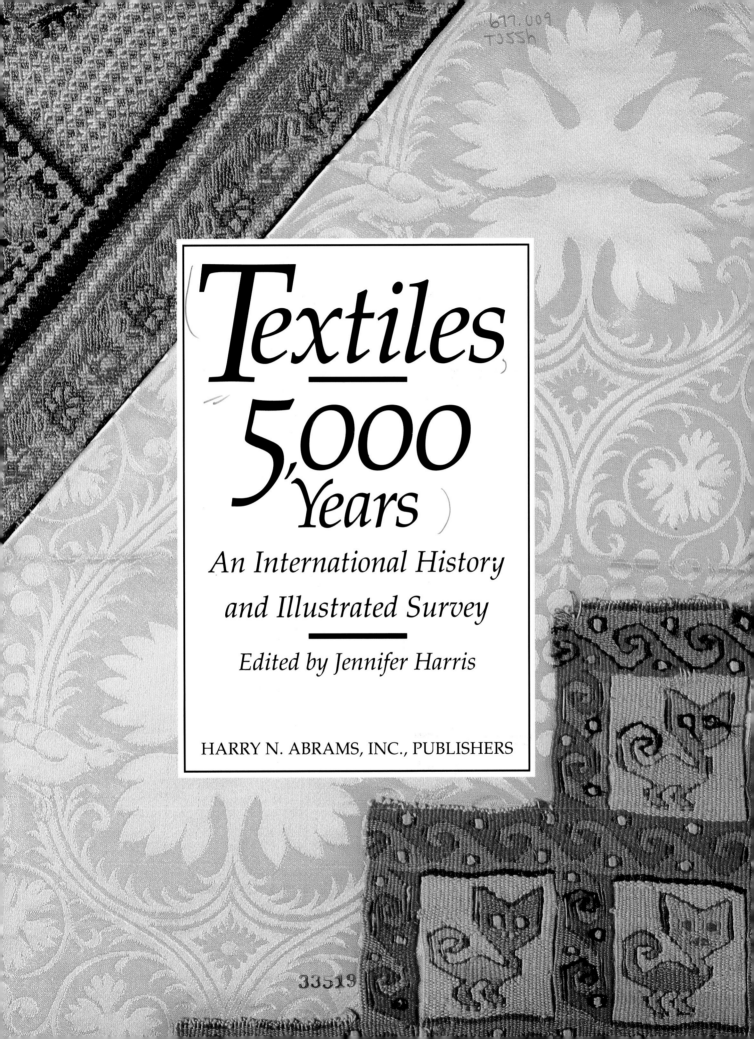

Textiles

5,000 Years

An International History
and Illustrated Survey

Edited by Jennifer Harris

HARRY N. ABRAMS, INC., PUBLISHERS

PREVIOUS PAGES Details of (*from left*) silk embroidered lady's trousering from Iran, 18th century; silk damask, early 20th-century reproduction of a 16th-century Italian silk, manufactured by Warner & Sons; slit tapestry fragment from Peru, central coast, 15th century.

RIGHT Detail of a lady's petticoat, painted and printed cotton. Made in India for the European market, 1750–55 (see II,11).

Library of Congress Cataloging-in-Publication Data

Textiles, 5,000 years : an international history and illustrated survey / edited by Jennifer Harris.
    p. cm.
  Includes bibliographical references and index.
  ISBN 0-8109-3875-8
  1. Textile fabrics—History.
  I. Harris, Jennifer.
NK8806.T45   1993
746'.09—dc20   93-16980
             CIP

Published in 1993 by Harry N. Abrams, Incorporated, New York
A Times Mirror Company

First published in Great Britain in 1993 by British Museum Press, London, in association with The Whitworth Art Gallery, University of Manchester, and the Victoria and Albert Museum, London

Designed by Harry Green
Maps drawn by Technical Art Services
Printed and bound in Hong Kong

Contents

List of contributors

EDITOR: JENNIFER HARRIS is Curator of Textiles and Deputy Director at the Whitworth Art Gallery, University of Manchester. She has published many articles and catalogues on fashion and textile subjects, and has curated several major exhibitions, including 'William Morris and the Middle Ages' (1984) and 'The Subversive Stitch: Embroidery in Women's Lives 1300–1900' (1988).

PATRICIA L. BAKER wrote her doctoral thesis on Islamic court dress. A former lecturer in art history, she teaches on the SOAS (London University)/ Sotheby's Asian Arts course and is writing a book on Islamic textiles for British Museum Press.

PENNY BATEMAN previously worked as a curator at the Museum of Mankind, London. She has carried out fieldwork in the Andes of Peru, acquiring contemporary textiles and pottery for the Museum. She now works in the British Museum Education Service.

SUSAN-MARIE BEST is a freelance lecturer, author and consultant on Japanese art and design, specialising in fashion and textiles.

THOMAS CAMPBELL is the founder and archivist of the S. Franses Tapestry Research Archive, London. He lectures regularly on European tapestries of all periods, and is researching a doctoral thesis on 16th-century tapestry collections.

SYLVIA FRASER-LU has written widely on Asian arts and crafts in the twenty years she has lived and worked in South-East Asia. Her publications include *Indonesian Batik: Processes, Patterns and Places* (1986) and *Handwoven Textiles of South-East Asia* (1988).

MARGARET HALL trained originally as a book illustrator but, since 1962, has worked almost continuously with John Irwin, Keeper of the Indian Department of the Victoria and Albert Museum, London, until 1978. Their published work includes *Indian Painted and Printed Fabrics* (1971) and *Indian Embroideries* (1973).

JACQUELINE HERALD is a freelance writer and lecturer in the history of fashion and textiles. Her publications include *Renaissance Dress in Italy 1400–1500* (1981), *Fashions of a Decade: The 1970s* (1992), and *World Crafts* (1992). She is currently preparing a book (with Susan Conway) on Indian textiles for British Museum Press.

SANTINA M. LEVEY worked in the Textiles Department of the Victoria and Albert Museum, London, specialising in European embroidery and lace, and was Keeper of the department from 1981 to 1989. Author of the standard work on lace, *Lace: A History* (1983), and many articles and catalogues, she now works as a freelance textile historian.

JOHN MACK is Keeper of the Museum of Mankind, London. His specialist interest is in the arts and cultures of central, eastern and southern Africa. His publications include *African Textiles* (with John Picton, 1991) and *Malagasy Textiles* (1989).

JOAN ALLGROVE McDOWELL (1928–91) was Curator of Textiles at the Whitworth Art Gallery, University of Manchester, from 1960 to 1981, specialising in ancient and Islamic textiles. Forced through ill health to take early retirement, she continued to lecture and publish until her death in early 1991.

LESLEY MILLER wrote her doctoral thesis on designers in the 18th-century Lyons silk industry. She is Senior Lecturer in Design History at Winchester School of Art and has recently published a book on Balenciaga (1993).

LISA MONNAS worked for four years in the Far Eastern Department of the Victoria and Albert Museum, London. She is currently preparing her doctoral thesis on Italian patterned silk fabrics from 1300 to 1500, and has published several articles.

ANNA MUTHESIUS is Fellow Commoner at Lucy Cavendish College, University of Cambridge, and Senior Lecturer in Textile History at the Surrey Institute of Art and Design. She has published extensively on the Byzantine silk industry AD 400–1200.

CHLOË SAYER is the author of several books on Mexico, including *Mexican Textiles* (1990) and *The Arts and Crafts of Mexico* (1990), and has carried out fieldwork for the Museum of Mankind, London.

MARY SCHOESER was educated in North America and the UK. A freelance textile historian, her publications include *Fabrics and Wallpapers* (1986), *English and American Textiles* (1989) and *French Textiles* (1991). She has curated many exhibitions, including Warner Fabrics plc, the Museum of London and the Crafts Council, London.

CAROLINE STONE is the author of *The Embroideries of North Africa* (1985). She lives and works in Spain.

COLIN and BETTY TAYLOR have researched many aspects of North American Indian material culture in the world's ethnographical collections. Dr Colin Taylor is Senior Lecturer at Hastings College of Arts and Technology, and has lectured and published extensively on the arts of the Plains Indians.

RODERICK R. TAYLOR is a management consultant specialising in international business strategy, and the author of *Ottoman Embroidery* (1993).

JENNIFER WEARDEN is Assistant Curator in the Textiles and Dress Collection of the Victoria and Albert Museum, London, specialising in east European and post-1500 Islamic textiles.

SHELAGH WEIR is Assistant Keeper at the Museum of Mankind, London, and the author of *Spinning and Weaving in Palestine* (1970), *Palestinian Embroidery* (1970) and *Palestinian Costume* (1990).

JOHN-PETER WILD is Senior Lecturer in Archaeology and a Director of the Ancient Textile Unit at the University of Manchester. An authority on archaeological textiles, particularly of the Roman period, he is the author of two books and numerous articles on early textile technology.

VERITY WILSON is Assistant Curator of the Far Eastern Collection at the Victoria and Albert Museum, London, and the author of *Chinese Dress* (1986).

Preface

The history of textiles is a wide-ranging subject which may embrace the study of archaeology, anthropology, social and economic history, and art and design history. Textile historians may be involved with any of these disciplines, and elements of the different approaches peculiar to them are to be found in the present volume, which reflects the varied backgrounds of the many authors who have contributed. It has meant, inevitably, some sacrifice of unity of approach and attitude, but what is gained in its place is, I believe, a wealth of varied expertise and some idea of the multi-faceted nature of the subject.

Twenty-four authors have contributed, all of them acknowledged experts in their field. They have been aware throughout of the necessary constraints imposed in trying to convey something of the complexity of their given areas of expertise concisely and in such a way as to entice readers, perhaps coming to the subject for the first time, to explore it further. This can be done through the works listed as further reading and by visiting specialist museum collections of textiles, many of which are noted in the illustration acknowledgements. Without making claims for this book as an exhaustive survey, we believe that it offers a more comprehensive and authoritative introduction to the history of textiles than has so far been available.

A number of people are owed my thanks for helping to make the book possible. My main debt of gratitude is to all the contributors. A survey of world textiles is not a task which I would have had the temerity to consider writing single-handedly, and the book would simply not have happened without their enthusiasm for and belief in the project. Tragically, Joan Allgrove McDowell, who had undertaken to contribute several chapters, died suddenly dur-ing the writing of them. It was the only time that I had worked with Joan, who was my predecessor as Curator of Textiles at the Whitworth Art Gallery, and she had generously given up much time to discuss with me some of the general issues surrounding the organisation of the book. Her wide-ranging knowledge of textiles is at least partly reflected in her contributions, which I hope stand as a fitting tribute to her scholarship and genuine love of the subject. Equally, I am greatly in debt to Jennifer Wearden and Patricia Baker for taking over those sections on Central Asian textiles and carpets which Joan had been unable to complete. I was astonished at and grateful for the speed and efficiency with which they produced their excellent chapters to meet an incredibly tight deadline.

I should like to thank the University of Manchester for granting the study leave in which to assemble and edit the book, and my colleagues at the Whitworth Art Gallery for holding the fort whilst I took my leave, especially Maude Wallace. A special note of thanks goes to Sue Mortimer for practical help on the word processor and for innumerable other kindnesses whilst the book was being written. I should also like to express my appreciation of the patience and imagination shown by Peter Burton and Michael Pollard, of the History of Art Department at the University, in producing many new photographs of textiles from the Whitworth's collection.

I have been assisted admirably at the British Museum Press by Deborah Wakeling and Nina Shandloff, who have been exemplary as editors and founts of publishing wisdom. I hold myself responsible, as academic editor, for any shortcomings in the conception and organisation of the book.

JENNIFER HARRIS

Introduction

This book depends for its subject-matter on the chance survival through the centuries of materials inherently prone to decay. Textiles are made to be used primarily as furnishings and dress, and are expected to wear out and eventually be discarded. It is for this reason that books like this are essentially histories of decorated textiles, since the ordinary or the everyday will rarely survive the lifetime of its user. In the major museum collections of the world christening robes, wedding dresses, festival garments, dowry items – in other words the special or the extraordinary made to be worn or used on only a few occasions – form a disproportionate percentage of the holdings. Thus museum displays of historical textiles and, to a great extent, written histories of the subject, which tend to draw heavily on them for their illustrative materials and research, can only ever provide a partial picture.

Britain, for example, had an important woollen industry from the medieval period but, in comparison with embroidered items, little survives, having succumbed either to the ravages of clothes' moth or been discarded as undecorated and thus not precious. And where plain cloths have survived in any number over a long period, as in the Egyptian burial grounds, these were often pillaged for the more decorative tapestry-woven ornaments on them and then tossed aside.

Textiles begin to deteriorate from the moment they are made, and even those chance survivals which make up the story of this book will have been subjected to some environmental damage. Those which were in constant use will almost certainly have suffered from exposure to light, particularly the ultraviolet rays present in both daylight and in artificial light. The greatest enemy of textiles of all kinds, light not only fades the dyes but also embrittles and thus weakens the actual structure of the fibres themselves, hastening disintegration. Climate has a similarly detrimental effect on textiles. Silk will become brittle in dry heat, whilst a humid atmosphere will rot fibres and cause mould to grow and fugitive dyes to 'bleed' into surrounding areas of cloth. When one further considers the damage

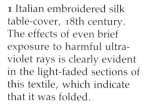

1 Italian embroidered silk table-cover, 18th century. The effects of even brief exposure to harmful ultraviolet rays is clearly evident in the light-faded sections of this textile, which indicate that it was folded.

greatest variety of textiles covering a long period of time. They include abundant quantities of plain linen from the Pharaonic period, decorated wool and linen dating from the Romano–Egyptian period right up to the eleventh and twelfth centuries AD (which include complete articles of clothing and accessories), and even silks, imported from Persia and Syria as well as of local manufacture. In South America, too, the sand of desert graves in the dry coastal areas of northern Peru has preserved a great many ancient textiles, again offering a more complete picture of the culture's achievements in the textile arts than is possible at even very much later periods in other parts of the world.

Very low temperatures have also proved an excellent means of conservation. In northern Mongolia and the Central Asian steppes important textile finds dating back to the fifth

ABOVE 2 William Morris, 'Kennet' woven silk curtains. Design registered 1883, fabric purchased c. 1915. Abrasion, caused by constant handling of the edges of these curtains when opening and drawing them, has reduced the silk to shreds.

ABOVE RIGHT 3 Part of a large plain-weave linen cover with tapestry-woven wool border, Egypt. Roman, late 3rd century AD. The bright colours in this textile fragment, excavated in the late 19th century from a Romano-Egyptian sand burial, are astonishing considering its age.

done to fibres by dust and attacks by clothes' moths and other pests, one begins to wonder that so many textiles have survived at all.

In comparison with objects of metal, stone, pottery or glass textiles represent only a small proportion of excavated material. In damp soil the vegetable fibres of which many textiles are made disintegrate entirely, although occasionally the copper salts from oxidised bronze or silver objects pinned to articles of clothing will act to preserve small fragments of cloth from decay. Nevertheless, special circumstances in several different parts of the world have meant that some textiles have been preserved over extraordinarily long periods of time.

The dry, dark and sterile sands of the desert have provided some of the best conditions for the survival of textile items. The Egyptian burial grounds have yielded the largest number and

century BC were recovered earlier this century from the frozen tombs of nomadic chieftains who dominated that area over a long period. Other fortuitous survivals include the textiles recovered from bogs in Scandinavia where it is thought that hermetic sealing from air, constant humidity and, possibly, the presence of methane combined to ensure their preservation over many centuries. As in Egypt, the bog finds include entire garments, ranging in date from the Bronze Age to the late medieval period.

Such excavations point to a considerable commercial interchange of textile products from a very early date. There is archaeological evidence of Middle Eastern trade as early as the second millennium BC, which formed the foundation of later trade around the eastern Mediterranean during the Hellenistic and Roman periods. In the course of time this embraced the whole area

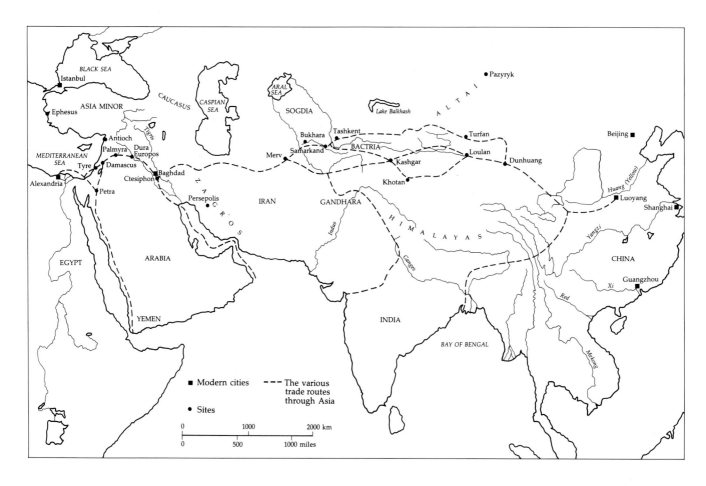

Map 1 The Silk Road.

from Egypt and Anatolia across Mesopotamia to Persia.

Textiles were easy to transport and soon became a primary medium of exchange in more long-distance trade. The overland routes between the Far East and the West were opened up a century or so before the Christian era, bringing China, Japan, Central Asia, India, the Middle East and all of Europe into contact. This Silk Road (see map 1) was in reality a number of trading routes through the deserts and mountains of Asia which conveyed silk, spices and other commodities from China to major Western markets such as Dura-Europos and Palmyra in Syria. Much later, from about 1500, the Spanish and Portuguese, followed by the English, Dutch and French a century later, began to trade with the East Indies by the sea route round the coast of Africa, increasing the demand for oriental goods among the western European nations.

It goes almost without saying that textile design reflects trading history. Egyptian textiles from the sixth and seventh centuries AD employ motifs borrowed from Persian silks. Many oriental silks are mentioned in medieval European church inventories, and Italian silks of the fourteenth century were clearly influenced by the motifs on Chinese silks (see II, 18). The influence

of the textile trade with India is evident throughout Indonesia, whilst the impact of Indian textiles on European textile design after the setting up of the various East India Companies is reflected in the many Indo-European motifs which have become part of the textile designer's repertory in the West (see II, 11 and 26). Many more examples of the influence of trade upon textile design are given in the chapters which follow.

These patterns of trade and distribution have largely dictated the organisation of this book. The first section is a survey of the main textile techniques, with some indication of their earliest appearance and distribution in the different cultures covered by the survey of world textiles which follows. In the latter the countries of the eastern Mediterranean and the Middle East are discussed first since many of the world's earliest-surviving textiles come from this area, which was also at the centre of some of the earliest trade routes. The textiles of India and the Far East are covered next since, again, very early textiles are known from China in particular and because the various trading routes across Asia described above brought them into relatively early contact with western Asia and Europe. The Americas and sub-Saharan Africa are placed last since those continents remained more isolated

10

4 Square pictorial badges displayed on the front and back of the surcoat (RIGHT), which was a required item of dress in the Chinese imperial wardrobe, identified the various official ranks at the imperial court. The golden pheasant (BELOW) denotes a second-rank civil servant.

geographically, although it is in South America that some of the earliest and technically most complex textiles have survived.

The role and function of textiles in any society is both general and specific. While textiles serve the everyday needs of people, literally from birth to death, they may also serve to distinguish individuals, and groups of individuals, in terms of social class, gender, occupation and status within the group. Textiles might be worn or displayed in an emblematic way, or their patterns might communicate such information.

In the hierarchical societies of Oceania differences in the quality and decoration of clothing denoted the social rank of the wearer. The *tiputas* (poncho-like garments) of chieftains and nobles consisted of paper-thin layers of *tapa* cloth (bark of paper-mulberry tree) felted and pasted together with a very fine, bleached top layer which was then decorated, whereas those of lower rank were obliged to wear undecorated *tiputas*. Red- and yellow-dyed *tapa* was also a prerogative of the higher ranks of society. Similarly, in the later years of imperial China embroidery on official robes functioned as a means of advertising status and authority within the

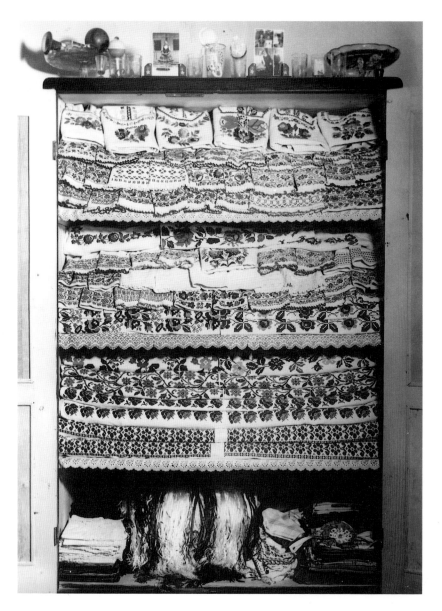

5 Linen cupboard packed with trousseau textiles, Slovakia. The bride would have spent much of her childhood and adolescence making these, while others would have been inherited from or made by her mother.

had meaning, and the wearer was expected to select a cloth appropriate to the occasion. These meanings are now largely lost, although the traditional patterns continue to be used.

Schuyler Camman (1972), in a lengthy survey of the symbolism in Islamic rug patterns, made an ambitious attempt to recover some of these specific meanings. He argues that the whole field pattern on many Persian rugs represents the Universe, or man's vision of the Universe, in flat form. The endlessly repeating patterns of the central field, which appear to run on under the borders and which sometimes seem asymmetric to Western eyes, he relates to the concept of endlessness (Infinity) in Islamic thought, whilst the rhythmically recurring elements of the border patterns suggest the orderly progress of time. In other words together they depict a combination of the finite and the infinite, the temporal and the spiritual, and thus represent a microcosm of the Universe.

Because textiles can have real as well as symbolic value they have often been used by those in power. Worn or displayed in quantity to indicate opulence and prosperity and to fill spectators with awe, they have also been distributed in pursuance of diplomatic ends, to attract or retain the loyalty of other rulers and regimes. Under the Byzantine emperors silk was a powerful political tool: a foreign government out of favour might be denied trading privileges, whilst another might be rewarded (or bribed) with precious and highly coveted silks (see II, 6). In Peru the Inca emperors required their subjects to produce cloth as tribute, which they then distributed to their army or used as gifts.

In many societies textiles have played a vital role in the social, economic and religious life of the community. They are essential accoutrements in all major life-cycle ceremonies such as births, weddings and funerals, when they are either bestowed as gifts, exchanged, burned, buried, or passed on to the next generation as the substance of dynasty. Mattiebelle Gittinger (1979) has explored at length the ritual use of textiles in Indonesia, which is also considered by Sylvia Fraser-Lu in this volume (II, 16).

In many parts of Europe and Asia a girl would spend months, if not years, preparing clothing and furnishing textiles for her trousseau, often displaying the contents publicly before the wedding to demonstrate both her skills as a needlewoman and the textile wealth she was bringing to the marriage (II, 10, 16, 27 and 28). The marriage ceremony itself would be marked by a ritual exchange of cloth by both parties, whilst the marriage suit or dress acquired quasi-sacred status. Worn subsequently for festivals and other special occasions, the marriage shirt or *chemise* was in some areas set aside for later use

court hierarchy. Official dress was rigidly controlled, and badges of rank worn at the centre of the back and on the front of the surcoat identified one's specific rank in either the military or civil hierarchy.

In South-East Asia textiles not only defined the status of the individual, but the layout of patterns might also denote family lineage and clan identity (see II, 16). Indeed, there was hardly any such thing in traditional societies as an object of daily life decorated merely for ornament and without some meaning. Designs tend to have a specific meaning for a particular ethnic group alone, however, and it was assumed that everyone within the group knew them; but once their meanings have been lost, it can become extremely difficult, if not impossible, for those outside the culture to reconstruct them. In Javanese batiks, for example, the motifs originally

as a funeral shroud. The consummation of the marriage brought its own cloth rituals, the most common being the public display of a shift or wedding sheet stained with blood to prove the girl's virginity, as in the Greek Islands. In North Africa belts are an important part of the marriage gifts and are ritually knotted or unknotted at weddings, in childbirth, at circumcisions and in mourning (II, 32).

Death and mourning have involved almost as many rituals using cloth. Some cultures have seen cloth as, literally, a thread binding the generations. The people of Madagascar produce fine silk burial cloths for reshrouding the exhumed corpses of their ancestors, hoping to please the latter and thereby ensure for themselves a continuing flow of good fortune (II, 33). In Hawaii and Tahiti inaugural regalia, in the form of feathered cloaks and girdles, were passed from generation to generation as the embodiment of power, in much the same way that regalia of office have been used in the royal families of Europe to transmit ideas of sanctity and majesty as well as status.

The introduction of a capitalist production system in so many parts of the world during the past two centuries has radically reordered the role of textiles in society. Jane Schneider and Annette Weiner, in a recent anthology, *Cloth and Human Experience* (1989, p. 11), suggest that, firstly, it eliminates the opportunity for textile producers (spinners, weavers, dyers, and so on) to infuse what they produce with spiritual value. Secondly, in requiring endless variation and rapid turnover capitalism has encouraged the growth of the modern fashion system, so that dress has now become the predominant means of expression.

Finally, the question of gender in the production of textiles is an issue which is raised in a number of the chapters in this book. Broadly speaking, women have played a far larger role than men in making textiles, and in some societies, such as those of South-East Asia, textiles are seen as specifically female goods. Schneider and Weiner (1989, pp. 23–4) point out that in societies where women are the main producers of textiles and control their distribution too they wield considerable power in social and political life, whereas under capitalism their contribution to textile wealth has been devalued.

There are, however, many instances of men being the main or predominant producers of textiles. In much of Africa, for example, it is men rather than women, or men as well as women, who produce both woven and dyed textiles and embroidery. Also in many urban or courtly textile traditions it was often men who were the main producers, examples being Asian rug weaving (workshop, not tribal rugs) and Euro-

pean tapestry. Nevertheless, a recurring distinction is that men make textiles professionally, for sale, whilst women's production is mainly domestic, although there have always been some women who enjoyed professional status or who were obliged to sell the fruits of their labour in order to survive.

There will be found within the pages of this book some suggestion of the many ways that textile history may be approached and its artefacts interpreted. A major component of material culture, textiles may be viewed as the products of technology, as cultural symbols, as works of art, and as items of trade. Indeed, the textile arts represent a fundamental human activity, as well as expressing symbolically much that is of value in any society.

I

A
Survey
of
Textile
Techniques

1 Weaving

A woven structure consists of two sets of threads, the warp and the weft, which are interlaced to form cloth. The warp threads are held parallel to each other and under tension, while the weft is worked over and under them, row by row. Weaving is the most universal construction method and probably developed some time before 6000 BC, when early neolithic peoples began to settle in permanent dwellings and to farm and domesticate animals. Indeed, in its simplest form weaving possibly pre-dated spinning, since early cultures doubtless interlaced with their fingers long fibrous stems (essentially basketwork) before they learned to convert short fibres into continuous yarn.

Weaving involves three basic operations. First, some of the warp threads are lifted to form a shed, which is the triangular space created between the warps that are up and those that are down. For example, in the case of plain weave, simple 'over one, under one' interlacing, half the warps are up and half down, and alternate warps are raised each time the shed is changed. Secondly, the weft, which is generally wound on to some sort of shuttle to speed the process, is passed through the shed. Finally, the weft is beaten or packed even with a comb.

Looms

The loom is the device for keeping the warp threads evenly spaced and under tension. Really very complex work can be produced on the simplest of looms, and, broadly speaking, developments in loom design have served the dual purpose of making certain processes easier and of increasing the speed with which they could be accomplished. The earliest looms of which we have knowledge are those of the Egyptians: a horizontal or ground loom (where the warps lie parallel with the ground) is depicted on Egyptian pottery of the pre-Dynastic period (c. 5000–3100 BC), and a vertical or upright loom is shown in tomb paintings from the Twelfth Dynasty onwards (c. 1900 BC).

The body-tension loom

The simplest loom is the backstrap or body-tension loom. Ancient in origin, it is still important in South and Central America and in many parts of South-East Asia (see 11, 16 and 31). At one end the warps are attached to a fixed beam or post and at the other to a breast beam held to the weaver's body by a belt or strap. The warp is held at an angle of about forty degrees to the ground, and the weaver controls the tension of the threads through the movement of his or her own body. Weaving proceeds away from the weaver towards the fixed warp beam. Cloth woven on a backstrap loom tends to be on a small scale since it is not possible to make a continuous length of cloth by rolling a long warp on the back beam. Although simple, the backstrap loom has been used to produce an enormous variety of complex weave structures (see 11, 31).

The warp-weighted loom

Also ancient in origin, the warp-weighted loom is closely associated with Greek wool weaving, appearing in illustrations on Greek vases from the sixth to fourth centuries BC. It was also the most commonly used type of loom in northern Europe before the Roman conquest and was still in use in Scandinavia and Iceland until recently. Another simple structure, two wooden uprights placed at an angle against a wall hold a horizontal beam which revolved to store the finished cloth. A set of odd-numbered warps, loosened and tied to weights made of baked clay or stone, was hung vertically behind a fixed shed rod. The even-numbered warps, also weighted, hung in front. To reverse the process the warps hanging behind the shed rod were attached by loops of thread (leashes) to another stick, which enabled them to be pulled forward to form a second shed, or countershed, in front of the other set. This device, known as a heddle, was placed between the shed stick and the finished cloth.

The warp-weighted loom generally required two weavers, standing, to manipulate the heddle rod and pass the weft. Beating the weft up against gravity made the task more difficult. During the early centuries of the Christian era the warp-weighted loom was gradually replaced by the vertical and horizontal loom.

7 Horizontal ground-loom depicted on a bowl found at Badari, central Egypt, c. 4000 BC.

ABOVE **8** Warp-weighted loom depicted on a Boeotian skyphos, Greece, 4th century BC.

RIGHT **9** Tomb model of a weaving workshop, with a horizontal loom, from Upper Egypt, Middle Kingdom period.

covery of some very long pieces of linen at Egyptian burial sites indicates that the Egyptians may have used roller beams.

A form of the horizontal loom is still used today by the Bedouin and other nomadic weavers of the Middle East, Pakistan and North Africa. The beams and sticks can be easily dismantled and packed for transport.

The two-beam, vertical loom

In the two-beam, vertical loom a lower beam takes the place of the weights in the warp-weighted loom and is used for rolling up the finished cloth. The weavers could therefore sit in front of the loom, always working from the same place, and beat the weft down instead of up. A two-beam, vertical loom appears in many wall-paintings of Twelfth Dynasty Egypt (*c.* 1900 BC) and is markedly similar to the vertical tapestry and rug looms still used today in Africa, Greece, the Near East and by the Navajo Indians of the American south-west.

FAR RIGHT ABOVE **10** Bedouin ground-loom.

FAR RIGHT **11** Drawing of a vertical loom as depicted on a wall-painting from the tomb of Thotnefer at Thebes, Egypt, *c.* 1500 BC.

The horizontal, ground loom

Used for weaving linen in ancient Egypt, the horizontal loom is the type which has been most highly developed in the course of history. The warp is stretched between two beams which are held in place by four pegs hammered into the ground. It has a fixed heddle, supported on stones several centimetres above the ground. The set of warps thereby raised forms one shed, while the other is formed by moving the shed rod and pulling the lower set of warps by hand to raise them above those held by the heddle. Each pass of the weft is beaten in firmly with a flat stick. The loom size probably determined the length of cloth to be woven, but the dis-

12 Horizontal loom
with shedding mechanism
operated by treadles,
depicted in a 13th-century
English manuscript.

The treadle loom

On all the looms described above the sheds are
formed by hand, which can involve considerable delay between the passing of each
weft. If, however, the loom is fitted with a
treadle, the shed is formed by the action of the
feet, leaving the hands free to pass the shuttle
with greater speed. It also allows far longer
pieces of cloth to be woven, since a very long
warp can be wound up on the warp beam.

The origins of the treadle loom go back to
Chinese silk weaving, which was at an advanced stage of development two or three centuries before the Christian era. It is thought to
have arrived in Europe in the Middle Ages with
the organised wool industry in the Low Countries and was certainly known in its fully developed form by the thirteenth century. The
treadle loom is still used by hand-weavers today, and a simple treadle mechanism is a characteristic of the narrow strip looms of West Africa
(see II, 33).

Complex, pattern looms

The treadle loom could be modified to produce
more complex weaves and to speed production

13 Water-colour drawing
depicting the weaving of
figured satins on a drawloom
in China, from *Silk Culture
and Manufacture*, dating from
the reign of the Qing
Emperor Kangxi
(1662–1722).

織更曲殷照心女時
作將折勤眼手工態攀

technology allowed the shuttle to be propelled mechanically and sheds to be selected automatically. The Jacquard loom, which was in use in English cotton mills by 1813 and which was adapted for fully mechanised operation during the 1830s, replaced the cords and drawboy by a mechanism driven by a single treadle and which could be operated by the weaver unaided. A series of linked, punched cards, with each punched hole corresponding to one warp end in a pattern unit, is mechanically matched to the heddles. When the card mechanism has completed a revolution, the different sheds have been passed and the pattern unit is complete.

During the same period water and steam were used to power the looms. However, the basic techniques of weaving remained unchanged. Industrialisation brought about greater speed of production and a reduction in the skilled labour required to operate the looms, rather than any improvement in the design or structure of the fabrics produced.

Simple weaves

The three basic weaves are tabby, twill and satin, and all require one set each of warp and weft threads.

Plain weave

The simplest and most universal weave is tabby, or plain weave, which is produced by passing the weft across the warp twice. On the outward journey it passes over all the odd warps and under the evens; on its return it passes over the evens and under the odds (fig. 1). Tabby thus requires only two shafts or lifting devices. Variety can be introduced to plain weave by changing the texture or colour of the yarns (to produce stripes and checks, for example), and also by changing the spacing of the warp threads in relation to the wefts. If the warp threads are packed closely so that the weft is hardly visible, a warp-faced construction with a crosswise rib called repp results. The opposite of repp is tapestry weave, which is weft-faced plain weave (see I, 2). A variation of plain weave is basket weave, or hopsack, where the warps and wefts are used in pairs but the proportion of warp to weft remains the same.

Twill weave

Twill weaves are characterised by a pronounced diagonal movement which is caused by starting the weave sequence one place to the right or left on each successive passage of the weft (fig. 2). If warp and weft are different colours, it produces a diagonal stripe. As in plain weave, there is only one set of warp and weft threads, but the binding system, or sequence of interlacing, may vary – that is, the weft goes over or under more than one warp.

Twill-woven fabrics have been found in neo-

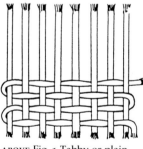

ABOVE Fig. 1 Tabby or plain weave.

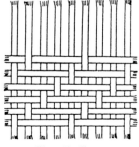

ABOVE Fig. 2 Twill weave.

by increasing the number of foot-operated heddles, but there remains a limit to the number of heddles which can conveniently be operated by foot treadles alone. The drawloom enabled an infinitely greater variety of sheds to be formed. Instead of heddles, the warps on the drawloom which were to be raised for each shed were attached by strings to a cord which passed over the loom. Each shed, therefore, had a cord which was numbered and which was pulled in sequence by a 'drawboy', while the weaver inserted the weft. As many different sheds were possible as there were combinations of draw cords. The drawboy first sat on top of the loom; later he could stand on the floor and pull down the cords.

The drawloom was developed in the Middle East for silk weaving during the sixth and seventh centuries AD, but its origins may lie even further back. Fragments of twill damasks dated to the second century BC in China suggest that some sort of pattern loom was known there by that time. It remained in use until replaced by the Jacquard loom in the early nineteenth century and was used to produce some of the most elaborate woven textiles ever known (see II, 17–21). The size and complexity of the drawloom demanded skilled workers and permanent positioning of the loom; thus commercial production of patterned textiles became not only possible but, indeed, necessary because of the time required to set up the loom.

During the Industrial Revolution of the eighteenth and nineteenth centuries developing

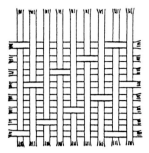

Fig. 3 Satin weave.

15 William Morris, 'St James', silk and wool damask, 1881.

lithic Swiss lake dwellings and in Bronze Age bog burials (see II, 3), and certainly the 2/2 (over two and under two) or common twill is as importantly historically as plain weave. In the 2/2 sequence an even-sided, reversible twill is produced if warp and weft counts are roughly equal. In others, however – say, 3/1 or 1/3 – one face will be predominantly warp, the other weft. Tartan is traditionally made in 2/2 twill, while denim is a warp-faced twill. Most twills are continuous, in that the diagonal goes from one corner to the corner diagonally opposite, but if the direction of the diagonal is changed, a herringbone – or diamond – twill pattern may be formed.

Satin weaves

Satin weave is distinguished by the spacing of the binding points, the normal sequence being over one warp, under four (or more, fig. 3). It required, therefore, at least a five-shaft loom. The warp 'floats' on top of the weft on the right side and is thus a warp-faced weave. A weft-faced satin, where the sequence is reversed to over four, under one, is known as sateen.

Simple pattern weaves can be formed by using different combinations of warp and weft floats. Damask, for example, combines warp-faced and weft-faced twill or satin sections and is always reversible, because a pattern area with warp floats on one side will have equal weft floats on the other. The earliest-known damasks were found in China, but the technique was also developed to a high level by the linen manufacturers of northern Europe from the sixteenth century (see II, 22).

Compound weaves

Each of the three basic weaves can be made into a compound weave by the addition of extra warps, weft or both. Unlike supplementary weft or warp floats (discussed below) which can be removed and still leave the ground fabric intact, these complementary sets of threads cannot be removed without destroying the fabric. Com-

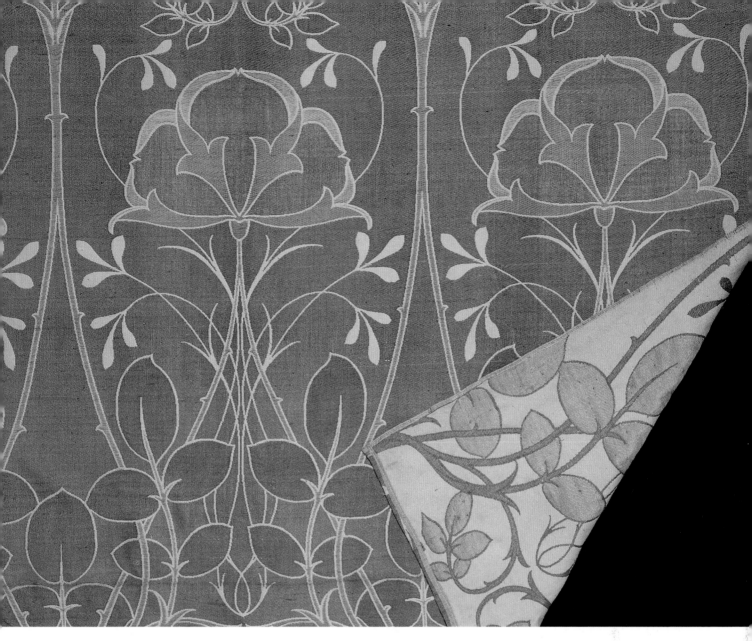

16 Gavin Morton, 'White Free Rose', silk and cotton double cloth manufactured by Alexander Morton & Co., 1900.

pound weaves are associated with the draw-loom and were especially important in European silks of the thirteenth to eighteenth centuries.

Double cloth is a compound weave which has two main warps and two main wefts, generally of contrasting colour. The two cloths are woven simultaneously but separately; when the pattern requires a change in colour, the back warps and wefts are brought to the front and the two cloths interlocked, while elsewhere the two layers remain separate. Double cloths are reversible, the pattern and ground appearing in one colour combination on the front, in reverse on the back.

Velvet

All simple or compound weaves can be elaborated into velvet by introducing a supplementary warp over a series of small rods; when the rods are removed small loops remain, which can then be cut if required. The extra warp beam

necessary to make velvet was not in use much before the fourteenth century. When the ground is entirely covered with pile, the velvet is said to be solid, whereas voided velvet has areas without pile. *Ciselé* velvet has areas of cut and uncut (looped) pile, and in pile-on-pile velvet the fabric is woven in two or more different heights to form a pattern. *Jardinière* velvets have multiple-pile warps, one for each colour.

All simple, compound or velvet weaves can be enriched by supplementary sets of yarns that float on the surface of the cloth, a technique commonly referred to as brocading. Brocading can be continuous – that is, the supplementary weft is carried across from selvage to selvage, coming to the surface only where the pattern requires it and floating between pattern areas on the back, or it can be discontinuous; here a small group of shuttles is required for the pattern to be put in by hand, and yarn floats on the back only within the pattern areas. Magnificent brocaded

17 Detail from a voided velvet cushion cover, Turkey, 18th century.

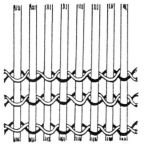

ABOVE Fig. 4 Weft twining.

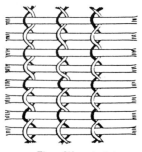

ABOVE Fig. 5 Warp twining.

OPPOSITE **18** Detail from a silk brocade skirt panel, British, Spitalfields, 1749–52.

silks, using gold and silver threads, were made in France in the seventeenth and eighteenth centuries (see II, 21).

Pile, or *bouclé*, weaves are achieved by means of additional wefts drawn up into loops. This was a technique known in Pharaonic Egypt, whilst post-Pharaonic finds include many examples of linen made with supplementary linen loops. The most sumptuous Italian velvets of the fifteenth and sixteenth centuries were often enriched with supplementary loops of gold and silver thread (see II, 18).

Finger-weaving techniques

Twining

Twining, sometimes referred to as finger-weaving, is closely related to weaving in that it uses two sets of yarn. In weft twining the warp is stretched between two bars and the weft worked across in pairs, one thread going over a warp, the other under, and taking a half-turn around one another between each warp (fig. 4).

As with weaving, many variations on this basic structure are possible: the number of wefts may be increased, more than one warp may be crossed at a time, or wefts may be worked discontinuously within design areas, as in tapestry. The Maoris in New Zealand used many variations of weft twining to produce cloaks, and it was a highly developed art among the North American Indians (see II, 30).

In warp twining pairs of warps were twisted around each other as the wefts were inserted (fig. 5). This technique was generally used to make narrow bands. Twined fabrics have been found at early sites in both Anatolia and Peru.

Braiding

Unlike twining and weaving, braiding uses only one set of elements which are interlaced diagonally from the outside in or from the centre outwards. Starting with a few threads, more and more threads or groups of threads are gradually drawn in. Braids have been made in many parts of the world from early times.

2 Tapestry

OPPOSITE 20 Detail from a tapestry-woven silk (*kesi*) rank badge, China, late 18th century.

BELOW 19 Detail from a slit tapestry *kelim*, Qashqa'i, south-west Iran, early 20th century.

The term tapestry is usually associated, by the layman, with the large pictorial wall-hangings of medieval and later northern Europe; in the past century or so it has been used to identify any pictorial weaving and, even, pictorial needlework. Strictly speaking, however, tapestry describes a distinctive woven structure, specifically a weft-faced plain weave with discontinuous wefts.

The technique is known in many different cultures and can be used to produce fabrics ranging from heavy, durable floor-coverings such as the Middle Eastern *kelim* to delicate Chinese silk *kesi*. The oldest-known tapestries are from the tombs of Tuthmosis IV and Tutankhamun, dating from c.1400 BC to 1330 BC, and it is thought that those from the latter may be of Near Eastern, possibly Syrian, origin. Tapestry-woven textiles of the first millennium BC, showing a high level of technical skill, have also been found on the west coast of Peru where, as in Egypt, they were preserved in desert graves.

Tapestry lends itself to complex pictorial and other patterning effects, yet it can be woven on the simplest of looms. Both a horizontal and a vertical loom have been used. The latter, which

21 Slit tapestry fragment from Peru, central coast, 15th century.

is basically a very heavy two-bar loom, is the older and is possibly a descendant of the warp-weighted loom; it was in use in Egypt from c.1500 BC. The horizontal or ground loom was also used in Egypt, as well as in China, Japan, and South and Central America. Both types were used in the manufacture of pictorial tapestries in Europe, where the high-warp loom was known as *haute lisse* and the low-warp as *basse lisse*.

In high-warp tapestry weaving the weaver works from the back, from a cartoon (an enlarged and colour-coded drawing of the design) which hangs on the wall in front of the weaving, as does a mirror which allows him to observe the progress of the weaving. In low-warp weaving the cartoon, where required, is laid on the ground under the warp. Both the vertical and horizontal loom allowed several weavers to

work side by side on a single tapestry, an undoubted advantage in such a time-consuming and labour-intensive craft. On the highly detailed European pictorial tapestries a rate of one square metre per weaver per month was not unusual.

Tapestry weaving is characterised by discontinuous wefts, which means that the weft crosses the warp only where its particular colour is required by the design. Discontinuous wefts can meet or join in a number of different ways. If they meet but do not join, a slit forms in the direction of the warp (fig. 6), examples of which may be seen in Middle Eastern *kelims* and in Chinese *kesi*. Slit tapestry is also the most common technique in European pictorial tapestries, where the slits were sewn up after the work was removed from the loom. A slit of any appreciable length tends to weaken the cloth struc-

26

ture, and so weavers have devised other methods of joining discontinuous wefts. These methods include interlocking, which links adjacent weft threads in the space between the warps, or adjacent wefts may share a common warp and be dovetailed.

In single interlocking adjacent wefts loop around each other on alternate passes (fig. 7). This method is much used by Navajo weavers. Double interlocking is a variant of single interlocking whereby the weaver interlocks the wefts on every pass (fig. 8). It slows the weaving, but the resulting join is very strong and the join line where the two colours meet is almost as clear as a slit, whereas the single interlock creates a slightly fuzzy line. Dovetailing uses the warps to interlock rather than the spaces between them. In single dovetailing the wefts are wrapped alternately around a common warp (fig. 9), a method widely used by Coptic and Peruvian weavers. Multiple dovetailing is a variation which allows slightly faster weaving, since two or three passes with weft of one colour are alternated with two or three passes with weft of the adjacent colour (fig. 10). With slit tapestry the design can be built up irregularly, leaving the weaver free to concentrate on one particular section of it. When interlocking or dovetailing, however, the weaver must maintain a more even cloth line and so forfeits the ability to concentrate on one section of the design.

The fact that infinite changes of weft are possible enables the tapestry weaver, when the subject is pictorial, to imitate the graduations of tone achieved by the oil-painter. This capability of the medium was fully exploited in post-medieval European tapestry (see II, 23). To enhance realism further the weaver may also batten the wefts into curves or pack them more tightly in some areas than in others; these are known as eccentric wefts. Tapestry can allow the weaver considerable creative freedom in comparison with other weaving techniques, although this freedom was not always granted to him.

BELOW **22** Weaver working at the high-warp tapestry loom, from Denis Diderot's *Encyclopédie, ou dictionnaire universel des arts et des sciences,* 1762–5.

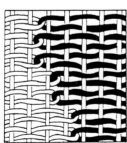

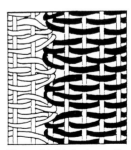

Fig. 6 Slit tapestry.

Fig. 7 Single interlocking tapestry.

Fig. 8 Double interlocking tapestry.

Fig. 9 Single dovetailing.

Fig. 10 Multiple dovetailing.

3 Rug weaving

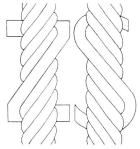

Fig. 11 Yarn spun or plied in an anti-clockwise direction follows the diagonal of a z (LEFT); clockwise, of an s.

Rugs can be made by a number of different techniques: they include flat-weave rugs (*kelims*), which are tapestry-woven (see 1, 2), felts, which are non-woven rugs (see 1, 9), and brocaded rugs. In the latter the design is added to a plain-weave foundation by means of supplementary wefts (see 1, 1, p. 21). The most common type of brocaded rug is the *soumak*, made over quite a wide area, though named after a town in the eastern Caucasus. However, it is pile rugs which are the type most closely associated with rug weaving. These are made of row after row of tiny knots tied on the warps of a foundation weave which *en masse* combine to

23 Detail from the Pazyryk carpet, from the Altai region of southern Siberia, 5th century BC.

form a thick pile. In rug-producing cultures they are put to many different uses – they serve as wall- and floor-coverings, prayer-mats, saddle-cloths, bags and cushion tops.

The history and origins of rug weaving are the subject of intense and lively debate amongst scholars. The earliest type of rug is probably the looped pile rug, which is made by sewing woollen loops into a simple flat weave or, alternatively, by using an extra weft which is pulled out in loops to produce a kind of single-sided towel fabric. Weft-loop pile fabrics were known in ancient Egypt, and a rug of this type was found in the famous frozen tombs of the Pazyryk valley in the Altai region of southern Siberia. It is one of a group of rugs found there

still encased in the solid ice which had preserved them since the fifth century BC. The group also included a border fragment from a felt rug and, most importantly, a knotted pile rug of high technical quality with a design of horsemen, deer and ornament relating to the art of Assyria and of the Achaemenian dynasty (550–330 BC). This pre-dates the oldest pile rugs otherwise extant, Islamic Seljuk and Mamluk carpets (see II, 13), by some 1,700–1,800 years. The origin of the carpet is unknown, but the design suggests south or west Persia. It is also reasonable to assume that a piece as technically accomplished as the Pazyryk carpet must have been preceded by a history of rug weaving in that area, stretching back perhaps as far as the second millennium BC.

The traditional 'oriental' rug was woven in a belt stretching from Spain and North Africa across to India and China, and it is interesting how many of the rug-weaving societies are, or were at some important stage in their history, governed by Islam (see II, 13). The materials used in rug weaving include wool (of the sheep, goat or camel), silk, cotton, linen and hemp. Of these wool is by far the most common, and many carpets are made entirely of it – the warp, weft and pile. Of the other fibres cotton is much used for the foundation – rugs with cotton warps and wefts are easier to weave and tend to lie flatter once completed. The pile is usually wool, although silk is much used in Chinese and sometimes in Persian carpets.

The wool fibres are converted into yarn by spinning: yarn spun in an anti-clockwise direction is known as z-spin; clockwise is known as s-spin (fig. 11). The spun yarn is then plied or twisted into thicker yarn by plying two or more strands together. Plying is generally the reverse of spinning; thus z-spin yarns would be plied in a clockwise manner to produce s-ply yarn. After spinning and plying the yarns were dyed, traditionally with colours made from locally available dye plants. Because skeins of yarn were dyed individually, there might be slight colour variations from one batch to the next, which were revealed in the finished rug. This phenomenon, known as *abrash*, is thought, however, to enhance rather than detract from the aesthetic appeal of a traditional oriental rug.

The carpet loom is, essentially, a frame for holding taut the warp threads which form the foundation and may be extremely simple in

FAR RIGHT 25 Qashqa'i girl
beating down carpet wefts at
the tribal weaving school in
Shiraz, Iran.

construction. Indeed, the village or nomadic
loom is little more than a rectangular, heavy
wooden frame which is laid flat or propped up
on a few bricks or stones. The more sophisticated version bears a close resemblance to the
tapestry loom and has two strong uprights
carrying a pair of rollers: the upper supplies the
warp and the lower gathers up the completed
work. A simple shedding device separates the
warp into two layers to allow the weft thread to
be passed after each row of knots.

The pile is secured to the warp by the knot.
Knots are basically of three kinds, which might
have minor modifications. The two main knots
are the symmetrical, or Turkish, knot (sometimes called Ghiordes, fig. 12) and the asymmetrical, or Persian, knot (often called Sehna),
which may be open on the left (fig. 13) or right
(fig. 14). Although the names suggest a specific
geographical origin, both Turkish and Persian
knots are used all over the Muslim world.

BELOW 24 Carpet knotting at
the tribal weaving school in
Shiraz, Iran.

To make a pile the weaver starts at one side of
the rug and ties a knot on the first two warps,
cuts the yarn and continues across, tying knots
on successive pairs of warps and using which-
ever coloured yarns are required by the design.
After completing a whole row of knots, the
weaver passes the weft through the shed between the warps and beats it into place with a
metal comb to make the fabric solid and com-
pact. The weft may be passed once or as many as
eight times, though most tribal rugs have two
wefts. The weaver then proceeds with the next
row of knots. When a reasonable length has
been knotted, the rug is trimmed with special
shears to the desired pile length. Sometimes
both Turkish and Persian knots are tied on more
than two warp threads, a technique which enables the weaver to proceed twice as fast but
which greatly weakens the fabric. A third kind
of knot is tied on a single warp thread: the knots
on one row are tied on every other warp, those

RIGHT Fig. 12 The
symmetrical or Turkish knot.

CENTRE Fig. 13 The
asymmetrical or Persian knot,
open on the left.

FAR RIGHT Fig. 14 The
asymmetrical or Persian knot,
open on the right.

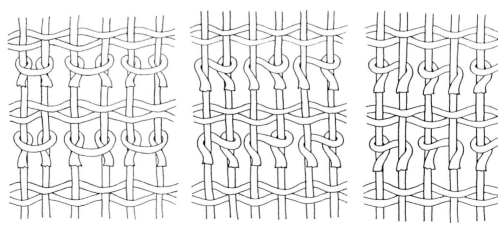

26 Detail from a carpet depicting peony blossoms, Ningxia region, western China, Qianlong period (1736–95). The large peony blossoms in the corner are carved into the pile, a technique peculiar to the Chinese and still used today.

on the next on alternate warps, and so on. It is much less common than the Turkish and Persian knots but is found on most Spanish carpets.

The ends of a rug may be finished off in a wide variety of different ways, which tend to follow local traditions, and may thus reveal a great deal about a rug's age and origins. Generally there is at each end a band of plain or tapestry weaving and beyond that there is often a fringe formed from the warp ends. These are sometimes left single but are more often twisted together in groups or knotted to form a network.

There are three main types of production relevant to rug weaving – that carried out by nomadic or village weavers, that done by craftsmen in small workshops, and that done to order and for sale in large, palace workshops. Generally only the palace workshops worked to a design, and even this might be just a small, cursory sketch, which demanded skill from the weaver in translating it into full size on the right scale. Nomadic weavers and village craftsmen, on the other hand, would employ familiar, traditional motifs and create the design as they went along, so that certain pattern elements, borders and repeating patterns became part of a standard repertoire. Most rug weaving was done by women.

Chinese carpets are quite different in both colouring and design from Near and Middle Eastern carpets. Colour schemes are paler, there are large areas of plain ground, and design motifs such as flowers are treated in a more realistic manner. Realism is further enhanced by the practice, in Chinese work, of shaving the pile with razors along the outlines of the design so as to form a deep groove and create a three-dimensional effect.

The first European-made pile carpets were produced in imitation of carpets imported from the East, although their designs soon became more vernacular. French Savonnerie carpets were produced from the late seventeenth century onwards, and English court production of pile carpets was set up in the eighteenth century along similar lines. Many attempts have been made in the West to reproduce by machine the effects of hand-knotted pile carpets. In mechanised carpet weaving, which has been done successfully since the late nineteenth century, a supplementary warp is woven into the foundation weave in such a way as to form loops, which are later cut to create a pile. It is not very different from the process by which velvet is made. By the mid-twentieth century a new technique had been developed, whereby the loops were fixed in a gummy background, obviating any weaving and producing the so-called tufted carpets which dominate the bulk of the carpet trade today.

4 *Embroidery*

Embroidery is a method of decorating with the needle an already existing structure, usually a woven foundation fabric, although embroidery can and has been done on other media such as parchment or bark. It can be done by hand or, since the nineteenth century, by machine. Unlike needlework, it excludes simple seaming and other basic stitchcraft, and also needleworked techniques such as knitting or crochet.

It is possible to confuse embroidery with certain weaving techniques, particularly brocade, but embroidery yarns are worked into the fabric after it has come off the loom, whereas brocade yarns are placed there by a moving shuttle or bobbin during the weaving process. Such supplementary-weft patterns can present problems of identification, but examination of the reverse of the fabric should reveal the difference between the two techniques since the brocade threads are carried loose across the wrong side of the fabric where the pattern does not require them. Tapestry and embroidery

have also frequently been confused since the nineteenth century, mainly because the word 'tapestry' has been wrongly applied to canvas-work or counted-thread embroidery, which was originally done in imitation of true woven tapestry.

The earliest-surviving embroidery is Egyptian, from the tombs of Tuthmosis IV (*c.*1412–1364 BC) and Tutankhamun (1334–1325 BC), but its origins are presumably even older. Embroidery also has a long history in China: embroidered silks and gauze have been found at archaeological sites dating from the fourth century BC onwards (see II, 14); and many examples of European and Islamic embroidery have survived from the eighth to twelfth centuries AD.

The main embroidery stitches, very generally speaking, may be classified as one of three types: flat stitches, loop stitches and knotted stitches. With flat stitches (fig. 15) the threads lie flat on the surface of the ground fabric, although the stitches may be side by side, overlapping or

BELOW **27** The reverse of a fragment of silk satin brocade, showing how the supplementary-weft threads are carried loose across the fabric where not required by the pattern. English, 1740s.

BELOW RIGHT **28** The reverse of a piece of floral silk embroidery, showing clearly how the threads are worked into the fabric. English, early 18th century.

RIGHT Fig. 15 Flat stitches
(a) satin stitch
(b) stem stitch
(c) long-and-short stitch
(d) cross stitch
(e) tent stitch
(f) couching

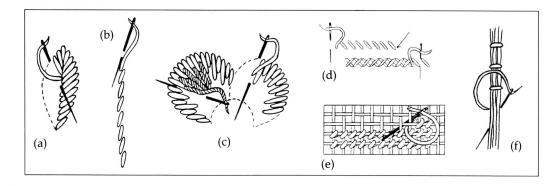

ABOVE Fig. 16 Loop stitches
(a) chain stitch
(b) buttonhole stitch

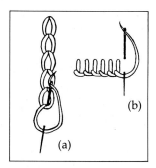

RIGHT Fig. 17 Knotted stitches
(a) Pekin knot
(b) French knot

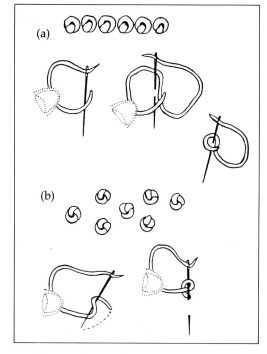

crossed. Among the innumerable variations of flat stitches are satin stitch, stem stitch, long-and-short stitch and couching. Counted-thread embroidery on canvas is also usually done with flat stitches such as tent or cross stitch. To form a loop stitch (fig. 16) the thread is brought to the front of the fabric, loosely looped and returned to the back. As the needle comes to the front a second time, it catches the end of the loop and secures it in place. Loop stitches may be open, as in buttonhole stitch, or closed, an example of which is chain stitch. In knotted stitches (fig. 17), such as the French or Pekin knot, when the needle is brought to the front of the fabric the thread is wrapped around it several times, then carried to the back again to secure the knot.

Although one generally associates embroidery with coloured yarns, the various forms of whitework are also usually classified as embroidery. They include not only white embroidery on white cotton or linen but also the techniques known as pulled- and drawn-thread work, where yarns are either pulled aside or withdrawn completely from the ground fabric to

RIGHT 29 Two women working waistcoat fronts in a professional embroidery workshop of the mid-18th century, from Denis Diderot's *Encyclopédie, ou dictionnaire universel des arts et des sciences*, 1762–5.

allow the remaining structural elements to serve as a framework for the insertion of decorative stitches. Embroidery may also be raised or in relief as well as flat, and techniques are known in many cultures which incorporate padded details, spiralled wires, beads or other materials to produce three-dimensional effects. Indeed, quilting is a form of embroidery which relies on an element of relief for its effect. To quilt, decorative stitches are made through two layers of fabric to join them together. A layer of wadding material between them, or a soft cord, throws the stitched patterns into relief. Quilting is sometimes combined with pieced or applied work (patchwork and appliqué).

Embroidery has been both a domestic craft and a professional activity. The former has, in most cultures, been carried out mainly by women, although some men have done embroidery as a hobby. Professional work, however, has been practised by both sexes. Although some contemporary embroiderers work without a pattern, embroidery has traditionally been carefully planned before stitching is begun. Designs might be drawn directly on to the ground or, more usually, transferred from a paper pattern. In counted-thread embroidery each small square on graph paper represents a stitch, so transferring the pattern to the fabric is unnecessary.

30 Corner of a kerchief of embroidered muslin, with flower and leaf motifs in drawn thread and shadow work, and a wide variety of different fillings. British, 18th century.

5 Lace

Lace is not easy to define. It is essentially an openwork fabric constructed not by weaving but by the looping, plaiting or twisting of threads using either a needle or a set of bobbins. There are a number of net-based fabrics – darned net or *lacis*, for example – which are traditionally classified as lace, and other techniques which can be used to produce an openwork fabric similar to lace but which are not normally classified as such – knitting, crochet, sprang, and macramé are just a few.

All true lace is either needle- or bobbin-made and is constructed independently of any woven surface. Although other looped fabrics are known from a very early date, true lace seems to

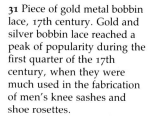

31 Piece of gold metal bobbin lace, 17th century. Gold and silver bobbin lace reached a peak of popularity during the first quarter of the 17th century, when they were much used in the fabrication of men's knee sashes and shoe rosettes.

Needle lace

Needle lace evolved from openwork embroidery. Most of the threads would be drawn out from a piece of cloth, leaving a grid of vertical and horizontal threads which were then strengthened with buttonhole stitches. The spaces created would then be bridged or filled with more stitches to form patterns. Lace thus worked within a skeleton of woven fabric was known as *reticella*. The starting-point for true lace came when the woven support was abandoned and the stitches began instead to be constructed on a temporary support of parchment, which was removed once the work was finished.

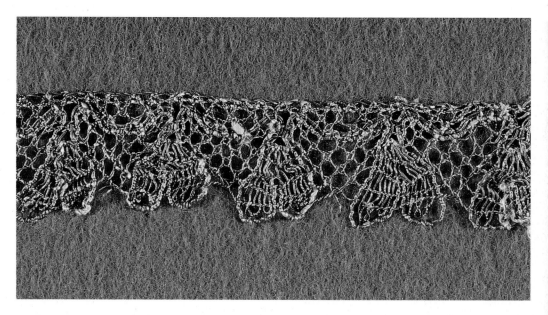

have been made no earlier than the late fifteenth or early sixteenth centuries. The finest-quality, fashion laces were made in Italy, France and Belgium, but lace has also been made in other parts of northern and southern Europe, in eastern Europe, in China, India, the Philippines, and in South and Central America.

Yarns used for lace include linen, silk and metal-wrapped silk, although the fine linen thread made in Belgium was preferred above all others. Cotton and wool are also found in 'peasant' laces. Lace-making is a time-consuming and highly skilled activity which has been carried out mainly by women. Progress on fine pieces might be as slow as a few centimetres per day.

To make needle lace the design drawn out on the parchment is first outlined with tacking stitches or a couched foundation thread. To the latter are attached the loops of the detached buttonhole stitches which form the solid or decorative areas. Each row serves, in its turn, as a support for the following row. It is possible to add three-dimensional effects by attaching shaped bundles of threads to the foundation and covering them with buttonhole stitches. When the patterned areas are complete, the background is filled either with small, linking bars oversewn in buttonhole stitch and sometimes ornamented with little stars (called picots), or with a net, usually also based on variations of the buttonhole stitch. When both

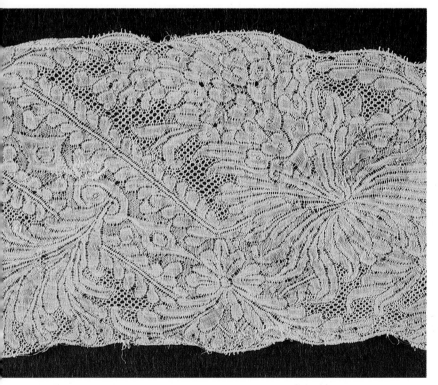

pattern and ground are complete, the tacking or couching threads are cut and the parchment can be removed, thus releasing the free-standing piece of lace.

Bobbin lace

Unlike needle lace which is made with one thread at a time, bobbin lace is constructed with many different threads, each wound on to its own bobbin, which are manipulated in a manner similar to that used in braiding, whence the technique derives. The bobbins function both as a weight and as a means of keeping the threads from tangling or unravelling. Bobbin lace is sometimes referred to as pillow lace, though a pillow is often used to support the parchment when making needle lace too.

As with needle lace, bobbin lace is constructed over a parchment pattern, but the design, instead of being drawn out, is marked by pricking holes. As the work progresses, pins are placed through the pricked holes to hold the 'stitches'; when a section has been completed, the pins can be removed without any danger of the lace falling out of shape (see p. 14).

The structures of all bobbin laces derive from the interlacing of four threads manipulated twice. With the four bobbins divided into two pairs, a z-cross of each pair is made first, followed by an s-cross of the two middle bobbins. By controlling the number of z- and s-crossings of the basic movements, and the number of bobbins, many different structures may be made. The pattern areas of bobbin lace are more densely constructed than the background net or bars, which are themselves made up of twisted strands.

Bobbin lace may be made in one continuous process (straight lace) or can be made up of a number of separately worked motifs joined up by bars or a mesh (part lace). Straight lace cannot be made very wide as it would require far too many bobbins. As it is, a band of lace 12 cm (4.7 in) wide might use up to 1,500 bobbins, depending on the complexity of the design. Part lace requires a comparatively smaller number of bobbins to make up the individual parts but it can be used to create larger pieces of elaborate lace.

Machine-made lace

Early in the nineteenth century the invention of a machine for making bobbin net led to repeated experiments to construct a machine for making patterned lace itself. This was achieved c.1840 when the Jacquard system (see I, 1) was adapted to the net machines (see II, 25). Thereafter, hand- and machine-made laces were produced alongside each other, rather than in direct competition, for the rest of the century.

TOP **32** Piece of *gros point de Venise* lace, late 17th century. This heavy, three-dimensional lace from Venice was well suited to the elaborately decorated baroque fashions of the day.

ABOVE **33** Detail from a Valenciennes lace lappet, early 18th century. The Flemish lace-makers perfected an incredibly fine yet densely-patterned bobbin lace which complemented the relatively simple styles and soft accessories of the era.

6 Dyeing and printing

Leaving aside effects achieved by exploiting the various shades of natural fibres, colour in textiles is produced by painting or printing, or by dyeing. Until the nineteenth century all dyes were derived from vegetable or, more rarely, animal or mineral sources.

The root of some species of the madder family was used from the earliest period to produce a whole range of reds, since it could be grown practically everywhere. Red animal dyes, derived from certain species of scale insect, were also highly valued from ancient times and right through the Middle Ages. Yellow dyes, whether from weld or some other plant such as saffron or turmeric, invariably fade or disappear, which accounts for the blueish tinge of what were once bright greens in woven tapestry, for example. Before the first, fast 'solid' green was invented in the early nineteenth century greens were achieved by the overdyeing or overprinting of yellow and blue. Blues were obtained from indigo, which was widely cultivated in India and exported from there, and from woad, a plant common in Europe and also used in the Near East from the beginning of the Christian era. Although these dyes were probably the most common, many others have also been used.

The range of natural colours was hugely expanded and, indeed, superseded by the chemical dyes developed during the nineteenth century. By 1900 a complete range of synthetic colours had been evolved, many of them reaching a standard of fastness to light and to washing greatly exceeding that of natural dyestuffs. Since then, the petroleum industry has added many new chemicals, and from these other types of dyestuffs have been developed. Much of the research was stimulated by the peculiarities of some of the new synthetic fibres: acetate rayon, for example, seemed at first to have no affinity for dyes and a new range of colours had to be developed; nylon and Terylene presented similar problems.

The printing of textiles has involved a number of distinct methods, all or some of which might be used in conjunction in producing a finished cloth. With the exception of printing directly on to the cloth (whether by block, roller or screen), all the other techniques for printing patterns are based on dyeing – that is, the immersion at some stage of the fabric in a dye bath. They may be more correctly described, therefore, as pattern-dyed rather than printed.

Direct printing

The three main methods of direct printing are by wooden blocks, engraved copper roller and screen. Block printing is the oldest method.

34 Block printing on calico, from John Barrow's *New Universal Dictionary of Arts and Sciences*, 1754.

Although printed cloths were practically unknown in the West before the seventeenth century, direct printing from blocks on to linen was practised in medieval Europe, having been probably introduced from Asia during the Roman period. Whether Persia or Egypt was the original source of the technique, it was in India that it was developed into a great art.

In block printing areas are carved away from a wooden block to leave the design for printing in relief. Alternatively, copper or brass strips and pins may be hammered into the block to produce finer lines or stipple effects. Blocks are rarely larger than 46 cm (18 in) square or 6 cm (2½ in) deep, since anything larger would be too heavy for the printer to handle comfortably. Once furnished with colour from a tub carried on rails alongside the printing table, the block is pressed firmly on to the stretched cloth by the printer who gives it a firm tap with the handle of a wooden mallet. This action is repeated until a whole length of fabric is complete. Pins hammered into the corners of the block are used to help position the block accurately and to ensure precise registration of colours. Each colour requires a separate block, and the colour on the fabric must be dry before subsequent colours are applied. It is a time-consuming and labour-intensive technique which can never really be applied to mass production. The slow build-up of one colour upon another in block printing, however, produces a rich effect, and the technique has survived into the twentieth century as a craft activity and for short runs of exclusive furnishing fabrics.

A technique for printing from engraved copperplates enjoyed a brief period of popularity in the second half of the eighteenth century. An intaglio technique related to etching, it enabled finely drawn images to be printed from hand-engraved copperplates measuring anything from about 30 cm (12 in) to 91 cm (3 ft) square. It made possible, therefore, much larger designs than could be achieved with blocks and much finer drawing. On the negative side, however, it was difficult to print in more than one colour, since the fine detail created problems with precise registration. Nevertheless, during the years between c.1760 and 1800 the technique was used to produce some of the finest printed textiles to have survived, notably those French and British monochrome pictorial prints of the late eighteenth century, commonly referred to as toiles de Jouy (see II, 26).

Cylinder or roller printing is, in a sense, a direct descendant of copperplate printing, since the rollers were engraved in the same way, the main difference being that the diameter of a roller was rarely larger than 76 cm (30 in) and often much smaller. It was the first fully mechanised process, allowing an entire length of fabric to be printed continuously. The first successful machine was patented by a Scotsman, Thomas Bell, in 1783 and was being used to print pictorials, as an alternative to copperplates, before 1800. The machine consists of a large, central pressure cylinder, around which are arranged the engraved rollers, each fed with colour from a colour-furnishing roller revolving in a tub of dye. A flexible steel blade, called a 'doctor', scrapes excess dye from the cylinders. The cloth for printing passes between the pressure cylin-

35 Vignette depicting copperplate printing, from *Les travaux de la manufacture*. The design, by Jean-Baptiste Huet, was produced to mark the award of the title of 'Manufacture Royale' to the Jouy factory outside Paris in 1783. It illustrates, almost in comic-strip form, the various printing and finishing processes in use there.

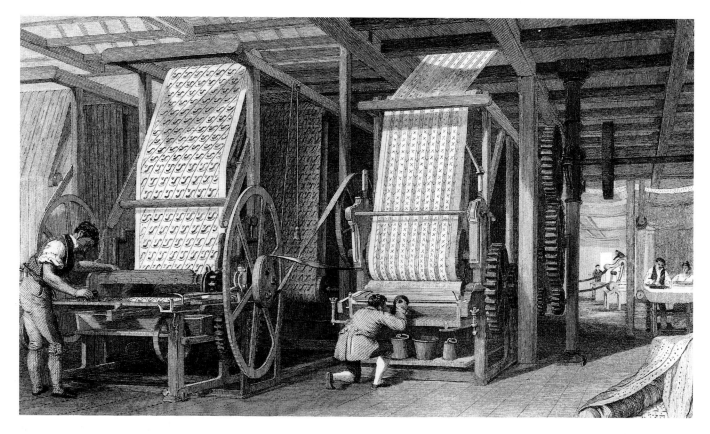

36 Calico printing by engraved copper rollers, from Edward Baines' *History of the Cotton Manufacture in Great Britain*, 1835.

der and the engraved roller and receives impressions in proportion to the number of engraved rollers in use. Initially only three or four cylinders could be combined in a machine, but this had increased to as many as twelve or fourteen by the second half of the nineteenth century. Like woodblocks and copperplates, the cylinders were originally engraved by hand, but methods of machine engraving were introduced early in the nineteenth century to speed up production.

Alternatives to the cylinder machine were a surface-printing machine, invented by a Frenchman, Rodolphe Ebinger, in 1800, where wooden rollers were carved in relief similar to blocks, and another French invention, the Perrotine, a block-printing machine patented by M. Perrot of Rouen in 1834. It effectively mechanised block printing, but the blocks, which were as long as the width of the fabric but only a few centimetres wide, were really unsuitable for large-scale furnishing fabrics, the mainstay of the hand-block-printing trade in England. Although widely used in France and elsewhere in Europe, the Perrotine therefore never challenged the cylinder-printing machine in England.

Roller printing revolutionised the industry, being capable of doing the work of about forty hand-block printers and of printing between 5,000 and 20,000 metres of cloth a day. With modifications and refinements the cylinder-

printing machine has remained in use to the present day, although it was largely superseded by screen printing during the 1960s.

Screen printing is based on the technique of stencilling, which has a long history in the Far East, particularly in Japan. It was introduced into commercial use in Europe during the 1920s and 30s and was at first a hand process. The screen is a shallow tray covered with nylon or polyester gauze (the 'silk'). The design is applied by coating with a special varnish those areas which are not to be impregnated by dye (now done commercially by photochemical techniques), and dye is forced through the screen by applying pressure from a squeegee, a wedge-shaped wooden bar with a rubber edge. As with blocks and rollers, each colour requires a separate screen, though there is almost no limit to their size or number, other than that directed by practicality. After each impression is made, the screen is lifted and moved along the printing table.

Flat-bed screen printing was automated in the mid-1950s, and instead of the screen moving the fabric itself moves along under each colour screen. Rotary screen printing, which has been in common use in Europe and the United States of America since the mid-1960s, has further improved upon the speed and efficiency of the technique. Here finely perforated cylindrical nickel screens take the place of flat screens, and

possible with either woodblocks or copper-plates; they are relatively cheap to initiate and thus allow short runs to be produced without too great a financial risk, and permit a manufacturer to respond more rapidly than with the other techniques to changes of fashion; and their output can compete with that of the cylinder-printing machine.

Pattern dyeing

Pattern dyeing has a longer history and broader geographical spread than the surface printing of textiles. Linen, and occasionally wool, with wax- or clay-resist patterns have been excavated from Egyptian burial grounds of the fifth to sixth centuries AD, and resist-dyed silks have been found in excavations in the Central Asian steppes of east Turkistan and the Kansu provinces, possibly imported from Tang dynasty China (AD 618–906). Important silk batiks of the Nara period (AD 646–794) are also preserved in the Shōsō-in Repository in Nara, Japan, again either imported from China or made by emigrant Chinese artists.

There are two principal procedures for pattern dyeing, depending on the capacity of the dyes employed to be absorbed by the fibre. They are resist dyeing and mordant dyeing; and the one is more or less the opposite of the other. In practice resist dyeing has been used mainly for indigo and related dyes like woad, whose properties are such that they cannot be used for direct printing since the dye quickly oxidises as soon as it is exposed to the air. A resist substance such as hot wax, rice paste or clay is therefore applied to those areas chosen to resist the dye and remain white. The cloth is then dyed and the resist later removed by tapping, scraping or boiling in very hot water. The resist may be applied with stamps, with large blocks or by using a stencil and brush. The technique is known in India, China, Japan and West Africa but is probably most closely associated with Javanese batik, where designs are traditionally worked free-hand with a *canting*, an onion-shaped receptacle with a spout that holds the hot wax (see II, 16). To simplify and accelerate the production of batik waxing by means of a *cap*, or stamp made of metal strips, was introduced in Java *c.*1850.

Another method of resist dyeing is tie dyeing, where parts of the cloth are tied with bast or waxed cord before dyeing; small stones or feathers may also be tied in to make other shapes (fig. 18). Dyeing is done quickly so that the wrappings are not penetrated and negative patterns emerge. The technique is known in India (as *bandhana*), Indonesia (as *plangi*), Japan (as *shibori*), South America, Central Asia and Africa (as *adire*). By a related technique, called *tritik* in

TOP **37** Hand-screen printing in the workshops at the Manchester Metropolitan University.

ABOVE **38** Modern rotary screen printing machine manufactured by Stork Screens B.V., Holland.

dye is introduced into the screen from a hollow tube inside it. As with flat-bed screen printing, the fabric is carried beneath the screens, although at a faster rate than with flat screen machines.

Screen printing of one sort or another now dominates the industry. Screens possess most of the advantages and almost none of the disadvantages of the other surface printing techniques: they can reproduce effects once only

Fig. 18 Diagrams representing some of the basic *plangi* resists.

RIGHT **39** Detail from a modern piece of tie-dyed (*adire*) cotton, Africa (Nigeria). The design is achieved by tying or stitching small stones into the cloth before immersion in the dye.

OPPOSITE **40** Detail from a kimono, showing *shibori* work and embroidery. Japan, 18th century.

Java, threads are sewn as patterns in the cloth which is then drawn up into tight folds which resist dye penetration, and a line of undyed dots is produced. In Africa the latter is often combined with tie dyeing (see II, 33).

The process for resist dyeing of yarns before weaving is now generally known as ikat (from the Malayan *mengikat*, 'to bind or tie'). The warp (hence warp ikat), weft (weft ikat) or both yarns (double ikat) may be wrapped to pattern in bundles and dyed before cloth construction begins. The technique produces a hazy, partially dyed effect when woven up, as the colours of the ikat-dyed yarns merge irregularly into each other. Ikats have been made in many parts of the world, and no single place of origin can be identified. Very fine examples are known from India, Indonesia and Japan, but the technique was also well developed in South America, Africa and Central Asia. Ikats have also been made in Europe, in France, where the silk warp ikats of Lyons were known as *chiné*, and in Spain, noted for velvet ikats.

An additional method of pattern dyeing with indigo is known as discharge. The cloth is first dyed, then the pattern is removed (discharged) by printing a bleaching agent from the block on to the dyed background. The discharged areas may subsequently be overprinted with other colours. This technique was not extensively de-

veloped until the early nineteenth century. It was much used in Alsace to discharge dye from Turkey red-dyed fabrics, which were then overprinted, and was also popular in England where later in the century its use was revived by William Morris (see II, 26).

Many dyestuffs will not be directly absorbed by a fibre, so mordants (from the French *mordre*, 'to bite') or fixing agents are used which combine with the dye and fibre to make the colour insoluble. Madder was an important dyestuff that could not be made colour-fast without the addition of a mordant. The mordant, or in some cases a variety of mordants, is applied to the cloth in similar ways to a resist, then the fabric is submerged in the madder dye bath; but where indigo resist dyeing presents the pattern in negative (white on a blue ground), a mordanted madder design appears positive (red on a white ground). Different mordants will produce a whole range of tones and shades within a group of colours (for example, black from an iron mordant; red, purple and brown from alum, etc.).

While most of the techniques described above are used singly, the master dyers of India frequently combined both direct printing and pattern-dyeing techniques in the production of their magnificent pictorial wall-hangings and floral chintzes (see II, 11).

43 Detail from a very large cotton hanging which in the one piece combines the techniques of batik, mordant resist and direct printing. India, first half of the 19th century.

7 Knitting

Knitting is a looped fabric made from a continuous supply of yarn, by hand with needles, or by machine. The yarn need not be continuous throughout the piece, however, if working with different colours or in fancy work employing different qualities of yarn.

The origins of knitting are rather obscure since so few early examples survive. It is possible that the technique was introduced into Europe from Asia via trade routes or as a result of the Moorish invasion of Spain (AD 711–12). Some of the earliest examples of true knitting are stockings from Egypt of the Islamic period (c.1200–1500) and late thirteenth-century cushions from royal tombs in the abbey church of Las Huelgas in northern Spain. Knitted liturgical gloves appear to have been relatively common in Europe after

1500, and hand-knitting flourished in the seventeenth and eighteenth centuries, when it became a suitable pastime for ladies.

In 1589 the Reverend William Lee invented a knitting frame which was used in stocking manufacture. It took another hundred years or more, however, until patterned knitting and a wide variety of shapes could be achieved on the frame. The frame may have been used in the manufacture of a group of 'brocaded' silk knitted jackets of the late seventeenth/early eighteenth centuries which survive in a number of European and North American museum collections.

Knitting's ability to stretch and insulate, without creasing, has made it popular for informal and sports wear in the West in the twentieth

RIGHT **44** Fragment of a knitted silk jacket, possibly Italian. Late 17th or early 18th century.

OPPOSITE **45** Judith Duffey, 'Sheep in Wolf's Clothing', 1986. A witty example of modern machine-knitted 'sculpture', though still based on the shape of a garment.

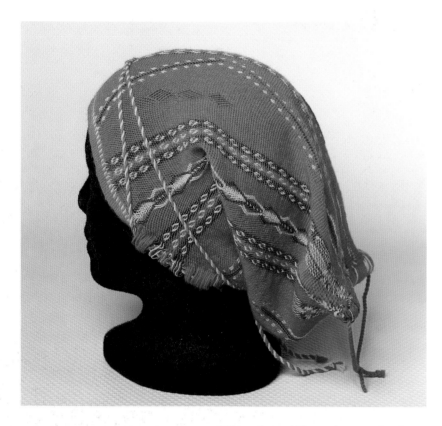

century. It has enjoyed even more popularity since the late 1960s, with a wider range of yarn types offering both professional and amateur knitters endless opportunities for creating variety in texture, pattern and colour.

A number of other fabric structures have sometimes been mistaken for knitting. Sprang is an ancient technique and a precursor of knitting, though it is made on a frame rather than with needles. The warp is fixed at both ends of the frame, and pairs of threads are interlaced working from the middle (fig. 19). Mirror-image patterns are formed simultaneously at the top and bottom of the frame. When the fabric is complete the frame, or rods composing the frame, can be withdrawn to leave an intact fabric. The technique seems to have been much used in the production of different types of head-covering, ranging from lacy openwork hairnets to densely constructed hoods. The earliest examples of sprang date from the early Bronze Age (c.1400 BC) in Denmark, but the technique has been practised widely and there are archaeological finds from ancient Peru (1100 BC) and post-Pharaonic Egypt (fourth to seventh centuries AD), as well as many more recent examples of the craft.

Items found in ancient Peruvian graves and socks from fourth- and fifth-century Romano-Egyptian burials also display a technique which resembles knitting, but which has been more precisely described as crossed-loop knitting (Burnham 1972). It was not done with a continuous length but with relatively short lengths which were threaded into a bone needle or cactus thorn and worked more like sewing (fig. 20). Loops were made one after another and packed against the preceding stitch.

ABOVE **46** Copy of a post-Pharaonic sprang hood excavated in Egypt. 5th–7th century AD. Reconstruction by Mrs Coby Reijnders-Baas, 1989.

Fig. 19 The method of working basic sprang.

BELOW **47** Child's sock in crossed-loop knitting from Oxyrhyncus, Egypt. Roman, 2nd century AD.

RIGHT Fig. 20 The method of working crossed-loop knitting.

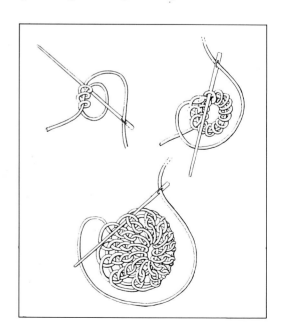

8 Netting, knotting and crochet

Netting

Netting is a technique of great antiquity and pre-dates weaving and twining. Netted fabrics have been found at neolithic sites and were presumably used for fishing nets, snares and, possibly, head-coverings.

Knotting

Knotting was a popular pastime for ladies in seventeenth- and eighteenth-century western Europe and colonial North America. Worked with a small shuttle, knots were made at intervals in lengths of string, linen, silk or wool, and the thread was then applied to a suitable ground fabric, forming patterns or covering it completely. Knotting has been popular in the twentieth century in the form of macramé.

Crochet

Crochet (in French literally 'a small hook') is a looped fabric which, like knitting, is made with a single continuous thread constructing horizontal rows but differs in that the loops are locked laterally as well as vertically. The technique was known in Britain by the end of the eighteenth century, and the great variety of modern crochet stitches developed during the Victorian period.

48 Detail from a crocheted antimacassar, British, 1900–10.

9 Felt and bark cloth

Felt and bark cloth are produced directly from the compression of fibres and do not involve any weaving or twining.

Felt

Felt is a fabric formed by applying pressure to hot, wet fibres (usually wool); the fibre scales become interlocked, and the process cannot be reversed. It is one of the earliest forms of textile and is known in many parts of the world, though it has been particularly important in the Middle East and Central Asia, where it is still made.

The Pazyryk burial mounds in the Central Asian steppes, which date to the fifth century BC, contained two fine felt rugs and several fragments. Since these show a highly developed technology and a great diversity of design and technique, it is reasonable to assume that the origins of felt probably go back much further. Indeed, Mellaart suggested that felt was known to the neolithic people of Çatal Hüyük (c.5800–

49 Qashqa'i shepherd wearing a protective felt coat (*kapanak*), 1970s.

5700 BC) on the evidence of textile-type patterns on wall-paintings at that site and the identification of actual felt among the grave finds (Mellaart 1966b, p. 180). Literary references to the use of felt in China go back to the third century BC, and felt objects are also included among the eighth-century AD textiles conserved in the Shōsō-in Repository in Nara, Japan.

Although not specially prized for its aesthetic qualities and not really flexible enough for general use as clothing, felt's ability to stretch and mould, and its excellent insulating qualities, have made it particularly suitable for saddle-covers, rugs, blankets, hats, footwear, waterproof cloaks and coats, and tent-like structures known as yurts, in areas of extreme cold. The technique was also widely used in the hatting industry in western Europe.

To make felt, wool is first carded on a large comb with two rows of fine metal teeth to make it fluffy and porous. Then the wool is spread out on a mat or old piece of felt (hatmakers use a metal former instead) and sprinkled with a mixture of very hot water and solid or liquid soap, before being rolled up tightly and rolled back and forth under pressure, or treaded with bare feet, to compress the wool. The whole process is repeated several times. Finally, the finished felt is rubbed smooth with a wooden roller or a polished, flat stone. In Europe carding machines and felt presses replaced the hand methods during the nineteenth century.

Felts do not lend themselves well to detailed designs, but they can be decorated in a number of ways. Designs may be created by adding dyed wool in patterns to the surface of the felt slab before the final steaming and pressing process. Alternatively, designs can be painted or printed on when the felting process is completed, or pieces of differently coloured felt can be sewn on (appliqué or intarsia). Mosaic patterns can be created by sewing many small pieces of felt together.

Although felt-making generally has seen a decline in the twentieth century, in Scandinavia and Britain it enjoyed something of a revival among craftspeople in the 1970s and 80s.

Bark cloth

Bark cloth has been made in Africa and South America, and its manufacture reached a high level of technical achievement in Indonesia. However, the technique is most closely asso-

rough outer bark was scraped from the inner. The soft pulpy strips of inner bark were then laid over wooden anvils and beaten continuously by groups of women with club-like wooden mallets to form sheets of cloth. The cloth was saturated with water throughout the beating process. The anvils might be highly resonant, and it is said

ABOVE 50 Hand-rolled felt hats by Heather Belcher, British, 1991.

ABOVE RIGHT 51 Detail of *tapa* cloth, Polynesia, late 19th century.

ciated with Polynesia since Captain James Cook (1728–79) and other white seamen visited the Pacific Islands in the late eighteenth century and recorded what they saw of its production there. *Tapa* has gradually come to denote all bark cloth, although this term originally described bark cloth from a particular group of islands. Bark cloth has been used for a wide variety of purposes both domestic and ceremonial, but its primary application was for clothing. The most important trees used in its manufacture are the paper mulberry, the bread-fruit and the fig-tree, all of which belong to the mulberry family (*Moraceae*). Paper mulberry produces the highest-quality cloth and was cultivated specially for the purpose of *tapa* production, whereas the bread-fruit tree was primarily a food source.

After the trees were felled the bark was stripped from the trunk and soaked for several days to make it soft and flexible, after which the

that *tapa*-making women were able to convey messages over great distances by beating in a rhythmic way and using a well-understood code of signals. Before it was decorated the cloth might be lengthened or made thicker by gumming or felting several sheets together. Pieces of *tapa* might also be sewn together using a bone, wood or bamboo needle and a thread from the same fibre. A small design might be engraved on the mallet or anvil to produce an all-over pattern called a 'watermark'. Otherwise, designs were either painted on free-hand or printed on with hardwood dies or bamboo stamps. The entire cloth might also be dyed with colours made from local plants. The range included red, brown, yellow and black, with a large number of varying shades of red and brown.

The craft of *tapa*-making has now disappeared from many parts of Polynesia, though in some areas there is a thriving tourist market for it.

II

A Survey of World Textiles

LEFT **52** Embroidered cover with carpet patterns. Iran, mid–late 16th century (see II, 7).

The Ancient World

1 Introduction

A century ago invaluable evidence of early civilisations was lost through poor excavation methods, and Egypt was thought to be the only ancient land to have preserved organic material such as cloth. Modern excavation techniques on new sites, however, together with greater awareness among archaeologists and better conservation methods, have revolutionised knowledge of textile production in the ancient Near and Middle East.

Fibres

Flax was the commonest ancient plant fibre, though hemp, rush, palm and papyrus were also used. Probably originating in west Asia, this plant requires a good water-supply and settled, organised communities for its cultivation. Seeds of domesticated flax (*Linum usitatissimum*), found with spindle whorls together on the same site, are indicative of textile activity. They have been found in north Syria (at Ramad), *c.*6000 BC, in Samarran villages in north Iraq (Tel-es-Sawan and Choga Mami), *c.*5000 BC, and in Egypt

neolithic Kom, in the Fayum, has yielded stone and pottery whorls of about 6000 BC, while at the pre-Dynastic sites of Omari, near Cairo, and Abydos, in Upper Egypt, both *c.*5500 BC, flax seeds, whorls, bone needles, cloth and matting were found. Spindles of wood and wooden whorls have not survived from these early times, nor have looms, which were also of wood.

The domestication of sheep, goats and dogs dates from *c.*9000 BC in the uplands of north Iraq at Zam Chem Shanidar, from *c.*7000 BC at Jarmo, in the Zagros Mountains of north-west Iran, and in Palestine and south Turkey from the seventh to sixth millennia BC. Sheep rearing became a major industry in Sumeria *c.*3500 to 3000 BC, by which time both hairy and the later woolly sheep were known. Wool became Ur's principal export, and the Law Code of Hammurabi, *c.*1800 BC, lists it as an export from Babylon. Sheep were also kept at Bougras, in Syria, from *c.*6000 BC, and in Jordan and Palestine from *c.*3000 BC, often simultaneously with flax cultiva-

53 Procession of tribal 'Aamu bringing tribute to Governor Chnemhotep, from his tomb at Beni Hasan, Egypt. 12th Dynasty. In their brightly patterned garments, possibly of wool, the figures may be ancestors of modern Bedouin.

Map 2 Upper Egypt in the classical period.

tion in mixed farming economies, and by pastoral nomads, including the Old Testament Jewish tribes, whose sheep provided wool for tents from time immemorial.

Cotton, native to India, with a variety growing in the Sudan and Ethiopia, is first documented in the 'Annals' of the Ayssyrian King Sennacherib, *c.*700 BC, where it is described as 'tree-bearing wool'. It was imported into the Levant in the Hellenistic period, *c.*323–30 BC, but became important only after the Islamic conquest, in the mid-seventh century AD. Silk, another early Western import, was originally exclusive to China, but the recent discovery of *Bombyx mori* silk thread in a German tribal chief's grave dating from the sixth century BC, at Baden-Württemberg, puts back the silk trade by at least four centuries.

Dyes

Although the ancient Egyptians and, later, the Jews preferred garments of 'white' linen and wool, often for religious purposes, there is plentiful evidence that others did not. They included those whom the Egyptians described as 'barbarians', tribespeople of Semitic origin, as well as Kushites, Nubians and Libyans. In ancient Egypt dyed textiles are rare, but Egyptian tiles and wall-paintings depicting these foreigners

survive. Most famous is the family group of tribal 'Aamu painted in the provincial Governor Chnemhotep's tomb at Beni Hasan, of the Twelfth Dynasty, who wear brightly striped garments, probably of wool. They have been claimed, wrongly, to be Israelites, but the Middle Kingdom date of these paintings is too early. It may be assumed that pastoral peoples of the Levant had similar tastes, but there it was shared by town-dwellers, particularly the wealthy and royalty.

The principal dye plants and mordants such as alum must have been known from early times. Leonard Woolley (1880–1960) found traces of red garments at Ur III from 2100 to 2000 BC, whilst the most celebrated dye, the 'royal purple', from murex, was produced in Tyre, the centre of Phoenician dyeing, and together with other, cheaper dyes and wool became the major trade goods of the adventurous Phoenicians. Recent excavations on the Syrian and Palestine coasts have exposed crushed murex shells, at Ugarit, *c.*1450–1365 BC, and at Byblos, a great trading port. Numerous later dyeworks discovered by Israeli archaeologists include Tell Beit Mirsin, of the eighth century BC, and Tell-Mor, near Ashdod, *c.*400–200 BC. Scraps of dyed wool were found on both these sites.

The earliest textiles

The title of 'earliest textile' has recently shifted from Egypt to Anatolia, with Egypt and Palestine close contenders. James Mellaart's dig at the neolithic village of Çatal Hüyük in southern Turkey, dating from the early sixth millennium BC, exposed fine-spun and plied-thread, plain-weave tabby cloths and garments, some of the latter showing darns, while others had been dyed with local dye plants. Remains of sheep but none of flax led at first to identification of fibres as wool or mohair, but this has been challenged by fibre tests also revealing flax. Çatal Hüyük opened up possibilities for other early finds, but few other Turkish sites have been excavated. However, a burial couch found at Gordion in ancient Phrygia, and dated to the late eighth century BC, was covered by some twenty layers of linen and wool cloth, together with traces of Tyrian purple cloth and fragments of hemp and mohair.

Widespread Israeli excavation has revealed that this country's deserts provide ideal conditions for the preservation of fibre. Finds from the neolithic Hemal Cave in the Judaean Desert, dating from *c.*7160 to 6150 BC, include rope, netting, matting, spun and plied thread, chiefly flax, and tabby-woven cloth, including a blue-dyed textile with shell and bead decoration. In the nearby Nahal Hemal Cave, dating from about the fourth millennium BC, similar finds emerged. Arad, a town site of c.3500—2650 BC, yielded whorls, linen thread wrapped round tool handles, and pottery impressions of fine plain weave. At the copper-mine of Timna, established by the Egyptians using local labour, c.1300 BC, rare fragments of a large tent-shrine of thick red and yellow wool tabby were found. Later town sites have all preserved textiles. Tell el-Hamah, dating from about the tenth to eighth centuries BC, and Tell Beit Mirsin, destroyed by the Egyptians in the tenth century BC, yielded tools and textiles, and large quantities of linen cloth fragments were found at Kuntillet Ajrud, in the Negev area, a trading settlement from the ninth to the eighth centuries.

Early trade

Archaeological evidence shows that trade was established as early as the neolithic period in the seventh millennium BC. Wool and cloth were important trade goods in the East–West trade. Maritime trade between south Mesopotamian cities and the Indus Valley is documented by tablets from Ur, dated c.2000 BC, which refer to trade with 'Dilmun' (Bahrain) and 'Makan' (probably Oman). Ur's textile goods were exchanged for raw materials. A tablet of c.2026 BC records a loan by Ur's Temple of Nanna to a merchant of 'sixty talents of wool, seventy garments and 180 skeins for buying copper from Makan'. Ur also traded up-river to Babylon and Mari in north Syria.

Wars and territorial conquests were largely motivated by trade. The warlike Assyrians consolidated their military expansion by building caravan routes and caravanserai long before the Arabs, with whom the caravan is usually identified. Assyrian merchants were established at Kanesh (Kultepe) near Kayseri in south Turkey in 2000 BC. The lucrative Phoenician trade in dyed wool, from c.1700 BC, relied on the wool of its hinterland, the profits from which were later shared by the Jewish kings. The 'Book of Ezekiel' records sheep and goats from Arabia, white wool from Hebron and Egyptian linen, all marketed in Damascus. These trade links were the foundation of later Hellenistic and Roman trade around the Mediterranean.

54 Tapestry fragment worked with the cartouche of Amenhotep II, and lotus and papyrus, the symbols of Upper and Lower Egypt, from the tomb of Tuthmosis IV, his son, at Thebes. 18th Dynasty.

2 *The Mediterranean*

Ancient Egypt

Egypt is unique in textile history. Her dry, sterile sands have preserved tools, textiles, documentary and pictorial evidence, making possible a cohesive account of her textile history which is lacking elsewhere.

Linen was the paramount fibre, and other plant fibres were used, though wool was very rare in the Pharaonic period, owing to a religious prohibition against wearing or being buried in animal fibres, mentioned by Herodotus (*The Histories*, Book II, p. 159). Flax cultivation and fibre preparation were men's work. A winter crop, it was harvested by pulling during March, and the soaking (retting) and beating (scutching) of the outer bast fibres are all recorded. Spinning and weaving were women's work until the end of the Middle Kingdom (Twelfth Dynasty, *c*.1786 BC). A flat, smooth, wooden disc whorl was used by this time, with a wood spindle, and the drop-spindle method was preferred as it gave a strong, even thread. Plying was done by placing feeder balls of spun thread in a pot with rings in its base; such pots have survived. Egyptian flax twists naturally to the right (s-twist) and was most commonly plied to the left (z-twist). Egyptian cloth's high quality was said to be due to careful fibre preparation.

The Middle Kingdom (Eleventh and Twelfth Dynasties, *c*.2133–1786 BC) is exceptionally well documented. Servant models from nobles' tombs show textile workshops with spinning, plying, warping and weaving in progress, information which is supported by similar scenes in tomb-paintings of provincial governors at Beni Hasan. In addition tools were found in the houses of Kahun, a contemporary workmen's town near by.

The two-beam horizontal (ground) loom was used in Egypt from the earliest times until the end of the Middle Kingdom. This is one of the watersheds of Egyptian textile history. By the early New Kingdom (*c*.1552 BC) a domed spindle whorl and a vertical two-beam loom were in use, and professional weavers were male. These were all foreign innovations, introduced during the Hyksos invasions, although the conservative Egyptians did not entirely abandon the old tools.

Simple plain-weave tabby predominated until the Ptolemaic period, but with a great variety of thickness and texture, and, as with other Egyptian crafts like stone-working, the finest cloth was made from the earliest times. Evenly spun and woven linen tabby cloths from Badarian burials, *c*.5000 BC, have a thread count of eleven to fourteen warps and twenty-four to twenty-eight wefts per square centimetre, and First Dynasty tabbies from Tarkhan have medium-fine counts of eleven to fourteen warps and twenty-four to twenty-eight wefts per square centimetre. Kahun's cottage industry produced coarse, medium-fine and fine cloth to meet all needs.

Linen cloth was finished by washing, and the finer types were bleached and sun-dried and even polished. The yellowish tint of some textiles may indicate the addition of saffron, which was used as an insecticide. Cloth was woven in the small home and on great estates, in royal and state workshops and in temples. The professional weaver's state was unenviable, according to the New Kingdom 'Satire on Trades' (Papyrus Sallier, 11.7, 2–4): 'The weaver in the workshop he is worse [off] than a woman. His knees are drawn up to his belly, he cannot breathe the open air. If he cuts short the day's weaving he is beaten with fifty thongs . . .'. Nevertheless, Egypt's linen industry was a vital one. Linen cloth was used for all household purposes, like bedding and hangings, and mountains of it were necessary for mummification, although old cloth was recycled for inner bandages, with new cloth on top. In the absence of coinage payment for work was made in the form of cloth or garments, together with food. The other main use of linen was for dress – even labourers wore brief white loincloths. Among royalty and the nobility plain white linen was a foil to the magnificent jewellery worn by both sexes, and fine, translucent linen half-revealed the wearer's limbs.

Dyed textiles are very rare. The ancient Egyptians, like the Israelites later, were obsessed by hygiene and preferred 'white' (bleached) linen. Linen, moreover, does not take dyes well. A few New Kingdom textiles with indigo selvage stripes, and cloth from Tutankhamun's tomb, reveal that the indigo dye has not fully penetrated the fibres. Nevertheless, coloured and patterned textiles are not totally absent. Foreigners are depicted in brightly patterned garments and, curiously, so are Egyptian gods, kings and priests in their ceremonial dress, doubtless preserved from Egypt's earliest history. A tiny ivory statuette of an unknown First

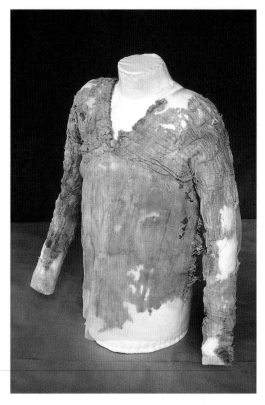

quiver and gloves are ornamented in soft blues, browns and reds, now much faded. The King's underwear, linen loincloths, kilts and a shirt were also in the tomb. The fine-woven shirt has on it the regnal year date of Akenaten, the 'heretic Pharaoh', and is another family heirloom, although Akenaten's family relationship with Tutankhamun is disputed. One kilt is made of coloured beadwork, and gold rosettes and sequins decorated clothing and palls. Although some garments may have been worn by the boy-king in his lifetime, it is thought that the 'dalma-

ABOVE 55 The so-called tunic of Tutankhamun, from his tomb at Thebes. 18th Dynasty. The applied ornament at the neck of the garment provides some of the earliest evidence for embroidery in Egypt.

ABOVE RIGHT 56 Pleated linen dress for a girl, from Tarkhan, Egypt, 1st Dynasty.

Dynasty king, *c.* 3050–2890 BC, shows the king in a lozenge-patterned cloak, perhaps the *heb-sed*, or Jubilee garment.

Four linen cloths with coloured tapestry of lotus and papyrus, symbols of Upper and Lower Egypt respectively, and royal cartouches were found in the Theban tomb of the Eighteenth Dynasty King Tuthmosis IV (*c.* 1412–1364 BC). Family heirlooms, three of them have the cartouches of the King's father, Amenophis II, and grandfather, Tuthmosis III. Tutankhamun's funerary wardrobe gives the most complete glimpse of royal finery, however, and includes garments unparalleled in Egyptian history. The famous sleeved tunic, or 'dalmatic', has applied decorative bands of embroidery and an unidentified warp-faced weave at each side, an *ankh* at the neck, the King's cartouche and motifs which are distinctly Syrian in flavour. The tunic, and a

tic' was for funerary purposes only. The sad condition of most of these textiles precludes closer study.

The presence of patterned textiles in these two tombs raises the issue of whether they may have been imported. The tapestry articles from Tuthmosis IV's tomb are the earliest found in Egypt, and Syrian/Mesopotamian motifs on Tutankhamun's tunic might suggest foreign workmanship. However, the Egyptians may have learned tapestry weaving in the New Kingdom, a time of eastward expansion.

Another famous patterned textile is the 'girdle of Rameses III', now in Liverpool Museum, identified by this king's cartouches and a date. Its weave, somewhat resembling tablet weaving, is still unidentified. On it are *ankhs* and small geometric motifs. It is certainly a girdle, which has been disputed, but not the wide,

EGYPTIAN PERIODS AND DYNASTIES

PERIOD	DATE	DYNASTY
Pre-dynastic period	c.5000–3100 BC	
Archaic period	c.3100–2890 BC	I
	c.2890–2686 BC	II
Old Kingdom	c.2686–2613 BC	III
	c.2613–2494 BC	IV
	c.2494–2345 BC	V
	c.2345–2181 BC	VI
First Intermediate period	c.2181–2173 BC	VII
	c.2173–2160 BC	VIII
	c.2160–2130 BC	IX
	c.2130–2040 BC	X
	c.2133–1991 BC	XI
Middle Kingdom	1991–1786 BC	XII
Second Intermediate period	1786–1633 BC	XIII
	1786–c.1603 BC	XIV
	1674–1567 BC	XV
	c.1684–1567 BC	XVI
	c.1650–1567 BC	XVII
New Kingdom	1567–1320 BC	XVIII
	1320–1200 BC	XIX
	1200–1085 BC	XX
Third Intermediate period	1085–945 BC	XXI
	945–730 BC	XXII
	817?–730 BC	XXIII
	720–715 BC	XXIV
	715–668 BC	XXV
Late period	664–525 BC	XXVI
	525–404 BC	XXVII
	404–399 BC	XXVIII
	399–380 BC	XXIX
	380–343 BC	XXX
	343–332 BC	XXXI
Conquest by Alexander the Great	332 BC	
Ptolemaic period	332–30 BC	Graeco–Roman period
Conquest by Romans	30 BC	
Roman period	30 BC–4th century AD	

Taken from A. Rosalie David, *The Ancient Egyptians: Religious Beliefs and Practices*, Routledge, London and New York, 1982

jewelled type worn by Pharaohs. However, it closely resembles the narrower, patterned girdles worn by women in New Kingdom wall-paintings.

Other known Egyptian weaves are weft-loop pile and a crimped fabric resembling seersucker, shown as an over-robe worn by ladies at a party in a tomb-painting of Neb-Amun at Thebes,

c.1400 BC. Pleating was an early skill. Royalty and nobles wore kilts pleated at the front. The earliest pleated garment is that of a teenage girl, from Tarkhan, of First Dynasty date, c.2800 BC. The top of the garment survives, with tightly pleated sleeves and yoke. Wooden objects identified as 'pleating boards' are not universally accepted as such, and some think that pleating was done with the fingers and some form of starch.

The Hellenistic kingdoms

The ancient world finally collapsed when Alexander, King of Macedon, conquered huge territories round the east and south Mediterranean and brought other lands much further east – Persia, Central Asia and part of India – into the Macedonian Greek sphere of influence. After his death in 323 BC his empire was divided among his generals, who founded feudal monarchies. The name 'Hellenistic' means 'Greek-ish'. Seleucus and his descendants ruled Syria and Iraq from 321 BC, the Attalids held Pergamum and Asia Minor until Attalus III bequeathed his kingdom to Rome in 133 BC, while Ptolemy took the greatest prize, Egypt, founding the most continuously successful dynasty from c.332 to 30 BC. Egypt thus became part of the Hellenistic world, and Alexandria, with Pergamum and Antioch, became one of its chief cities.

Textile industries grew where the climate and water-supply were suitable, and where a skilled labour force and trade connections existed. Once established, there would be little reason for them to move unless the political climate changed. Egypt's production, for instance, was to be harnessed by her various conquerors – Greek, Roman, Byzantine and Arab. Hellenistic rulers consciously encouraged trade throughout their world and beyond, since the potential profits were enormous. Syria's wool, woollen goods and dyestuffs were widely exported, even into Egypt, although Tyre's leadership ended when Alexander destroyed the city in 332 BC. Damascus, on the other hand, continued to handle textile specialities from elsewhere, wool from Miletus and towels from Ephesus (presumably a pile cloth).

Macedonians in their native land were considered barbarians by the Athenian Greeks, who criticised their taste for richly coloured fabrics. Among the rare surviving pieces is the cloth which wrapped the cremated bones of King Philip II, father of Alexander (died 330 BC), and was found in a gold casket in his tomb at Vergina. It is a wool tabby of Tyrian purple with a wide tapestry of gold metal thread, with mythological creatures and scrolls similar to those on contemporary jewellery.

This would have been very much to the taste of peoples in the later Hellenistic Empire, however, a period characterised by the development of pattern weaving. Syria is credited with the beginnings of twill weaving during the third century BC and with early damasks. It is also thought that tapestry weaving developed there, though these theories cannot be sustained without firm evidence, and textile finds are negligible. However, it does seem reasonable to concede that tapestry was woven in this large area, then adopted wholesale under the Romans. It is the earliest and simplest way of producing a complex pattern and, before the drawloom, the only one.

Once again, it is necessary to turn to Egypt for information and textiles. The Ptolemies brought coinage with them, increased the Delta's fertility by better irrigation, and extended its area by land reclamation. They imported Miletus sheep from Asia Minor to improve the native stock and introduced cotton. Their capital city, founded by Alexander himself, rivalled Rome and, later Byzantium, in its intellectual and artistic activity and world trade. Its chief products were glass, papyrus paper and linen. Although both Hellenistic Greeks and Romans embraced Pharaonic religious and burial practices and built 'Pharaonic' temples, the native Egyptians and Egypt's Jews were denied citizenship and heavily taxed.

Mummification was still practised, even among the Greeks, requiring plain linen cloth in abundance. A Greek feature was the winding of outer wrappings into decorative checked patterns. A linen tabby with regular rows of weft-loop pile has been wrongly attributed to the Greeks. In fact, examples of this technique date back to the Old Kingdom in Egypt, where it was used to make warm garments in parts of the country which have chilly nights. Wool became more common, for warm clothing, rugs and mattresses, and the tapestry technique developed. Together with fine linens it became one of Alexandria's specialities.

The Roman period

The Hellenistic kingdoms became the Roman Empire's Eastern Provinces, where efficient taxation became the keynote. Subject peoples had to endure a regular census – hence Joseph and Mary's journey before Christ's birth – and the Edict of Diocletian in AD 30–1 fixed prices throughout the Empire for common goods, including cloth.

The caravan cities of Petra, Palmyra and Dura-Europos handled overland trade from China, India and Iran. The wars waged against Iran over control of western routes were not always victorious for the Romans. Exotic goods, chiefly spices and silk, were sent on to Antioch, Alexandria and Rome. Plain and striped fabrics and garments of tabby, and twills and compound cloths, dating from the first to the third centuries AD, were found at Palmyra, and whole linen and wool garments, woven in one piece, and a rare weft-faced compound wool cloth with a reversible key pattern were discovered at Dura.

The At Tar Caves, in west Iraq, an ongoing excavation at a Silk Road site, have revealed similar textiles in thousands, from the late second century BC to the fifth century AD. When fully published they should provide a firmer chronology for other, undated material. The textiles are principally wool, with some linen and cotton, and patterned pieces include twills, tapestry, embroidered fabrics and resist-dyed cotton. Tapestry 'portraits' in square frame borders resemble other contemporary output. The pile fragments will expand knowledge of carpet history. Among them may have been trade goods, the textiles travelling east and some, at least, of the carpets to the west.

Textiles found in Israel obey the Jewish Law (Shaatnez), prohibiting the mixing of animal and vegetable fibres, but otherwise are similar to textiles elsewhere. In the Cave of Letters, 132 BC–AD 35, indigo- and purple-dyed yarns, white wool tent yarn, plain and striped tabbies, garments and linen scroll-wrappers were found. At Masada, destroyed by the Romans in AD 273,

57 Tapestry hanging depicting Hestia Polyolbos, goddess of the domestic hearth, with her attendants, Light and Poetry, and putti bearing the gifts of Peace, Progress, Virtue and Wealth. Alexandria, 3rd–4th century AD. H: 1.13 m (3.6 ft).

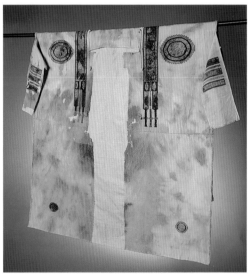

papyri also record small town enterprises, like that of Tryphon, in the first century AD. His was the fifth generation of his family to own a weaving workshop, and he employed paid labour and apprentices. Guilds existed, their chief function to organise larger government orders and guarantee quality. Even temples still played a part. Two temples in Karanis each owned a weaving workshop, and the Temple of Serapis in Oxyrhynchus was the town's bank and tax office.

An abundance of textiles survives from this period, principally from cemeteries; poorly excavated in the nineteenth century, the material cannot be accurately dated. Although mummification was adopted by some wealthy Romans, the commonest type of burial was in a pit, the body in everyday clothes with a shroud, or shroudless. Household textiles were often used,

ABOVE **58** Child's tunic, wool with tapestry-woven ornament. Egypt, 9th–10th century AD.

ABOVE RIGHT **59** Man's tunic, wool with tapestry-woven ornament. Egypt, 6th–7th century AD.

the baskets and mats of the Zealots who died there were preserved with household cloths, tapestry, clothing and sandals.

Egypt again has preserved papyri at Oxyrhynchus, Karanis and Antinoopolis (Antinoë), recording administration, lawsuits and personal correspondence. Alexandria was still the capital, and Egypt supplied military and civilian clothing to the rest of the Empire. Rural life continued much the same as ever for the Egyptians. Remote from the capital, the Egyptian farmer may have been aware only that his masters had changed. Roman technical innovations were the distaff, which made spinning faster, sheep-shearing, which superseded plucking of wool, fulling and new methods of bleaching and dyeing. Weaving remained a cottage industry, and on country estates, which the Romans encouraged by granting land to retired soldiers, sheep were kept and their wool woven. The

as a shroud or cushions supporting the head. Only one large hanging with portraits of Aurelius Colluthus and his wife, from Antinoë, can be dated from AD 454 to 456 by dated material also in their tomb. Nevertheless, large tapestry hangings have survived, of the type admired by Theocritus' two Syracusan ladies at a Festival of Adonis: 'the figures stand and turn so naturally, they're alive, not woven . . .' (*Idyll*, 15, 82–6). They were an Alexandrian speciality, showing Graeco–Roman mythological scenes and celebrations of the Nile-god, with his attendant Nereids, finely and evenly woven in polychrome wools from competent designs. They probably competed with paintings to decorate the walls of wealthy homes.

The largest number of tapestry fragments were dress ornaments. Some whole garments survive, and Roman mosaics at Piazza Armerina in Sicily show unshaped tunics with varied

60 Tapestry fragment depicting a mounted huntsman with putti, Roman. Egypt, 4th century AD.

ornament of bands or medallions of geometric motifs. Surviving garments show that tunic and decoration were woven while the garment was on the loom. Warps were of linen or wool, and the tapestry in polychrome colours or indigo on white. A feature of the 'blue and white' style is the fine detail worked with the tapestry, at the front, using supplementary weft wrapping with a hand shuttle and a single linen thread. The belief that polychrome and 'blue and white'

tapestry are of different dates is untrue. In Roman mosaics, which they resemble, the two styles appear contemporaneously.

Geometric patterns, and mythological, hunting and bucolic scenes predominate, often with vine-scrolls, and another favourite was the portrait personification in a square 'frame'. This theme is the subject of a small group of embroideries, of which the finest depicts 'Autumn', with a companion season, 'Winter', of the fourth

century AD. 'Autumn' represents a peak in Roman imperial art; 'Winter' is less well drawn but of special interest. Both embroideries are close to contemporary Roman mosaics, but 'Winter' strongly resembles a mosaic in Bignor Villa, West Sussex, the two providing evidence that design pattern-books circulated round the Roman Empire.

Weft-loop pile was also used for similar 'portraits' and scenes, although the reason for using this technique for pictorial textiles is unclear. Knitting should also be mentioned, for Roman socks, even for children, survive, made with a separate big toe to accommodate a sandal.

Coptic textiles

'Coptic' is a nineteenth-century blanket term for post-Pharaonic textiles, and a new definition is needed. Egypt after the Pharaohs became a land of 'layered' cultures, of foreigners isolated from natives. 'Post-Pharaonic' seems apt for the entire group, subdivided by 'Ptolemaic', 'Roman' and 'Coptic', the latter referring only to those with Christian subjects or in the Coptic figure style.

Christianity came early to Egypt, possibly at St Mark's first visit in AD 41. The first converts

ABOVE **61** Embroidered panel depicting 'Autumn', Roman. Egypt, 4th century AD.

62 Tapestry hanging depicting huntsmen, warriors and dancers. Egypt, 5th century AD.

were Greeks and Jews in Alexandria, and this city became a prominent theological centre from the second century. The Egyptian populace was slower to convert, from the third century, although an estimated eighty per cent of the country's population was Christian by the end of the fourth. Except for provincial towns rural Egypt was deeply divided from the capital, and in rural areas monasticism took hold, with largely peasant monks who worked and prayed, unambitious and, on the whole, lacking wealthy patronage to produce great art or libraries. Monks made baskets and cloth for sale, and tapes for binding shrouds. Weavers were absorbed, and in some communities unskilled novices were taught to weave. Papyri so far discovered are religious texts.

Paganism did not finally disappear until the sixth century, so it is not surprising that the familiar classical themes continued, albeit in increasingly diluted form. The great tapestries of Alexandria perished and, in fact, the city declined in importance with the growth of Byzantium. Most of the surviving fragments derive from everyday dress, buried with their owners as before. The Coptic figure style, fully developed by the sixth century, followed contemporary trends in painting and sculpture. Figures are in frontal view, with large heads and eyes, and seem to shed their years, whether the subject is religious, like the Joseph story, or pagan, like the Labours of Hercules. Early bishops deplored the tendency to wear brightly patterned dress, but this favourite fashion endured into the Islamic period. Religious subjects are, in fact, fairly rare. 'Joseph's Dream' has been found decorating tunics, one even with a Hebrew inscription; indeed, Joseph became patriarch of the Coptic Church. Nameless Coptic saints, usually on horseback, standing priests and devotees and the Coptic cross, which derives from the Pharaonic *ankh*, form the range. Otherwise the repertory is much as before, with the Coptic *horror vacui* adding crowded plant and flower ornament. Without accomplished designers and fresh inspiration these motifs metamorphosed into a folk art which, nevertheless, survived until the twelfth century.

LEFT **63** Tapestry roundel depicting the story of Joseph, Coptic. Egypt, 7th century AD.

TOP **64** Curtain fabric in weft-loop pile and wools on linen depicting a woman praying, from Schech Sayet, Egypt. 6th century AD.

ABOVE **65** Tapestry medallion, Egypt, 6th–7th century AD. The design is a Coptic version of a Sassanian drawloom fabric.

3 Central and northern Europe

Prehistoric archaeology in Europe begins with the first traces of man on the continent around 600,000 years ago and lasts in the south until Rome's colonial expansion in the first century BC, but in the north until the advent of Christianity nearly 1,000 years later. For what we know of the earliest textiles and allied structures we are reliant on archaeological finds of fabrics and textile implements – and on the vagaries of their survival in the special conditions which inhibit decay, such as wet bog deposits. A handful of important discoveries allows us a mere glimpse of early man's textile technical achievements.

The Stone Age

Fragments of fishing net from Finland dating to the eighth millennium BC show that the bast fibres from the stem of the willow and other trees were the first material in Europe to be twisted into yarn. However, textiles properly speaking are not attested until c.4200 BC, when the mesolithic inhabitants of Tybrind Vig, now a submerged site off the Danish island of Funen, spun willow bast and grasses into yarn and from it constructed with a needle bags and possibly clothing in several forms of knotless netting. Although culturally earlier, they were working over 2,000 years later than the neolithic weavers of Çatal Hüyük in Turkey, referred to earlier (see II, 1).

66 The Egtved girl in her oak coffin. Denmark, Early Bronze Age, c. 1400 BC.

By far the most significant early European textiles are the technically sophisticated examples from the later neolithic (4000–2000 BC) villages on the shores of the Swiss lakes. Elm, oak and especially lime bast fibres were woven into fine tabby cloth, decorated not only with elaborate borders but with remarkable fleecy surface effects, and weft-wrapped and brocaded to render complex designs. Netting, basketry and matting were much in evidence too. Pottery spindle whorls and loom weights coupled with the characteristic flat-woven starting borders on some textiles point to a thriving industry based on the upright warp-weighted loom. Flax was grown, spun and woven, but wool is not found before c.2400 BC; for the first domesticated sheep had hairy coats and only later were bred for wool.

The Bronze Age (2000–700 BC)

In the Bronze Age the centre of interest shifts to north Germany and Denmark and to a series of graves containing bodies fully clothed. The girl's ensemble there consisted of a tight-fitting bodice with embroidery round the halterneck, a short openwork corded skirt and sometimes a hairnet. The corresponding male costume included a loincloth, a heavy cloak (oval in outline) and a bonnet. The last two sometimes had added pile. Only tiny fragments of textile survive elsewhere in Europe (including Britain). Wool was now the principal fibre of northern Europe, and by 700 BC its quality had been enhanced by selective breeding; flax remained the preferred fibre of the south. Tabby weave, often coarse, was almost universal, but 2/2 twill had arrived by 800 BC. The warp-weighted loom was standard, but the upright two-beam loom, lacking weights, was found locally.

The Iron Age

Before the Romans (700–50 BC)

Danish bog finds of the early Iron Age feature twill skirts, scarves and leg wrappings with checked designs and plaited ('sprang') hairnets, all in wool. Central Europe from 500 BC had a different and richer tradition with greater local diversity: 2/2 twill (occasionally diamond twill) is strongly represented, and patterns are based on checks of dyed and naturally pigmented yarns or yarns with contrasting spin-directions. The contents of the princely tomb at Hochdorf, Stuttgart, including brocades, fine embroidery

rectangular cloaks demonstrate most vividly the versatility of the warp-weighted loom on which decorative fringed tablet-woven selvages were woven *pari passu* with the main web of cloth and were matched by tablet-woven starting and finishing borders. The warrior's fitted trousers, on the other hand, were a tribute to the tailor's art.

For all garments 2/2 twill weave – and often its developed form, diamond twill – had become the norm, and measured by any criterion cloth quality had reached a peak. Improved fleeces from this period onwards were regularly white, an encouragement to the dyer: woad gave blue, lichens a purple, and some red and yellow dyes have not yet been identified. The famous mantle from Thorsberg, Germany, for instance, was a three-tone woad-blue check, and the girl's costume from Lønne Hede, Denmark, included a blue- and red-checked wrap and blouse with white and red tablet-woven edging. Flax, used for simple tabby weaves, was a subordinate fibre with a central and southern distribution; hemp cultivation had only just begun in Europe. There was a good deal of technical overlap between the weavers inside and outside the Roman frontiers; for they enjoyed a common heritage from the earlier Iron Age distinct from that of the Mediterranean.

After the Romans (AD 400–800)

As the Romans withdrew from western Europe after AD 400, they were replaced by vigorous new Germanic kingdoms whose textile technology was partly inherited Iron Age and partly informed by new trends from the Byzantine east. The Anglo-Saxons in Britain continued to weave good-quality wool cloth in tabby, 2/2 and 2/1 twill and fine tabby linens on the warp-weighted loom; loom weights are regularly unearthed in Anglo-Saxon huts. However, their luxury products now included gold-brocaded, tablet-woven braids and some outstanding silk and gold embroideries. On the Continent Alamannic weavers developed decorative rosette twills and ribbed twills in wool, and the contents of Frankish and Anglo-Saxon royal tombs demonstrate their taste for Byzantine silks, Coptic tapestry and pile rugs. The simple Iron Age clothing styles inevitably yielded to the influence of these new luxuries.

The Vikings (AD 800–1000)

Trade in exotic and expensive textiles owed much to the Vikings who roved freely across Europe after AD 800; but Viking 'homespuns' included some exceptionally fine worsted diamond twills and high-quality linens dyed with both local and imported dyestuffs. The tablet-woven braids which edged their tunics were minor works of art, as were the hangings in wrapped and woven tapestry technique.

67 Modern reconstruction of the Thorsberg mantle. Iron Age, *c.* AD 200.

and complex tablet-woven bands emphasise the remarkable quality of sixth-century textile art.

Alongside the Romans (50 BC–AD 400)

The powerful image of the Iron Age warrior-aristocrat of barbarian Europe, clad in long wool trousers, and long-sleeved shirt and cloak, is echoed in the ritual deposits of weaponry, accoutrements and cloth cast into the Nordic bogs and lakes to celebrate local victories. The large

The Near and Middle East

4 Sassanian textiles

Sassanian textiles, with heraldically treated creatures in repeating pearl roundels, were arguably the most influential in weaving history, yet some scholars doubt that any have survived. Those claimed to be authentic came from Egyptian sites, notably Antinoë, from Western tombs and church treasuries, and Silk Road burials. None has been found in Iran, where the only evidence for them is late Sassanian royal rock reliefs.

Iranian textile production is recorded from the Achaemenid Dynasty (c.559–330 BC), and Herodotus (*The Histories*, Book I) testifies to the Persian love of brilliantly coloured finery, even among the military. After the Seleucid Empire collapsed in the early third century BC two native dynasties of nomad origin, the little-known Parthians (c.211 BC–AD 224) and the Sassanians (AD 224–642), restored Achaemenid concepts of kingship and religion to reinforce their own claims. Both dynasties exploited Iran's strategic role in the lucrative Silk Road trade, threatening Roman and Byzantine control of the Western land routes. At its fullest extent in the mid-sixth century the Sassanian Empire stretched from west Iraq to Central Asia.

68 Rock relief (RIGHT) of King Khusrau II at Tāq-ī-Bustān, Iran. Late 6th century AD. The king's clothing is patterned with *senmurv* (FAR RIGHT), as seen on a silver-gilt dish of the 7th century.

The Persians possibly knew the secret of sericulture by the third century AD and probably wove with Chinese yarn before that. Where the drawloom system originated is unknown, but Iran's previous claim has now yielded to Syria, still without firm evidence. However, suspect Arab accounts that King 'Shāpūr' settled captive Western craftsmen in Iran are now vindicated by a Pahlavi inscription of King Shāpūr I (AD 241–72) at Naqsh-i-Rustam, and these prisoners-of-war, including weavers, were Syrians captured by this king at Antioch. Using their skills,

Shāpūr developed sericulture in the Caspian satrapies, exporting silk yarn to Byzantium and Central Asia, and fostered weaving in Susiana (now Khuzistan), founding new cities there.

However, there are no known textiles from this mid-dynasty period. Only on later royal reliefs, of King Khusrau II (AD 591–628), does any evidence for patterned clothing appear. There are three rock reliefs at Tāq-ī-Bustān. The King, armoured and mounted, dominates one relief, and the other two show a royal boar hunt and a deer hunt respectively. The boar hunt was a Zoroastrian concept, the boar both god and sacrifice. The King's role was as Divine Ruler, and only he wears garments patterned with large *senmurv*, a mystic creature, half-bird, half-dog. Not to be confused with the griffin, in the *Zend Avesta* (the sacred book of Zoroastrianism) the benevolent *senmurv* roosts on the tree which grows between heaven and earth, sending rain and seed to humankind below.

Two surviving *senmurv* silks may be Sassanian. Found in a reliquary in the Church of St Lieu in Paris, one fragment is now in Paris and the other is in London. They are closely identified with Sassanian royalty by crescents of the

moon goddess, intersecting the pearl borders, also found on Sassanian crowns. Previously thought to come from the same silk, the Paris fragment has only two crescents to the London piece's four, suggesting different loom widths. This powerful symbol was much copied after the fall of the dynasty. The 'Shroud of St Rémi', now in Rheims, may be a ninth-century Central Asian version, and a tribal chieftain's caftan, from his grave at Mochtchevaya Balka, in the Caucasus, certainly is. Recently discovered and of about ninth-century date, this silk garment

69 Compound weft-faced silk twill depicting *senmurv* in pearl-bordered roundels, from the relics of St Rémi, Paris. Iran, Sassanian, late 6th century AD.

70 Compound weft-faced silk twill depicting a ram wearing the Sassanian royal collar, from Antinoë, Egypt. Iran, Sassanian, late 6th century AD.

has five large *senmurv*, each confronting or addorsing its neighbour, across the garment's width, suggesting a loom width of 80 cm (31.5 in). The Sassanian royal crescents have been replaced by innocuous four-lobed rosettes.

Silks and a Persian 'riding-coat' found at Antinoë may have the best claim to Sassanian origin, although found in an undated context. One shows a magnificent ram, with the royal collar and fluttering ribbons. The ram and the boar represent the god Verethragna, who punished evil-doers in the *Avesta*. The boar's head was a personal device of Khusrau II, and boatmen wear it on their livery on the boar hunt relief. The famous boar's head silk from Astana, excavated at a Silk Road site in east Turkistan (now in the National Museum, New Delhi), is a degenerate eighth- to ninth-century Central Asian version but retains much of the animal's menace. The large repeat, 19 × 20 cm (7.5 × 7.9 in), is a feature of Sassanian textiles, to judge by those worn on the reliefs, and remained a feature of later copies.

Birds, harbingers of good fortune, appear at Tāq-ī-Bustān, where cocks, ducks and waterfowl ornament servants' dress. A silk with rows of cocks standing on jewelled plinths which resemble Sassanian metalwork (Vatican Library, Museo Sacro) is likely to be a Byzantine version, with a border no longer of pearls but otherwise close to the original. Early Islamic versions were discovered at Fustāt. Birds holding necklaces or garlands in their beaks are common motifs in Sassanian silver (which has its own problems of identification). A silk with a pheasant holding a branch in its beak (Vatican Library, Museo Sacro) is very similar to a ninth-century fresco at Varaksha. The duck with an object in its beak, the *tse-naio* (gnawing bird), is of Chinese Buddhist origin and was adopted by Sassanian, Byzantine and later Spanish-Islamic designers.

Some believe that the pearl roundel also reached Sassanian Iran from China. It seems more likely that Sassanian kings, who wore pearl collars and diadems on their crowns,

investiture scenes in which the King receives the royal diadem from the god Ahuramazda. Usually mounted, the figures face each other across the central diadem, their horses nose-to-nose. Hunting was an obsession of the Persians and was closely linked with their religious beliefs; such scenes were depicted in fresco in mid-dynasty palaces. One silk, a Byzantine copy, certainly has a purely Persian subject (Sant' Ambrogio, Milan). It shows the legendary feat of King Bahram V (Gor) killing a lion and a wild ass (*gor*) with a single arrow. Other silks show kings in pseudo-Iranian dress. One of the famous Byzantine chariot silks has, in the spandrels, tiny figures of charioteers wearing pseudo-Sassanian royal crowns (Musées d'Art et d'Histoire, Brussels). Hundreds of other silks, dating to the eleventh century, testify to the lasting popularity of these motifs.

71 Compound weft-faced silk depicting Bahram Gor killing a lion and an ass with one arrow. 8th century AD. These poorly preserved fragments are both right-hand sides of two repeats. Probably woven in Byzantium or Syria, they are based on a Sassanian original.

adopted this symbol of power from Assyrian royal crowns and from Hellenistic coins, on which the rulers' heads are framed by circles of discs. The circle itself reflects the circular diadem of kingly power, so that not only in their iconography but in their actual composition the silks, too, are overt royal propaganda.

Many textiles survive with hunting and battle scenes, showing a pair of figures confronted on either side of a central axis. They are known through Byzantine and Central Asian – and even Coptic – versions. Although this composition does not appear at Tāq-ī-Bustān, earlier rock reliefs at Naqsh-i-Rustam, in south Iran, feature

Sassanian textiles remain shrouded in mystery for lack of firmly attributable pieces and of historical evidence. They live largely through Byzantine silk weaving, but relations between Byzantine and Sassanian courts, both of which supported State weaving industries, remain unstudied. Later Persians regarded the Sassanian period as a golden age and perpetuated it in textiles, miniature painting and literature. Their iconography of kingship, battles and hunting, and their heraldic imagery, appealed outside Iran to feudal societies as widespread and varying as those in early Islam, in Christian Europe and in Tang China.

5 Early Islamic textiles

When the Prophet Muhammad died in AD 632 he left an undivided state and a religion, based on the Koran, the Word of God revealed to him. However, he left no sons, and the first three caliphs were chosen from his Companions in Medina as the spiritual and temporal leaders of Islam. But 'Ali, his son-in-law, claimed the succession through his wife Fatima, the Prophet's daughter, and founded a separatist movement, Shi'ia. In the ensuing wars 'Ali and his son, Hosein, were killed. The orthodox Sunni and the Shi'ia remain separate sects today.

Muhammad's plans to spread Islam by conquest were carried out by the early caliphs, whose small Arab armies rapidly conquered a vast empire. Syria, Palestine and Iraq were theirs by AD 635, Egypt by 641–2 and Iran by 651. Later campaigns swept westward along the African coast and to southern Spain, and eastward to Central Asia. Their small numbers encouraged the early Arabs to impose only loose control in conquered lands, leaving administration and industries in local hands, under a Muslim governor. However, some of these were able to assume personal control, and the caliphs gradually lost their political power over their empire of disparate races, though in religious matters they remained supreme.

The Muslim prohibition against natural forms in art has been misunderstood in the West. It does not appear in the Koran, and early decoration, even of mosques, borrowed from existing art forms, chiefly Byzantine. It does appear in the Hadith (Tradition), a corpus of Muhammad's own teachings codified up to 200 years after his death, which refers particularly to religious art. The doctrine reveals the deepest split between the two major Islamic factions, for the Shi'ia Fatimids in Egypt and Iranian rulers favoured the human form, while the Sunni tolerated only abstract and geometric motifs. Surface decoration, whether of buildings, ceramic tiles or textiles, became the chief expression of the Islamic style, with designs common to them all. In no other cultures have textiles been more highly valued, for their own sake, as an important adjunct to court ritual and as precious trade goods.

Textile industries are well documented by Arab writers, particularly the *tirāz* system, developed from Byzantine and Sassanian imperial workshops, which worked solely for the ruler. It is associated particularly with the Abbasid dynasty, from the late ninth to the eleventh centuries AD. Clothing had changed to looser garments of thin cloth, the male dress consisting of a shirt, a long gown, baggy trousers and a turban, while women wore garments of similar cut and covered the head with a shawl or veil. Sleeves, necks, turbans and veils bore inscribed bands, the nature of which seem to indicate that they were worn by the moneyed classes. Most surviving pieces were found at Fustāt, the first Arab settlement in Egypt and now part of Cairo. The earliest probably came from Iraq, where

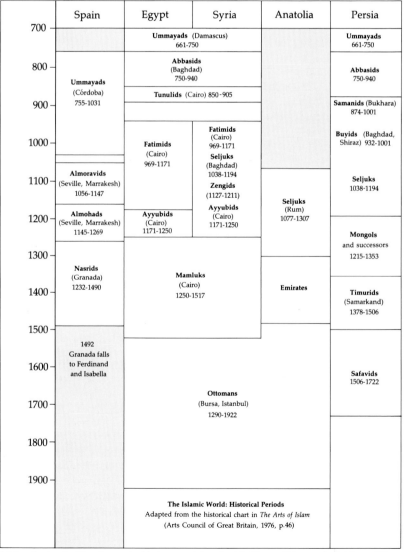

	Spain	Egypt	Syria	Anatolia	Persia
700		Ummayads (Damascus) 661-750			Ummayads 661-750
800	Ummayads (Córdoba) 755-1031	Abbasids (Baghdad) 750-940			Abbasids 750-940
900		Tunulids (Cairo) 850-905			Samanids (Bukhara) 874-1001
1000		Fatimids (Cairo) 969-1171	Fatimids (Cairo) 969-1171		Buyids (Baghdad, Shiraz) 932-1001
1100	Almoravids (Seville, Marrakesh) 1056-1147		Seljuks (Baghdad) 1038-1194 Zengids (1127-1211)		Seljuks 1038-1194
1200	Almohads (Seville, Marrakesh) 1145-1269	Ayyubids (Cairo) 1171-1250	Ayyubids (Cairo) 1171-1250	Seljuks (Rum) 1077-1307	
1300	Nasrids (Granada) 1232-1490				Mongols and successors 1215-1353
1400		Mamluks (Cairo) 1250-1517		Emirates	Timurids (Samarkand) 1378-1506
1500	1492 Granada falls to Ferdinand and Isabella				
1600					Safavids 1506-1722
1700		Ottomans (Bursa, Istanbul) 1290-1922			
1800					
1900					
		The Islamic World: Historical Periods Adapted from the historical chart in *The Arts of Islam* (Arts Council of Great Britain, 1976, p.46)			

Only the ruling dynasties of those places mentioned in the text are cited, not the whole of the area which came under the influence of Islam.

72 Detail of a *tirāz* band, Iran, AD 896. Possibly made in Merv for the Abbasid Caliph al-Mu'tadid (AD 892–902). At the bottom the inscription is laid out ready to be embroidered: 'In the name of God, the Merciful, the Compassionate. Happiness from God to the servant of God, Ahmad, the Imām al-Mu'tadid billah, Commander of the Faithful, may God strengthen him. This has been ordered by the Amir. Year 283.'

Baghdad was the capital of the caliphate from AD 762. They have single-line inscriptions embroidered with coloured silks on cotton or *mulhām* tabby. Only stitching could produce a non-repeating inscription, and embroidery was apparently introduced from Iraq into Egypt for this purpose. The principal stitches were back stitch, chain and blanket stitch. Inscriptions usually give the ruler's name and titles with a pious greeting, and perhaps the name of his vizier, who supervised *tirāz* production, and the place and date of manufacture. It was thought that cotton grounds meant Iraqi workmanship as compared with Egyptian linen, but recent research shows that cotton was widely diffused in the Islamic world by the tenth century.

The term *tirāz* itself drives from *tarz*, a Persian word for the embroidery used for these bands and, later, for the ateliers which made them. These were usually a State monopoly whether private, Dar al'Khassa, working for the ruler, or Dar al'Amma, which could sell cloth. The early inscribed bands were 'an emblem of dignity reserved for the sovereign [and] for those whom he wishes to honour . . .', according to Ibn Khaldun (1332–1406), the Arab philosopher and historian, in the *Muqaddimah*. In a society where clothing indicated rank robes of honour, with the ruler's insignia, which he presented at the New Year Festival, bound to him in loyalty those whom he thus rewarded. Wealthy noblemen also dispensed robes of honour among their dependants and even owned *tirāz* workshops. Egyptian weavers later adapted the style into silk tapestry of almost unbelievable fineness, their designs still horizontal bands but with more perfunctory repeat inscriptions such as 'good fortune', 'prosperity' and 'power', but no insignia and, since the Shi'ia Fatimids condoned natural forms, rows of tiny birds and animals enclosed in roundels, and geometric ornament.

Factories producing other fine textiles also assumed the name *tirāz* and flourished, until the thirteenth century and the crumbling of the caliphate, in ancient textile centres such as Alexandria, Akhmîm and Bahnasa (Oxyrhynchus) in Egypt, at San'a in the Yemen, Antioch and Aleppo in Syria, Sūs and Nishapūr in Iran, and the newer Arab cities of Baghdad (the most important), Cairo, Córdoba and Palermo. Their fabrics and clothing were sent as annual tribute to the caliph and traded widely. Each had its speciality – Baghdad's *mulhām*, a mixed silk and cotton cloth, Yemen's gold-printed ikats, Upper Egypt's fine, plain fabrics and Iran's figured silks. The latter are recorded in the documents as *khusrawani* ('of the old Persian kings') and were still made in the former Sassanian royal workshops. They are described as patterned with animals, birds and humans in roundels, and were exported all over the caliphate, where they were very popular even in Sunni provinces, and to Byzantium which sent its own silks in return. Alone among the Arab conquests Iran preserved her national identity, established by the Sassanians, and in her literature, language and imagery, particularly the use of the human form in manuscript painting and textiles, became a unique force in Islamic culture.

Sericulture continued in north-west Iran, supplying the numerous *tirāz* workshops. Their products have, unfortunately, not been identified. More is heard of Khorasan, the north-east province with Merv its capital, and of Transoxiana, ancient Soghdia, the furthermost Islamic province, and its capital Kokhara, an ancient Central Asian market. Textiles have survived from both areas. The 'Shroud of St Josse', now in the Louvre, Paris, thought to have reached France just after the First Crusade, was probably woven in Khorasan and bears the name of the Turkish military commander of the province, who died in AD 961. A thick silk twill, it has an unusual carpet composition with two rows of paired elephants, by this time commonly used as power symbols, with cocks and a border of camels. Silks, chiefly weft-faced compound

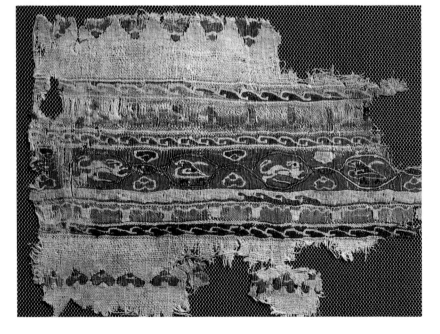

73 Border fragment of silk tapestry. Fatimid, 11th–12th century AD.

74 Compound weft-faced silk twill depicting a pair of confronted lions. Transoxiana, 8th–9th century AD.

twills dating from the fifth to the tenth centuries AD, which have been found at Silk Road grave sites, can be attributed to Transoxiana. They include the Astana boar's head silk (see II, 4) and other versions of this evidently popular subject, of which one is dated AD 661. Others have etiolated versions of Sassanian animal and bird designs, single and paired. They are lively but clumsily 'drawn', suggesting imperfect skill

with the drawloom. Their popularity is shown in contemporary Central Asian frescos, notably one at Afrasiab (Samarkand) depicting dignitaries who wear long caftans with boars, cocks and *senmurv* in roundels. Documents mention *zandaniji* cloth and garments, recently identified as silks woven in Zandana, a village near Bukhara.

With a huge variety of fine textiles to hand,

the ruling class lived in ostentatious luxury. The Fatimids were notorious high livers. Their entire court, including servants, received new outfits every summer and winter, and their Cairo warehouses held every kind of cloth and garments, some of them gold-embroidered. They included trappings not only for horses and camels but elephants too, with howdahs *en suite*, complete furnishings for audience chambers, and tents – small campaign tents, larger military tents, audience tents and pleasure pavilions, some decorated inside and out.

A unique glimpse of this finery survives. The Norman rulers of Sicily, a Fatimid province until they conquered it in AD 1071, adopted their predecessors' life-style. The Palazzo Normani, the Royal Palace in Palermo, was built around the former Fatimid Palace which housed the royal *tirāz*. To it Roger II (1130–54), the first Norman king, added the Capella Palatina, the Palace Chapel, with its Arab ceiling of carved wood and 'stupendous mantle' of Byzantine mosaics covering its walls. Another mantle was made for the King himself to wear – the so-called 'coronation mantle' of Roger II, now in Vienna, but made in the Palermo Dar al'Tirāz (see II, 17 and II, 24). Its brilliant design, of a camel and a maned lion fighting on either side of a palm tree, is in the *khusrawani* style, though its subject is more ancient, going back to ancient Mesopotamia. On red silk twill the embroidery of coloured-silk chain stitch and gold-thread underside couching is enriched further by double rows of pearls as outlines and applied enamel discs and precious stones. Along the edge of the mantle is a long Kufic inscription, embroidered with pearls, beginning 'Made in the royal *tirāz* for him in whom dwell fortune and honour, prosperity and perfection . . .' and ending 'In the capital of Sicily, in the year 511' (AD 1133–4). Roger was crowned in 1130, and the mantle is now thought to have been worn by the King at the consecration of the Royal Chapel, though that did not take place until 1140. Together the building and the mantle are reminders of the all too brief 'Golden Peace' in Sicily and south Italy, between Christian and Muslim.

Through well-established trade networks Islamic textiles were dispersed beyond Islamic lands as far as China and western Europe; not even major upheavals such as the Crusades interrupted the trade. Until Italian silk weaving began to develop in the fourteenth century Europe relied upon Byzantine and Islamic silks, as countless fragments found in churches, reliquaries and burials testify.

75 Lining from the 'coronation mantle' of Roger II, Palermo, Sicily. First third of the 12th century. Probably produced by Islamic weavers in Sicily.

6 Byzantine silks

Byzantine silks evoke images of splendour, but the term 'Byzantine' itself is a modern-day misnomer. Byzantine silks were textiles of the east Roman Empire, whose capital lay at Constantinople (f.AD 324). From the sixth century onwards Constantinople grew in power and prestige, and administrative, political and commercial activities were increasingly centred in the capital. By the tenth century the silken magnificence of the Constantinopolitan court embodied the power and prestige of the Byzantine Empire. It was a mark of the importance of silk to the Empire that manufacture continued even after the fall of Constantinople to the Latins in AD 1204.

Byzantine silk weaving can be divided into two phases before the thirteenth century, and these clearly mirror the changing political fortunes of the Empire. Phase one, from the fourth to the seventh centuries, witnessed the establishment of imperial workshops in the capital and in important provincial centres in Egypt and Syria. By the sixth century some private silk-weaving workshops were documented in Tyre and in Beirut also, but the origins of non-imperial silk manufacture are shrouded in mystery. After the Islamic conquests of Byzantine territory, including Egypt and Syria, in the seventh century, private silk weaving seems to have declined and imperial production was centralised in Constantinople. Gradually private silk-weaving workshops were established in the capital also, and in the tenth-century 'Book of the Prefect', a document detailing metropolitan guild regulations, no fewer than five private silk guilds were represented. Private silk-weaving workshops flourished in the Peloponnese in the twelfth century, but nothing is known about the types of silks that were produced there for sale in the capital.

To support the Byzantine silk industry originally raw silk from China had to be imported via Persia; but increasing conflict between the Persian and the Byzantine Empires represented a serious hazard to raw silk supplies, and Byzantium determined to introduce sericulture into her Empire. A Chinese source, the *San-kuo-chih*, compiled before AD 429, recorded that sericulture was practised in Byzantine Syria in the fifth century, and it is evident from Byzantine sources, including Procopius (AD 500–65) and Theophanes of Byzantium (end of the sixth century), that sericulture penetrated further into the Byzantine Empire during the course of the sixth century.

Our knowledge of imperial as well as private silk manufacture in the Byzantine Empire between the fourth and the twelfth centuries depends on both documents and surviving silks. Historical sources include legislative codes which describe the types of silks restricted to imperial manufacture and use. Between the fourth and the sixth centuries the Theodosian and the Justinianic Codes illustrate an imperial monopoly over the production and use of silks dyed with imperial murex purples in particular, and this embargo was repeated in the *Basilics*, the Law Code of the Macedonian dynasty from the tenth century onwards. The 'Book of the Prefect', too, clearly defined the many different shades of imperial purple that were forbidden to private manufacture, as well as certain types of tailored silk garments reserved for the imperial house.

Silks were important to the Byzantine court from an early date. The establishment of imperial silk factories in Constantinople and the provinces in the fourth century was intended to cater specifically for the silken requirements of the court. By the tenth century the elaborate place reserved for silk vestments and furnishings in the life of the court is clearly reflected in the intriguing accounts of palace life documented in the 'Book of Ceremonies'. Here not only magnificent silk curtains and cloths but also the most elaborate and ornate imperial costumes were described. There were silks of imperial purple alongside golden, green, blue and red ones; some were plain, others were decorated with eagles, griffins, bulls and hornets or foliate motifs. The silken magnificence of the Byzantine court was conveyed to foreign nations via diplomatic channels, both through the attendance of envoys from far and wide at suitably festooned silken palace ceremonies and by the dispatch of Byzantine silks as gifts to foreign courts. Moreover, silks were an important economic asset in their own right and were frequently exploited purely for political ends by the Byzantines.

At a time before the Latin West in particular had established its own silk-weaving workshops there was an overwhelming demand for imported, rare and precious Byzantine silks. The Italians, as well as the Bulgars and the Russians, were willing to, and indeed did, provide military and naval support to defend threatened Byzantine territories, in exchange for privileged silk-trade concessions and impressive silken gifts. The Venetians, especially, carried Byzantine silks to the West in exchange for naval assistance against enemies of the Empire, while the German emperors provided moral support to Byzantium in the face of Arab, Norman and Turkish threats against Byzantine territories, right through from the eighth to the twelfth centuries. During that period no fewer than sixteen marriage alliances between Byzantium and the West were negotiated.

Given the enduring alliance between Byzantium and the West from the eighth to the twelfth centuries it is perhaps appropriate that the Byzantine silks which have best survived the ravages of time are to be found mainly in the ecclesiastical treasuries of western Europe. Liège Cathedral Treasury possesses a silk with a Greek monogram of seventh-century date, traditionally associated with the Emperor Heraclius (c.575–641), although it should be noted that the monograms on silver pieces of this emperor do not compare. Silks with religious, narrative themes, in both twill and in tabby weave, were also woven around the sixth to seventh centuries. Two silks at Sens Cathedral Treasury with scenes from the life of Joseph have Greek inscriptions, and they may have been woven in Egypt before the Islamic conquest of AD 640.

During two periods of iconoclasm in Byzantium (c.AD 726–87 and 815–43) narrative Christian themes were banned from production, and it is to be expected that Byzantine silks with religious themes were no longer woven in the Empire. The silks with Christian scenes documented in the eighth to ninth centuries in the *Liber Pontificalis*, the book of the Popes, may have been commissioned in Syria under Muslim rule. In Byzantium charioteer and hunter themes were encouraged. An important Byzantine silk woven during the first period of iconoclasm is the splendid imperial hunter fabric in the Textile Museum of Lyons. This silk was taken from the relics of St Austremoine at Mozac and may have been a gift from the Emperor Pépin (c.715–68), who is known to have presented a silk to the relics of the saint in AD 764. The silk was probably a diplomatic gift sent over from Byzantium in connection with the proposed marriage of the daughter of Pépin to the son of the Byzantine emperor.

A series of five inscribed, purple, imperial Byzantine lion silks from Rhenish church treasuries may also have been produced as diplomatic gifts. Of these five silks, two are documented and three survive in fragmentary condition. The series of lion silks can be variously dated between the eighth to ninth and the

76 One of two silks with scenes from the life of Joseph. 6th–7th century.

RIGHT 77 Lion silk from St Servatius, Siegburg, 921–3.

OPPOSITE 78 Hunter silk from Mozac, 8th century.

eleventh centuries on the evidence of their inscriptions in combination with other stylistic and technical data. Only one of the five known lion silks has an imperial inscription that yields a precise date – the Siegburg lion silk which bears the name of Romanos I and Christophoros, his son, who jointly reigned only from AD 921 to 923. The Siegburg lion silk was removed from the shrine of St Anno (d.1075), Archbishop of Cologne, in the late nineteenth century and was rediscovered in 1980, in a forgotten drawer of the museum of Schloss Köpenick in East Berlin. The silk was perhaps amongst gifts sent from Constantine VII (913–59), son-in-law of Romanos, to Otto I (962–73) in AD 945 and was probably stored for centuries in the West before being presented as a shroud for Anno.

Two only slightly different imperial lion silks were woven under the Emperors Basil II and Constantine VIII (976–1025), and the better preserved of them is in the Diocesan Museum, Cologne. The second lion silk is fragmented and is divided between Schloss Charlottenburg's Kunstgewerbemuseum in West Berlin and Düsseldorf's Kunstgewerbemuseum. Further fragments of the same piece were once in the Kunstgewerbemuseum, Krefeld, but today are presumed lost. These Basil II and Constantine VIII lion silks may have reached the

West between 1000 and 1002 when there were plans for the marriage of a daughter of Constantine VIII to the German Emperor Otto III (996–1002). Ties between Byzantium and the West certainly were very close from the time of the marriage of the Byzantine princess Theophanou and the German Emperor Otto II (967–83) in 972. Wentzel (1972) has suggested that a vast body of silks in Aachen Cathedral Treasury reached the West as the dowry of Theophanou, but the silks range in date too widely for this to be plausible. Nevertheless, Theophanou no doubt did have Byzantine silks at her disposal in the West. A bullock silk with a background diaper of heart motifs at St Servatius, Maastricht, might be linked to her, for instance. The use of such bird and animal motifs is typical of the tenth century. Two Byzantine

79 Bullock silk, 10th century.

BELOW **80** Elephant silk, first half of the 11th century.

eagle silks at Auxerre and Brixen Cathedral Treasuries belong to the same period of manufacture.

The height of technical achievement was reached with the early eleventh-century elephant silk at Aachen Cathedral Treasury, an inscribed piece woven in an imperial Byzantine workshop at Zeuxippos, a district of Constantinople. Like the lion, bullock and eagle silks described above, the elephant silk was woven in twill weave with paired inner or 'main' warps. The single elephants are housed in foliate medallions 91 cm (3 ft) across. The hand draw-loom required to produce the silk was from 1.8 to 2.7 m (6 to 9 ft) wide, and the design was tied to a special pattern-producing device that required 1,440 manipulations for the production of a single medallion repeat. The silk was found in the twelfth- to thirteenth-century shrine of the Emperor Charlemagne (800–14) at Aachen Cathedral in the late nineteenth century.

A rare Byzantine tapestry-weave silk survives at Bamberg Cathedral Treasury. This resplendent silk hanging, almost 2 m (7 ft) square, depicts a victorious emperor on horseback accompanied by two female figures offering

crowns. Beckwith (1971) plausibly identified the scene with the triumphal entry of the Emperor Basil II into Constantinople and Athens following his defeat of the Bulgars in 1017. The tapestry served to shroud the body of Bishop Gunther (d. 1065), who died after a diplomatic mission to the Byzantine court. The silk was probably intended as a gift for the German Emperor Henry IV (1056–1106) from the Byzantine Emperor Constantine X (1059–67).

In marked contrast to the polychrome silks, monochrome twills and lampas-weave silks were in evidence from the eleventh century onwards. The same panther and griffin medallion design, with birds in the spandrels, occurs on two silks from the grave of Pope Clement II (d. 1064) in Bamberg Cathedral. One of the silks is a twill, the other a lampas weave, which suggests that the two techniques were being developed side by side. Large-scale ogee and foliate motifs were popular on the monochrome twills in particular. Two such silks were used for chasubles of Archbishop Willigis of Mainz (d. 1011).

By the eleventh to twelfth centuries an international style of silk weaving pervaded the Med-

iterranean area, and Byzantine and Islamic silks of the period are sometimes difficult to distinguish from each other. Undoubtedly, Byzantine silks, and particularly imperial pieces, played a significant part in establishing stylistic trends in silk weaving in the Mediterranean region. In addition, the export of Byzantine silks to the West, both as items of trade and as diplomatic gifts, had a profound effect on the ecclesiastical and the secular uses of silk by the Latins, up to the time of the establishment of silk weaving in Norman Sicily in the second half of the twelfth century. It is sad that the catastrophic fall of Constantinople to the Turks in 1453 erased all traces of the silken heritage of the capital. Only those pieces of Byzantine silk that reached the West appear to have survived to bear witness to what is surely one of the most remarkable chapters in the entire history of silk weaving.

7 Safavid Iran (1499–1722)

OPPOSITE 84 Tent roof with hunting scenes. Cut and voided silk velvet, Iran, mid-16th century. Diameter: 98 cm (38.5 in).

Persian silk production continued until the thirteenth-century Mongol invasions destroyed entire cities, their populations and industries. Yet the Mongols were eventually seduced by the cultures of their conquered lands and became great patrons. Timurid rulers of the fourteenth to fifteenth centuries, in their capital Herat, fostered silk weaving, so early Safavid silks did not appear without precursors: Tabriz, Kashan and Yazd already supported textile industries, and the principal Safavid weaves – twill, lampas, satin, brocade and velvet – were already known.

The Safavid dynasty (1499–1722) united Iran and made the Shi'ia rite the State religion. Surviving textiles date from Shah Tahmasp's reign (1524–76). Ruling from Tabriz, this shah was a notable patron, particularly of miniature painting, and his interest is reflected in contemporary silks, which took on complex and witty narrative designs at a time when other Islamic textiles – Mamluk and Ottoman – and even European silks favoured formal, non-figural designs. Shi'ia belief permitted this unique development, and weavers interpreted designs by court artists in their own way. Early lampas silks, in many colours and metal threads, are 'drawn' with such virtuosity that they compete with the pen.

Narrative scenes were also woven in velvet, with fine cut pile and voided satin grounds. Hunting was still a favourite pastime, and a circular tent roof of the mid-sixteenth century shows a mêlée with huntsmen, some on horseback with hunting leopards perched behind them, others on foot carrying firearms, with gazelles and lions all in a rocky landscape. The most beautiful velvet of all has repeating hexagons enclosed in leafy ogives of palmettes with spotted snakes entwined in them and, at the intersections, lion masks in spiky thistle palmettes. In each hexagon is an elegant young man holding a falcon, which has spotted a duck overhead, while a servant carries a game bag. Each young man wears a different coloured robe from his neighbour.

Shah Abbas I (1587–1629) moved Iran's capital to Isfahan. Under his personal supervision silk weaving became the country's chief industry. He moved Armenians, renowned merchants, from the north to New Julfa, in Isfahan, and settled in another quarter Jews whose traditional crafts were dyeing and gold embroidery. The Shah, who collected Chinese porcelain,

83 Cut and voided silk velvet known as 'The Falconer'. Iran, mid-16th century.

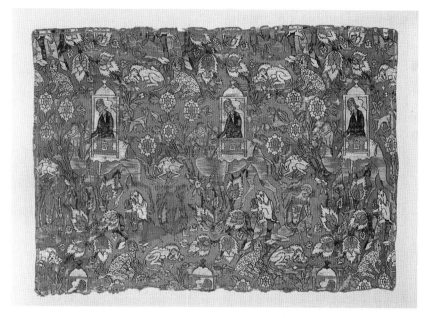

85 Satin lampas depicting the story of Layla and Majnun. Iran, late 16th to early 17th century. Layla visits Majnun in the desert, travelling by camel in a howdah which bears the inscription 'Ghiyath', a Yazdi designer.

welcomed foreigners, including European craftsmen and travellers who left accounts of the city. At the end of the seventeenth century the Frenchman Jean Chardin (1643–1713) in his *Journal du Voyage* (1686–1711) described thirty-two weaving ateliers in the palace grounds, just off the *maidan*, the city's main square. Court architects, artists and craftsmen were expected to be versatile, and painting and book design, textile manufacture and carpet weaving flourished side by side.

Silks were put to many uses. At first long, supple coats covered men's shirts and trousers, worn with the elegant baton turban; women wore garments of similar cut with a white headcloth tied under the chin, the *chaqād*. Seventeenth-century coats were waisted, with bell-shaped skirts, and were worn with a wider turban or a brimmed hat by men and with the *chaqād* by women. Coats were often of patterned silks, which were also used for furnishings, for ceremonial tents, and to line the streets during festivals. Narrative scenes continued into Shah Abbas's reign in lampas weaves with very complex repeats. Persian poetry and national legends are frequent subjects, one silk lampas depicting the love poem 'Majnun and Layla' (late sixteenth to early seventeenth century), with the visit of Layla to the lovelorn hero Majnun in the desert. Other silks have simpler scenes, with young men drinking wine and chatting in dark, cool gardens.

Velvet became even more fashionable and gained from simpler designs, which allowed scope for textural variations. By the mid-seventeenth century weaving design was closely related to painting, which was focusing on peaceful pursuits and single figure studies.

RIGHT **86** Cut and voided silk velvet depicting ladies beside a pool. Iran, early 17th century.

RIGHT **87** Cut and voided silk velvet coat. Iran, first half of the 17th century. The coat was a gift to Queen Christina of Sweden from the Czar of Russia in 1644. In the design, young men are depicted wearing similar coats.

88 The Esterházy appliqué. Silk and leather on cotton, Tabriz, Iran, mid-16th century. The embroidery contains numerous Chinese motifs, while the winged figures are *peris*, spirits who accompanied Muhammad on his flight to Heaven.

The court painter Riza Abbāsi introduced a new, languorous figure style, adopted by his son, Safi Abbāsi (1642–66), who also designed textiles and carpets. Typical of his work are cut and voided velvets with pairs of graceful ladies standing beside pools of silver, among flowering plants. Their hair and low-cut bodices show European influence. Similar velvets show young men in long coats and dashing brimmed hats. A magnificent seventeenth-century coat

with elongated sleeves is made of just such a velvet, patterned with youths drinking wine – an elegant sartorial joke to the young dandy who wore it.

From the mid-seventeenth century the bell-skirted coat was fashionable, and small pattern repeats were better suited to its cut. This coincided with a new floral style, influenced by the style of the lacquer painter 'Ali Ashraf, which ousted the human figure. A different weave was

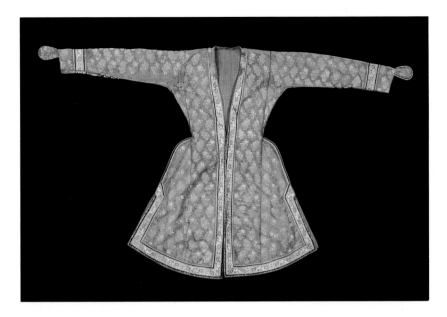

developed, a compound plain weave with inner warps and extra wefts, its main feature a shimmering ground of metal thread wound round a yellow silk core. This provided a foil to delicately drawn flowers – roses, irises, poppies and flowering bushes resembling English embroidered 'slips'. They are free-standing or enclosed in stripes or an ogival lattice. The same gold ground fabric also made a decorative edging used to border coats and precious textiles. The borders are difficult to date, as they were copied until the nineteenth century, and the coats themselves present problems since Indian fabrics which were used in Iran to make coats are similar.

Embroidery was an ancient craft in Iran. Safavid embroidery designs resemble those of woven textiles and carpets, an example of further links between the crafts. A mid-sixteenth-century appliqué panel, of leather and silk on cotton, formerly owned by the Hungarian Esterházy family, has a subject familiar from miniature painting – a garden reception, *madjlis*, with a young ruler, probably Shah Tahmasp, enthroned under a canopy and attended by musicians and courtiers who offer him wine and fruit. The embroidery may have been designed by the court painter Sultan Mohammed, for miniatures by him show the same subject. A unique circular cover of the late sixteenth century, embroidered with carpet motifs, was probably made in north-west Iran, for it resembles carpets from the Caspian region and the south Caucasus, with its eight-pointed star, palmettes and serrated leaves (see p. 52).

Later Safavid textiles showed a decline as Iran faced growing political and economic problems. The last Safavid shah, Sultan Huseyn (1694–1722), still lived in some splendour but wore less costly fabrics, woven in simpler point repeats with less gold. Nevertheless, the fabrics had their own charm and designs were meticulously 'drawn'. Flower-brocaded taffetas with calendered grounds were typical.

TOP LEFT **89** Coat of silk taffeta with brocaded floral repeat. Iran, 17th–18th century.

LEFT **90** Compound plain-weave metal-ground silk. Iran, 18th century.

8 The Ottoman Empire

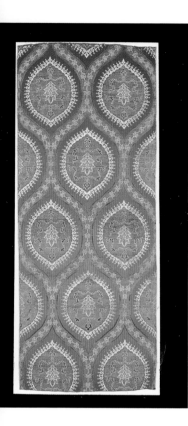

ABOVE **91** Satin twill lampas with gold thread. Ottoman Turkish, mid-16th century.

92 Imperial Ottoman silk velvet caftan associated with Sultan Mehmet II, the Conqueror (1451–81), though some would ascribe it to the 16th century.

In the sixth century AD Turkic tribes began a centuries-long migration from north-east Siberia into Asia. Seljuk Turks founded dynasties in Iran and Anatolia; the Seljuk Sultanate of Rum (literally Roman, that is, Byzantine) ruled from Konya from 1077 to 1307, and a few Seljuk silks survive with paired creatures in roundels in Sassanian/Byzantine style. However, the followers of Othman (Ottomans) gradually seized power in Anatolia. In 1338 Orkhan captured the Byzantine city of Bursa, making it his capital. The final prize, Constantinople, fell to Mehmet II, the Conqueror, in 1453 and was renamed Istanbul. The Ottoman Empire at its greatest extent included the Levant, Arabia with its holy places, Mamluk Egypt and North Africa as far west as Morocco, Iraq and (temporarily) part of north-west Iran, and the Balkans. The Ottomans were turned back in Europe at the siege of Vienna in 1683. This huge, polyglot Empire lasted until 1918.

Bursa had been an important Byzantine silk-weaving city. In the fourteenth century it was a principal world silk market, handling raw Persian silk for export to Italy or for use at home, for Turkey never produced enough for her own needs, although sericulture dating from Byzantine rule flourished in west Anatolia, Aydin, the Morea and Amasya. This trade flourished until the late nineteenth century, with the customs duty on exports being reaped by the Ottoman rulers. In 1502 Bursa had over 1,000 looms, and an inventory of 1504 lists ninety-one types of fabric made there, many still unidentified. Bursa's chief specialities were lampas and twill, velvet, the costly *seraser* and gold embroidery. Other weaving centres were Smyrna (Izmir), Amasya and, later, Scutari, together with Chios and Rumeli (north-west Greece).

Fifteenth-century silks are of the *chintamani* type, with three discs ('leopard spots') and waving lines ('tiger stripes'). Most plausibly these were reminders of the Ottomans' tribal past, for Turkic nomads commonly took a wild animal or bird as their *tamgha*, or totem. Mehmet II (1451–81), the Conqueror, adopted the *chintamani* design as his personal emblem, and it appeared on woven and embroidered textiles, carpets and ceramics.

In the early sixteenth century imperial looms were established in Istanbul, though Bursa continued to supply the court. The silk industry worked under tight governmental control: guilds of spinners, dyers and weavers worked in cottage industries and were supplied with raw materials by middlemen, the *khamdjis*. There were controls over loom widths and the quality of gold and silver used; cloth was stamped and prices fixed. In 1574 gold was confined to imperial use, in the ateliers at the Topkapi Saray. This was the Empire's powerhouse as well as the sultan's palace, where officials commissioned weavers and tailors, and where the Weavers of Silver Thread worked next to the Mint, which provided the metal. The Topkapi Saray today houses the largest collection of Ottoman silks and imperial caftans.

The Anatolian climate, cold in winter, influenced dress. The long, dignified caftan could be quilted or lined with fur for winter. Men wore large, impressive turbans. Ottoman dress silks are heavier than Safavid, with large, formal patterns in limited colours and with subtle textures, enhanced by metal thread. Certain garments and colours were reserved for the sultan and his court, and *khil'a*, robes of honour, were recalled by the Treasury on the death of an owner. Expensive metal thread was wound around a silk core. *Zenbaf* was possibly a gold lampas, *chatma* a fine brocaded velvet, and

seraser was a thick weft-faced compound weave with velvet pile and gold or silver. The latter was used chiefly for long cushions, with a single large motif, narrow borders and lappet ends. Similar rich fabrics and carpets lined the streets during court processions and were even used underfoot.

The mid-sixteenth century saw the introduction of the ogival repeat. Its exact origins are difficult to ascertain – it may have reached Turkey with fourteenth-century Chinese imports or fifteenth-century Mamluk silks. Early Ottoman ogival designs show a marked Italian influence, with lotus and artichoke palmettes, crowns and acanthus. A distinctive Ottoman style soon developed, however, retaining the palmette but with favourite Turkish flowers, the hyacinth, tulip, rose and carnation, exquisitely drawn. Seventeenth-century silks added star and rosette lattice repeats, with spiky outlines. Technically the most breathtaking is the *saz* style, which has curling, serrated leaves, lotus palmettes and hybrid flowers, and which was influenced by the work of two Persian artists. Shah Kuli joined the palace studio in 1525 and Wali Jan in 1580, at a time when palace registers record 156 weavers, sixteen designers and some fifty draughtsmen who presumably drew up point papers. Sketches of *saz* leaves are preserved in the Topkapi, and two magnificent imperial caftans display the ultimate in *saz* silks. In seven colours and gold no motif is exactly repeated, requiring a very large loom. With cream and green grounds respectively, they are now assigned on stylistic grounds to a period between 1550 and 1570. *Saz* silks with conventional repeats were also woven for general consumption. Such magnificence was short-lived, and a century later silk contained less metal, or none, as the Treasury was unable to supply it.

Military textiles, of which many surviving examples were captured in 1683, include armour, horse-trappings, campaign tents and *san-jaks*, banners carried into battle. Of lampas weave, usually white on red, these bear the Muslim star and crescent, the miraculous two-bladed sword of 'Ali, the Prophet's gift, and the Koranic 'Victory Sura' (verse from the Koran): 'Verily, We have granted thee a manifest Victory.' Talismanic shirts which were worn under armour and bear protective Koranic verses also survive. Tomb-covers, with pious inscriptions, were produced in the same weave.

93 Imperial Ottoman lampas silk caftan in the *saz* style, now associated stylistically with the early years of Shezade (later Sultan) Murad III. Third quarter of the 16th century. The elongated ceremonial sleeves are detachable.

94 *Sanjak* military banner in lampas weave silk with gold and silver thread, captured at the Battle of Vienna by Mancin Zamoyski in 1683.

Embroidery was no poor relation. Male professional embroiderers made large hangings, bed curtains and covers of several linen loom widths joined. These emulated woven patterns in silk pattern darning and couching, though their designs were closer to ceramics than to carpets, and their floral ornament, like that of Iznik wares, reflected the cult of gardening to which Sultan Murad III (1574–95) was devoted. The apogee of Ottoman embroidery is represented by the great military tents, 200 of which were captured after the siege of Vienna. Plain outside, their interiors are magic gardens of floral appliqué, of linen, cotton, satin, velvet, leather and spangles, on red or blue grounds. Another class of professional embroidery, in which Bursa specialised, was gold embroidery and couching on velvet for women's coats and jackets, which were worn with trousers (*salvar*) at weddings and other festivities.

Much embroidery, however, was domestic, done on linen or cotton with silk laid and couched

95 Interior of an Ottoman military tent captured at the Battle of Vienna, 1683. Canvas, silk, satin, gilded leather and appliqué. Wall H: 3.2 m (10.5 ft), W: 28.5 m (93.5 ft).

OPPOSITE **96** Detail from a large hanging, silk embroidery on fine linen. Turkish, mid–late 17th century.

work, pattern darning and couched metal threads, sometimes edged with *oya*, gold or silk crochet. Among household items bed-linen and pillows, napkins (*peshkir*) and larger towels (*havli*), both with embroidered borders at each end, and square *bohça* were the most common. Cloth *bohça* were all-purpose wrappers (a tribal tradition) used to cover anything from clean clothes taken weekly by women to the bath to gifts of fruit and sweets. Clothing such as women's trousers, headscarves (*cevres*) and sashes (*uckur*) for both sexes received similar treatment. The garden repertory flourished in a folk art which lasted well into the nineteenth century. The rose spray, tulip and hyacinth remained favourites, with individual districts developing their own designs, and flowers and colours took on special meanings. These Ottoman embroideries strongly influenced those of mainland Greece and the Greek Islands (see II, 28).

ABOVE **97** Towel end, silk embroidery on fine linen. Turkish, 18th century.

98 Fragment of silk-embroidered woman's trousering. Turkish, 18th century.

9 Central Asian textiles

Central Asia has evocatively been called 'the land of furs and fans': it is a land of contrasts, of immensely high mountain ranges – the Pamirs, the Tien Shans and the Hindu Kush, where nomadic tribes struggled to exist in the high valleys – and it is a land of vast deserts – the Kara-Kum and the Kizil-Kum, where oases provided rich agricultural land amid barren scrub and where other nomadic tribes struggled against the environment. Reaching from the eastern shores of the Caspian Sea to the borders of China, Central Asia is presently divided into the Republics of Turkmenistan, Uzbekistan, Tadzhikistan, Kirghizia and Kazakhstan and reaches over into north-eastern Iran and northern Afghanistan. The names reflect some of the ethnic groups and tribes which once ruled the area, frequently warring with each other, until they were swallowed into the expanding Russian Empire in the middle of the nineteenth century.

It is an area with rich textile traditions, although few pieces have survived from before the nineteenth century. The majority of its inhabitants followed a nomadic way of life, travelling with herds of horses and camels and flocks of sheep and goats from one pasture to another. They lived in tents and possessed nothing which was not portable: clothing, bedding and utensils were stored and moved in wooden chests or in strong woven bags which could be slung over the back of a pack-animal. Even in the loam dwellings of settled herdsmen and farmers the only item of furniture was a bed. The many brightly coloured textiles which adorned both tents and houses were primarily functional; used as covers and containers, when they were worn out they were discarded.

Most of the pieces which have survived were made by the sedentary population of the large oasis towns and trading centres such as Bukhara, Tashkent and Samarkand. Of these textiles the most important ones produced within the home were the embroidered covers, sometimes called *susani* (meaning 'needlework'), which formed part of the bridal trousseau. These varied in size according to function and were used as simple covers, bedspreads, decorative hangings, prayer-mats and shrouds. The cotton cloth used for the ground was woven

Map 3 Central Asia.

91

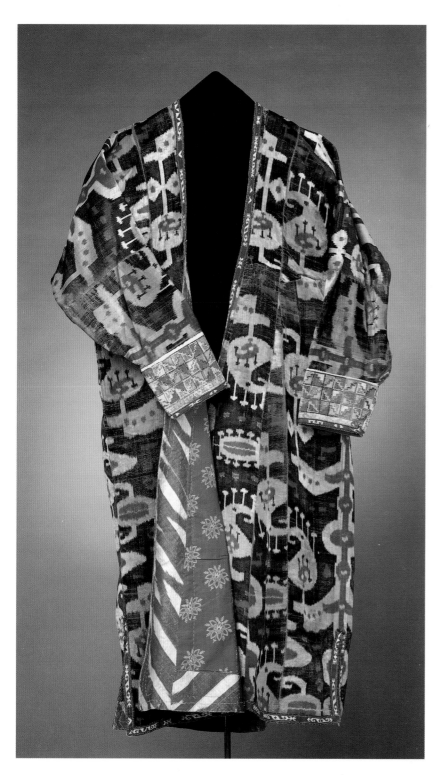

OPPOSITE **99** Large embroidered hanging (*susani*). Turkistan (Nurata), late 19th century.

ABOVE **100** Man's coat (*chalāt*) of ikat velvet. Turkistan, early 20th century.

on narrow domestic looms, and several widths had to be sewn together to form a piece of the desired size; silk was rarely used. Someone in the family or in the neighbourhood would draw large floral designs on to the fabric, which would then be unpicked. Frequently each width would be embroidered by a different woman, all of them using coloured silks with a marked preference for red. The fact that several hands might have been involved in the working of one piece explains why the colours, the stitches and even the pattern often did not match properly once the widths had been rejoined. It is thought that each of the main towns had its own particular design: those of Bukhara were often divided into a lattice formed by serrated leaves, those of Tashkent were dominated by dramatically large red circles, while, in contrast, those of Nurata were based on naturalistic sprays of flowers and leaves.

Curtains, cloths and simple robes were made from ikat, sometimes from pure silk, but more usually from a silk and cotton mixture. The breeding of silkworms and the production of silk thread were done in most homes, but the manufacture of ikat was undertaken by craftsmen working within a well-organised guild system. The designs dyed on to the warp varied from simple two-colour stripes to complex patterns based on floral motifs using up to seven different colours. The most expensive type was ikat

velvet which combined time-consuming dyeing processes with a slow weaving technique. Lengths of ikat and ikat coats were given to merchants, courtiers and ambassadors by the local khans and emirs as marks of distinction or as rewards for services rendered; and as the ikat patterns seemed to have changed almost annually, a man's wealth and social status were indicated by his being robed in the current fashion.

It was not uncommon for very wealthy men to wear five or six ikat coats one on top of the other as a way of proclaiming their position in society. An embroidered velvet coat was even more coveted, and early photographs of the rulers of Central Asia show them wearing heavy velvet robes embroidered with metal threads in preference to ikat. It is difficult to embroider velvet, especially with gold and silver threads, and the more difficult a fabric is to make the more expensive it is to buy and the more status is attached to wearing it. Such embroidery would probably have been done within the emir or khan's own workshops alongside looms which produced gold and silver brocades in European styles for use in his court and household. Imported fabrics from Persia and India were used by those who could afford them, and towards the end of the nineteenth century large amounts of fabric, especially roller-printed cotton, were imported from Russia and used in both costume and furnishing.

Unlike the men, most townswomen dressed soberly in simple cotton robes, and it was the tribal women who wore richly embroidered clothes and large quantities of jewellery. Their most striking garment was a hip-length mantle, worn over the head like a cloak, which was called a *kurteh* and formed part of a married woman's costume. The colour of the ground fabric changed according to the age of the wearer; dark blue was for a young woman, yellow was for the middle-aged, and white was for the old. The *kurteh* had false sleeves hanging down the back, indicating that it originally evolved from a coat, and it was always densely embroidered with coloured silks in a variety of stylised floral patterns said to be based on the 'Tree of Life' motif; more lavish embroidery was to be found on the dark blue examples than on the white. Unmarried girls (and boys and many men) wore round caps which were often embroidered in a variety of colours and styles and from which jewellery and amulets could be hung. The use of garments to measure a man's position in society was virtually restricted to urban settlements; tribesmen preferred to express their wealth and power in the use of beautifully decorated animal trappings – bridles, harnesses, saddles and saddle-cloths.

OPPOSITE **102** Woman's mantle (*kurteh*) of embroidered silk. Turkistan, early 20th century. The sleeves are purely vestigial.

The Hungarian Arminius Vámbéry (1852–1913), an early traveller in Central Asia, was amused by the appearance of ragged-looking men astride superbly decorated horses. Although leather decorated with silver ornaments and cornelian was most commonly used, saddle-covers and -cloths made from knotted pile, *kelim* or appliquéd felt were used to add colour.

Undecorated felt was made by the women of the family and was used to cover the collapsible wooden frame which formed the circular tent, or

ones made from woven cloth must also have been used.

When most of the textiles within a society are functional they do not survive for more than one or two generations, and so it is impossible to obtain a complete picture of the variety of fabrics, techniques, colours, designs and shapes which were available to the people in Central Asia in the nineteenth century. However, textiles may have helped to make a very hard life more comfortable. Since the 1920s most tribes-

103 Caps embroidered with silk. Central Asia, 1850–75.

yurt, in which they lived; it was warm and waterproof but had to be replaced every few years. Patterned felts were used as floor-covers and were cut to make appliqué and patchwork covers, curtains and hangings. Mattresses, pillows, quilts and clothing made from a variety of materials – whatever was available – would have been stacked around the inside of the tent and covered to protect them from the smoke of the fire. When not in use most utensils and foodstuffs – spoons, dishes, grain, salt, and so on – would have been stored in a variety of woven bags designed specifically to hold them. The bags which have survived are the strongest and made from knotted pile, but less durable

men have been compelled by economic and political pressure to adopt a sedentary existence, but two of the main textile traditions of the area are still alive. Ikat, using synthetic fibres as well as cotton and silk, is still made, and a simple ikat dress has become a form of national dress in Uzbekistan. The technique is being revived by aid agencies in Pakistan who are working with north Afghan refugees in an attempt to enable small communities there to be productive and eventually self-sufficient. *Susanis* are still produced in Bukhara, but they are now made in factories using industrial sewing-machines – one of the most popular *susanis* is a cover for the television set.

10   Palestinian embroidery

At some period prior to the early nineteenth century the seeds of a beautiful costume art took root in rural Palestine and reached a spectacular efflorescence during the first half of the twentieth century. Dresses, coats and flowing head-veils of hand-woven cotton and linen in natural shades or dyed indigo blue or rusty red were richly embellished with an extraordinary profusion of brilliantly coloured silk embroidery and taffeta and satin patchwork.

This artistic tradition developed among the Arab farmers who formed the majority of the population of Palestine until the middle of this century, and was an exclusively female art form, created and sustained by peasant women in hundreds of small villages throughout the country. Each region and even each group of villages had its own distinctive styles and patterns, all subject to constant changes in fashion.

We do not know when these village artists began to adorn their costumes, nor can we document the earliest sources of their techniques and patterns. The oldest garments from this tradition which have been preserved are probably no older than the early nineteenth century, and travellers and historians of earlier periods do not describe women's costumes in informative detail. All we can assume is that the decorative panels of embroidery and patchwork which are the most striking feature of village women's festive garments evolved originally from functional stitching and protective patchwork on everyday working clothes, and that costume styles and embroidery patterns, techniques and colour schemes were all affected by a multiplicity of local and foreign influences. Historically many thousands of Christian and Muslim pilgrims have visited Palestine wearing or bearing as gifts or for sale costumes and textiles from many different countries; some female visitors married and settled in Palestine and passed on their embroidery skills and ideas; cloth and clothing have long been imported from Europe and Asia as well as other parts of the Middle East; and Palestine has been conquered and administered by a succession of foreign powers, each of which left some mark on local fashions. However, many peoples are exposed to similar influences without developing such a complex and lavish costume art, so the impetus and sustaining roots of the Palestinian embroidery tradition must be sought within the culture and society of the Palestinian villagers.

The beautiful, colourful and ornate art of embroidery is in striking contrast to the otherwise humble material culture of the Palestinian peasantry, and could have developed only in a culture where women's skill and creativity were admired and encouraged by both sexes. Women maintained embroidery's rigorous aesthetic standards by appreciating and criticising each other's work, while fathers and husbands generally provided the money to pay for the expensive materials – no small consideration for peasant farmers. Embroidery was also sustained by the desire to gain prestige from the display of wealth – not only the expenditure of surplus cash but also women's precious time and labour.

The most admired embroidery was executed with small, neat stitches, had well-planned patterns, and conformed to local conventions in its choice and arrangement of colours and motifs. Embroidery was an important expression of village identity and pride, and women relished even small differences between their embroidery and that of other villages. It was important for young women that their embroidery be in the latest fashion, and for older women, for whom the flamboyant styles of youth were considered unsuitable, that it should be subdued. Richly embroidered garments were not, of course, worn for toiling in the fields or the home – embroidery was too precious to risk its being spoilt during everyday chores. It was reserved for embellishing garments worn for special social and ceremonial occasions such as formal visits, religious feast days and, above all, the most important family celebrations – circumcisions and weddings.

A girl prepared her first embroidered garments for her wedding trousseau, and wore the most richly decorated dress in her collection for the first time during her wedding ceremonies as a dramatic and colourful proclamation of her new marital status. Girls began to embroider around the age of six, learning from their mothers and other older women the techniques, the large vocabulary for embroidery stitches and motifs, and the combinations of colours and patterns peculiar to their village. At the same time they absorbed the exacting standards of the art, some excelling more than others according to natural talent. Acknowledged experts, who were usually also innovators always on the look out for new motifs to introduce to their villages, were admired and copied by other women.

104 Ceremonial costume from Upper Galilee, Palestine, late 19th or early 20th century. The arms and back of the coat are richly embroidered in silk thread, as are the cuffs of the trousers, and the front of the coat is embellished with appliqué patches of satin and taffeta.

BELOW **105** Silk embroidery on the back of a woman's ceremonial coat. Upper Galilee, Palestine, late 19th or early 20th century.

In the late nineteenth century there were two major styles or traditions of embroidery in Palestine, corresponding to major differences in women's costume between the north and south of the country. In the hills of Galilee in the north women wore a short-sleeved, calf-length coat, most often made of blue or russet-coloured cotton, hand-woven and dyed locally (with indigo and kermes), over white or blue ankle-length pants of similar cotton and a long-sleeved tunic of fine white cotton or silk. A colourful, checked or striped cotton or silk sash was wrapped round the waist over the coat, and the head was covered with a bonnet bedecked with coins, and over it a scarf or veil, usually of maroon or black silk, tied above the forehead with a headband.

The most beautifully ornamented garments were the coats of indigo-blue cotton which the embroidery artists of Galilee treated like a painter's canvas, embellishing the fabric so heavily with appliqué patchwork and silk stitching that most of it was concealed. Rectangular and irregularly shaped patches of red, yellow and green taffeta and striped or ikat-patterned satin were applied on the sleeves and on the front of the coat, or inside the front so they would be glimpsed when it flapped open. The silk fabrics and threads for decorating these outfits were imported from the great Syrian weaving centres of Damascus, Aleppo and Homs.

As if this flamboyant decoration were insufficient to attract attention, the lower back and sides of the coats were beautifully embroidered in lustrous floss silks, mainly in satin stitch combined with a variety of other stitches – running stitch, cross stitch, satin stitch, hem stitch and drawn-thread work, often all combined on the same garment. As in all Palestine, the predominant embroidery colour was red enlivened with touches of other colours. The patterns used were mainly geometric, with various combinations of diamonds, triangles, rectangles and chevrons arranged in rows. On some coats the embroidery was worked as an unbroken panel concealing the background material. More commonly the hand-woven blue cloth is revealed between discrete motifs, contrasting with and accentuating the smooth, lustrous texture of the embroidery. The pant legs were embroidered in a similar manner.

We know from travellers' accounts that these splendidly ornate and colourful costumes were being worn in the 1860s, but as with all Palestinian costume we cannot now trace the origins or early development of styles of dress and ornamentation. We can be sure, however, that they will have been affected by the same (universal) principles that governed costume styles during the better-documented and -researched period from the end of the nineteenth century –

OPPOSITE **107** Embroidery on the back of a woman's ceremonial dress, from the coastal plain south of Ramleh, Palestine, *c.* 1920s.

BELOW **106** Ceremonial costume from the southern coastal plain of Palestine, *c.* 1920s. The skirt, arms and chest panel of the dress are heavily embroidered in silk thread in cross stitch, and there are cross-stitch patterns on the edge of the veil which is also adorned with a silk fringe. The front of the skirt and the hem are decorated with taffeta appliqué which is also lightly embroidered in silk thread.

the desire to display wealth, good taste and skill, and the ever-present drive to emulate the changing fashions of social superiors. Thus by the early twentieth century new styles of costume based on the fashions of the Turkish ruling class had been adopted by the Galilee village women, and embroidered coats and pants ceased to be worn.

In southern Palestine (south of the Nablus area) Turkish fashions had little influence on village costume. Until the 1940s the village women wore ankle-length dresses of locally woven natural (creamy white) or indigo-blue cotton or linen with tight-fitting or triangular sleeves, bound round the waist with a colourful silk, cotton or woollen girdle. Various regional styles of coin-bedecked bonnet were worn by married women until recently, covered with flowing white cotton or linen head-veils. Festive dresses were as lavishly and colourfully embellished with embroidery and appliqué as the ceremonial coats of Galilee, and often bonnets and veils were embroidered as well. In some areas women also embroidered cushion-covers of red, green and yellow taffeta to decorate their homes. On dresses the embroidery was arranged symmetrically in panels on the chest, sides and lower back of the skirt, and sometimes on the sleeves. The shapes and sizes of the embroidered panels, as well as the motifs employed, varied from area to area. Head-veils worn for festive occasions were embroidered in bands round the edge and were sometimes sprinkled all over with motifs.

The main embroidery stitch of southern Palestine is the cross stitch, with a variety of other stitches playing a supporting role – satin, herringbone, running and special stitches used for oversewing edges, joining seams and attaching patchwork. Until the 1930s Syrian floss silk was used, as in Galilee, which gave a thick stitch usually concealing the cross shape of the stitch, and yielding embroidery with a rich sheen and voluptuous texture, especially when it was executed in solid blocks as on the most magnificent dress in the bridal trousseau in certain regions. The patterns were executed from memory, or copied from another garment, and were sewn directly on to the material, the open weave of the hand-woven fabrics enabling the embroideress to count the warp and weft threads and plan her motifs and overall design.

The oldest cross-stitch embroidery motifs are simple geometric shapes used alone or in rows, or combined with others to make more complex patterns. Most are abstract, but some clearly represent trees, plants and flowers. Many of these designs were inspired by the decorations and patterns village women saw on buildings, tiles, carpets and textiles when they visited the

OPPOSITE **109** Chest panel embroidered in Bethlehem or a nearby village, Palestine, *c.* 1930s or 40s. The panel is sewn on to a dress of black velvet, a style worn in the village of 'Ain Karim, near Jerusalem.

BELOW **108** Detail of the cross-stitch embroidery on a dress from Ramallah, Palestine, early 20th century. Floral and foliate motifs such as this were introduced to Palestine in the late 19th century by European missionaries and teachers who set up schools in predominantly Christian villages such as Ramallah.

towns and their markets. In the late nineteenth century curvilinear and naturalistic motifs depicting subjects like flowers and birds were introduced by European missionaries who set up schools and embroidery classes in predominantly Christian villages such as Ramallah, and these new motifs eventually spread throughout southern Palestine.

Various shades of the dominant red embroidery colour and different combinations of subsidiary colours were preferred in different areas, and like other features of costume and embroidery were self-conscious expressions of local identity. Chemical- (aniline-) dyed silks were not widely available in Palestine until the 1920s, when small touches of brilliant greens and pinks became common in the embroidery of certain areas.

From the 1930s closely woven machine-made cottons and later man-made fibres imported from Europe and Asia replaced local materials, mercerised (*perlé*) cotton threads replaced floss silk, and many new embroidery patterns were imported in European pattern-books sold with the embroidery threads. These new patterns, which had to be executed using waste canvas, became very popular during the 1950s, as did others imported in magazines later, and they predominate on the embroidered dresses worn today. There was also a shift from the dominant red of the older embroidery – yellow, orange, green, blue and pink, alone or combined in the same dress, all becoming popular.

The other main southern Palestinian embroidery technique, strikingly different from cross stitch, was couching in silk, silver or gilt cord. This was twisted into elaborate floral and curvilinear patterns, which were filled and framed with satin and herringbone stitches in brilliantly coloured floss silk. This expensive and luxurious style of embroidery was initially a speciality of Bethlehem, Beit Sahur and Beit Jala, mainly Christian villages south of Jerusalem, where women used it for decorating the best dresses in their trousseaus, for broadcloth or velvet jackets and for their distinctive fez-shaped head-dresses. The people of these villages were wealthier and more urbanised than those of other villages who looked up to and wanted to emulate them. So as village people became financially better off from the late 1920s, Bethlehem-style embroidery became more and more fashionable in southern Palestine, and wedding trousseaus often included one or more dresses ornamented with panels of couching. This embroidery was produced commercially by women in Bethlehem and its neighbouring villages, and by professional embroideresses in other villages.

In many villages of the coastal plain of the

Mediterranean and in the hills north and south of Hebron the most important trousseau dress was also embellished with appliqué panels of red or orange taffeta sewn on to the front of the skirt between the panels of embroidery. These were shaped and slashed in a variety of ways to reveal the indigo-blue fabric of the dress beneath, and were sometimes lightly embroidered. The front edges of a short-sleeved coat dress worn in the villages of the Jaffa area until the 1920s were also edged with taffeta or satin patches, and were sometimes tied with silk tassels and sprinkled with sequins. In many areas decorative satin or velvet patches were also sewn on the yokes of the finest dresses, and in the Bethlehem and Jerusalem areas striking chest panels in red, yellow and green taffeta with zigzag appliqué borders were attached to dresses of luxurious fabrics of mixed silk and linen. Zigzag appliqué was also widely used to edge neck openings, cuffs and hems.

Palestinian culture and society were severely disrupted by the establishment of the State of Israel in northern, western and parts of southern Palestine in 1948. During the hostilities surrounding this event nearly half the rural population fled in fear or were driven out of their villages and became refugees in eastern Palestine (now called the West Bank) or in neighbouring countries. Many more became refugees as a result of the 1967 war. Despite these calamities, traditional costume and the art of embroidery still flourish in the early 1990s, albeit greatly changed, in the villages and refugee camps of the Israeli-occupied territories of Gaza and the West Bank, and among southern Palestinians in the refugee camps of Jordan and Syria. Many new embroidery patterns (such as large flowers and birds) and colours (especially shaded threads) of foreign origin are popular across the whole spectrum of village and refugee camp society; at the same time subtle features have been retained to indicate a woman's original village or region in Palestine. Other distinctive new embroidery patterns and colour combinations (the white, black, green and red of the Palestinian flag) have been created since the start of the Palestinian uprising (*intifada*) against Israeli occupation to express national identity and aspirations.

India and Pakistan

11 Historical development and trade

Interest in historic Indian textiles tends to focus on the painted chintz which traders of the East India Companies brought back to Europe in the seventeenth and eighteenth centuries. After Vasco da Gama (*c.*1469–1525) landed at Calicut in 1499, traders followed in search of the re-ported riches in gold, jewels and spices. They found an already flourishing trade in painted cotton textiles between India and Persia, and further to the south-east between India and the Spice Islands. The Europeans' first interest in those cotton textiles, however, was as profitable

Map 4 The Indian sub-continent.

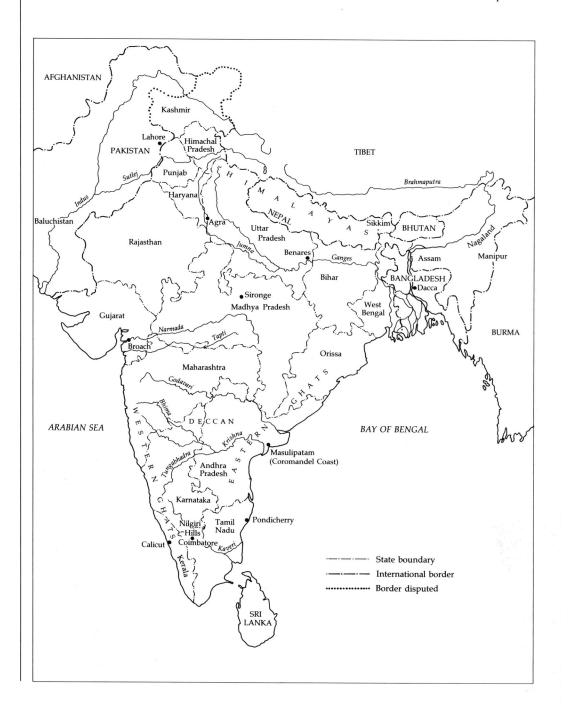

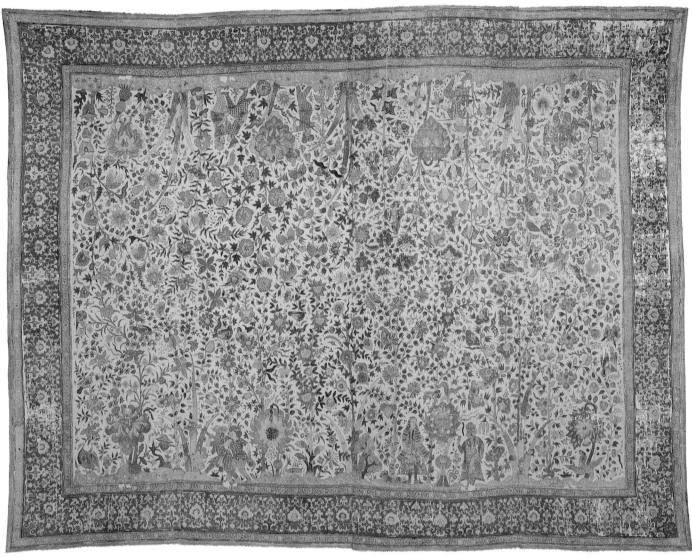

110 Cotton floor or bedspread, painted and dyed. Made for the Indo-Persian or the Persian market, and formerly in the stores of Amber Palace, Rajasthan, India. From Golconda, Coromandel Coast, *c.* AD 1630.

commodities for sale or barter in the conduct of their oriental trade.

Owing to the ravages of the Indian climate very few textiles survive in India from earlier than the eighteenth and nineteenth centuries. A beautiful *kalamkāri* (painted cotton cloth), acquired by the Victoria and Albert Museum in 1929, was originally in the *toshkhāna* (wardrobe store) of the palace of Amber, in Rajasthan, and is dated to about 1630. The Museum's registration noted that upon the back of the cloth were '. . . a series of stocktaking dates and data, ranging between 1639 and 1650' (Irwin and Brett 1970, p. 64). The design is of Indo-Persian flowering trees; within the border are small groups of courtiers hunting and at play, with one delightful detail of a courtier dallying with an Indian serving-girl.

The Indians were intrigued by the newcomers, with their strange customs and dress. The *kalamkāri* hangings made for Indian use in

the mid-seventeenth century often depict Europeans in a purely Indian setting. On a hanging composed of seven panels sewn together, for the Indian handloom could weave a narrow breadth only (Culin 1918), each panel had a different design, most being of Europeans and Indians; but one unique panel shows tribal people of the forest and jungle, far from the centres of trade, wearing garments made of leaves. Both *kalamkāris* were painted in the state of Golconda, on the Coromandel Coast, south India, where the port of Masulipatnam had a flourishing trade all over India and by sea to Persia.

Trade in Indian textiles is very ancient. We are dependent, for early history, upon records: *Periplus Maris Erythraei* was originally written in the first century AD, by a Greek working as a master-mariner in Egypt (Schoff 1912), when the ancient trade routes across the Mediterranean to Egypt were venturing further east to the Persian Gulf. There, meeting traders from India, the

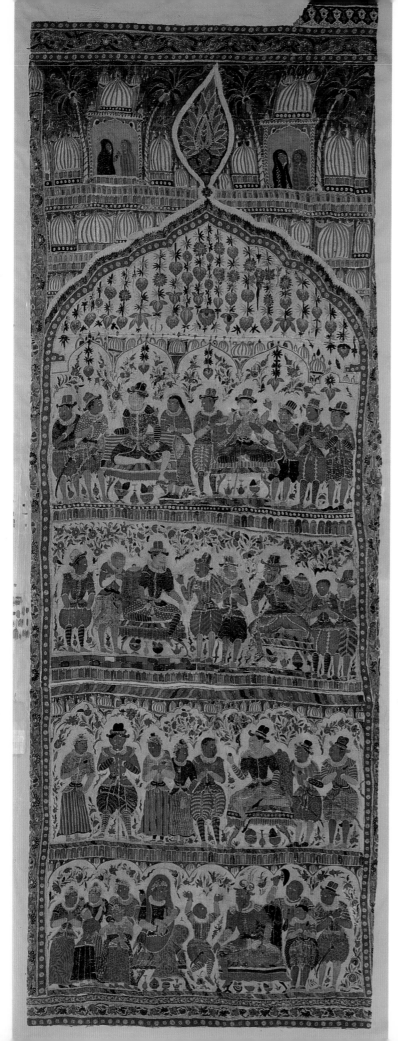

Greeks sailed on to the western coast of India. A *periplus* is a guide for mariners and while the manuscript provides a wealth of practical details, in the present context its importance lies in the extensive information about articles of trade and the ports at which they could profitably be sold. There are constant references to 'Indian cottons' and other textiles brought from Barygaza (Broach), on the estuary of the Narbada River, to ports in the Persian Gulf and on the Red Sea. The source of many textiles in India is often mentioned, confirming an extensive network of trade routes overland to the ports of western India.

Thus by the first century AD India was already producing woven cottons of noteworthy quality in the fertile plains of Gujarat and the valleys of the Narbada and Tapti Rivers, still a fine cotton-growing area today. Continuity of the Indian textile trade has been independently confirmed by the discovery of numerous fragments of printed cottons of Indian origin at Fustāt, south of Cairo, the site of a traders' caravanserai throughout the medieval period. The fragments have been dated to various periods between the eighth and the fifteenth centuries (Irwin and Hall 1971, pp. 1–13). The majority were clearly textiles of moderate price, for purchase by the ordinary people in the market-place. Some are dyed with indigo, with patterns made by resist dyeing, using a paste to resist the penetration of the dye, then washing it out, leaving the pattern in white. Others are block-printed in shades of red, black, brown and brownish-violet, fast colours obtained from alizarin-bearing vegetable dyes, using an alum and an iron mordant. The craft of mordant printing is still practised in western India today.

The records of the seventeenth-century European traders confirm that they found printed cottons in western India, but they were of inferior quality compared with the painted ones. The earliest textiles to be brought back to England, however, were embroideries from Gujarat, in coloured silks upon white cotton, in fine chain stitch. The early examples were in the Indo-Persian style, but the traders began to take out designs in the English fashion, which the Indian embroiderers executed beautifully (Irwin 1948/52). In Bengal, eastern India, embroidered quilts were made for Portuguese traders with a blend of Indian and Portuguese motifs (Irwin 1952).

Trade between Europe and western India was interrupted in 1631 by a terrible famine in Gujarat, after the rains failed for two years. Already the ships plying round the coast of India had found that the *kalamkāri* cloths of the Coromandel Coast, south India, were better suited to their needs for trade with the Spice Islands. The

Two panels from a hanging originally consisting of seven panels. Painted and dyed cotton. From Golconda, Coromandel Coast, *c.* AD 1630–40. Each whole panel: 230.7 × 96.5 cm (90.8 × 38 in).
OPPOSITE **111** Indians with Portuguese travellers.
RIGHT **112** Detail showing tribal people of the Indian forests and hills, wearing leaf-dress.

special qualities of Indian *kalamkāris* were the beauty of colour and the fastness of the dyes. The craftsmen were not only making them for Indian use as hangings and covers but were also producing patterns acceptable to the traditions of the islanders of South-East Asia and, separately, cloth of the fine quality required for the Persian trade. The English, the Dutch and the French recognised the potential for their own home trade and began to send out designs in their own fashions for bedspreads and sets of curtains for four-poster beds. By the end of the seventeenth century Indo-European styles were emerging to the individual taste of those three countries (Irwin and Brett 1970, *passim*). A favourite subject was the Indo-Persian 'Tree of Life' bearing many kinds of leaf, flowers and fruit. European flowers appear amid the Indo-Persian conventions (see illustration on pp. 4–5); but it is in the border designs that European influence is often most evident, with classical garlands draped in swags and tied with ribbon bows. During the eighteenth century a prosperous trade in such designs developed.

The beauty of the *kalamkāris* of the Coromandel Coast lay in the quality of the dye from the alizarin-bearing tap-root of a plant called *chay* (*Oldenlandia umbellata*). Used with an alum mordant, it produced glowing red; with iron, a soft brownish-black; and with a mixture of alum

and iron, a range of violets and browns. Other alizarin-bearing dye-roots were used elsewhere in India, notably *al* or *saranguy* (*Morinda citrifolia*), but none matched the purity of *chay*. Greens and yellows were painted from less fast local vegetable dyes. European observers began to enquire into the techniques of Indian cotton-painting with a view to improving their own textile industries. The earliest account, by Captain Beaulieu, an officer in the French navy (d. 1764), on behalf of the French dye-chemist Charles François du Fay de Cisternay (1698–1739), was written about 1734, near Pondicherry. Beaulieu gave the cotton-painter a length of cloth and cut off a sample piece at each stage to illustrate his account (Irwin and Brett 1970, Appendix 'A', pp. 36–41, illus.). Other accounts followed during the eighteenth century (ibid., pp. 42–58).

The development of copperplate printing in Europe and the invention of cylinder printing on textiles (see II, 26) led to a decline in the demand for Indian chintz. There was, however, renewed interest in Indian printed cottons, which were purchased with a view to studying the designs in order to produce cylinder-printed calicoes which would be acceptable as exports to India. The end of the nineteenth century was a period of extreme difficulty for all Indian craftsmen, endeavouring to compete with cheap imports

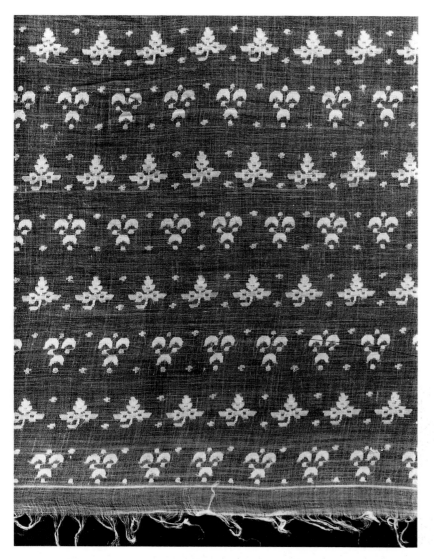

113 Detail of patterned muslin (*jamdani*), fine white cotton brocaded with thicker white cotton. From Dhaka (Dacca, Bangladesh), mid-19th century.

from Europe and eventually the establishment of factories in India itself.

The former caste system in India (abolished in 1947) was, so far as handcrafts were concerned, the key to India's consistency in craft traditions. The extended family was a closely integrated community, whether weavers, dyers, painters or printers. They married within their own caste, and the children followed the family tradition, helping with simple tasks from a very young age. Thus manual dexterity and knowledge of local materials were inborn and practised for one's lifetime – and then, in turn, passed on to a new generation.

The Great Exhibition in Hyde Park, London, in 1851, enabled the fine crafts of Britain and of her colonies to be seen in the magical setting of the Crystal Palace. The Indian *sārīs* and shawls of silk brocaded with silver and gold were marvels of exoticism, but to Victorian taste it was the hand-woven muslins from Dacca (now the capital of modern Bangladesh) which captured

special interest. Of pure white cotton, they appeared as fine as a cobweb, with dainty *būtīs* (floral sprigs) brocaded in thicker soft white cotton, and it was considered a marvel that human hands could have woven them. They became a popular article of trade in subsequent years.

The Royal Society of Arts published a small monograph by James Taylor (*c.*1802–79), a medical officer who had resided in Dacca between 1828 and 1846 (Taylor 1851). The waters of the Brahmaputra River and its tributaries flood annually, covering the land with fine silt when the waters subside. The cotton plant in this region was cultivated with special care and yielded a boll with a very fine fibre and long staple. The spinning of the thread was done by the women of the villages, the supple fingers of the younger women providing the best yarn. The *tukū'ā*, a small, light spindle of iron, rested upon a hollow in a piece of shell, embedded in a board, to take the weight as the deft fingers worked. The weaving was done by the men upon a very simple loom. Before setting up the loom the warp threads were steeped in rice paste to make them firm enough to withstand the tension of weaving; the humid climate kept them supple as the work progressed. When taken from the loom, the finished cloth was washed in the running waters of a stream, so that all trace of the rice starching was removed. The soft, fine cloths, laid to dry and to bleach in the fields in the early morning sun, brought such descriptive terms as *baft-hāna* (woven air) and *shab-nām* (evening dew), and were traded all over India and abroad.

Small details in Taylor's account confirm an ancient origin for fine weaving at Dacca. For cleaning and carding the cotton bolls in preparation for spinning the women used the jawbone of the *boalee* fish (*Siluris boalis*); the small, finely spaced teeth were perfect for the job, and this ancient 'tool' had never been surpassed. Muslin was woven at other centres in India, notably at Sironge in Rajasthan, but the special quality of Dacca cloth could never be equalled.

The soft woollen shawls of Kashmir became known in Europe in the late eighteenth and early nineteenth centuries, when these long, gracefully patterned wraps blended perfectly with the elegant classical-style dresses of the period. The *shāls* (shawls) of Kashmir were originally traded throughout north India and Central Asia as luxurious shoulder-wraps for men in the cold season. From the *Āīn-i-Akbarī*, the annals of the Mogul Emperor Akbar (1556–1605; Blochmann and Jarrett 1927–49), we know that the weaving of shawls was already long-established in Kashmir. At *Āīn* 32 the historian Abu'l Fazl states:

ABOVE **114** Shawl fragment of the late Mogul period, from Kashmir, c. 1680.

115 Woven Kashmir shawl, early 19th century.

In former times shawls were often brought from Kashmír. People folded them up in four folds, and wore them for a very long time. Nowadays they are generally worn without folds, and merely thrown over the shoulder. His Majesty has commenced to wear them double, which looks very well. His Majesty encourages, in every possible way, the manufacture of shawls in Kashmír . . .

Kashmir is a fertile valley in the Himalayas, and Persian influence in design and technique was evident in all her arts from an early period. A shawl fragment of the late seventeenth century is now in the Victoria and Albert Museum (Irwin 1973, pp. 11, 40 and pl. 1). The end-borders are much shorter, and the row of *būtās* (conventional flowering-plants) have a characteristic drooping bud at the top. By the end of the eighteenth century the *būtās* were becoming larger and the style more conventionalised (Irwin 1973, pp. 11–14, figs 1–8), leading to the development of the style where the 'drooping bud' typical of Indian design has become the curling tip of the motif widely known in Europe as the 'Kashmir cone'.

The shawls were woven from *pashm*, the fleece of the mountain goat *Capra hircus*, the finest shawls being from *asli tūs*, the soft, fine inner fleece which the animal grows during the winter and sheds by rubbing off on the rocks and bushes in the spring. The *asli tūs* was collected, washed and spun, then dyed with soft colours from local plants. The loom itself was comparatively simple: the basic web of the cloth was twill-woven, each motif being worked by hand in the twill-tapestry technique. The early

būtās were well within the limitations of the technique. The larger motifs, designed to satisfy European demand, with their small-scale infilling, brought increasing strain upon the weavers, who were under constant pressure for speedy completion.

The invention of the Jacquard loom in Europe enabled elaborate patterns to be achieved quickly, and the style of the Kashmir shawl was copied, first in Paris, then in Norwich, and finally at Paisley in Scotland. In a desperate effort to fulfil the desire for increasing elaboration of pattern the Kashmir weavers found by the late 1860s that it was often quicker and cheaper to work a shawl entirely by needlework upon plain *alwār* (shawl cloth). The early *amli* (embroidered shawls) are often of high quality, but by the end of the nineteenth century standards had declined.

The shawl weavers, impoverished and crippled by ruthless taxation in Kashmir, were emigrating to Amritsar and other towns in the Punjab. The available wool was coarser, but the weaving of *jamawār* (a length of patterned shawl cloth for a garment) and *alwār* remained reasonably profitable.

An important innovation under Emperor Akbar was the introduction of the weaving of silk brocades. The *Āīn-i-Akbarī* records at *Āīn* 31 (Blochmann and Jarrett 1927–49):

> His Majesty pays much attention to various stuffs; hence Iráni, European and Mongolian articles of wear are in abundance. Skilful masters and workmen have settled in this country, to teach people an improved system of manufacture. The Imperial workshops, the towns of Láhór, Ágrah, Fathpúr, Ahmedábád, Gujrát, turn out many masterpieces of workmanship; and the figures and patterns, knots and variety of fashions which now prevail, astonish experienced travellers . . . and on account of the care bestowed upon them, the intelligent workmen of this country soon improved. All kinds of hair-weaving [weaving with wool] and silk spinning were brought to perfection, and the imperial workshops furnish all those stuffs which are made in other countries. A taste for fine material has since become general, and the drapery used at feasts surpasses every description.

The trade in silk from China along the old Silk Road had enabled Persia to develop skills since the medieval period. During boyhood Akbar had lived at the Safavid court of Persia while his

116 Woven Kashmir shawl, mid-19th century. At this period the Indian weavers were forced to compete with the complexity of the Jacquard-loom woven shawls from Paisley in Scotland.

OPPOSITE 117 Brocade (*kimkhab*), silk brocaded with silver-gilt thread, the border brocaded in the *minakari* ('enamel-work') style in coloured silks on a gold ground. From Burhanpur (central western India), mid-19th century.

father Humayūn (reigned 1530–40, restored 1555, d. 1556) was in exile. Akbar's development of *khārkanas* (court workshops) '. . . to teach people *an improved system of manufacture . . .*' brought the introduction of the more sophisticated looms used in Persia for weaving brocaded patterns and the employment of *ustāds*, Persian master-craftsmen, to supervise and instruct the Indian weavers in the new techniques – and

Lahore, Agra and other cities declined, and the craftsmen returned to their own towns and villages. A new generation of Indian weavers became *ustāds* themselves, and the techniques of brocade weaving spread to central India and Bengal, the natural habitat of the Indian wild silk-moths, where silk cloth of simpler design had been woven for generations. Bengal, which produced the finest wild silk, is renowned for soft brocades of pure silk, mellow in colour. The weaving of *kimkhab*, silk brocaded with silver and silver-gilt thread, flourished in central India, and since the seventeenth century Benares has been the most renowned centre (Krishna and Krishna 1966). In southern Rajasthan and central India the lovely *minakāri* (enamelled work) style, where the motifs were brocaded in coloured silks upon a field of gold, is a truly Indian expression.

Towards the end of the nineteenth century the import of machine-woven brocades from Europe put severe pressure on the weavers to achieve greater complexity of design. From about the 1870s the *kimkhābs* of Benares are a profusion of birds and animals amid flowers. At the end of the nineteenth century the growing preference of men in India for wearing European-style dress in the towns, and ceremonial uniforms at court, led to a decline in the demand for brocade lengths for men's dress, but the grace and charm of the Indian brocaded *sārī* remain fashionable until the present day.

The craft of ikat in India is reputedly of very ancient origin, though examples survive only from the nineteenth century. The silk *patolas* of Gujarat, woven as traditional marriage *sārīs* for some communities (Bühler, Fischer and Nabholz 1980, pp. 7–67), are extremely skilled work. The elaborate patterns are tie-dyed in both the warp and the weft (double ikat), and much care is needed when setting the warp threads on the loom. The earliest designs are *pan bhat* (leaf pattern), possibly originally a fertility symbol, but by the end of the nineteenth century the motifs included other auspicious symbols, such as *popat* (a bird), *kunjar* (elephant) and *nārī* (a doll, a woman).

Ikat silks and cottons, including *patolas*, were among the textiles exported from India to South-East Asia. Weaving by the ikat technique is practised elsewhere in India, notably in Orissa, eastern India, where the dyeing may be on silk or cotton, sometimes in the weft only.

Another form of tie-dyed work is *bandhana*, in which the finished white cloth, whether cotton or silk, is tied in tiny bunches to resist the dye, leaving the pattern in white dots on the coloured ground. In Rajasthan turban-cloths with *bandhana* patterns were traditionally worn by men at festivals, and the red *chundārī* (spotted head-

ABOVE 118 Detail of the border of a woven cotton sari, tie-dyed in the warp and the weft by the ikat technique. From Orissa (eastern India), 19th century.

'. . . the intelligent workmen of this country soon improved . . .'.

Indian medieval poetry and drama reveal the splendid life of the Indian Hindu and Buddhist courts before Akbar's innovations. References confirm the wealth of fine silks, cottons, muslins and textiles ornamented with silver and gold (Chandra 1960). We have no means of knowing the techniques; silver and gold may have been applied by embroidery.

India has the capacity in the arts of absorbing new influences – and making them her own. Brocade weaving became one of India's finest textile crafts. Under the puritanical Aurangzeb (1658–1707) the Mogul court *khārkanas* at

119 Silk head-veil for a woman (*orhni*, or *odhani*), tie-dyed by the *bandhana* ('knotted') technique. From Gujarat State (possibly Jamnagar, Saurashtra), *c.* 1867.

OPPOSITE 120 Dress (*kira*) for a woman, white and coloured cotton, woven in patterned stripes, with parts of the design further embellished by embroidery. The dress is pleated and draped around the body, fastened by clasps of metal at the shoulders, and then bound at the waist by a broad sash. From Bhutan (north-east India), late 19th or early 20th century.

veil) often features in Indian poetry, as worn by a woman when meeting her lover. The finest expression of India's regional textile crafts – whether brocaded, tie-dyed or embroidered – is often found in the marriage *sārī* which is draped around the bride, for in town and village a marriage is the greatest social festival. In the long ceremonies of a Hindu wedding the actual moment of marriage is when the *brāhmin* (priest), speaking the sacred *mantra* (prayer), ties a corner of the marriage *sārī* of the bride to the ceremonial scarf worn by the bridegroom, and 'wearing one garment' the couple walk seven times around the sacred fire.

Each region of India has evolved its own local style from long-established traditions in the textile crafts of home and village (Gillow and Barnard 1991, *passim*, and Plates). Embroidery in coloured silks on unbleached or coloured cotton cloth is the finest homecraft in north and western India (Irwin and Hall 1973, pp. 73–147, and Plates; Grayson 1982, pp. 32–3, illus.), and in Bengal (Irwin and Hall 1973, pp. 171–93, and

Plates). The *chhipas* (cotton printers) of a few villages still practise their art for traditional garment cloths for the local people, and at Sanganer, Rajasthan, a flourishing trade developed in the 1950s in traditional hand-printed cottons for export (Irwin and Hall 1971, pp. 110–32, and Plates). At Kalahasti, in Andhra Pradesh, south India, the *kalamkāri* painters continue to produce cotton temple cloths, painted with images of the gods, and scenes from Hindu legend (Irwin and Hall 1971, pp. 74–9, and Plates; Grayson 1982, pp. 17–21, illus.).

The woven textiles of Bhutan, the small mountain kingdom in the eastern Himalayas, have been little known until recently. The northern boundary with Tibet is the mighty natural barrier of the Himalayan peaks and ranges, from which great spurs extend steeply southwards, crossing the entire kingdom with high ridges separated from each other by deep valleys, each with its river rushing down a steep gradient southwards, an impassable torrent in each season of rain and at the melting of the snows. Each valley is thus isolated for much of the year and must be self-sufficient. Because of its isolation Bhutan has been free from the influences of foreign trade which so radically transformed local textile styles and traditions elsewhere.

Weaving is a homecraft, not only in the villages but also in the larger houses of the landowners where one room is always set aside for the looms. Traditionally a Bhutanese woman weaves for the needs of her own household, but the wealthier homes sometimes employ professional weavers in the house. The textiles are woven on a narrow handloom, and several widths of fabric must be sewn together to make a larger cloth. The Bhutanese exploit this feature by variations of colour and pattern on each of the pieces. Though tradition is respected by everyone in this sparsely populated country, it is the beautiful cloths of the aristocracy of Bhutan which have attracted collectors.

The present landowners of Bhutan are descended from a band of Tibetan soldiers who subjugated the country almost three centuries ago, settled there, and intermarried with the earlier inhabitants. In this way the ancient homecraft tradition of the women became blended with the deep regard for ceremonial of the men. The presentation of a woven scarf is a social obligation when meeting a religious or a civic official. The dress of the men of all classes, worn over a cotton shirt, leggings and boots, is the *koh*, a sleeved coat, about knee-length, with the separate *kera* (sash) binding the waist. It is the *kira*, the graceful draped dress of the women, which has attracted most interest by the richness of woven pattern, sometimes further enhanced by embroidery.

12 Tribal textiles

The hills and forests of central India were formerly rich in tribal life, of which only vestiges remain. India's turbulent history since ancient times of the rise of powerful kingdoms and empires – only to disintegrate in internecine warfare – had through the centuries forced frequent migration of tribes and the formation of numerous sub-tribes, often far from their place of origin. The development of roads and railways accelerated changes. Thus peoples of central India claiming the same tribal origin – Bhils, Gonds, Kolis and others – are now found very widely scattered. The Kolis can be traced in southern Rajasthan, Gujarat, Maharashtra and the northern and western Deccan. They were originally the great huntsmen of the forest – old photographs show them posing with bows and arrows – but those who settled in villages along the west coast of India became communities of fishermen.

The tribespeople traditionally fulfilled their needs by food-gathering in the forest. In the hot climate of central India clothing was simple and basic – a cloth for the loins, giving freedom of movement for speed and agility. Even a simple cloth of plain cotton gained arrogance and style by the mode of tying. In remoter parts of India, where tribal life had been less disturbed, traditions of pattern weaving emerged. There is not, however, any great tradition of woven textiles among the tribes of central India, though colourful decoration is found using shells, seeds and applied scraps of coloured cloth, and bold stitchery in coloured yarns.

The Bhils, who are widespread over Rajasthan, Madhya Pradesh and the northern Deccan, have tended to find local environments where they could settle, to till the land and raise their livestock. However, a late Mogul miniature painting of the eighteenth century, now in the Victoria and Albert Museum, shows Bhils hunting deer in the forest at night, wearing only skirts of long, pointed leaves. Painted manuscripts of the *Aranya-kānda* of the *Rāmāyana*, wherein Rāma and Sīta are banished to the forest, usually depict them wearing leaf-dress.

BELOW LEFT **121** Cotton bag, with pattern of geometric and stylised plant ornament, and symbols of birds and humans or gods woven in coloured silks. From Assam, mid-19th century. The bag was shown at the Great Exhibition in London, 1851.

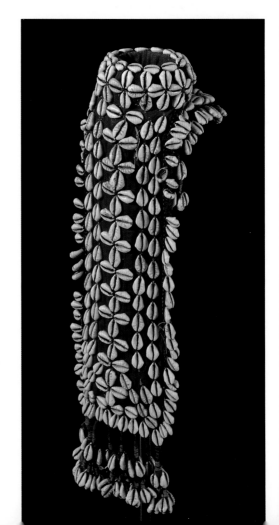

RIGHT **122** Cotton head-dress with padded ring for carrying loads, decorated with cowrie shells. From Banjara (central India, Gond tribe), early 20th century. L: 55 cm (21.6 in).

114

123 Cotton jacket for a man, embroidered with coloured cotton. From Banjara (central India, Gond tribe), early 20th century.

By the end of the nineteenth century, however, the tribal life of central India was rapidly merging into village life.

The Nilgiri Hills in south India, rich in flora and fauna, and with a temperate climate which contrasts with the hot plains below, are the home of a number of tribes who until this century have preserved an independent life of primitive simplicity. The Todas have excited the most interest by their strictly regulated pastoral life centred upon the care of their magnificent herds of sacred buffaloes, which provide rich milk and curd. The work of the *pali* (*paḷḷi, paḷthḷi* – dairy) within each Toda *mad* (*mand* – village of huts) entails ceremonial for each daily task and stages of initiation to qualify a man for entrustment with each type of work.

The distinctive dress of the Toda tribe is the *putkuli*, a large white mantle which enwraps the entire body, worn by both men and women. The *putkuli* is made from a long piece of cotton cloth, folded at the middle of its length so that it is of double thickness and stitched together at the edges, leaving, however, an opening at the upper edge of one side, which is stitched to form the *kudsh*, a large, deep pocket at the front edge of the mantle.

Below the *putkuli* a man wears the *tadrp*, a straight loincloth from the waist to the knee. Below this he wears the *kuvn*, a tiny breech-cloth held in place by a string at the waist; this string is often of the bark of a plant. A woman wears a slightly longer *tadrp*, tied under the armpits so that the breasts are covered, and reaching almost to the ankles.

The Todas have no known tradition of weaving. Rivers (1906) informs us that the white cotton cloths for the *putkuli* and the *tadrp* had for centuries been procured from weavers who came from Seramuge, in Coimbatore, but more recently these garment-cloths were bought in the bazaars. The cloth lengths for the Toda *putkuli* were specially woven with distinctive bands of blue and red to hang at the front end of the mantle (where the *kudsh* was constructed). The Toda women embellished these traditional

124 Woollen salt-bag (*wādān*), plain weave with pattern wefts floating on reverse, decorated with tassels of wool, cotton bindings and bone and shell ornaments. From Nushki, Chagai, Baluchistan (Zaggar Mengal tribe), early 20th century. 51 × 35 cm (20 × 13.8 in).

The textiles of the nomadic tribes are woven by the women for the practical needs of their daily life from the wool and fleece of their own herds of sheep, goats and camels. The beauty of colour and pattern transcends the simplicity of the weaving equipment, easily set up in the camp and quickly dismantled to transport when they move on. The larger articles, such as the *kōnt* (floor-cover), *katpōsh* (bed-cover) and *shaffī* (a large cloth to cover the pile of blankets and bedding stacked in the tent), or the *asp-e-jhul* (saddle-cloth for a horse), *khōrjīn* (pair of saddle-bags) and *ushtar-e-jhul* (saddle-cloth for a camel) can be woven only when the tribe expects to be settled in a camp for a long period. An infinite variety of smaller articles, such as *ghindrī* (corn sack), *wādān* (bag for storing rock-salt), *tūrag* (nosebag for a horse) and many types of bag for foodstuffs and personal possessions, can be woven when the encampment is for a comparatively shorter time.

The horizontal ground loom, constructed from straight branches and sticks, is described in I, 1 and in Konieczny 1979 (pp. 16–21 and figs 7–15). The loom is set up to the length and breadth of the cloth, and the warp threads are stretched upon its beams. The geometric patterns are woven by the floating-weft technique, the unwanted weft threads passing from motif to motif on the underside of the cloth, and the fabric made firm with a beating-comb. The finished articles are decorated with tassels of wool, ornamented with shell and bone.

The natural colours of the yarns provide a harmonious scheme: sheep's wool is white or off-white; goats' fleece may be fawn, brown or black; the hair of the camel yellow or brown. Aniline dyes have been in use in the towns of Baluchistan since the late nineteenth century, but natural dyes from local plants are still used by some nomads who are too poor to purchase commercial dyes. A list of the main natural dye plants is given by Konieczny (1979, pp. 15–16).

Among the most interesting tribal textiles of India are those of the Naga tribes of Assam and Manipur. The numerous tribes maintain their own individual traditions within a broadly common culture. They now mainly occupy the Naga Hills of Assam, their distinctive villages crowning the ridges; each tribe cultivates the ground below their village and hunts in the adjoining forests.

Wild cotton grows in the hills. A woman has the responsibility to weave for her husband and family. The warp beam at the top of the *tsirochunglung* (a simple loin-loom) is securely tied to a wall or a tree; the tension is maintained by a leather or cloth belt around the weaver's hips. The shed is formed by a heald-stick, a very simple device for making a shed on a primitive

bands of colour with embroidery, called *pukuru*, forming a broad decorative border of geometric ornament.

Tradition tells of an older cloth, called *an*, which the Todas formerly made themselves 'from the bark of a plant', but the method is not described. A 'dark cloth', required in certain ceremonials, notably for enwrapping the dead, should be of *an*, but today a cloth of grey colour is sometimes used.

Baluchistan, the arid mountainous country to the west of Sind (Pakistan), is a harsh environment where, even today, nomadic tribes glean a frugal existence travelling from season to season in search of fresh pasturage for their flocks and herds. Isolated river valleys provide a more fertile and settled existence for some people: the Baluchis are famous for fine woven rugs; the Brahuis, who were formerly rulers of Baluchistan, have a superb tradition of embroidery.

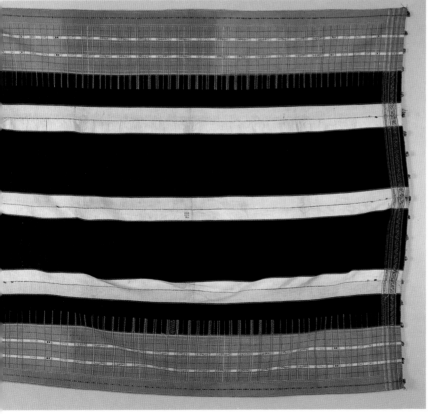

loom; simple geometric patterns are picked by hand. Only a narrow breadth can be woven; larger cloths require several breadths, which are stitched together. Some cloths are ornamented with tufts of dogs' hair dyed red or with cowrie shells.

Traditionally the Nagas used only two dyes, from local dye plants. Dark blue – almost black – was made from the leaves of *Strobilanthes flaccidifolius*, pounded up and boiled with water. A light blue was obtained from leaves saved from the dye bath, dried, kept for a year, then reused. Red was obtained from the root of *Rubia sikkimensis*.

The basic garment-cloth for a Naga man is the *lengta*, a long, narrow loincloth of white or blue cotton, with a long striped or patterned border at one end. The *lengta* is folded and tied around the waist and between the legs; the patterned end-border hangs as a flap in front. The body-cloth, worn as a mantle, signifies a man's wealth, social status and prowess in warfare, and must be earned by fulfilment of the appropriate social *genna*, a series of rituals usually involving the sacrifice of an animal to provide a feast for the extended family, or even for the whole village.

A Naga woman wears the *sürham* (*sübeti*, *sitsükam*), a short skirt-cloth tied at the waist; the free end is sometimes decorated with yellow orchid stem. Her body-cloth is usually white or dark blue for working days. At festivals the cloths worn by women of all tribes of Assam and Manipur are patterned or decorated.

This brief summary outlines the main tribal cultures of India where a textile tradition can be traced, often with primitive origins in leaf-dress and bark cloth, or animal skins in a cold climate, prior to any development of weaving. Many former tribal traditions have now merged into folk art. Modern political boundaries have meanwhile obscured influences from earlier times when the tribes moved freely over the adjacent lands.

TOP LEFT **125** Cotton body-cloth, woven in the pattern traditionally permitted only to a head-hunter, but which may now be earned by the appropriate social *genna*. From Assam (Naga tribe), early 20th century.

LEFT **126** Cotton dancing-cloth for a girl. From Kakadan village, Manipur (Kanui tribe), early 20th century.

The carpets of the Islamic world have always possessed a great fascination for the European observer. Western painters such as Holbein, Delacroix and Matisse were attracted by the exciting interaction of motif and colour. To nineteenth-century critics and designers like William Morris Islamic carpets also offered a solution to contemporary design problems, while the general public saw them as products of exotic, primitive societies. In sixteenth-century Europe the Turkish carpet was paramount, but three centuries later, with the Ottoman sultanate seen as a decadent despotic power controlling the former lands of Christian Byzantium and classical Greece, the Persian carpet became fashionable. More recently Western dissatisfaction with mass production has led to a growing interest in the craftwork of rural or 'tribal' communities apparently so divorced from the pressures and demands of urban civilisation.

Archaeological finds, such as the finely woven Pazyryk carpet discovered in 1949 (see 1, 3) and the small fragments from various sites along the Silk Road, prove that carpet weaving was firmly established in Central Asia many centuries before the Islamic era. Early Arabic chronicles record the magnificent bejewelled carpets of the Sassanian palaces captured by the early Muslims, but nothing remains of these nor of the 22,000 carpets seen by the Byzantine envoys in AD 917 at the Abbasid palace in Baghdad. Fragments of eleventh-century Islamic carpets have survived, but perhaps the earliest known Islamic carpet design is depicted in mosaic, at the eighth-century Umayyad 'royal' bath complex at Khirbat al-Mafjar, Israel.

Court patronage remained an important element in the development of carpet weaving, along with the contribution of the court artist to the design. However, the output from the royal workshops formed only one section of production. In urban and rural communities throughout the Islamic world pile and flat-woven items were made in the home and in small workshops, where the designer and weaver were generally one and the same person and the product was destined for either personal use or sale in the immediate locale, as floor-coverings, furnishing fabrics and drapes, storage containers, riding and pack-animal trappings, and so on.

In the home or nomadic encampment the weavers were usually women, but in the workshop situation, where guild regulations pertained, men were more frequently employed. The social status of the weaver, although higher than, say, the dyer and yarn-twister, was comparatively low. The last two centuries have seen radical social changes and population movements throughout the Middle East which, along with the introduction of chemical dyes and, more recently, of alkaline finishing washes, have influenced the development of regional carpet production. However, the greatest impact has been on design and colouring, with Western taste and preferences dominating selection.

In the past it was the court artist, often inspired by the poetry and literature of his period, who determined the design and motif in court carpets. As for local weavers, it is thought they adopted and adapted much of this metropolitan style in time, but not all critics accept this association, preferring to find exclusively tribal and cultural origins for individual patterns. At times this has resulted in highly imaginative interpretations of certain motifs and their perceived symbolism. Certainly the Muslim prayer-rug possesses a definite iconography, but even so the meaning and, indeed, shape of some of its pattern elements are ambiguous.

Egypt

While the medieval Arabic chronicles are crammed with details of the textile industry during the Fatimid period (AD 969–1171), there are only occasional references to carpets. A few actual fragments have survived, but it was presumed that all these pieces, whether or not they had the so-called Spanish knot (an asymmetrical, single-warp type) and utilised cotton yarn (cotton cultivation in Egypt was considered to post-date the Fatimid regime), were imported from Spain and Anatolia. However, finds from the Fustāt archaeological excavations and recent research into medieval tax records relating to Egyptian cotton are prompting a revaluation. Certainly there was thriving Spanish manufacture and export trade in carpets, as several Arab writers noted, and it is known that Spanish rugs decorated the streets for the wedding of Edward I of England to his Castilian bride in 1254. The Fustāt and other fragments are too small to allow any useful comparison with the famous Spanish fourteenth-century 'Synagogue' rug now in Berlin, with its large stylised 'blossoms' placed either side of a central 'tree', but by the late fifteenth century the Spanish carpet weavers were producing work similar to Egyptian Mamluk and Anatolian 'Holbein' rugs.

In Egypt of the Mamluk period (1250–1517) there were definitely one or more workshops, presumably in Cairo, producing court-quality piled carpets in the third quarter of the fifteenth century. Carpet manufacture continued despite the 1517 Ottoman conquest of Mamluk territory, as in 1585 some of the Cairene weavers were sent to Istanbul. The workshops still existed sixty years later and were evidently making costly pieces to special order as the 1674 mosque inventory of the Istanbul Yeni Cami records a

127 Egyptian Mamluk woollen carpet, c. 1500. If viewed vertically, the arrangement of pattern zones resembles the layout of 15th-century Mamluk manuscript frontispieces.

huge prayer-carpet with 132 separately delineated 'niches' for individual prayer prostrations, as made in Cairo.

Mamluk carpet design was not as varied as that of contemporary Anatolia but the daring use of colour and line sets these pieces in a category apart. The intense jewel-like shimmering colour comes from juxtaposing, without a single-knot outline in brown or black as in Anatolian examples, a cherry-red field with a great amount of leaf green, with occasionally some blue, along with touches of yellow, ivory white and brown wool. The simultaneous visual contrast (retinal after-image) is thus immediate and unimpeded. The spatial arrangement of the classic Mamluk carpets has reminded more than one scholar of contemporary marble-mosaic fountain surrounds, but the most striking resemblance is to fifteenth-century Mamluk manuscript frontispieces. In both a wide border, often with cartouches, frames the inner central

area which has been reduced to a square by the addition of two further bands, top and bottom; this inner area is filled with an intricate square- or star-shaped arrangement. The whole surface is covered with complex geometric compositions, themselves containing a mass of stylised floral elements, such as palm and cypress trees, lotus plants, and single and double rosettes.

This group of carpets shares more or less a common structure: s-spun wool with a four-ply wool warp, and the use of the asymmetrical knot. Until recently another set of carpets characterised by a grid or lozenge chequerboard design and with similar colouring was classified as Mamluk, but because this group is made with a symmetrical knot and z-spun wool with s-ply warps, most carpet historians now prefer to assign an Anatolian provenance to these 'chequer-board' pieces.

The making of woven floor-coverings has continued in Egypt, the coastal city of Alexandria being known, for example, in the early twentieth century for some stylish art deco carpets. However, present-day interest has focused on flat-woven rugs, particularly those produced by the Wissa Wassef foundation at Harraniya, Giza, near Cairo. Set up in 1952 to provide a training for children in the area, the school has become famous for its vegetable-dyed *kelims* with naïve images of everyday life.

Anatolia

Medieval European and Muslim travellers alike recorded that Anatolia was famous for carpet weaving, and fortunately a few pieces have survived from that period. Most of these Seljuk fragments, discovered in the Konya region, possess a deep border, with meaningless Kufic inscriptions, which seems to dominate the main field. In this field, generally cream, deep pink, or blue in colour, are placed separate stylised pattern motifs arranged rather in the manner of tile, metal or mother-of-pearl inlay, within a diagonal grid or in staggered rows. Similar stylisation is found in the later, fifteenth-century Anatolian 'Animal' rugs, but there the deep border has been rejected for a series of narrow bands leading the eye immediately into the main field which is occupied by two large octagons, containing angular representations of birds or animal forms. Only two of these striking rugs have survived, one in Berlin and the other in Stockholm, but a number of fifteenth-century Italian paintings feature such patterned floor-coverings in the composition. In both the Seljuk and the 'Animal' rug examples symmetrical knots make the pile but, unusually in the latter, occasional lines of knots are found on the reverse side; z-spun wool was used for both warp and weft.

128 Anatolian 'Animal' rug. Several contemporary Italian paintings depict floor-coverings with similar stylised animal forms held in octagons, and indeed this early 15th-century woollen rug was found in an Italian church in 1886.

Turkish carpet production increased at a phenomenal rate during the sixteenth and seventeenth centuries. Large numbers of rugs were exported to Europe to grace the residences of the powerful and the rich. Cardinal Wolsey handed over 230 to Henry VIII in the 1520s, and although not all were Turkish, it seems at least four carpets were of the 'Lotto' kind, so-called after the sixteenth-century Italian artist Lorenzo Lotto, who frequently used these bright red and yellow carpets in his paintings. Presumably also one, if not more, was a 'Holbein', so named after Holbein's portraits which often show this type of carpet. With a possible ancestry in earlier Central Asian floor-coverings, as illustrated in certain thirteenth-century Chinese scrolls, these 'Holbeins' have the central area covered in a series of highly patterned octagons, sometimes with decorative lozenges in between; a narrow border often containing interlaced 'knots' surrounds the field. The vibrant colours of the woollen pile and the intensely complex patterning would normally provide the observer with conflicting retinal images, but the essentially simple geometric forms and their disciplined spatial arrangement, along with the use of a narrow (single-knot width) line of brown or black to separate each strong colour, prevent this occurring. The same device is used in the 'Lotto' carpets, so allowing the vivid red of the field to sit alongside the bright yellow of the

129 *The Somerset House Conference*, 1604. Oil-painting attributed to Marcus Gheeraerts. A 'Holbein' carpet is shown covering the table.

ABOVE 130 'Ottoman Court Manufactory' rug. The sophisticated patterning of these rugs is drawn from the decorative repertoire of the Istanbul court.

ABOVE RIGHT 131 'Ghiordes' prayer-rug. This is a fine example of the 'classic' 'Ghiordes' type, showing the stylisation of motifs derived from earlier 'Ottoman Court Manufactory' rugs.

skeletal 'arrow-headed' octagons and quatrefoils, with their powder-blue and leaf-green accents.

It is not certain where these carpets were made; Uşak (Ushak) in western Anatolia has been suggested, and indeed there are structural similarities with another sixteenth–seventeenth-century group called 'Star Ushak', thought to have come from that region. In all three groups a number of carpets have warps of white wool, with two shoots of red wool after each row of symmetrical knots; knot density is low. All three designs had a long production life, at least seventy years, and have continued to inspire modern work.

With the 'Star Ushak' and 'Medallion', another type of Ottoman Anatolian carpet, the impact of court or metropolitan taste is more apparent; the composition and the more fluid linear approach to motifs relate closely to contemporary bookbinding decoration. However, it is in the rugs classified as 'Ottoman Court Manufactory', produced around the same time, that the influence of the Istanbul court artists is clearest. An illusion of depth is created by the scrolls moving across the surface with rhythmic, controlled energy carrying broad fronds and stylised flowers which fall gracefully across the stems. Here, as in the 'Ushak' and 'Medallion'

rugs, it can be said that pattern rather than colour dominates the field, for although the individual wool colours (six to nine in all) are rich and vibrant, the visual effect is quiet and dignified. It is thought these 'Manufactory' rugs were made in at least two, if not three, centres as two different weave structures have been employed. Istanbul was one centre along with perhaps Bursa; this production is characterised by the use of s- and z-spun yarns in the warp and pile, and an asymmetrical knot (opening to the left). The other structure closely resembles that of Mamluk carpets, and so indicates the work of the Cairene workshops or Egyptian weavers working in Ottoman Anatolia.

However, many Ottoman carpets show only tenuous links with court designs. In seventeenth–eighteenth-century 'Transylvanian' rugs, so called because many pieces were found in eastern Europe, the central medallion with the four corner areas, and the cloud-band and floral motifs, are so stylised that perhaps it is misleading to relate them with earlier court 'Medallion' carpets. Some enthusiasts prefer to describe the composition as double-niche, so associating it with contemporary prayer-rug design, like the 'Ghiordes', 'Ladik' and later 'Milas' work which possess broadly similar spatial and

132 Anatolian *kelim* prayer-rug.

OPPOSITE 133 The Ardabil carpet. A small panel carries the information that it was made by Maqsud of Kashan in 946/1539–40. The knot count is 5,100 per square decimetre (340 per square inch).

examples can now be securely assigned by design or colouring to a particular weaving centre.

To some extent this state of affairs also pertains to the present-day production of flat-woven rugs in Anatolia. Few historic pieces have survived, but that is no reason to assume that *kelim* weaving was a late Ottoman innovation; indeed, some enthusiasts see a direct, sustained link from neolithic times to the present day. The patterns of these early fragments again show evidence of the two traditions, metropolitan and provincial. The Vakiflar Kelim Collection, housed in the crypt of Sultan Ahmet Mosque, Istanbul, includes a fine eighteenth-century 'court' piece decorated with three large medallion forms on a blue-green ground, itself patterned with tulips, lotuses and other blossoms carried on curving stems. Alongside, others of comparable date and of similar high technical quality are in the 'provincial' style with stylised angular motifs, placed in sizeable areas of one colour; there is often a clear emphasis on horizontal and vertical axes for both motif and field.

It is possible to argue that there is a third tradition, the weaving of nomadic or semi-nomadic peoples, but as with Persian carpets our knowledge of these 'tribal' weavings is virtually confined to the last 100 years. It is accepted practice to identify two main nomadic groupings – those living in the black goats'-hair tents as found in North Africa, the Levant, the Hijaz and western Iran, and those using the domed felt or trellis tents (yurts) as seen in the Caucasus, Iran and Central Asia across to north-west China. Generally speaking, although the piled and flat-woven pieces from both feature small, simple, repeating elements, the Anatolian black-tent group appears to have a preference for dark, sombre fields with the pattern motifs held in a series of horizontal or vertical bands, while more strident coloured work with diagonal composition is more associated with the other group. However, concerted government policy over the last fifty years to settle these groups and promote intermixing has naturally led to a blurring of distinctions.

Persia

Medieval Persian manuscript painting is presently the primary source of information for the designs of early Persian carpets, a bitter legacy, perhaps, of the urban devastation wrought by the numerous military campaigns by Timur Leng (Tamerlane, d. 1405) and his successors across the central Islamic lands. In such miniatures as those in the 1396 'Khawju Kirmani' manuscript (British Library) the floor-coverings are shown in colourful detail with their plaited Kufic borders and the fields of repeating oc-

linear qualities, although the actual composition and pattern elements vary considerably. With the strong angular treatment and larger areas of one colour, softer shades of red, yellow and blue wool along with cream are used.

Both traditions, which perhaps may be classified for convenience as metropolitan and provincial, continued to evolve with many variations and combinations. The Hereke production centre established in 1844 and that of Kum Kapu, in Istanbul, carried on the metropolitan style, which in the nineteenth century was greatly influenced by the more intricate patterning and colouring of contemporary Persian manufacture; here, as elsewhere, chemical dyestuffs were extensively used. Carpets woven in the Anatolian provinces, then and now, show a heavy reliance on historical patterns and compositions with little, if any, reinterpretation. Population movements in the early twentieth century and a massive increase in carpet production throughout Turkey to satisfy an ever-growing demand from the West mean that few

tagons and squares containing stylised stars and rosettes; the similarity to later Anatolian carpet design is noticeable. However, by the late fifteenth century both border and field are depicted with more curvilinear patterns, as found throughout Timurid surface decoration, from bookbinding to metalwork, from ceramic tiles to manuscript illumination. This elegant decorative style, developed by the Timurid court artists, is characterised by the arabesque scroll, fine but controlled, carrying delicate half-leaves and chinoiserie floral elements, such as lotuses and peonies. With its illusion of depth created by various 'levels' of arabesque and the use of 'deeper' colour tones in the background, this style was to remain influential in the world of Persian carpets for centuries.

The involvement of the court artist in carpet and textile design continued and increased throughout the sixteenth century. The court carpet workshops established by Shah Tahmasp (1524–76) of the Safavid dynasty in such centres as Tabriz, Isfahan, Kirman, Yazd and Kashan worked to cartoons supplied by the royal atelier, so the weaver's contribution was confined to production and interpretation. In some examples this working arrangement led to overdecorous designs in which the vigour of the composition was submerged, but at best yielded magnificent results. An outstanding example is the pair of Ardabil carpets dated 1539–40 in the Victoria and Albert Museum, London, and the J. Paul Getty Museum, Malibu, USA.

The output of the court workshops was not confined to the 'Medallion' composition of the Ardabil carpet, even if the designs continued to be based on the decorative repertoire of manuscript illumination. The main pattern element of the 'Herati' carpets, for example, consists of dignified, elegant arabesque scrolls moving quietly across the dark field, while the designs of the 'Polonaise' rugs exploit the special two-dimensional quality of illumination ornament through the use of gold and silver metallic thread, and the play of light on the silk pile, with the consequent startling colour changes. There were also pictorial compositions depicting Safavid horse-riders pursuing wild animals across the main field (the 'Hunting' carpets), or the 'Animal' carpets in which the beasts, both mythical and real, tumble over the field, locked in fights to the death, or the highly detailed 'Multiple-medallion' rugs with their series of ogival medallions containing human figures, interspersed with animal forms. Other designs emphasise floral motifs such as the famous 'Garden' carpets in which a complete Persian garden layout forms the composition, or the 'Vase' group with its understated lattice arrangement holding masses of stylised flowers,

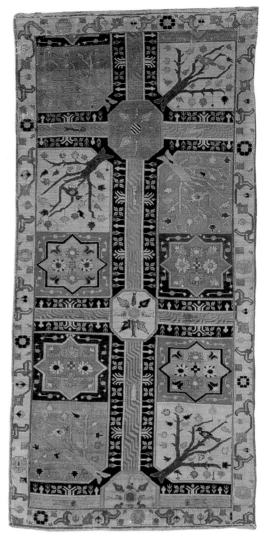

along with the 'Sickle Leaf' design characterised by large, curved leaf forms sweeping decisively in circular movements across the field, from a central 'stem'. The variety seems endless.

Structural analyses of these court carpets show that no design was exclusive to any one workshop, as a number of pieces, while sharing common technical features, have markedly different patterns. Likewise carpets closely related in pattern and motif display no similarity in the warp and weft structure nor in the employment of cotton, wool and silk, although most feature the asymmetrical knot (opening to the left), whether in wool or silk. Indeed, some of these compositions were produced as flat weaves of incredible fineness, perhaps for use as canopies. A splendid early seventeenth-century silk *kelim* which incorporates the Polish royal coat of arms, now in the Residenz Museum, Munich, closely follows the classic 'Polonaise' pattern, while another, the 'Figdor' silk *kelim* in the Thyssen-Bornemisza Collection, Lugano, features the 'Multiple-medallion' composition.

OPPOSITE FAR LEFT 134 Detail of a silk Persian 'Animal' carpet dating from the second half of the 16th century.

OPPOSITE 135 Late 17th- or 18th-century 'Garden' carpet. Its structure suggests Kirman production. The irrigation channels and the individual flower-beds are clearly shown.

RIGHT 136 The Corcoran 'Vase' rug. Persian, early 17th century. The border and field motifs show the strong connection with 'Vase' carpet design, although the latter's formal lattice arrangement has been rejected in favour of circular sweeps from the vertical axis.

Political turmoil throughout Iran in the late seventeenth and early eighteenth centuries resulted in the withdrawal of court patronage, and it was only with the Qajar dynasty (1789–1925) that the manufacture of large, costly 'court' carpets was revived. The Qajar weaver and designer looked to the classic carpets of the Safavid period for inspiration but adapted composition, motif and colour to suit contemporary tastes, both home and abroad. Leaving aside the problems concerning the use of imported chemical dyes in the second half of the nineteenth century, the technical standard of production of these late carpets from Tehran, Kashan, Isfahan and Kirman is high, but there is a certain loss of clarity and movement, with the mass of intricate detail tending to overwhelm the composition in which colour is relegated.

ABOVE **137** Persian silk *kelim* rug, early 17th century. This may be one of the four carpets specially ordered in Kashan for the Polish court in 1601–2 as, instead of the usual central medallion, the arms of the Vasa royal family appear.

ABOVE RIGHT **138** Qashqa'i tribal rug from western Iran, late 19th century.

While these pieces have a peculiar charm of their own, as their continued production suggests, many observers think that the real achievements in nineteenth- and twentieth-century Islamic carpet designs are to be found in the work classified as village and tribal products. The contrast with the 'court' product is immediate. While there are perceivable links with the decorative repertoire of the 'classic' carpets – the 'Medallion' composition, for example – pattern, motif and colour combinations have been vigorously developed in their own right, with many variations. Baluchi work, for example, has a subtlety of dark rich browns, reds and blues arranged in a series of narrow bands filled with small understated motifs, whereas the Qashqa'i weavings possess an energy with strong yet intricate designs, rendered in flowing, vibrant colours. Stylisation, often implicit from the rather coarse knotting and weave structure employed, is emphatic, and while the weavers sometimes refer to the individual pattern motifs by specific names, these rarely, if at

all, indicate any symbolic meaning. In a similar way the many tribal or regional classifications of the pieces are becoming increasingly invalid with radical social changes over the last forty years.

The Caucasus

The most famous pile carpets generally attributed to this region are the 'Dragon' rugs, originally dated to the fifteenth century but now usually assigned three or more centuries later. The stylised character of dragon and other animal motifs, contained within a generous lattice of serrated leaf forms, has led various authorities to suggest links with early Scythian work, pre-Christian Armenian motifs and Chinese decorative arts, but Safavid 'Animal' carpet design seems to have been the immediate inspiration. The earliest examples in this group of some 150 rugs generally have cream-coloured z-spun woollen warps, with similarly spun wefts in single or double shoots between the rows of symmetric knots. The knot count varies from

LEFT **139** Caucasian 'Dragon' rug, 17th century. The motifs include dragons, birds and gazelles.

BELOW **140** Early 19th-century Caucasian 'Sunburst' rug.

525 to 1,800 per square decimetre (35 to 120 per square inch), and usually eight or more intense colours are employed on the red or blue-green field.

Similar stylisation of leaf and floral elements, but without the animal forms, is found in other contemporary carpets from the region, such as the 'Kuba' and 'Kazak' pieces. As in Caucasian embroideries of the same period, these strong palmette and sunburst motifs are clearly outlined with 'latch-hooks'. A parallel treatment of motif and its placing in the main field are visible in the woven textiles, knotted, *kelim* and *soumak* (weft wrapping), emanating from the Shahsevan tribal confederation, whose nomadic migrations take in sections of the western Caspian shores, as well as the north-west Iranian border regions.

India

There is no evidence of an indigenous pile carpet-weaving tradition existing in the Indian sub-continent before the reign of Akbar, the

was modified and dissipated with the development of a distinct Mogul style, which rejected the Safavid, rather mannered formality for a livelier, more energetic approach, as seen in Mogul 'Animal' carpets.

As elsewhere in the Islamic world, the court artist contributed to carpet (and textile) design. Early seventeenth-century Mogul pictorial rugs, probably made in Lahore, show the same concern for animal and bird subjects as in contemporary manuscript painting. In Mogul floral carpets and a small group of prayer-rugs, with z-spun cotton wefts and often warps, there are also clear links with architectural decoration of the Shah Jahan period. Their designs may be directly related to marble carving and *pietra dura* work at the Taj Mahal mausoleum, Agra, and other seventeenth-century buildings.

Sharing a similar structure of cotton warps and wefts, and asymmetrical knot type (opening to the left), is another seventeenth-century group. Carpet enthusiasts have variously assigned the production centre of these 'Portuguese' rugs to Gujarat or Goa, and also to north, south or east Iran, despite the uncharacteristic colour combinations. Persian-styled borders are overshadowed by a large central multicoloured medallion in the field, while in the four corners boats holding European figures 'float' uneasily. It was first thought that these rugs celebrated the coming of the Portuguese envoys to India (hence the classification), but then it was suggested that the composition depicted the drowning, in 1537 while on a Portuguese ship, of the Gujarati ruler Bahadur Shah. More recently the scene has been interpreted in terms of a mandala relating to Shamanist, Buddhist and certain mystical Islamic philosophical beliefs.

From 1739 court patronage decreased as the fortunes of the Mogul dynasty waned. Although certain princes continued to commission carpets from their local workshops, by the mid-nineteenth century only Kashmir and Warangal, near Hyderabad, were producing high-quality work. Examples from these centres were displayed at the 1851 Great Exhibition in London, and the great public interest they provoked was instrumental in causing a revival of carpet weaving in northern India. For designs the weavers drew heavily on historical Persian and Mogul pattern repertoires, and up to the present day this reliance on established decorative tradition has continued and widened to include Chinese, Tibetan and Central Asian designs as commercial weaving shops seek to satisfy market demands from the West.

Regarding *kelim* weaving in the Indian subcontinent, the first unmistakable references to flat-woven rugs are found in the early seventeenth-century records of such foreign

third Mogul emperor (1556–1605). He 'caused carpets to be made' and 'appointed experienced workmen, who have produced many masterpieces', in the words of the court historian Abu'l Fazl, who also noted that the most important carpet-weaving centres were Agra, nearby Fatehpur Sikri and Lahore. Bearing in mind that his father, Humayun (r. 1530–56), returned from fifteen years of Persian exile with two Safavid court painters to establish his own court atelier, it is very probable that Akbar's carpet weavers were brought in from Iran. Indeed, there is a strong Persian element in the patterning of carpets depicted in the *Hamza-nama* paintings (Victoria and Albert Museum, London), begun in Humayun's court and completed during Akbar's reign. However, this overt influence

travellers as Pietro della Valle, but it was over 250 years later that the Indian dhurrie was introduced to the British public by Sir George Birdwood (1832–1917). Their functions were varied as suggested by the many variations in size, from the small prayer-mats for Muslims and Hindus to the 18 × 8 m (60 × 25 ft approx.) Rajasthani palace floor-coverings. Recognition of this textile art came with the Delhi Imperial Exhibition of 1903, despite the fact that the dhurries exhibited were the products of prison workshops, and since then there has been an active European market for these weft-faced, cotton-warp rugs.

Central Asia

As one would expect, fragments of woven silk have been found at archaeological sites along the Silk Road, and also a few knotted pieces have survived. Unfortunately, these third- and fourth-century remains are too small to allow any reconstruction of the overall design, let alone any comparison with later depictions of carpets in Timurid paintings. Indeed, the paintings and the occasional documentary reference are our only sources of information regarding carpet design in medieval and later Central Asia. The term 'Central Asian carpets' is therefore generally used for products of the nineteenth and twentieth centuries.

The relationship between the Timurid depictions of carpets and later Ottoman and

Safavid designs, along with textiles illustrated in certain Chinese scrolls, has already been mentioned (see pp. 120, 123). Parallels can also be drawn with the geometrical patterning seen in certain nineteenth-century Turkoman carpets from Central Asia. The characteristic Turkoman polygonal motif, or *gul* (literally, 'flower' or 'rose'), with its projecting 'latch-hooks', 'clover-leaf' or 'clove' stems, could well be an adaptation of carpet patterns as portrayed in Timurid painting; after all, such transmission of design elements from court to 'provincial' carpet production occurred elsewhere in the Islamic world. However, some critics argue that the wide dissemination, from Anatolia to China, of motif and pattern points to a common inherent (and ageless) decorative tradition, springing from the Turkic-speaking nomadic tribal families of pre-Timurid Central Asia, and that the *gul* with all its variations possesses heraldic significance, reflecting the changing fortunes of the individual tribe. More recently it has been suggested that one should look further east, to imperial China, for the origins of the motif, to the Chinese 'pearl-roundel' patterned silks woven for several centuries, and perhaps more controversially to the cloud-collar of the Chinese imperial garments.

The function and placing of the *gul* in the composition is perhaps best seen in 'Tekke' carpets, popularly and misleadingly known as 'Bukhara', although the city was never the centre of production. The red field is regularly divided into rectangles; over the intersections are placed the *guls*, with a secondary motif, either quatrefoil or lozenge in shape, sitting in the enclosed space. There are only three main colours in the pile (asymmetrical knot) – red, brown and blue – but two or three shades of each are used along with some yellow and touches of green. With later pieces their visual appearance is muted, the rich red seemingly replaced by a golden-brown colour, but this fading is the result of the unstable dyes introduced from Europe in the last years of the nineteenth century. Ironically, this colouring, so atypical of Turkoman weaving, proved to be extremely popular in the West, and production of such 'Golden Bukharas' continued for some time.

Weaving associated with the Saryk, Salor and Ensari tribal groups is closely related in style to Tekke work, although there are differences in weave and knot structure, colour and yarn use, and the shape and complexity of the *gul*. Although most of the Turkoman weaving has a field of red, varying from bright, rich red to dark blue-purple, certain smaller items were made with a cream or white ground, flat-woven or piled, with the main decorative pattern of red-brown stiff, stylised leaves held on angular

143 Central Asian 'Tekke' carpet, late 18th century.

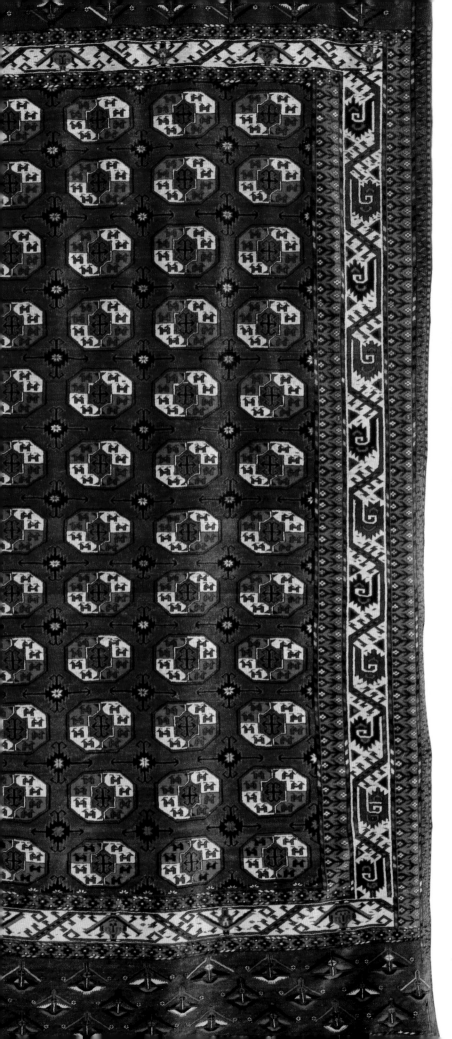

stems rendered in pile. In all these groups and others in the region weaving was not restricted to the production of rugs and carpets; there was a wide range of work, including tension bands, of various widths, used in the erection of the trellis or domed felt tents (*kibitkas*), storage bags of all shapes and sizes, animal-trappings and door-hangings. The sheer volume and variety raise the problem of whether all pieces should be regarded as solely the work of these nomadic tribal groups, as generally assumed. Increasingly from the 1840s these communities, along with the rest of the rural and urban population, were severely affected not only by radical political and social changes but also by widespread migratory movements, both voluntary and enforced, in the region.

Further east, on the west and east sides of the Tarim Basin, astride the major silk-trade routes, between Russia, Kashmir, Tibet and Mongolia, is a Turkic-speaking region, the present-day Chinese province of Xinjiang; its carpet designs ('Eastern Turkistan') show both Turkoman and Chinese influence in treatment and individual decorative elements. Enclosed by a series of significant borders often featuring stylised 'rams' horns' or rosettes, the field in early

146 Co-operative carpet workshop in Urumqi, western China. The weaver works according to a design cartoon, seen upper left.

147 Chinese carpet, 19th century. The design of 'One Hundred Antiques', 'Eight Immortals' and 'Four Elegant Accomplishments' is rendered in approximately 735 knots per square decimetre (49 knots per square inch).

nineteenth-century examples is a rich red or deep blue with an essentially simple motif, either three medallion forms ('Kashgar' design) or a pomegranate branch theme ('Khotan' pattern); the warp and weft are cotton and the knot asymmetrical. Today carpet-making is an important industry in the area. Co-operative workshops in Urumqi, for instance, produce a wide variety of good-quality rugs, copying Chinese, Persian and Turkish designs as set out on working cartoons; but there is also a thriving village industry with vertical looms set up in domestic houses whose output is rather coarse work with low knot counts, in strident (but locally popular) colour tones produced by chemical dyes, with the women weavers working without cartoons.

China

It may be that the occasional mention of carpets in Tang documents referred to felt rather than woven pieces as a number of felt rugs, datable to the eighth century, still survive in the Shōsō-in Repository at Nara, Japan. There are also a few references to silk floor-coverings in use in official buildings in late ninth-century Manchuria. However, by the mid-seventeenth century there was clearly an established production of piled carpets in Jingyuan and Taiyuan, in Gansu and Shanxi provinces (north-west China) respectively, as several Jesuit priests mentioned these carpets as being 'such as the Turkey ones, of all sizes'; this could mean that either the pattern or the structure was similar to Turkish pieces. Two centuries later other commercial workshops were in operation including one in Beijing. Export markets in the USA expanded as a result of the 1903 International Exhibition in San Francisco and the disrupted supply of Middle Eastern carpets during World War I.

A comparatively low density of asymmetrical knots is often found in both old and modern pieces, approximately 600 per square decimetre (40 per square inch), so the design tends to have an angular quality. In nineteenth-century Chinese rugs the field is generally light in colour, although Baotou work, influenced by eastern Turkistan production, often has dark blue or red grounds. Similarly, Baotou rugs frequently utilise Turkistan motifs and compositions, but generally the Chinese carpets are patterned with isolated elements found in the established decorative repertoire: floral (lotus, 'immortal' fungus, peony); geometric and calligraphic (for example, frets, swastikas, *shou*, or long life character); and religious symbols (Eight Daoist Immortals, Eight Buddhist Symbols, Eight Precious Objects).

The Far East

14 *China*

Chinese textile history largely focuses on silk. Although other fabrics do not now survive in such quantities as silk, three types of bast-fibre material were in use from neolithic times up to the thirteenth century. These were ramie, hemp and *ge* from the fibres of *Pueraria thunbergia*, the vine-creeper. Cotton, an import from India, grew in economic importance during the fourteenth century and remained the everyday material of the Chinese people. The Chinese invention of the spindle wheel during the Zhou dynasty (*c.*1050–221 BC) was first applied to bast fibres and then adapted for silk, and it is this lustrous fabric, primarily produced for the prosperous sector of society, that concerns us here.

The earliest woven silk fragments found to date come from the period between 2860 and 2650 BC. Although these examples were in plain weave, it is supposed that fabrics with patterns followed on soon after. The tomb of an unknown lady provides us with truly astonishing proof of the early range of textile techniques and the intricate patterns that were employed. Dating to about 300 BC, the excavated chamber at Mashan in what is today Hubei province in south central China was, at the time of the woman's funeral, in the powerful state of Chu. This state, known for its evocative poetry and its singular decoration on bronze vessels, must now rank high in any world view of the textile arts. The excavations revealed garments and bordered shrouds as well as other smaller textile pieces, and the find is arguably the largest and

earliest group of intact textile items ever recovered. Except for a miniature ritual robe, all the gowns found were on the woman's corpse, and these, together with the wraps that also enveloped her body, are decorated mostly with complex embroidered designs in rows of close chain stitch. The ground material of these is of even, plain-weave silk, and the embroidery spreads across the surface on the diagonal. On some of the robes the pattern repeats are long and, although the symmetrical organisation of the designs is immediately apparent, the axes about which the patterns turn are often hard to pick out. The twining foliage and fantastic birds and beasts dissolve into each other in sinuous curves giving the impression that the design scheme is freer than it actually is.

The silks patterned on the loom provide a contrast to the embroideries by virtue of their different technique and motifs, although many of them have diagonally arranged designs. These loom-patterned textiles fall into two main groups. Those which have their patterns formed by the warp are the antecedents of the similar and better-known bicoloured and multicoloured weaves of the Han dynasty (206 BC–AD 220). The most frequently occurring designs on the Mashan warp-patterned silks are different configurations of the diamond shape. A stepped tower design appears on the silk used as ties for the outermost shroud, while the shroud itself, a *tour de force* of woven patterning, is decorated in green and cream with confronting birds, beasts

148 Detail (LEFT) of a woman's embroidered shroud (RIGHT) from Mashan, *c.* 300 BC.

and reptiles, as well as paired dancers holding their arms aloft. Warp-patterned silks have been found at other sites dating from the Warring States period (475–221 BC), the timespan within which the Mashan finds fall, but up until now Mashan is the only excavation from this period and for some time after to have yielded a second and unexpected group of loom-patterned textiles. This second group, narrow in width and used for edgings, is weft-patterned. The designs are both geometric and figurative, one of the latter showing a hunting scene with chariots, charioteers and wild animals. A feature of this textile group is the use of thick pattern wefts which make the motifs stand out from the ground. Although these early borders can in no way compare with the weft-patterned silks woven on a drawloom around 700 years later, they do extend the repertoire of known textile types in early China. Braiding and a technique somewhat akin to knitting, as well as gauze-weave silks, are all also described in the Mashan site report.

Embroideries, gauze weaves and polychrome warp-patterned weaves continued to be made in the Han dynasty, and during this period monochrome figured silks and silks with a looped warp occurred. Unlike the earlier period there are many specimens of Han textiles in collections outside China, but, as with Mashan, Chinese archaeological exploration has provided an abundance of whole silk artefacts the like of which do not exist elsewhere. Another noblewoman's burial, that at Mawangdui on the outskirts of Changsha in Hunan province, given a date between 174 and 145 BC, revealed chainstitch embroideries with designs of a more abstract and swirling appearance than the earlier needlework. In general the fantasy creatures and personages of the Mashan period textiles are not so prominent on those of the Han era. Gauze weaves, both plain and figured, are sometimes additionally embroidered, painted

or printed. The figured gauzes show diamond shapes in various forms. Some of these give the impression of being arranged in alternate bands of light and dark tones. Only one colour is in fact present, the diamonds being woven so that some of them have thick outlines and some fine. These gauzes are presumed to have been dyed after weaving. Modern-day weavers, although now able to reconstruct the handloom methods used to make these gauzes, are none the less amazed at the Chinese craftworkers' skilful manipulation of such very fine thread.

The same is true of the monochrome figured silks whose single colourway and straight-line patterning are deceptive. They are of extreme fineness and show several ingenious variations in weave structure to create the pattern. To date no systematic study has been made concerning the use of the different kinds of textile known to exist in early China; however, there is now sufficient data to begin such a study. For example, a monochrome figured silk, partly embroidered, was used for a woman's skirt at a double burial at Niya, a site along the Silk Road in the north-west province of Xinjiang dating from the Eastern Han (AD 25–220). A flaring robe, a pair of mittens, two pairs of socks and pillows from the same Niya entombment were all made from multicoloured warp-patterned material, whereas at Mawangdui, further south, the tomb-occupant's gowns were of embroidered silk and the polychrome silk finds here were rather few. Together with a number of pieces from elsewhere the Niya silks form a select group distinguished by ideographs woven into the patterns. This constitutes a design variation only. Technically the group does not deviate from the binding system to which all warp-patterned silks mentioned so far adhere. The looped-warp weave, found at only a very few sites of Han date, is also based on the same weave structure. On these silks, which seem to have been used sparingly because of the arduous labour involved in their production, the décor stands above the background in loops.

The period between the Han and Tang dynasties – the third to sixth centuries – witnessed a changing aesthetic in textile design as well as a major change in loom arrangement for patterned silk manufacture. The Silk Road, in reality several East–West routes across the north of China and beyond, continued the exchange of goods and influences between east and west Asia and, ultimately, Europe. Buddhism spread to China from India this way, and a dedicatory textile found at Mogaoku in Gansu province in the Silk Road region represents the first securely dated silk connected with this great faith. Dated to AD 487, the textile shows part of a Buddha figure with a Bodhisattva standing to one side of

149 Gauze-weave silk from the tomb of the Marchioness of Dai at Mawangdui, *c.* 168 BC.

RIGHT **150** Robe in polychrome patterning from Niya, Eastern Han dynasty (AD 25–220).

RIGHT 152 Cover for a *biwa*, a stringed musical instrument. 8th century. Believed by some scholars to be a Japanese import from Tang China, it fully exploits the weft-patterning technique, combining ten or more colours easily into the design. The central floral roundel alone is 53 cm (21 in) across, suggesting an unusually wide loom-width of around 110 cm (43.3 in).

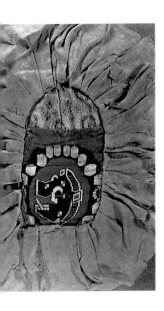

ABOVE 151 Face-cover for the dead showing a pearled roundel silk. Tang dynasty (618–906).

DYNASTIES

BC

c.1700–1050	Shang
c.1050–221	Zhou
475–221	Warring States
221–207	Qin
206 BC–AD 220	Han

AD

220–580	Six Dynasties
581–618	Sui
618–906	Tang
907–960	Five Dynasties
960–1279	Song
1279–1368	Yuan
1368–1644	Ming
1644–1911	Qing
1912–1949	Republic
1949–	People's Republic of China

early and middle years of that dynasty. The long history of warp patterning in China was due to the availability of strong silk thread which, because it did not need laborious spinning, could be used for closely set warps.

It has been said that every advanced weaving technique known in the world at the time was practised by Tang weavers, and the warp- and weft-patterned silks, both of which display variations, have already been mentioned. Judging by the number of surviving examples, monochrome figured silks continued to be appreciated. Tang weavers built on the knowledge of their Han forebears and continued to develop self-patterned silks with plain-weave grounds. They also took over ideas from their Western near-contemporaries and created monochrome damasks which have both the ground and the décor in twill weave, thus showing off the silk's sheen to best advantage. Figured gauzes in clear, strong colours also survive.

A major departure from loom patterning was the production of refined resist-dyed textiles. This involved tying off or masking out with wax or rice paste areas of pattern before immersion of the textile in the dye. A process whereby selective areas of the silk are degummed so that they accept the dye more readily than the parts where the gum remains seems also to have been employed, as does a method which used paired wooden boards, identically carved in relief. Folded silk was laid between these two boards and dye poured through holes drilled in the top

it, and below is a row of monks, nuns and donors. The whole picture is executed in chain stitch which completely covers the ground.

Other votive textiles were to have a high profile from this time onwards, and secular silks show new motifs adapted from Sassanian (Iranian) and Soghdian (western Turkistan) designs. Perhaps the most enduring of all these designs was the pearled roundel, a circular or oval cartouche bordered with spots and containing bird or animal motifs. Face-coverings for the deceased were made from pearled roundel silks right through the Tang dynasty (618–906), by which period the drawloom had been introduced to or independently developed by the Chinese. This meant that multicoloured patterns could now be created by the weft, giving smoother design outlines and greater sophistication in patterning. Despite the advantages of weft patterning, the changeover from warp to weft ornamentation was a gradual process, and both methods existed alongside each other in the centuries before the Tang and on into the

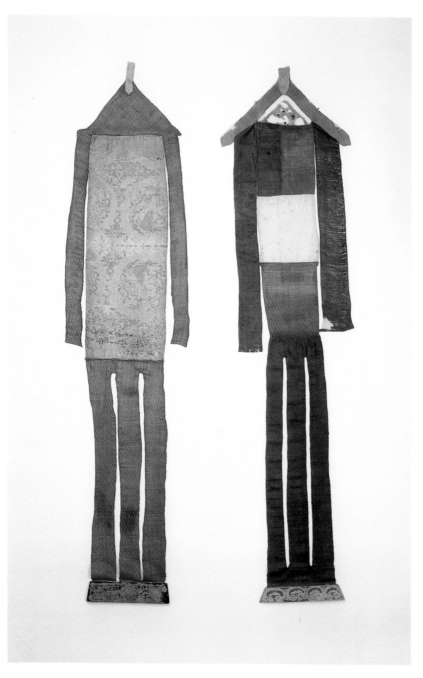

153 Two Buddhist banners from the Cave of the Thousand Buddhas, Dunhuang, Gansu province. Tang dynasty (618–906). The banner on the left has a resist-dyed central section, while the other silks are plain or self-patterned.

emerges when reports from Song archaeological sites of the last thirty years are consulted. Recorded finds of *kesi* pieces are negligible. Instead there are sheer plain weaves, figured gauzes in a proliferation of technical variations and damasks, one of which, from the tomb of a lady called Huang Sheng who died in 1243, may be the earliest-known Chinese example of a satin weave. Also from this burial came gold-printed and -painted silks and embroideries. The designs are dominated by graceful floral branches flowing across the surface with much greater fluidity than any ornamentation encountered so far. Tiny figures and small birds often appear between the boughs lending a pleasing oddity to the scale of the design.

Birds and flowers are perhaps the most recurring motifs found on *kesi* pieces of this time, but these textiles belong firmly in the Chinese painting tradition and are of a very different order from the textiles recovered from tombs. Despite being woven, they resemble paintings and some of them are in fact copies of famous paintings. The picture-making opportunities of the *kesi* technique were utilised to the full to produce these valued scrolls and album leaves. The method is akin to that used for the great wool tapestries of Europe. The picture is formed by coloured weft threads, each colour being wound on to a small shuttle which is then manipulated by the weaver across sections of the warp according to the dictates of the design. The wefts do not pass from selvage to selvage but turn back around the warp that marks the limit of that particular colour.

Although gold and gold-coloured threads were not unknown prior to the twelfth century, it is true to say that these were used sparingly in earlier times. The twelfth to the fourteenth centuries saw an increased use of metallic yarn, both flat gold strip and wound gold thread, for weft-patterned textiles. A royal tomb from the Jin dynasty (1115–1234), which ruled in the north simultaneously with the native Chinese Southern Song dynasty (1128–1279), contained many garments and other textiles whose decoration solely consists of gold thread. It appears that on these articles the additional gold wefts are bound in with the plain-weave ground, but other gold textiles, usually of a later date in the Yuan dynasty (1279–1368), have a supplementary set of warps to bind the weft threads that form the pattern. These Yuan silks are structurally and decoratively different from those of the Tang, the latter having no warp threads visible on the face of the textile. A shaped collar with streamers down the front connected with Buddhist ritual provides a sumptuous example of Yuan gold patterning. It is composed of several figured silks each with a

one. The colour penetrated the silk only at the points where it was not clamped tightly.

For the post-Tang era silks which have survived above ground as opposed to those from excavations have to be taken account of in any overview of Chinese textiles. Generally, their numbers increase the closer they are to the present. The Song dynasty (960–1279) is always thought of as the era when silk tapestry weave, often referred to by its Chinese name *kesi*, or *k'o-ssu*, reached unprecedented heights. The *kesi* pieces which confirm this have been held by collectors down the centuries and preserved as works of art. However, a different picture

月玩物乐

LEFT **154** *Kesi* hanging-scroll entitled 'Accumulating Counters in an Immortal Abode'. Song dynasty (960–1279). This picture has an inscription added in 1344 during the Yuan dynasty which informs us that *kesi* began in the Song dynasty, and claims later examples cannot compare in refinement. Examples of *kesi* prior to the Song are in fact known, but they are not of this kind.

BELOW **155** Gold-patterned Buddhist collar. Yuan dynasty (1279–1368).

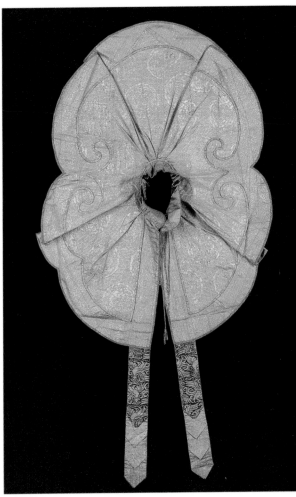

different design, and some of these design elements, notably the swooping birds, recur on European silks not very much later. We know of actual Yuan period Chinese silks preserved from that time in Europe, often in church treasuries, and these are both gold-patterned, sometimes against a satin-weave ground, and satin damasks.

The Ming dynasty (1368–1644) and the succeeding Qing dynasty (1644–1911) had flourishing textile industries in a number of places throughout the Empire. No single technique or group of textiles is more noteworthy than the rest during these centuries for there is a mass of

ABOVE **156** Length of velvet with added embroidery from an imperial robe, early 17th century 3.09 × 2.72 m (10.13 × 8.92 ft).

RIGHT **157** Robe in *kesi* technique, *c.* 1600.

extant material, all equally interesting. The so-called fine-art tradition continued with the production of *kesi* pictures, but increasingly this weave was applied to garments and furnishings as well. It is pertinent to raise the subject of velvet here. Chinese sources mention the Yuan dynasty as the starting-date for this warp-pile weave, and there is some indication that a robe from a tomb dated to 1365, very late in the Yuan, was made using this technique. More pieces survive from the Ming and Qing, and at least one of these, a yellow uncut length for an imperial robe dated to the early seventeenth century and now in the Royal Ontario Museum, Toronto, shares technical features with Spanish velvets indicating a possible Western influence.

It is perhaps surprising that so few velvets were found in the Dingling tomb of the Emperor Wanli (1573–1620) and his two empresses. Satins, damasks and embroideries form the majority of the textile finds from there, and, as far as it is possible to tell at present, silk from the reigns of the Ming and Qing emperors housed in the Palace Museum, Peking, the former imperial residence, consists of all the kinds found in the Wanli tomb as well as quantities of what the Chinese call 'brocade'. This covers a broad span of technical variants of polychrome loom-patterned fabric with an array of designs, some geometric and some figural.

An intriguing inventory drawn up in 1562, comprising a list of the total possessions of Yan Song, a former Grand Secretary, affords us another view of the textiles from this period. The overall quantity involved is 14,331 lengths and 1,304 items of dress, although it becomes clear that most of the lengths are in fact dress lengths which had not been made up. The list is arranged according to technique, and the order seems to represent a hierarchical ranking, an understood importance attached to certain intrinsic qualities of each silk object. The satins are placed first, and the gauze weaves and velvets appear before the 'brocades'. Embroidery, seemingly so favoured during the Ming and Qing, does not feature as a separate category. However, as all of the pieces have their ornamentation described, it is hard not to conclude

ABOVE **159** Painted silk for export, *c.* 1770.

OPPOSITE **158** Embroidered sleeve-bands for women's robes, late 19th–early 20th century.

that at least some of these must be embroidered. This staggering quantity of luxury textiles must, in part, have been used as a sort of currency, but, more than that, they enjoyed a special role in the creation and extension of *guanxi*, a word which literally means 'connections' and which might be categorised as bribes.

The commercial aspects of textile manufacture in China have only been hinted at. Undoubtedly, the type of fabrics under discussion were made in professional workshops with a high degree of specialisation. Some of these were tied to the needs of the imperial court, while others were mercantile enterprises making their products available to those who could afford them. Within the Empire the dividing line between the two kinds of business was, in reality, blurred at least for the later period. The products of factories that turned out export textiles from the seventeenth to the twentieth cen-

turies were not at all sought after by well-to-do Chinese or members of the aristocracy. It is unlikely that they would have recognised them as Chinese at all, for they were adapted to European taste yet satisfied the customer by their perceived 'oriental' touches. In the late eighteenth and into the nineteenth centuries embroidery and painting were the predominant methods used to pattern export silks. Both techniques covered the silk's surface with less effort than loom patterning. Satin stitch, used for domestic-market silks ever since it displaced chain stitch in the Tang dynasty, is employed on export textiles too. These latter commodities do not generally have the rows of small knot stitches found on late nineteenth-century native embroideries, many of which are now, however, in the West having been brought back by European visitors at the turn of the nineteenth century.

15 Japan

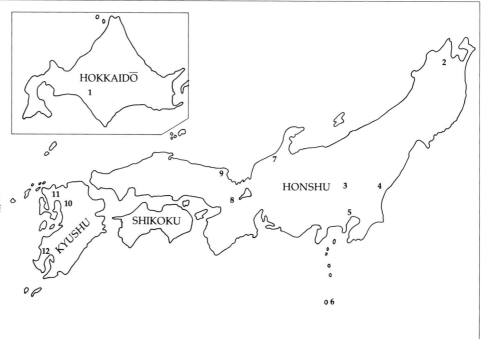

1. Hiratori (Hokkaidō)/*Atsushi ori* (Ainu elm tree bark fibre)
2. Hirosaki (Aomori)/Tsugaru *kogin* (decorative stitching)
3. Kiryu (Gunma)/*Omeshi chirimen*
4. Yuki (Ibaraki)/Yuki *tsumugi*
5. Tokyo (Tokyo)/Edo *yūzen,* Edo *komon*
6. Hachijo Island (Tokyo)/*Kihachijo*
7. Kanazawa (Ishikawa)/Kaga *yūzen*
8. Kyoto (Kyoto)/Kyo *yūzen,* Kyo *kanoko shibori, kinran, kara-ori, tsuzure ori* (tapestry weave)
9. Mineyama (Kyoto)/Tango *chirimen*
10. Kurume (Fukuoka)/Kurume *kasuri*
11. Saga (Saga)/Saga *nishiki*
12. Kagoshima (Kagoshima)/Oshima *tsumugi*
13. Naha (Okinawa)/*Bingata,* Ryukyu *kasuri*

Map 5 Major textile-producing areas of Japan. Each place is listed with its prefecture and products.

Beyond their customary use in dress, accessories and furnishings the textile arts are esteemed in many aspects of Japanese culture and society. Religion and mythology have endowed fabrics with talismanic qualities. The standardisation of cut and making methods of the principal garment, the kimono, focuses attention on the weave, use of colour and applied decorative techniques. Silk provides the artist's canvas and the picture's mount, and rare brocades wrap precious Tea Ceremony wares. The design, production and use of textiles in Japan demonstrate a continuous process of refinement through the centuries.

Evidence of textiles in the proto-historic period can be seen in the impressions from braided cords on earthenware pottery of the Jōmon period (*c.*10,000–300 BC). Clothing styles of the fourth and fifth centuries are shown on excavated *haniwa*, clay figurines left at important burial sites. Written comments appear in third-century Chinese accounts of Japan (in the *Wo-jen chuan* and the *Wei-shih*), and in the eighth-century chronicles compiled by Japanese historians (in the *Kojiki* of AD 712 and the *Nihon Shōki* of AD 720).

Actual textiles survive from the mid-sixth to late eighth centuries, notably in the Hōryūji Temple, which houses a Sassanid temple banner from the Asuka period (AD 552–646), and the Tenjukoku Mandala (*c.*622) kept in the Chūgūji convent. The latter is the oldest embroidered fabric in Japan. A varied collection of religious and secular, imported and domestic *jōdai-gire* (ancient textiles) dating from the Nara period (AD 646–794) are kept in the Shōsō-in Repository of the Tōdaiji Temple. The introduction of Buddhism (*c.* AD 538) and relations with Tang dynasty China (AD 618–907) via Korea brought many cultural innovations to Japan at the far end of the Silk Road. Textile history sources, some accurate, some romantically embellished, reveal the evolution from these foreign models of design to a recognisably Japanese style during the Heian period (AD 794–1185).

Silk was used for all important garments and furnishings, with the exclusion of carpets which were not used in Japanese interiors. Among the early textiles the predominant techniques were *nishiki*, a polychrome warp-, or more advanced weft-patterned brocade; *aya*, a monochrome patterned twill weave; and a method of resist dyeing called *kyōkechi*, which produced symmetrical repeat patterns by clamping folded

142

fabric between two carved boards, the dye being introduced through tiny holes. This technique was also practised in Tang dynasty China (see II, 14).

Textile motifs were derived from geometrical, abstract, natural, imaginary and mythological forms and appear in mirror-image, radial, revolving, pictorial and scattered arrangements. Sassanid Persian influence shows on designs such as pearled medallions enclosing hunters, or of animals under trees. Among floral compositions the fluid arabesques and scrolling vines, especially the Buddhist-associated honeysuckle and the Chinese *kara-hana*, are particularly significant. The development of the imaginary many-petalled *kara-hana*, which was created partly from real flowers such as the peony and the lotus, reveals Japan's transition from dependence upon foreign motifs. Originally the motif was used in characteristically small formalised patterns, then subsidiary motifs were added close to the central *kara-hana* motif, gradually becoming more decorative elements in themselves. These subsidiary motifs became more dominant, eventually displaying the characteristic Japanese taste for naturalistic motifs.

Liberation from devotion to China can graphically be seen in the styles of eleventh-century imperial court dress. The softly draping multi-coloured *nishiki* clothing of Tang dynasty China was replaced by voluminous *ōsode*, large-

HISTORICAL PERIODS		ERA NAMES*	
Jōmon	*c.*10,000–300 BC		
Yayoi	*c.*300 BC–AD 300		
Kofun	*c.*300–700		
Asuka	552–646		
Nara	646–794		
Heian	794–1185		
Kamakura	1185–1333		
Nambokuchō	1333–1392		
Muromachi	1392–1573		
Momoyama	1573–1600		
		Keichō	1596–1615
Edo	1600–1868		
early	1600–1688		
		Kanbun	1661–1673
mid	1688–1781		
		Genroku	1688–1704
late	1781–1868		
Meiji	1868–1912		
Taishō	1912–1926		
Shōwa	1926–1989		
Heisei	1989–		

* Used to denote period specific styles in textile and fashion history.

sleeved, kimono-style robes made of stiff figured gauze in two-tone twill weaves with warp of one colour and weft of another. Worn several layers at a time, the textile interest was expressed through the contrasting weaves and colour combinations rather than forms of applied ornament.

Since the early seventh century the Japanese had followed the principles of Chinese cosmology. The five agents of fire, water, earth, wood and metal were associated with the directions of the compass, the seasons, the basic virtues and the primary and intermediate colours. The Japanese taste was for the intermediate hues which they creatively combined in an elaborate system called *kasane-iro*, in which kimonos were worn in layers of acutely gradated shades and varying degrees of translucency. With names like 'azalea layers', shades from palest to deepest vermilion-pink, or 'maple layers', shades from crimson to faded ochre, this display of colour in dress was part of a profound sensitivity to the transient beauty of the four seasons. The medicinal properties of dye plants and the emotive symbolism inherent in colour were further explored in the literature of the period. Just as the arrangement of *kasane-iro*

160 Seated court lady displaying the many layers of her Heian-period court dress. The colour combinations at the neck, sleeves and hemlines are attuned to the season.

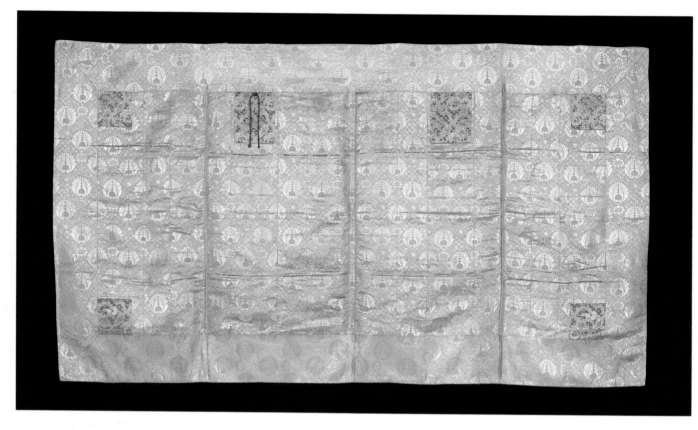

161 Sumptuous gold-leaf silk *kesa* woven with a pattern of repeating leaf medallions and flower scrolls. Constructed with reference to the complexities of Buddhist numerology, a *kesa* is considered as a mandala. The additional brocade patches represent the Four Guardian Kings of Heaven at North, South, East and West.

OPPOSITE **162** The suit of armour, like the samurai's sword, is both aesthetically pleasing and a highly effective weapon. It is worn over fine silk under-garments. Silk is also used for the decorative tassels and braided cords which lace together the gold-lacquered rows of iron and leather armour plates.

became standardised, so did the construction of textile patterns. The repertoire of patterns on dress and furnishing textiles for use at the imperial court were called *yūsoku*, and these patterns remained a primary design source thereafter. Containing several hundred designs from some twenty-seven basic groups, *yūsoku* motifs were inspired by natural forms and geometrically stylised to accommodate contemporary weaving techniques.

The main *yūsoku* patterns used in isolation, repeat or combinations were of the following varieties: diagonal-shape lattices; parallel, undulating lines arranged regularly along the warp so that the adjacent lines define oval lozenges often enclosing other motifs; arabesques and scrolling vines; small hollyhock background motifs; tortoise-shell hexagons; chequer-board patterns produced by raised weft threads; interlocking circles in a chain-mail pattern; and various floral, plant, bird and insect-derived medallions. Such enclosed motifs developed into *monshō*, family crests used for identification and ornament. Other important motifs were birds like the crane and auspicious combinations such as paulownia with bamboo, phoenix and *kirin*, a mythical beast. Mist and cloud clusters were often seen on Buddhist priests' robes and stoles, *kesa* and *ōhi*. The *kesa* is made from square patches of fabric which symbolise found rags; these are pieced together into a large rectangle of

five, seven, nine or more panels and worn under the left arm and fastened on the right shoulder. This patchwork style symbolised the Buddhist vows of poverty, even when the 'patches' were made from fine silk brocades, as when a deceased woman's garments were donated to her local temple for remaking into *kesa*, or altar cloths and temple banners. Sometimes the patches would be darned all over with coarse linen thread to create a soft rippled surface evocative of distant mountains.

The weakening of authority at the imperial capital of Kyoto was paralleled by the growth of an independent provincial military class. In 1192 the first of successive shoguns (military dictators) was installed at Kamakura (1185–1333) and then at Muromachi (1392–1573). Building on the aristocratic Heian period aesthetic, the military élite developed values of austerity and frugality which incorporated the new ideals and art forms of Zen Buddhism. In a way of life dominated by bloody civil wars the exquisite styles of court dress were inappropriate, and the warrior class adopted a mix of court and commoners' clothing. Armour was of paramount importance and combined the skills of the weaver and braid-maker, the lacquerer, metalworker and leather-worker. The finicky court system of rank colours was broken down, and popular colours for armour and accessories such as 'head bags' (to carry the severed head of an opponent) included

red, purple, yellow, white and evocative shades such as 'rotted leaf colour', deutzia blossom, wistaria, cherry blossom, fern, water plantain, or jay's feather blue. To the *yūsoku* motifs were added bold geometric patterns and objects from the warrior's life such as arrows, sword-guards and horse-trappings. Many motifs became simplified for use as *monshō* on armour or large scale on battlefield banners.

In women's dress the *kosode*, a small-sleeved under-kimono, had become commonly worn by both commoners and upper classes, status being denoted by the fabric, technique and design. The close-fitting *kosode* was made of soft silks that did not suit the woven repeat motifs of Heian period gauze *ōsode*. Free-style patterns executed in dye work and embroidery using tightly twisted silk yarns became increasingly popular for garments and items such as *furoshiki*, square carrying-cloths. Early free-style motifs depicted plants, animals – real and mythical – and objects, often grouped in seasonal or auspicious combinations, or with implied literary meaning. For example, *ashi-de*, reed-style designs depicting grasses in a water landscape, sometimes with plovers flying above, and with scattered characters from poems describing such a view incorporated into the design, had first appeared on decorated papers and lacquerware of the Heian period. The pine, bamboo and plum, individually, together or with the tortoise and crane, are among the most felicitous and oldest of grouped textile designs and appear in myriad different forms.

Owing to the financial burden of the civil wars domestic textile production dwindled, and once again Japan turned to China for exquisite silks. Renewed contact with Ming dynasty China brought *kinran*, a gold brocade twill woven with mulberry-bark paper-backed gold thread on a plain-coloured ground. *Kinran* along with *donsu*, a plain or multicoloured figured damask, were among the fabrics much prized for mounting paintings or storing Tea Ceremony wares. Alongside the Tea Ceremony, another entertainment of the military élite was the Noh drama. The various types of Noh costumes required the finest textile artisans and combined styles of everyday dress with the theatrically fantastic. Fabric, colours and motifs were chosen to represent the male, female or supernatural character of the actor's role, but were classified not by role but according to the technique by which they were made.

Kara-ori, for example, denoted a 'Chinese weave' brocade characterised by floating wefts, with a design in satin weave on a twill-woven ground; this type of fabric was originally imported for exclusive use by the shogun. Often *kara-ori* were ikat-dyed into rectilinear areas of

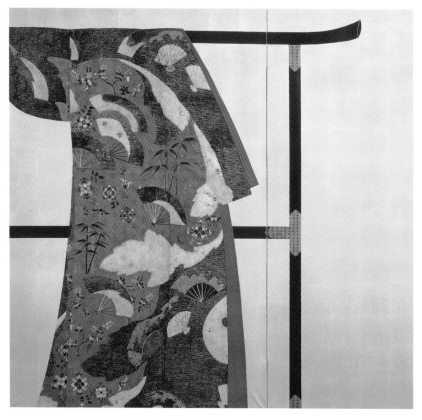

different background colours with elaborate brocading using both floating and tight threads of glossed and raw silk. A delicate floral pattern such as autumn grasses and the use of scarlet denoted a youthful female character. By contrast, the *atsu-ita* denoted a thick brocade with a twill geometric-patterned ground, dynamic motifs of a martial, surreal or Chinese flavour, and was associated with a robust male character. To enhance the gorgeous costumes on an austere and dim stage further, applied gold leaf or metallic thread added lustre to the coloured silk threads.

The Momoyama period (1573–1600), prior to the unification of Japan under a centralised feudal regime, was an age of splendour. The ascending *daimyō* (feudal lords) and their samurai enjoyed a sumptuous decorative style of castle architecture and interior paintings on screens. The textile industry was revived, and contemporary taste was echoed in dress fabrics that were coloured in warm safflower reds and gleaming golden hues, and copiously embroidered with plant motifs in long float stitches of glossy untwisted silk floss.

One technique unique to the period, later named *tsujigahana*, shows the contrasting aesthetic for subdued and rustic design as favoured for the Tea Ceremony. Geometric patterns and floral motifs, such as camellias and worm-eaten leaves, were executed in a mix of *shibori*, sewn tie dyeing, the delicate washes and lines of *kaki-e*, ink painting, *surihaku*, impressed metallic leaf, and *nuihaku*, embroidery with metallic leaf on *nerinuki*, plain, lustrous crisp silks, or ramie.

From 1544 European traders and missionaries brought foreign goods to Japan, but the most significant textile import had been cotton which later replaced hemp and other bast fibres, and was well suited to the economical techniques of decoration by paste-resist-dyeing, quilting and decorative stitching. However, by 1638 the government established in the new capital of Edo (now Tokyo) enforced a policy which virtually excluded all foreign contacts, and until 1853 Japan developed in cultural isolation.

Despite this and a rigid social hierarchy which prescribed the minutiae of daily life – not least of all dress – according to one's status, gender, age and occupation, the Edo period engendered spectacular creativity and cross-fertilisation in the arts. Celebrated painters covered white kimonos with monochrome ink landscapes, while favourite textile patterns decorated lacquer and ceramic wares. The shogunate sponsored textile production into a full-scale industry which included regional manufactures. Along with textiles predominantly patterned on the loom, for theatre or court robes, the main produce of the weaving industry was loom-width

OPPOSITE TOP **163** Brocaded *Atsu-ita* Noh robe. The
bold texture enhances the dynamic pattern of
scattered round cart-wheels against diagonal links
and alternating squares in a lattice design.

OPPOSITE BOTTOM **164** *Kosode* (on a screen) made from
red, black and white figured satin in a key fret and
chrysanthemum design. The intricate decoration,
with motifs in contrasting scale, includes
chrysanthemum leaves, fans and abstract shapes in
stitch resist and capped *shibori*. *Kanoko-shibori* is also
used inside the fan shapes. Characteristic of early
17th-century *kosode*, the embroidered bamboo and
plant motifs are confined to the red and white areas,
while the black ground is almost covered with
geometric patterns in gold leaf.

165 A young woman's long-sleeved,
special-occasion kimono (*furisode*) in
figured red silk. The overall,
geometrically stylised hemp-leaf
pattern and roundels composed of the
auspicious pine-bamboo-plum motif
are created in *kanoko-shibori*, giving a
uniquely crimped surface texture.

silks for making up into kimonos and *obi*
(kimono sashes), and suited to ornament by
dyeing, painting, embroidery and appliqué.

Nishiki and gauze fabrics endured, but
nerinuki was replaced by more durable silks such
as *rinzu*, a figured silk satin, *mon aya*, a figured
twill, and *chirimen*, fine or heavily textured silk
crêpe. The transitional style of the Momoyama
to Edo periods was characterised by strongly
asymmetrical designs and the use of figured
silks. The kimono ground would be divided into
irregular colour areas, predominantly black, red
and white, with additional motifs almost concealing the ground. Shapes and motifs were
realistic and abstract representations of natural
forms with a juxtaposition of unnatural sizes.
Frequently size and technique correspond. For
large areas *shibori* was used; for medium-sized
motifs *kanoko-shibori*, 'fawn dappled', a polka-
dot effect; and for small motifs *surihaku* or embroidery in tight satin stitch and long-and-short
stitch with glossy untwisted silk yarns and a
sparing use of couched metallic threads. A
kimono decorated all over by *shibori* became the
ultimate in luxury. The complex technique involved tying thread around each of those areas
which the dye should not penetrate; in a *kanoko-
shibori* pattern this might mean a kimono with
300,000 polka-dot areas. After dyeing came the
equally laborious task of removing the threads
to reveal the uniquely dyed and textured surface.

Not surprisingly the popular paintings and
woodblock prints of the period often depicted
the fascinating world of textiles, with specially

166 Woodblock print depicting a stylish young man accompanied by ladies of the *demi-monde*. The man's kimono is *kasuri*-dyed (see p. 150), and the woman peeking through his gauze silk jacket wears a kimono stencilled with *komon*, small repeating motifs. The girl apprentice has a *chugata*, middle-sized motif print – such patterns are still used today on indigo and white summer kimono. The flamboyant kimono sashes are characteristic of late 18th-century style.

OPPOSITE **167** Silk crepe kimono, *yuzen*-dyed with views of eastern Kyoto against golden cloud shapes. Embroidered cherry and plum branches both separate the scenes and unify the composition.

printed pattern-books devoted to new fashions. By the mid-Edo period (1688–1781) it was the colourful characters from the *demi-monde* of desirable courtesans, vivacious geishas and idolised Kabuki actors and their fans from the newly rich merchant classes who set the style. New themes and objects from ordinary urban life appeared in the design repertoire, and a trend towards realism and narrative as well as abstract and decorative designs grew.

The standardised use of colours and combinations of motifs such as pine, bamboo and plum were freely interpreted through a remarkably inventive use of form and also empty space offered by the kimono field – both two-dimensional when being made or displayed and three-dimensional when worn. Gradually the taste for opulent technical display and large-scale patterns was replaced by subtlety conveyed through a rather snobbish wit. Sumptuary laws were daringly circumvented: for example, when *shibori* was prohibited to the merchant classes, a stencilled or waxed fake form appeared, or a plain striped kimono con-

cealed the prohibited gold figured gauze on an undergarment.

Methods of paste-resist dyeing became increasingly attractive, replacing more costly techniques. *Kata-zome*, dyeing through mulberry-paper stencils, created all-over repeat patterns. The motifs of *komon*, minute patterns first appearing on samurai men's *kamishimo* (formal garments), were so intricate that from a distance they looked like solid colour. The eighteenth-century method called *yūzen-some* imitated the detailed effect and colour of embroidery. Characterised by a background that is brush-dyed – not dip-dyed as in *shibori* – resist paste is used to define motifs and separate colour areas so that each colour – dyes and pigments – can be brushed in. Echoing the subjects of popular paintings, *chirimen* kimono were decorated with *yūzen*-dyed landscapes peopled with bustling figures – a new addition to the textile repertoire. In 1879 a method of applying pre-coloured paste as opposed to resist considerably simplified this still popular technique. The women of the samurai élite preferred the more subdued appeal of

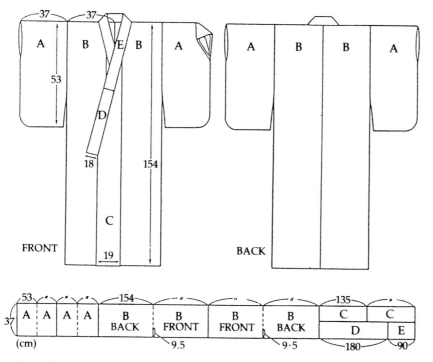

Fig. 21 Pattern for cutting a kimono.

chaya-zome paste resist which created refreshing Tea Ceremony garden views in shades of indigo on fine white ramie for elegant midsummer attire.

Challenging the urban centres of production were the country textiles such as the pampas grass-dyed yellow plaid of Hachijo Island, outside Tokyo, or *oshima tsumugi*, slub silk spun from left-over floss and dyed a unique reddish-brown in the local Kagoshima mud of Kyūshū Island. In particular, varieties of *kasuri*, ikat-dyed fabrics, especially in blue and white, were made throughout the Japanese archipelago. Whether in cotton or silk gauze, *kasuri* fabrics were favoured for both work and best attire and for household items such as quilt-covers. The uniquely blurred outline of *kasuri*-dyed geometric or pictorial motifs results from weaving yarn that has been resist-dyed with a pattern before being dip-dyed and woven.

By the late Edo period (1781–1868) the range and use of techniques were considerable. Embroidery might be used sparingly to enhance a

168 Quilt cover in *kasuri* technique. Pre-dyed and patterned indigo and natural-coloured cotton yarns are here woven with an alternating pattern of check squares and images of a Chinese Immortal riding a carp.

ABOVE **169** Embroidered gift-cover. Beautiful gift-covers became an essential element in the ceremonial presentation of gifts. Designs varied according to the season and occasion, and this example is embroidered with motifs associated with the New Year festivities – the turnip, bee-nettle, chick-weed, shepherd's purse, parsley, cotton-weed and radish comprise the seven herbs and vegetables traditionally eaten on the seventh day of the new year. The tassels were used to handle the *fukusa*, and the red border defined the design as the red under-kimono enhanced the outer garment.

ABOVE RIGHT **170** Child's kimono, Ryukyu Islands. Because of the southerly location, Ryukan textile crafts developed independent traditions. *Bingata*, brightly coloured stencil and paste-resist dyeing on ramie, hemp, cotton or silk, was originally reserved for Ryukan royalty. This example reflects the local landscape.

dyed kimono pattern or be lavish couching in metallic threads splendidly displaying the auspicious motifs on *fukusa*, the gift covers which were draped over a present on special occasions such as weddings or New Year festivities. Even after the repeal of some particularly stringent sumptuary laws in the mid-nineteenth century textiles for everyday use were sombre in colour and sparsely decorated. This contrasted with the fussy designs being made for export as Japan resumed contact with the Western world.

Following the restoration of imperial rule in 1868 and the resumption of foreign relations, the ensuing period of Bunmei Kaika, the 'civilisation and enlightenment' of Japan, resulted in the successful mechanisation of the textile industry – though not without cost to the traditional crafts. As the semi-automated Jacquard loom gradually replaced the drawloom, so muslin and wool became more popular than gauze and crêpe silk for both kimonos and Western-style clothing. Foreign contact brought synthetic dye colours, new graphic styles and themes to the textile repertoire, while a Japanese influence was seen on British, European and American textiles and fashions of the late nineteenth and early twentieth centuries. There was a revival of interest in Japan's country textile traditions including the colourful *bingata* stencil-dyed fabrics of the southernmost Ryukyu Islands (now Okinawa), and the unique symmetrical pattern forms and appliqué techniques of the Ainu peoples of Hokkaidō, Japan's northernmost island.

In the years after World War II Western-style fashions and conventions became common in Japan, and textile production, design and use

LEFT 171 Working within the centuries-old tradition of *yuzen* dyeing, Kunihiko Moriguchi has developed his own unique techniques. Perceiving the kimono as both garment and work of art, Moriguchi creates up-to-date patterns that distill nature's essence into geometric abstraction – a concern of Japanese textile artists for centuries.

TOP RIGHT 172 The owner and designer of Comme des Garçons, Rei Kawakubo, seeks innovation, from the first visualisation of her ideas through a specially created fabric and the pattern-cutter's realisation of a garment, to the presentation of her clothes in the precisely designed shops and through innovative graphic media. This machine-knitted 'lace' sweater challenges our concept of lace as intricate and hand-made.

ABOVE RIGHT 173 Kimono made from elm-tree bark with symmetrical appliqué designs in imported cotton. Textile crafts were an exclusively female occupation. Yarn-dyed fabrics were woven from plant fibres and animal hairs and decorated with appliqué or embroidery. Patterns were strategically placed to ward off evil spirits.

responded accordingly. During the 1980s, however, Japan's avant-garde fashion and textile designers were seen to challenge the European conventions of clothing construction and ideas about what constituted the medium of fabric. Contemporary practitioners of the traditional crafts are now State supported under the designation of National Living Treasure. From the ceremonial weaving of the Emperor Akihito's Heian period-style coronation robes to the mass production of synthetic fibres scented with fragrance micro-capsules for tights, textiles in Japan today reveal a respect for tradition allied to a fascination with innovation.

16 South-East Asia

Suspended between the two great civilisations of China and India, and populated by culturally diverse groups of people, South-East Asia has an extremely rich and complex textile tradition. A lush tropical environment has provided a variety of bast fibres, cotton and silk yarns, innumerable dyestuffs and the wood and bamboo for looms. Indigenous genius fuelled by complex belief systems, coupled with widespread historic trading contacts and a history of migration, have given rise to a wide variety of patterning techniques and myriad design motifs.

Textiles in South-East Asia also yield interesting information about the region's historical development. Vestiges of the dawn of civilisation may be seen in primitive anthropomorphic and reptilian figures which appear on the textiles of the outer islands to this day. Links to the region's neolithic–bronze age past are evident in the strongly geometric hook, spiral and rhomb patterns which persist in the textiles of the Thai-Lao of mainland South-East Asia, the Dayaks of Borneo, the Toraja of Sulawesi, and the Pammingir and Batak peoples of Sumatra.

Map 6 Main textile centres of South-East Asia.

153

Widespread cultural and trading contacts with India, in addition to spreading the Hindu and Buddhist creeds, introduced key motifs such as the lotus, the heavenly mountain, 'Tree of Life', *naga* snake and garuda bird (the mount of the Hindu god Vishnu) into local design repertoires. From Hindu and Buddhist mythology came epics such as the *Rāmāyana*, the *Mahābhārata* and *Jātaka* tales (stories of the previous lives of the Buddha), all of which have furnished subject-matter for both the performing and decorative arts.

Indian influence may also be seen through the famous double-ikat *patola* cloths from Gujarat, which at one time were widely traded throughout South-East Asia. *Patolas* were highly prized by the local inhabitants for their bright glowing colours, their superbly arranged geometric and floral motifs, and clearly demarcated design areas which made them ideal for sarongs and shawls and other wraparound clothing widely worn by various South-East Asian ethnic groups. *Patolas* have greatly influenced the layout of South-East Asian textiles throughout

niques such as couching, satin stitch and Pekin knots also enriched local embroidery traditions.

The arrival of the Muslim faith in South-East Asia during the fourteenth to sixteenth centuries led to the introduction of the weft-ikat technique and the incorporation of metallic threads, sequins and mirror glass into local weaving traditions. Over the traditional sarong newly converted Muslims began wearing a loose tunic, a garment probably inspired by the Middle-Eastern *galabiah*. The Muslim proscription against the realistic representation of living things led to the development of a wide range of intricate, beautifully integrated floral, vegetal and geometric scroll motifs. Muslim traders have also been credited with popularising the wearing of plaids throughout South-East Asia.

European presence in the region is reflected in the incorporation of naturalistic floral bouquets and heraldic and Christian motifs into textile patterns. Beginning in the late nineteenth century the introduction from the West of chemical dyes, synthetic yarns and spinning and loom innovations, accompanied by widespread social

174 Silk *patola* cloth, double ikat, India (Gujarat). 4.11 × 1.07 m (13.5 × 3.5 ft).

the region. On the outer islands where ownership of *patola* cloths conveyed wealth and status they became highly prized, sacred heirlooms in many communities. Chintzes and other Indian fabrics, created with South-East Asian preferences in mind, were also widely traded throughout the archipelago, and their design motifs have influenced local fabrics such as Javanese batik. The kings of Thailand were known to commission court fabrics from India patterned with Thai designs.

A penchant for aromatic woods and esoteric jungle produce drew the Chinese to South-East Asia at first as traders and later as settlers. In return for these products they traded their highly prized metalwares, textiles and pottery. As a result cloud and rock formations, dragons, phoenixes, the Buddhist Eight Precious Objects, swastikas and other auspicious symbols seen on Chinese imported objects entered the South-East Asian design repertoire. Chinese tech-

and economic change, has caused far-reaching modifications to local textile traditions.

In addition to supplying the family with clothing, bedding and towels, textiles in South-East Asia have traditionally played a vital role in the social, economic and religious life of the people. The presentation of cloth was *de rigueur* in marriage and gift exchanges. Textiles defined the status of the individual in terms of both costume and wealth; cloth layout and motif arrangement might denote family lineage and clan identity. Special sacred cloths were woven according to a set of strict taboos for religious ceremonies. Certain weavings conferred invincibility on warriors during battle, while others protected against illness and misfortune. At the time of death textiles covered the bier of the deceased and were essential accoutrements to a fitting send-off. Small, colourful, intricately patterned weavings such as bags, belts and scarves were offered as tokens of affection between a

175 *Acheik*-patterned silk *lon-gyi*, Burma (Amarapura/ Mandalay).

young weaver and her suitor. In traditional South-East Asian society weaving skills and design motifs were passed down from mother to daughter. A girl was not considered of marriageable age until she was a proficient weaver.

Myanmar (formerly Burma)

Tang Chinese historical accounts attest that the ancient Pyu (AD 500–900), the earliest Burmans, were weavers of fine cotton clothing. As devout Buddhists they avoided silk because it involved the taking of life. Seventeenth- and eighteenth-century Ava period panoramic wall-paintings depict stylishly coiffured women resplendent in a long, open, trailing sarong called *hta-mein*, a *tabet*, or breast cloth, and an *ein-gyi* fitted jacket. Accompanying men are shown in a long, ample sarong called the *pah-soe*, an *ein-gyi* jacket and *gaung-baung* turban. The *hta-mein* and *pah-soe* are the forerunners of the more practical, narrow, tubular *lon-gyi* which continues to be the national dress to this day.

Most highly prized for traditional *hta-mein* and *pah-soe* was *lun-taya*, a boldly coloured luxurious, expensive silk fabric created by an interlocking tapestry weave, a technique thought to have been introduced to Myanmar in the eighteenth century by captive weavers from Manipur in north-west India. Working on the wrong side of the cloth, 100–200 small metal shuttles bearing different brightly coloured silk yarns and silver-wrapped thread are laboriously manipulated through the warp by two girls to create traditional wave-like cable patterns called *acheik*, sprung with floral appendages.

Ikat patterning is practised by different ethnic groups in eastern Myanmar. The Inthas of Inle Lake and the Karen decorate their striped *lon-gyi* with small bands of 'arrowhead' and 'python' patterns in warp ikat, while the Shan (a branch of the Thai race in eastern Burma) weave sophisticated weft-ikat silk *lon-gyi* called *zin-me* in a twill weave embellished with hook and rhomb patterns in green and yellow on a red warp. The *zin-me* (Chiangmai) design arrangement and distinctive border areas have been influenced by Thai-Cambodian textiles and *patola* cloth. In recent years European-style floral-sprig designs have largely replaced the traditional geometric motifs.

Supplementary-warp and -weft-patterning methods are known to almost every ethnic group in Myanmar including the Burmese, Shan, Karen, Mon and hilltribe peoples. The

176 *Kalaga* wall-hanging from east Burma (Shan states). The techniques employed include embroidery, appliqué and beadwork.

finest Burmese examples come from the Gangaw district, in central Myanmar, which specialises in silk and cotton *lon-gyis* with discontinuous supplementary-weft geometric and small floral motifs. Better known, however, are serviceable, boldly patterned and loosely woven supplementary-weft-patterned floral *lon-gyi* produced by Arakanese weavers living along the coastal littoral bordering the Bay of Bengal. Geometric patterned *lon-gyis* and distinctive shoulder-bags with colourful silver bosses, woven by the Chin and Kachin peoples of the far north, are a familiar sight in markets throughout Myanmar.

Visually arresting wall-hangings called *kalaga*, which depict episodes from Buddhist mythology, the *Rāmāyana* epic, local folk-tales and traditional art motifs in appliqué, quilting and couching on a velvet ground, are unique to

Myanmar. Gold and silver sequins, strips of tinsel cloth, lamé ribbon, lace trim, glass and pearl beads, metallic threads, wool yarn and flannel cut-outs have been artfully combined on *kalaga* for a sumptuous effect. In addition to wall-hangings *kalaga* were used as room-dividers and coffin-covers for monks. *Kalaga* embroidery techniques were also formerly used to make heavy elaborate costumes, shoes, head-dresses and shawls for Burmese royalty.

The weavers of Myanmar at one time supplied their highly revered Theravada Buddhist monkhood with all their textile needs, which included saffron robes, waistbands, crocheted holders for their bowls and bamboo-stiffened cloth covers for their sacred books, secured with closely patterned ribbons called *sa-si-gyo* woven on a card loom. Today these articles are purchased rather than woven.

177 Detail of a Thai *pha-sin* with a *tdin-jok* border, Chiangmai province.

Thailand

Early fabric finds at bronze-age sites in the north-east and seventeenth- to nineteenth-century temple frescos provide tangible evidence of Thailand's long history of textile production. A history of migration, interspersed with invasions and warfare with neighbouring states, followed by forced resettlement of the vanquished, has led to the widespread dispersion in Thailand of various Thai-Lao groups, each of which is noted for its distinctive textiles.

Woven articles include traditional clothing such as the *pha-sin* and *pha-sarong*, ankle-length tubular cloths for women and men respectively, which are worn with a blouse, shirt or jacket. A rectangular shawl which varies in size and method of decoration among the various Thai-Lao groups is worn on formal occasions. Both sexes at one time wore the *pha-nung*, a cloth 3 m

(10 ft) long which was wrapped around the body and pulled through the legs to form knee-length pants.

The Thai-Lao people of Esarn (north-east Thailand) weave cotton and silk weft ikat called *mud-mee*. Ikat-patterned cotton on an indigo ground predominates in Nongkhai and Udon Thani provinces; elsewhere locally grown silk mixed with imported yarns is the preferred fibre. Traditional *mud-mee* is patterned with intricate geometric designs. Natural phenomena such as stars and running water, plants, including the lotus, jasmine, the pine, bamboo and banana, and the snake, squirrel and household implements have all lent their names to traditional textile patterns. *Mud-mee* motifs may be arranged in a closely patterned interlocking overall design finished with wavy borders or be set in bands between weft stripes, to appear vertically aligned when made into a sarong. Thailand's early links with Khmer culture may be seen in the predominantly rich red-brown, striped, plaid and *mud-mee* textiles of the Surin area made by weavers of Cambodian ancestry.

By contrast horizontal warp stripes are the predominant form of decoration for *pha-sin* made by the Thai Yuan and Lao groups living in Lan La (northern Thailand). Stripes may be created from bands of contrasting colours, two-colour twisted yarns and supplementary-warp motifs. The Thai Lu, a minority group formerly from south-west China, enliven their stripes with bands of zigzag tapestry weave called *pha-naam lay*, or flowing water patterns.

Various Thai-Lao groups embellish the foot of their *pha-sin* with a wide band of *tdin-jok*, closely patterned supplementary-thread geometric decoration in various colours painstakingly inserted into the weft with the aid of a porcupine quill. Differing colour combinations and the arrangement of motifs make it possible to distinguish regional styles in *tdin-jok*.

Similar in appearance to *tdin-jok* decoration, but more boldly conceived in pictorial terms, is *pha-kit*, a sturdy supplementary-weft-patterned cloth traditionally woven from handspun unbleached cotton. It is patterned with horizontal bands of loosely woven, colourful, geometric, vegetal and realistic animal motifs rendered in various colours with red and black predominating. In traditional Thai-Lao society the ability to weave fine *pha-kit* was an indicator that a girl was ready for marriage. In addition to weaving *pha-sin* for her future female in-laws, the bride-to-be would busy herself weaving *pha-kit*-decorated mattress-covers, pillows, blankets, sheets and towels as part of her trousseau. *Pha-kit* 'linen' was also presented to monasteries as an act of merit along with bamboo-reinforced *pha-ho-khampi* wrappers for sacred palm-leaf

178 *Pha-kit* textile of unbleached cotton with different-coloured supplementary-weft threads depicting horses and other patterns, north-east Thailand. 74 × 28 cm (29 × 11 in).

manuscripts and long, colourful *pha-tung* temple banners patterned with pagodas and other motifs of religious significance.

Sophisticated supplementary-weft patterning of small repetitive Thai floral motifs in metallic-wrapped yarns for formal attire is woven in a number of workshops in the north-east, Chiangmai and Bangkok. Some of the best-known work is from Pum Rieng in south Thailand, where descendants of nineteenth-century captive weavers from Kedah, Malaysia, produce *pha-yok*, a fabric which, in terms of cloth layout, bears striking similarities to *kain songket*, the sumptuous gold-patterned cloth of north-east Malaysia and coastal Indonesia.

Laos and Cambodia

Although not as well known as the weavings of Myanmar and Thailand in terms of technique, motif, application of colour and design sophistication, the textiles of the various peoples who inhabit the land-locked republic of Laos and Cambodia to the south have exerted a significant and lasting influence on the textile traditions of their neighbours.

Being more isolated from external trade influences than their lowland compatriots, the peoples of north-eastern Laos have retained their banded cloth layout and ancient geometric lozenges, scrolls and abstract anthropomorphic and animal motifs to this day. These are rendered in weft ikat or a supplementary-thread technique on a dark indigo or rich red ground of cotton or silk. On ceremonial and ritual textiles groups such as the Lao Neua, Tai Lu, Tai Puan and Tai Daeng apply dashes of colour to the predominantly white motifs in a non-symmetrical and haphazard way to enhance the abstract dimension of a design, so creating an illusion of change and impermanence, a key Buddhist concept. The select combination of motifs and the choice and arrangement of colour make it possible to distinguish textiles between the various Lao groups. Women traditionally wove to meet the textile needs of their immediate family only. Textiles were never sold or traded and consist of the *sin*, a calf-length sarong, the *pha-biang* shawl, headcloths, blankets, sheets and towels.

Textiles of central Laos, like those of Nongkhai and Udon across the river in Thailand, are predominantly weft-ikat geometric motifs on an indigo cotton ground. Weavers in the Vientiane and Luang Prabang areas, who at one time wove sumptuous textiles for royalty, now weave bridal *sin* of red and green silk yarns, patterned with either vertical stripes and scattered supplementary-weft or -warp motifs in boldly contrasting yarns or gold metallic threads finished with a *jok* brocade-weave border of colourful, repetitive, geometric and vegetal motifs. Weavers at Pakse in the south specialise in finely crafted, tightly woven weft ikat from imported silk yarns. Being close to Cambodia, their textiles also reflect influences from that country.

Cambodia also has a tradition of making fine silk weft-ikat ceremonial cloth called *samphot-hol* which was either worn as a sarong or pulled between the legs to create trousers. Geometric hook and lozenge patterns in deep reddish-brown hues touched with yellow and green predominate. In its design traditional *samphot* is strikingly similar to Indian *patola* cloth. The weaving of this style of cloth has recently been revived in north-east Thailand.

The Cambodians also wove a special funerary textile in weft ikat called the *pi-dan* which depicts bands of people, temples and elephants. *Pi-dan* were placed over the corpse prior to cremation or displayed as a hanging to remind participants of the impermanence of life. Replicas of these textiles, although now woven in brighter colours, are currently being made by Lao weavers from Pakse.

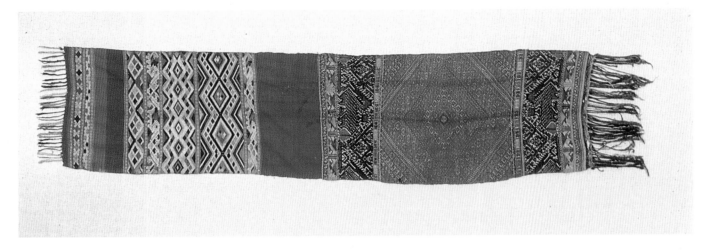

ABOVE **179** Silk shawl, warp ikat-dyed, with supplementary-weft patterning. Laos (Lao-Neua), first quarter of the 20th century. 247 × 43 cm (97 × 17 in).

180 Silk weft ikat *samphot-hol*, Cambodia.

Hilltribes

The various hilltribe peoples of western and northern Thailand, upland Laos and central Vietnam continue to create their distinctive clothing from home-grown cotton and hemp on body-tension or simple frame looms. Black-and-red-striped cotton sarongs enlivened with bands of ecru-coloured warp ikat are worn by the Lawa, Karen and Kayah peoples of Myanmar and Thailand. The Jarai of Vietnam decorate their loincloths and sarongs with bands of geometric supplementary-weft decoration, while the Hmong women continue to batik the central panel of their distinctive skirts with geometric patterns applied with a bamboo pen and beeswax.

Chinese influences may be seen in the tailoring of jackets, trousers, pleated skirts, aprons and caftans worn by the Lisu, Akha, Hmong and Mien peoples. Indigo-dyed cotton is the predominant cloth, which is intricately embellished with colourful bands of appliqué, cross-stitch embroidery, tufts of wool, seeds, buttons, and cascades of silver bosses and small club-shaped pendants. Motifs used by hilltribes people are strongly geometric and draw their inspiration from the local environment.

Clothing is worn with pride and as a mark of ethnic identity amongst the various hilltribes and their subgroups. In most cases a full complement of ceremonial clothing and jewellery is worn at the big events of life such as marriage,

the attainment of a position and by the deceased at the time of interment. A change in status from single to married may require a different costume, as in the case of the Karen woman. A skilled weaver or needlewoman is highly valued in hilltribe society and at the time of marriage can command a higher bride-price. A young woman's handiwork may also be examined by prospective in-laws to furnish 'clues' to her character.

The Philippines

Weaving in the Philippines today is largely confined to groups of people living in the northern and southern extremities of the archipelago. These include the Kalinga, Tinguian, Kankanay, Bontoc, Gaddang and Ifugao in the north. Until about 1900 the use of bark for clothing was widespread amongst the inhabitants of the highlands of northern Luzon. Traditional northern Philippine textiles are of cotton and woven on a simple body-tension loom.

Warp stripes are the major form of decoration and may enclose small, woven, embroidered or warp-ikat figures, which include geometric, rhomb and zigzag patterns, stylised renditions of natural phenomena such as reptiles and human figures, and cultural phenomena such as weapons, household utensils, farm implements and houses. Woven articles include the *tapis*, a short, knee-length wraparound skirt for women, a loincloth for men, and belts, jackets,

181 Isinai funeral blanket, decorated with patterns in white warp ikat on an indigo ground. Such motifs were at one time 'read' by knowledgeable persons as depicting the journey of a man through life.

bags and blankets for both sexes. Clothing for ceremonial events may be elaborately embellished with stitchery, seeds, beads, buttons, slivers of shell, brass and tufts of yarn.

Textiles traditionally were important items of trade throughout the cordillera. The colours and pattern arrangement not only defined tribal groups but also status within a group. Textiles were essential accoutrements in rites of passage, especially in death rituals which entailed the weaving of special clothing and blankets. The number of blankets surrounding a corpse as it lay in state was a tangible indication of the standing of the deceased within the community at large.

The upland peoples of the southern island of Minadanao such as the T'boli, Mandaya, Bagobo, Manobo, Bukidnon and Bila'an weave *tapis* skirts, loose trousers, bags, jackets, and blankets from banana fibre called *abaca*, which may be patterned with ecru-coloured motifs on a black and maroon-red ground. Motifs include human and reptilian forms skilfully integrated with rhomb and saw-tooth elements. Ceremonial cloth may be further embellished with geometric and curvilinear forms highlighted with masses of sequins, beads, coins and tiny brass bells. Cloth amongst these peoples is an important item of exchange in marriage negotiations and is an indicator of status and wealth.

Their lowland Muslim neighbours, the Maranao and Magindanao, have a tradition of weaving brightly coloured cotton and silk textiles in the form of large tubular sarongs called *malong*, colourful sashes and large headcloths. Worn as a dress by women and over trousers by men, the *malong* may be decorated with plaid designs, supplementary-weft metallic threads and weft-ikat patterns. Plainer-coloured *malong* may carry large cross-shaped strips of *langkit* decoration, curvilinear tapestry-weave patterns which are woven separately and attached later. The Tausug of Jolo use the same technique to create magnificent sashes and headcloths which cleverly integrate geometric design elements into a complex interplay of colour evocative of an oriental carpet. The Yakan of Basilan Island render related motifs in a supplementary-weft technique to produce their closely patterned *sinaluan* cloth which has the highest thread count in the Philippines.

Echoes of southern Filipino Muslim traditions may be seen amongst the Kadazan of Sabah Borneo, who decorate their black clothing with colourful *langkit* stripes, and the Bajau, who wear the *kain destar* turban headcloth patterned with motifs common to their ancestors of the Sulu archipelago.

Textile artistry of the lowland Christian Filipino has traditionally been expressed through embroidery. Local diaphanous cloth such as *pina*, woven from pineapple fibre, and *jusi*, a combination of pineapple and *abaca*, was used to fashion Catholic vestments, altar cloths and gossamer-like garments for the rich. These were painstakingly embellished with Western-inspired floral motifs rendered in satin stitch, open cut-work and shadow embroidery with an intricacy that almost defied belief.

Indonesia and Malaysia

A full flowering of the textile arts in South-East Asia may be seen in the Indonesian archipelago, which is unrivalled for the scope and variety of its weavings. Virtually every known patterning technique from decorative dyeing, such as ikat, batik, tie-dye *pelangi* and *tritik*, block printing and painting, to extremely complex supplementary-warp and -weft techniques, twining, couching embroidery, appliqué and beadwork are applied to a wide variety of yarns which include homespun and imported cotton, silk and synthetic threads, wool, bark-cloth bast fibres, animal and human hair. Textiles here assume an even greater ritual importance than elsewhere and have been referred to as the 'warp and weft of life', with the warp representing that which is pre-ordained and unchangeable, while the weft is synonymous with the variations and vagrancies of transient existence.

On the outer extremities of Indonesia textiles are the principal means of artistic expression and their use continues to permeate all aspects of the socio-religious life of the people. Regarded as 'female' goods, they are important in gift exchanges, particularly at the time of marriage. They also serve as banners and shrouds in mortuary rites and as baby-carriers for young children. In some societies prestige was gauged by the number and type of textiles an individual possessed.

Warp ikat on cotton fibre, woven on a simple body-tension loom, is the prevalent method of patterning on the outer islands. Supplementary-warp and -weft techniques, *nasa* shells and embroidery are also widely used to embellish textiles. Because of their relative isolation the various ethnic groups have developed and maintained their own distinctive textile traditions. The Atoni of Timor are noted for their indigo-coloured blanket-sized wraparound cloths patterned with neolithic-style composite hook and rhomb motifs, humanoid and stylised lizards and birds set between bands of brightly coloured warp stripes. The Dayaks of Borneo, using hook-like forms, integrate similar motifs in ecru and dark blue on a brick-red ground into their sacred *pua*, a large textile, which is an essential accoutrement to important rites of passage. Striking hook-arrow and zigzag motifs in

182 Cotton warp ikat Iban
pua, Borneo (Sarawak).

183 *Palepai* or 'ship cloth'
from south Sumatra, plain-
weave silk and cotton with
supplementary-weft
patterning in gold gimp.
19th century. 224 × 56 cm
(88.2 × 22 in).

warp ikats from Roti, Savu, east Flores and the
Solor archipelago.

The Batak of north central Sumatra weave
sombre indigo- and maroon-coloured cloths
called *ulos* decorated with stripes of simple geometric patterns in warp ikat or supplementary-
weft patterning. These cloths, in addition to
serving as clothing, are presented by the female
side of the family at rites of passage, to convey
protection and define social relationships. The
famous pictorial 'ship cloths', at one time made
by the Pammingir peoples of southern Sumatra,
were also important in reaffirming social relationships. These remarkable weavings patterned with ships, 'Trees of Life' and a
menagerie of animals against a background of
hook and meander forms in a supplementary
weft on an unbleached cotton ground were important in rites of passage. The ship motif,
formerly associated with death and the afterlife,
symbolised the transition from one stage to
another. Recent research by textile scholars suggests that there may be some links in design
motifs between these ship cloths and ritual *pha-
kit* textiles of north-east Thailand and possibly
Laos.

The Muslim coastal peoples of Indonesia,
being exposed to foreign contacts, have developed their own distinct textile traditions.
Weft ikat and a form of supplementary-weft
patterning called *kain songket*, using imported
metallic wrapped thread, are the most popular
methods of embellishing cloth which is made
into distinctive sarongs, shawls and headcloths.
Weft ikat is woven at Sengkong, south Sulawesi,
Samarinda Kalimantan, Gresik Java, Nusa Peni-
da, and in Palembang, south-east Sumatra,
while *kain songket* is woven on the islands of
Sumbawa, Lombok, and by the Achehnese, the
Minangkabau, at Palembang in Sumatra and by
the coastal Malay communities of Borneo. *Kain
songket* is also woven in the states of Kelantan
and Terengganu in north-east Malaysia. Being

white and red against a blue or purplish ground
comprise the key elements in the magnificent
funerary textiles of the Toraja of central Sulawesi. Ceremonial textiles of east Sumba, formerly reserved for the aristocracy, favour bands of
naturalistic motifs such as deer, dragons, coats
of arms, crustacea, skull trees and crocodiles,
royal paraphernalia and *patola* elements in
lighter colours against a background of rust and
blue. *Patola* and Western floral elements have
also been integrated with local motifs in the

185 Double ikat cotton *geringsing*, woven by the Bali Aga of Tenganan Pageringsingan village, east Bali.

184 Silk *slendang* (shoulder-cloth) with supplementary wefts in gold metallic yarns, Minangkabau.

staunchly Muslim, motifs on weft ikat and *kain songket* are largely floral and geometric. *Patola* influence is evident in cloth layout. Gold *songket*-patterned textiles are perceived as symbols of wealth and prestige and provide a fitting display of affluence at important ceremonial events.

The Hindu island of Bali, in keeping with its vibrant culture, at one time possessed an extraordinary array of textiles ranging from brightly coloured cottons and silk weft ikats, gold-painted *prada* cloth and richly patterned *kain songkets*. Being Hindu, the Balinese did not proscribe the use of human and animal motifs. In addition to ceremonial garb, textiles in Bali were traditionally used in rites of passage, at rituals

honouring ancestors and invoking favours from the gods. Certain textiles such as the unique double-ikat blue- and rust-coloured *geringsing* cloths from the remote village of Tenganan Pageringsingan, because of the complex technique and taboos associated with their manufacture, were regarded as effective in warding off illness and misfortune not only by the Balinese but by other groups of people as well.

Wax-resist batik on previously woven cotton cloth is the chief medium of textile expression on the highly populated island of Java. The art of batik has reached its zenith in Java owing to the use of the *canting*, a thin-walled spouted copper vessel with a short bamboo handle to hold

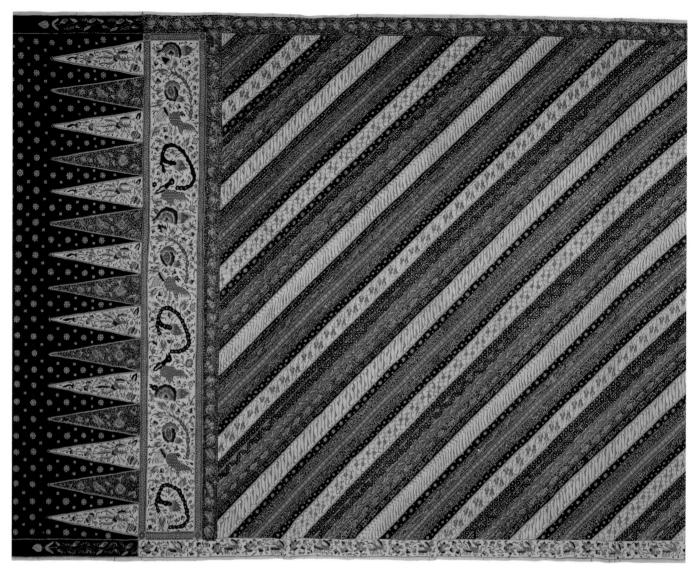

186 Detail of a batik sarong, Java (north coast), 1900–20.

molten wax. With this instrument the batik artist is able to draw intricate freehand *tulis* patterns with great precision. Batik is used to pattern material for sarongs, *selendang* shawls and male headcloths. These cloths are marked by distinct borders and a visual centre called *kepala* bounded by a series of triangular *tumpul* motifs.

There are two distinct traditions of batik in Java: that of the central region and that of the north coast. The 'classic' batik of central Java which uses only three colours – blue, brown and white – is closely associated with the courtly traditions of the sultanates of Jogjakarta and Surakarta. Patterns are traditional, featuring a range of slanting, geometric and strongly symbolic motifs set against a dense tendril-like ground. Designs originally had meaning, and the wearer was formerly expected to select one appropriate to the occasion. There were also sumptuary laws in effect which made certain patterns the preserve of royalty.

Unfettered by sumptuary laws and ritual requirements and wide open to foreign trade, the north coast batik tradition, which is centred on the towns of Pekalongan, Cirebon and formerly Lasem, by contrast with central Java is more entrepreneurial in spirit. To increase profits entrepreneurs in the industry have experimented with new techniques such as the use of a metal stamp, the *cap*, for applying wax which is faster but not as fine as hand-drawn *tulis* batik. Chemical dyes were introduced and batik workers were organised as a cottage industry. The north coast also used Chinese-, Arab- and European-inspired motifs, which were modified to suit the traditional cloth layout. They were used in combination with central Javanese designs.

These colourful, extremely popular batiks were widely exported throughout South-East Asia. Along with central Javanese batik they were at one time closely imitated by neighbouring Malaysian batik entrepreneurs. Over recent years talented Malaysian artists experimenting with chemical dyes on modern fabrics have worked to create their own distinct batik traditions and motifs with considerable success. Batik today is also considered the 'national' cloth of Malaysia.

164

Western Europe | 17 Sicilian silks

Sicilian silk weaving is a controversial subject amongst textile historians largely because Sicilian silks are so difficult to identify positively. It is certain, from historical documentation, that the first Latin silk-weaving workshop was established in Sicily by Roger II (1130–54) at Palermo in AD 1147 and that Byzantine weavers captured in the Peloponnese served in the manufacture of the earliest Sicilian silks, alongside native Islamic embroiderers of the island.

A mixture of Islamic and Byzantine designs and techniques is likely to have been used in Sicily in the late twelfth century, and the types of fabric produced were indicated by Hugo Falcandus in a description of 1190:

> Nor is it appropriate to pass over in silence those noble workshops which adjoin the palace, where the silk fibres are lately spun into threads of various colours and then are intertwined in many types of weaves . . . Here are garments worked in a remarkable way with a variety of circles and these desire or require greater industry on the part of the artists and greater richness of materials and consequently they sell for a greater price. And there you may see many other things and ornaments of varied colour and type in which gold is woven into the silks and you will see a manifold variety of designs adorned with translucent gems,

pearls also are either included whole in golden settings or are perforated and connected by a slender thread, and are turned into a picture by some elegant effort of disposition, to show the form of the work as it was commissioned.

Only one silk, a twill with paired inner warps, has a woven inscription that clearly states it was woven in Palermo in the royal workshop established under Roger II. This silk (Hanover, Kestner Museum, inv. 387) depicts part of a medallion design. The lower half of the medallion survives with the feet of a pair of rearing quadrupeds, and in the spandrel area there are birds. The medallion border houses the inscription 'OPERATUM IN REGIO ERGAST [erio]', that is 'Made in a workshop of the realm'. The style of the silk is comparable with that of twelfth-century mosaics in Palermo. The light blue and purple ground in combination with a deep brown, pink and off-white colour scheme is quite distinct from the usual red, blue, yellow and green permutations of Byzantine silks. The Palermo silk also has areas of brocading with silver gilt on a leather strip, unlike the gold parchment strips wound around a silk core on Byzantine silks.

A silk from the grave of Henry VI (d. 1197) in Palermo Cathedral is a red tabby, tabby lampas-weave silk with paired gazelles and birds in a foliate setting. Grönwoldt (1964) has suggested that this is a Sicilian piece and she has related a group of further silks to it.

Perhaps best known of the Sicilian silks is the so-called 'coronation mantle' of Roger II in the Weltliche Schatzkammer in Vienna (see II, 5 and II, 24). This magnificent semicircular mantle shows lions attacking camels, and the motifs are embroidered on a red twill silk, itself patterned with small, woven foliate scrolls. Around the lower hem of the piece is an Islamic inscription that can be translated to read '[Made] in the royal workshop of the capital of Sicily in the year 528 H [1133/34 AD]'. On the mantle the appearance of small pearls, gold threads and translucent gems recalls the description of Hugo Falcandus cited above. The mantle is lined with a red and a green silk as well as with a curious tapestry-weave silk. This tapestry is decorated with small figures, geometric trellis designs and also animal and foliate ornaments set on a gold ground. The richness of the fabric has led some to suggest a Sicilian provenance for the tapestry as well as the mantle, which itself may include pieces of earlier and of later manufacture.

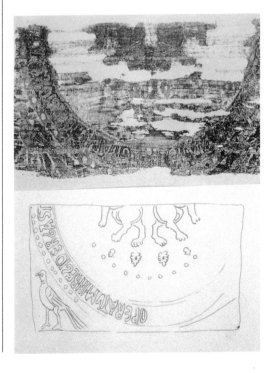

187 Silk fragment woven in Palermo, second half of the 12th century.

188 The so-called 'coronation mantle' of Roger II of Sicily, embroidered in Palermo in 1133–4.

The coronation mantle of Roger II, together with other Sicilian silks, an alb, a tunic, a lengthy belt, silk buskins and gloves, served as the main items of coronation regalia for the Hapsburg emperors. Among these pieces only the alb has been significantly restored. The body of this vestment has been recut from a later silk, on to which the Sicilian embroidered panels have been reset. These panels bear Latin and Kufic inscriptions, which indicate that the embroidery was carried out in the royal workshop in Palermo in 1181. The blue dalmatic with panels of foliate and geometric embroidery can be dated to the first half of the twelfth century. The red buskins with gold embroidery belong to the second half of the twelfth century, and red silk gloves with elaborate pearl embroidery and attached enamelled plaques and gems are twelfth to thirteenth century in date. The belt, or cingulum, of blue, red, white and yellow silk, like the other Sicilian pieces, boasts a rich array of pearls and precious jewel plaques.

The sumptuous use of gold on the coronation silks has encouraged the belief that a number of rich golden silk borders may also be of Sicilian manufacture. These include examples in the Victoria and Albert Museum in London (inv. 8227-1865 and inv. 8229-1863). Grönwoldt (1977) suggested, too, that a large mantle in Metz Cathedral, decorated with impressive eagle motifs, is a Sicilian work of the late twelfth to the early thirteenth centuries.

18 Italian silks (1300–1500)

The fourteenth century

During the later Middle Ages Italy was a leading producer of both woollen and silk textiles. Florence produced fine-quality cloth, made from imported English wool, some of which was woven in Florence, and other cloth which had been woven in Flanders and was finished in Florence. Despite the economic importance of wool in this period, it is the silk textiles woven in Italy during the fourteenth and fifteenth centuries which achieved lasting fame, and which have influenced textile design well into the present century.

To speak of Italy as a homogeneous centre of textile production is slightly misleading because there was great competition between weaving centres; and although certain towns and products developed distinctive styles, much imitation went on. By 1300 silk manufacture was focused in the north, in Venice, Genoa and Tuscany, with Lucca the leading centre of production. During the course of the fourteenth century, however, Lucca's political fortunes declined and her silk industry went into severe recession. In contrast, the industries of Venice, Florence and Genoa were set to enter a period of prosperity during the late fourteenth and early fifteenth centuries.

A group of silk-weaving statutes from 1265 shows the diversity of cloths being produced in Venice. These included pure silk fabrics such as *diaspers*, and mixtures of silk and linen, '*sarantasimi* of linen', together with samites, which could be all silk or a mixture. They were produced in broad widths, approximately 127–91 cm (50–75 in) and were woven with foliate, animal and heraldic designs, as well as human figures. The latter ranged from small, repeating patterns to specially commissioned woven scenes, such as the magnificent altar frontal showing Bishop Heinrich von Rotteneck (1277–93) kneeling before the Crucifixion, with the Virgin and Saints, in Regensburg Cathedral (King 1969, fig. 5).

An inventory taken of the Holy See in 1295 records only one silk from Genoa but many from Lucca and Venice (Molinier 1888, *passim*). There were Venetian cloths with roundels containing griffins, and many containing lions, the symbol of Venice. Amongst the silks from Lucca were some with griffins in circles, perhaps resembling the Venetian fabrics. The inventory also lists a Lucchese *diasper* with birds in roundels whose

189 Samite of silk, linen and gold thread. The ground is covered by faded red silk wefts and the pattern is in filé membrane gold thread. Venice (?), late 13th century. Venetian silks with lions in roundels were recorded in the inventory of the Holy See of 1295. 17 × 15 cm (6.7 × 5.9 in).

heads and claws were brocaded with gold (Molinier 1888, no. 1229). This description can be matched to some existing lampas silks (Falke 1936, fig. 229) with a pattern bound in tabby upon a tabby ground, either monochrome or in two colours, and brocaded with gold. A papal inventory of 1361 records Lucchese *diaspers* with parrots and lambs of God or deer, flanking floral motifs, with details brocaded in gold (Muentz and Frothingham 1882, pp. 34–7). A group of lampas silks – again mainly with a tabby pattern on a tabby ground – woven between the late thirteenth and early fourteenth centuries have related designs, with animals and birds flanking stylised plant motifs (Wardwell 1976–7, pp. 179–82). Lucca was not the only centre of production; both the papal inventory and one taken of St Paul's Cathedral in 1295 mention similar *diaspers* woven in Antioch, and some of the existing silks are thought to have been woven in Spain. *Diaspers* with bird and plant designs were purchased for the English court well into the 1320s.

From the early fourteenth century the Italians began weaving silks influenced by textiles imported from the Mongol Empire, which had been created during the thirteenth century by Genghis Khan and his descendants and stretched from China through Central Asia to Persia. The imported silks, generally referred to as 'tartar cloths' in early sources, ranged from fine linings and light twill damasks to heavy lampas cloths of gold and velvet (Wardwell 1988–9, *passim*). Important examples of tartar cloths found in Italy include the so-called funerary vestments of Pope Benedict XI (d. 1304; Magagnato 1983, pp. 164–79) and the clothing found in the tomb of Cangrande della Scala, the ruler of Verona (d. 1329; Magagnato 1983, p. 75 ff., *passim*).

The impact of such oriental fabrics cannot be overestimated, for they irrevocably changed the face of European textile design. By introducing principles of asymmetry and dynamism they heralded a break with centuries of dependence upon Sassanian-inspired roundel patterns. Animals, previously disposed in symmetrical, static designs, began to be arranged diagonally, in dynamic interaction. Exotic oriental motifs were readily adopted by Italian weavers, who produced animal silks displaying a fusion of elements directly transcribed from eastern models together with European motifs.

ABOVE **190** Italian lampas silk, tabby pattern, on a ground of five-shaft satin, c. 1380. By alternating rows of censing angels with other angels carrying instruments of the Passion, effective use has been made of the drawloom's repeating mechanism to create a tall pattern unit with maximum economy of labour. 57 × 34.6 cm (22.5 × 13.6 in).

ABOVE RIGHT **191** Italian lampas cloth of gold, second half of the 14th century. The design shows the influence of silks imported from the Mongol Empire. The ground has faded from bright red. 82.6 × 31.7 cm (32.5 × 12.5 in).

Gradually the Italians began creating versions of these designs with motifs drawn entirely from their native tradition. For example, there is a group of silks with designs of vine leaves, sometimes with small birds or animals, dating from the 1320s onwards (Wardwell 1976–7, p. 182). Sources from the mid-1320s to the late 1360s describe Lucchese silks woven with vine designs, either in red and white, or green and red, some of which may correspond to the existing

group. These were joined by fantastic, witty animal designs and, during the second half of the fourteenth century, by silks showing human figures – hunters and huntresses and scenes of courtly romance, or religious subjects.

The 1376 statutes of the Merchants' court at Lucca record the many types of silk being woven in Lucca towards the end of the fourteenth century. Under the influence of imported textiles the range of lampas weaves had increased, and six or seven kinds are mentioned. The Italian lampas silks which survive from the later fourteenth century show a correspondingly expanded range of weaves. These include various twill and satin grounds, instead of tabby which predominates in the earlier lampas groups. While the lampases of the Dugento show mostly only one or two colours (besides gold or silver brocading), those from the fourteenth century frequently have three. The most expensive of these silks were the cloths of gold, woven with gold pattern wefts made from *filé* threads of narrow gilt membrane or parchment strip wrapped around a silk or linen core. For the finest cloth a more expensive thread was used, made from gilt metal around a yellow silk core.

The 1376 statutes list ten plainer silks, some of them striped. Woven upon treadle looms, these silks, consumed in vast quantities, formed the bulk of contemporary silk production. Among the most costly of these was five-shaft satin, an important innovation for Italian weavers of the fourteenth century. Damask, a type of figured silk, long known in a 3:1 twill version, began to be woven in a five-shaft satin in Italy during the fourteenth century. A notable omission from the statutes of 1376, it was certainly known in Lucca by 1390, when a silk merchant, Domenico Lupardi, bought a loom 'to weave damask cloths' with four repeats across the width (Bini 1883, p. 66).

The most luxurious silk cloth of the late medieval period was undoubtedly velvet. Plain velvet had been woven in Italy from at least the thirteenth century, but during the fourteenth century, perhaps inspired by imported examples, Italian velvets began to be figured (Monnas 1986, *passim*). Initially woven with simple stripes or checks, by the middle of the century there were velvets with simple floral patterns in gold. By 1376 the Lucchese were weaving several kinds of patterned velvet, including velvet in three colours. These costly fabrics were worn throughout the courts of Europe. In the 1390s Richard II of England (1367–1400) – notorious for his extrava-

192 Solid cut-pile silk velvet woven in red (faded to beige), white and green. Italy, late 14th century. Whole: 14.5 × 24 cm (5.7 × 9.4 in); pattern: 7.7 cm (3 in) wide.

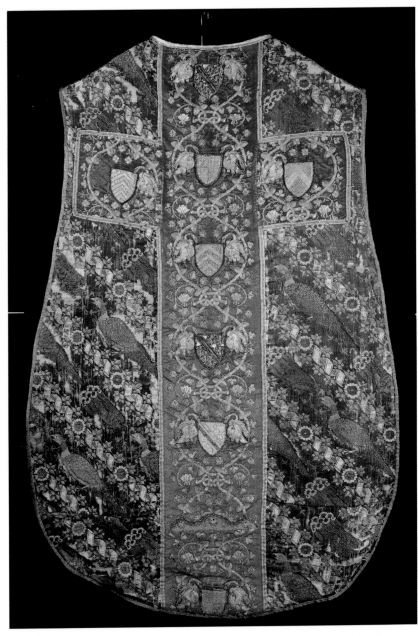

193 Chasuble with English orphrey embroidered with the arms of Edmund, 5th Earl of Stafford (d. 1403) and of Anne Plantagenet (d. 1438), whom he married in 1398. The woven material, of Italian lampas silk, has a pattern arranged in diagonal bands typical of the very early 15th century. Whole: 109.3 × 73.7 cm (43 × 29 in).

gance and personal vanity – purchased many fancy velvets, including a piece woven in two heights of pile, an early example of the fabulous pile-on-pile velvets which were to gain such renown during the fifteenth century.

The fifteenth century

The dawning of the Renaissance saw the consolidation of advances already made by Italian weavers, together with some glamorous additions to their repertoire. The interest in perspective and in the natural world which accompanied the Renaissance had its own repercussions upon textile design. Furthermore, the political framework of Italy of autonomous city-states fostered the spread of silk weaving, as their rulers vied with each other in attempting to set up local silk industries. During the century Florence and Genoa emerged as important

centres, and silk weaving was instigated in Milan, Siena and elsewhere in Italy (Herald 1982, p. 70).

The chief textile motif of the fifteenth century was undoubtedly the pomegranate (together with related forms – pine-cones, thistles or pineapples), but it did not become predominant until about the 1430s. The first two decades saw both lampas silks and velvets woven in a variety of plant and animal designs with a strong diagonal axis, often forming distinct bands. These patterns made a bold impression, but the actual repeats were still quite small, often only about 12–15 cm (4.5–6 in) wide.

Silks with animals continued to be woven throughout the century. Animals, recycled from fourteenth-century models, were drawn in a calmer, more naturalistic style and combined with updated foliate motifs (Santangelo 1964, col. pl. 29). As the century wore on, however, the animals played a diminishing role, while the foliage became increasingly prominent. The tomb of Archduke Ernest I of Austria (d. 1424) contained a splendid polychrome, brocaded velvet, voided upon a satin ground, with a design of knotted headbands and floral sprigs (Smola 1969, *passim*). A group of voided satin velvets, both monochrome and polychrome, with small floral designs is thought to date from the 1420s. Although voided satin velvets are recorded during the fourteenth century, the earliest surviving seem to date from the early fifteenth century, with repeats of about 22 × 15 cm (8.5 × 6 in).

As velvet weavers grew more proficient, they were able to produce broader designs which better suited the technique. These were woven with large undulating stems bearing cusped forms often containing pomegranates. Such a design can be seen on the canopy over the tomb of Pope John XXIII by Donatello and Michelozzo in the Baptistry in Florence (c.1427), and voided satin velvets with similar designs survive (Klesse 1967, cat. no. 458).

The largest group of monochrome, voided velvets to survive are the *feronnerie* velvets, which have tracery-like patterns produced in fine outlines of satin, normally depicting pomegranates enclosed by cusped leaves. Although their frequent appearance in Venetian paintings, particularly those of Carlo Crivelli (fl. 1457–93), might suggest a Venetian origin, it seems likely that these velvets were reproduced in many centres. A Florentine treatise of the fifteenth century refers to voided satin velvets woven in Florence *alla viniziana* (in the Venetian manner). A particularly splendid *feronnerie* velvet of the later fifteenth century, with a broad pomegranate design woven in two heights of crimson pile, is preserved in the Museo Civico, Turin (Santangelo 1964, col. pl. 56).

194 Cope of Henry VII (1457–1509), orphrey, hood and morse (not original) of English embroidery, late 15th century. Cloth woven *c.* 1499–1502, with the King's devices of Tudor roses and portcullises, bordered by a collar of SS. Made from Florentine *riccio sopra riccio* cloth of gold, with cut and uncut silk pile, brocaded with seven different gold and silver *filé* threads, and woven to shape with an integral border. Whole: 1.48 × 3.15 m (4.87 × 10.33 ft).

Italian weavers developed more complex brocading skills during the course of the fifteenth century. Not only were *feronnerie* velvets and damasks brocaded with coloured silk and gold thread, but cloths of gold were enriched with gold weft loops. In velvet these occur either as *allucciolato* wefts – individual loops glistening in areas of pile – or as massed gold loops, which could be woven in two heights, giving the effect known as *riccio sopra riccio* (loop over loop). Gold loops were introduced into velvet weaving by the late 1420s (Monnas 1989, pp. 291–2). They can be seen on the velvet worn by the donor in Jan Van Eyck's *Madonna of Chancellor Rolin*, of *c.*1435, in the Musée du Louvre. There is a group of velvets resembling Rolin's fabric, with a large pattern unit spanning half the width of the cloth – approximately 30 cm, (12 in) – and measuring up to 2 m (6.5 ft) high.

A major technical change in weaving cloth of gold was that the metal thread became shown to maximum effect upon the surface of the cloth. The gold cloths of the Trecento had been shot through with a continuous gold weft, much of which was concealed upon the rear. The 'Rolin' velvets of the 1430s show broad expanses of gold

in which the precious metal thread is eked out by 'accompanying wefts' of yellow silk. As a result, weavers were able to produce patterns with increasingly broad areas of gold thread, in which the velvet pile or the ground weave of a lampas silk was ultimately reduced to a fine outline. These outline techniques lent themselves to the increasingly intricate pomegranate designs with a proliferation of subsidiary leaves and flowers, found from *c.*1450 onwards, of which examples may be seen in the gold-brocaded cape found in the tomb of Sigismondo Pandolfo Malatesta (d. 1468; Flury-Lemberg 1989, cat. no. 22) and in lampas and velvet cloths from booty taken from Charles the Rash of Burgundy in 1476–7, preserved in the Historical Museum, Berne (Deuchler 1963, cat. nos 93 and 94, figs 124–7).

Riccio sopra riccio velvet, with extensive gold looping, was so expensive that it was frequently made to commission, sometimes woven to shape to avoid wasting precious gold thread. From the second half of the fifteenth century there remain several examples of such cloth woven to shape with heraldic designs, thought to have been made in Florence. These include

the dossal executed for Matthias Corvinus of Hungary (1458–90; Falke 1936, fig. 482), the altar frontal at Assisi showing Sixtus IV (1471–84) kneeling before St Francis (Falke 1936, figs 479–80) and the vestments of Henry VII of England (1457–1509) at Stonyhurst College, documented as woven in Florence, c.1499–1502 (Monnas 1989, *passim*). Although weaving to shape seems to have been a Florentine speciality, heraldic cloths of *riccio sopra riccio* velvet were also woven elsewhere in Italy. Notable examples are the

chasuble documented as woven in Venice, given to the Basilica di S. Antonio in Padua by Pope Sixtus IV (Monnas 1982, *passim*), and a beautiful Milanese altar frontal woven with the devices of Lodovico il Moro, the Duke of Milan, and his wife Beatrice d'Este, upon the occasion of their marriage in 1491 (Podreider 1928, fig. 186). These precious cloths of gold, woven by the most highly skilled weavers of their day, represent the apogee of Italian weaving during the fifteenth century.

RIGHT **195** Rear of a chasuble, with English orphrey embroidered with the arms of Henry de Beauchamp, Duke of Warwick (d. 1445), after his marriage to Lady Cecily Nevill in 1434. The woven material, of Italian velvet cloth of gold, incorporates six pattern effects in its weave, including a lozenge design formed by the gold pattern weft.

19 Italian silks (1500–1900)

FALLAX·GRATIA·ET·VANA·EST·PVLCHRITVDO

196 Angelo di Cosimo di Mariano Bronzino (1503–72), portrait of Eleanor of Toledo, the wife of Cosimo de Medici, Grand Duke of Tuscany. Her dress is of Italian silk velvet with rich weft-loop decoration and applied gold cord, indicative of Spanish taste.

By the sixteenth century the principal figured weaves – velvet, lampas and damask with brocaded effects, and *brocatelle* – had been developed. During the century the scale of design, types and weights of textile became more diverse. In general the larger, heavier textiles were reserved for furnishings, ceremonial and ecclesiastical use, and more exclusive clothes worn by the wealthiest of families. Many of the most lavish silks – for example, the *riccio sopra riccio*

velvets with silver and gold weft looping – shared characteristics with the velvets of Spain and Turkey, with which Italy traded actively through the ports of Genoa and Venice respectively. On the other hand, the new sprigged floral patterns, developed from *c*.1580, represented a new approach to figured textile design.

The pomegranate motif persisted in the richest of silk and gold textiles; around 1500 it appeared at the pivotal points of the branches which turned to right and left of a vertical axis. In some designs a single branch meandered across the width of the textile, though the dominant pomegranate punctuated the rhythm of its path, and was balanced by smaller vegetal growths from secondary stems – often thistle-flower pine-cone-type motifs, looking quite Islamic. In other designs a pair of branches, moving in the same vertical direction, and crossing at the centre, formed a symmetrical unit, the ogee.

The ogee lattice is the principal design composition of the sixteenth century. The pomegranate might be framed by the branches forming the ogee, or, alternatively, these branches enclosed heraldic motifs: increased wealth within society led to specially commissioned silks incorporating family emblems. The branches themselves became increasingly elaborate, composed, for example, of a central vein of guilloches enclosing tiny flowers, or embellished by spiralling acanthus leaves. The decoration generally feels more classical. Furnishing designs gradually became more architectural, juxtaposing natural and man-made elements – the vase, for instance, out of which grew an inflorescence. Sometimes the vase was flanked by animals, an arrangement reminiscent of late fourteenth-century designs, but more immediately, perhaps, a reflection of Renaissance painted wall decoration, notably Raphael's grotesques in the Vatican. Certainly there is a direct link, for *brocatelles* and other figured silks used for wall-hangings were conceived as panels proportionate to the architectural interior.

In fact, engravings of ornamental designs became a key source of decorative ideas. Several books of them were published in Venice – Tagliente 1527, Zoppino 1529, Vivassore 1537, Pagano 1543, Vecellio 1591, Parasole 1594. Though originally intended for metalwork, embroidery and lace, the motifs could be adapted to woven textiles and featured grotesques, arabesques, birds, hunting scenes and cherubs.

In the latter half of the sixteenth century the interlaced stems which defined the ogee lattice became simplified and narrower. The curving stems were often surmounted at the top of each ogee by a crown. This is really the formalised head of the thistle flower, pine-cone, or pomegranate, rising out of the central vase motif in a symmetrical palmette sprouting into a halo of carnations or other florettes. The reading of the design was coming to depend less on textural variations and increasingly on colour contrasts; red and cream, green and golden yellow were common combinations. Chequered fillings to little details created a flickering effect and marked the transition to the more geometric floral sprigs produced towards the end of the century.

Though the lattice framework remained the principal system of repeat, in many designs the branches became discontinuous, and the whole effect was simplified. From around 1580, and during the following fifty years, little floral motifs, increasingly geometric, were produced. New compositions appeared, combining either a floral sprig or the rectilinear broken-branch motif entwined with the curvilinear 's'. These were arranged in endless variations on a theme – in parallel rows, staggered rows, zigzags, diamond lattices and cruciforms.

The flowers – tulips, carnations and others featured in herbals – invariably change direction from one row to the next; sometimes the colours also alternate in horizontal bands. These patterns were imitated in knitted silk jackets. As well as stylised plant motifs, another group of patterns emerged, based on the repetition of minute geometric forms. Such small-scale scattered patterns were used especially in dress, as painted portraits of the sixteenth and seventeenth centuries record. These fashionable dress silks were lighter versions of damask or lampas, or the new qualities of brocaded satin or taffeta. They may have been manufactured in response to the preference for less durable fabrics of the French, quick to change with the mood of fashion, referred to in sixteenth-century commentaries.

During the seventeenth century, from about 1630, woven flowers became much more naturalistic and animated, with more sinuous stems and leaves – species like the peony and chrysanthemum enhanced the baroque style. The device of chiaroscuro and juxtaposition of complementary colours (green/red, bright yellow/blue, purple/gold) heightened the contrast between background and motif. By the mid-seventeenth century damask created a dynamic play of light on the background surface, against which motifs with a strong diagonal orientation were brocaded in coloured silks or metal

ABOVE **199** Lampas weave silk, probably from a chasuble. Italy, late 17th century.

RIGHT **200** Banded decoration from two 16th-century Perugia towels. Linen decorated with supplementary-weft patterns in indigo-dyed cotton.

changes in textiles for dress, but Genoa, in particular, was known abroad for its distinctive – and very expensive – *jardinière* velvets. These were sometimes monochrome in kermes red or rich blue with several heights of pile, but often rendered in red and green silk velvet on an ivory-coloured satin background. The flowers were simply drawn on a bold scale. The richest patrons of Europe appreciated their softness, depth and lustre; the pinkish tint of kermes red is said to have distinguished Genoa velvet from its French and English imitations. The heyday of the *jardinière* velvets was around 1670 to 1750, though the demand for Genoa silk damask continued longer.

Venice competed with Genoa in the art of velvet weaving, but Venetian design had different characteristics, appearing more dependent on French design. Whether a floral design, or a cartouche enclosing a *trompe l'oeil* glimpse of a classical ruin, the brocaded silks were drawn in fantastic colourways, very heavy

threads. Dyestuffs were mixed into a new colour palette – salmon pink, lime green, lemon yellow, turquoise blue. Meanwhile the duality of seventeenth-century taste was reflected by a second, much more sombre group of shades – dark red, dark brown, dark green, black and grey.

The 1660s marked a crucial turning-point for Italy's role within the European silk industry. At the beginning of the decade Louis XIV's minister Jean Baptiste Colbert (1619–83) ordered for the French royal household large quantities of Italian silk furnishings. In 1664 he sent French designs to be woven in Italy; but no more Italian silks were purchased for Louis after 1666. French State support favoured its home industry instead. Ironically, many of France's weaving establishments had originally been set up by Italian craftsmen.

From the late seventeenth century Venice and other Italian centres were led by Lyons design. From the 'bizarre' to the naturalistic style of the Lyonnais designer Jean Revel (?1684–1751) of the 1730s, Italian silks were subject to the changes in French fashion, though Italian weavers never pushed the use of *points rentrés* and multicoloured effects to the degree of richness and three-dimensionality of the French (see II, 21). Some Italian producers invited Frenchmen to train their apprentices and supply designs, but despite this, Savary de Brulons, in his *Dictionnaire de Commerce* of 1723, commented: 'Although Italy still exported large quantities of gold and silk fabrics to France, Italian persons of rank preferred to buy the elegant silk for their clothing from France.'

France may have monopolised the seasonal

and elaborate in style. Moreover, although French visitors considered Venice's products inferior to those of Lyons, Venetians valued their industry. In 1763 Piero D'Avanzo, himself an accomplished designer and author of a treatise on textile composition, established an academy of design for silk weavers.

Despite the dominance of France in the eighteenth century, and the contraction of the Italian silk industry from the Renaissance

ABOVE **201** Genoa *jardinière* velvet upholstery used on an early 18th-century French day-bed and sofa *en suite*.

onwards, Italy's textile output was still considerable. Thrown silk and metal threads were exported throughout Europe. Some Italian designs have become classics: the flame or Florentine pattern, now more commonly associated with embroidery, was woven into silks and mixed fabrics. Delicate *chiné* patterns for women's clothing and dynamic spotted and striped velvets for male dress were part of the repertoire. The latter were particularly admired by the macaronis, young men whose dapper spotted coats were inspired by fashions and fabrics observed during their Grand Tour.

In addition to figured silk weaving many types of mixed fabrics were produced. Perugia is the town associated with the linen 'towels' patterned with indigo-dyed cotton supplementary weft; their paired birds and figured designs are reminiscent of folk embroidery on the one hand and fourteenth-century Lucchese silks on the other. In Tuscany a wide range of mixed fabrics was manufactured for furnishing use – for example, heavyweight silk/cotton or silk/linen *sciamiti*, sometimes made with a napped surface, for canopies, bed curtains and coverlets. Also linen/wool and silk/linen fabrics, based on medieval Lucchese designs, or the smaller-scale abstract

florals of the seventeenth century, with horizontal bands of colour, were produced for many years.

Some Italian workshops produced lightweight plain silks, notably taffetas and gauzes. These seem to have been imported into France and were possibly copied by the French, whilst the Italians felt obliged to imitate French brocades. In 1755 Madame de Pompadour (1721–64) had in her boudoir at Bellevue 'A [roller] blind of Italian taffeta, painted with bouquets of flowers and garlands that are transparent'. Another category of Italian furnishing textiles included figured borders in *brocatelle*, possibly hung alternately with wider panels on the walls or used as borders in another context.

Certainly France dominated the field of figured silks from the later seventeenth century; but owing to increased demand for all kinds of textiles, at many different levels of the market, the Italian textile industry nevertheless had an important part to play within the European scene. With the growing interest in furnishings and interior decoration historians are now considering the aesthetics and use of linen and wool fabrics more seriously; no doubt this area will receive greater attention in the future.

20 Spanish silks

Before the Moorish conquest of AD 712 textile production in the Iberian Peninsula was confined to wool and linen, and figured silks were imported from the eastern Mediterranean. The Moors shaped the hillsides of Andalusia in southern Spain, where they introduced sericulture. By the ninth century there is documentary evidence for figured silk textiles, embellished with silver thread, which were recognised abroad as Spanish: Pope Gregory IV (AD 827–44) gave fourteen of them to the Church of St Mark in Rome.

In AD 756 Córdoba, 'the Bride of Andalusia', was established by the first Ummayad caliph as Spain's Islamic capital. *Tirāz* workshops and the

202 Silk woven in *taqueté* technique, with banded decoration bearing a *naskhi* inscription referring to happiness, good fortune, thanks and lasting fortitude. Spain, 13th century.

exchange of raw silk were integrated into the administrative and commercial structures of Córdoba and several other Andalusian cities, including Almería, Granada, Málaga, Murcia, Seville and Toledo. The Ummayad dynasty (AD 755–1031) set a shining example of Arab culture, craftsmanship and decoration. Spanish visitors were impressed by the richness of the caliphs' surroundings - the decorated architecture, textile hangings and carpets, and the shapes of their garments. Many aspects of Arab culture and style were adopted in the interior decoration and clothes of Spanish royalty and the wealthy, and Arab craftsmanship in silk weaving was highly prized.

Spanish silk production was influenced by the shifting balance of Arab and Christian rule within Iberia. Following the fall of the caliphate

Christians took advantage of the Arabs' political disarray and began the reconquest of northern Spain. Meanwhile the south of the country was subjected to two successive waves of invasion from North Africa – the Almoravides from the Sahara in the late eleventh century and the Almohades from the Atlas Mountains in the twelfth. The Jews and Mozarabs (Christians converted to Islam) fled to Castile and Aragon, where they translated Arab texts and practised traditional Arab skills including silk weaving. By the mid-thirteenth century northern Spain was reclaimed for the Christian Church, though it was still divided into the small, independent kingdoms of Navarre, Aragon, Castile and Catalonia. Crafts executed by Arab craftsmen under Christian rule between the thirteenth and sixteenth centuries are known as *mudéjares*. In 1469 the marriage of Ferdinand (1452–1516) and Isabella (1451–1504) united the kingdoms of Aragon and Castile. The Christian reconquest of Moorish territory was completed in 1492, when Granada surrendered. The Spanish Inquisition then began. Some Arab weavers were given asylum to run the textile workshops which contributed to Catholic luxury; others fled to North Africa where they continued to weave in the *mudéjar* style.

The designs and techniques of silk weaving were also determined by Spain's cultural and commercial relations with other Mediterranean countries. Samite, a weft-faced compound twill, is the dominant construction of the early period. It may well have been woven by weavers from Baghdad who set up workshops in Spain during the ninth century; these cloths feature roundels enclosing paired birds and animals, similar to silks of Syria, with whom the Ummayads had close ties. Later, following the Catholic expulsion of Moorish craftsmen, the silk industry depended on an influx of Italian weavers to set up velvet-weaving workshops in the fifteenth century and, in the eighteenth century, French weavers and designers from Lyons.

At certain periods Spanish silks can be difficult to distinguish from Middle Eastern, North African and Italian ones. Nevertheless, characteristically Spanish is the detailed geometric infilling of framework, interstices and features such as birds' wings. Colour is a particularly vital component, enhanced in samites by the twill weft floats of lustrous silk, with a negligible amount of twist, creating a wonderful sheen.

Many designs are of two strongly contrasting colours, accentuating the profile of the motifs and making them stand out from the background; the contours may be further enhanced by an outline of black or white, as in an Islamic carpet (see II, 13).

ABOVE 203 The complementary blue and orange, woven in the samite technique, create flat shapes and vibrant tones. The paired birds and animals also attest to east Mediterranean influence. 12th century.

ABOVE RIGHT 204 Silk textile of the type referred to in medieval inventories as 'cloth of aresta'. Such heraldic textiles were used for items such as seal bags, clothing and cushion covers. This one resembles many found in the royal tombs at Las Huelgas, Spain. Probably Spanish, 13th century.

During the tenth and eleventh centuries veils, cushion-covers and other cloths designed as units were woven with bands of Kufic script, also inserts of tapestry containing stylised animals and human figures revealing 'Coptic' influence. The repeating patterns of roundels resemble Byzantine silks and their ancient Sassanian prototypes in form, though the iconography of animals is closer to that of a medieval bestiary; they include the double-headed eagle, griffins, lions and peacocks.

Early inscriptions were in Kufic script, which is angular; gradually, however, the characters were embellished with flowers, scrolls or palmettes and arranged in different combinations. After the twelfth century *naskhi* cursive script became increasingly popular. Arranged in wide bands cutting across fields of vibrant pattern, or

fitted inside interstices and motifs, it could no longer be read as pure inscription. In other words, around the time of the Crusades the sacred calligraphy of Islam turned into mere conventionalised pattern.

By the mid-twelfth century designs combined geometric and stylised inscriptions, resembling the textiles of Sicily and Fatimid Egypt, countries with analogous cultures. These might be alternated with bands featuring motifs of confronted animals, or peacocks flanking a palmette symbolising the 'Tree of Life'. The composition was divided into horizontal bands of alternating colours, sometimes arranged as chevrons.

Sumptuary legislation of the early thirteenth century, restricting the use of gold thread in weaving and embroidery, suggests that cloths became increasingly expensive and elaborate.

The law embodied in *Las siete partidas* compiled by Alfonso X the Wise (1221–84), King of Castile and León, stated that a monarch must dress in silk with gold and silver and precious stones in order to distinguish his rank from the clothing of commoners. Alfonso's burial clothes of silk and gold were woven into a rich chequer-board of heraldic castles and lions, looking something like a game of chess: indeed, there is a connection, because in 1283 Alfonso X edited a book on chess, dice and draughts.

The Arabic element in design strengthened through the thirteenth century giving rise to the term Hispano-Moresque. Patterns include complex interlacing lines in the horizontal, vertical and diagonal axes to form square grids, stars and rosettes. The effect is highly stylised and geometric. Under the Nasrid dynasty (1232–

ABOVE 205 Spanish silk with pronounced geometric interlace pattern, of the type associated with the tile and stucco decoration in the Alhambra Palace, Granada. 14th century.

1492) in Granada the decorative style employed at the Alhambra was reflected in silks. Their arrangement resembles the horizontal divisions of the interior walls of the Alhambra Palace, colourfully faced with highly glazed ceramic tiles. These silks were greatly appreciated abroad, being described in the inventories of the Cathedral of Angers and of King Charles V of France (1337–80).

During the fourteenth century there was a notable departure from the animal-bird theme, as in Italy: there were many variations on the lozenge and eight-pointed-star patterns in which elements are frequently interlaced. Less calligraphic decoration was used, bands of intersected arches sometimes taking its place. Gradually more vegetal forms appeared, arranged in increasingly naturalistic rhythms and shapes, to disguise the geometric nature of the repeat. By the end of the century many more designs incorporated arabesques and floral forms. The lotus motif, having previously been combined with the palmette or Almohade-like leaf, was developed into simple inflorescences of large multilobed medallions and small eight-lobed circles, and in addition gothic trefoils and quatrefoils were incorporated into some designs.

Although Hispano-Moresque patterns of Alhambresque decoration were still made, in the fifteenth century new small-scale *jardinière*-type designs, invariably red or green on ivory grounds, appeared. These tended to be made in half-silk or wool. Ogee forms and pomegranate-type silks featuring stems which undulate about a vertical axis are all similar to those made in Italy. Compared with the Italian products Spanish textiles have more pronounced linear effects, and in brocaded velvets they use greater quantities of gold and silver thread.

The evidence for Spanish textiles is varied, demonstrating the wide range of fabric types and uses. *Tirāz* scarves are worn by oriental characters in Italian Renaissance paintings. Rich in heraldry, burial textiles from the royal tombs of Las Huelgas, the Cistercian convent near Burgos, founded by Alfonso VIII (1155–1214) of Castile and his English wife, Eleanor, in the early thirteenth century, demonstrate the value placed on textiles in life. They include fine tunics, coifs, shrouds, cushion-covers and linings to coffins, some of which were trimmed with tablet-woven braids. From written records we know that samite was used for hangings of state beds and clothes, the lighter-weight sendal for banners, curtains and some clothing. Church treasuries of Europe possess examples of the less expensive half-silks, woven without gold thread, used to line vestments and even portable altars.

BELOW 207 Detail of a late 17th- or early 18th-century silk with masquerading figures brocaded in silk and chenille threads. Possibly Portuguese.

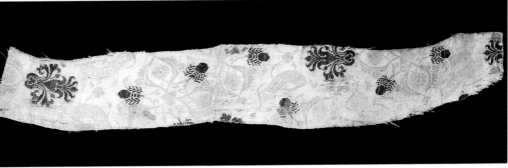

RIGHT 206 White silk lampas brocaded in gold. The design is gothic in taste but is deliberately Islamicised, with scrolls incorporating pseudo-Arabic inscriptions. Spain, 15th century.

The paths of acquisition are equally varied: some silks were commissioned, others were received as gifts, and some were acquired as booty. Las Huelgas offered shelter for pilgrims on their way to the nearby sanctuary of Santiago de Compostela, whence the half-silks of Burgos, possibly given to important pilgrims as gifts, may have been diffused. Pilgrims and newly appointed priests would donate sets of vestments to churches. Sometimes Muslim garments were given to Christians as gifts. Splendid Moorish tents and banners of gold and silver cloth were taken as trophies of Christian victory. One early fifteenth-century chasuble,

said to be Saint Euphemia's and treasured in the Church of San Sebastián at Antequera (Málaga province), was made from a banner surrendered by Muslims at the Battle of Chaparral in 1424 and bears an inscription commonly associated with silks made in Granada: 'Glory to our Lord, the Sultan.'

Spain sank into relative obscurity as France began to dominate the history books from the seventeenth century. Nevertheless, silk textiles of the Iberian Peninsula as a whole await further research, and Spain and Portugal's contributions to the cotton and woollen industries of Europe also deserve fuller recognition.

21 French silks (1650–1800)

From the seventeenth century French government regulations and patronage encouraged and supported the development of the existing native silk-weaving industry, and French patterned silk fabrics of the eighteenth century are some of the most spectacular surviving examples. The industry went into decline during the French Revolution, but in the early years of the nineteenth century Napoleon I (1769–1821) echoed Louis XIV's (1638–1715) late seventeenth-century sponsorship in his attempts to revive the ailing industry by commissioning furnishings for his imperial palaces.

The *Almanach des Négociants*, published in

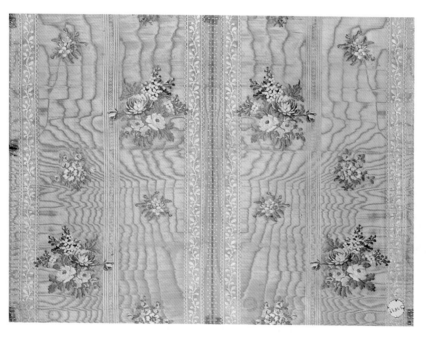

208 Striped brocaded *gros de Tours* with a moiré ground. Watered silks were produced in greater quantities in Lyons from the early 1750s onwards after the arrival of the Englishman John Badjer.

Brussels in 1762, offered a useful guide to the quality and success of various European silk-weaving centres, noting the place and output of the various French centres. It considered Lyons superior to all other cities because of the wide range of fabrics produced there, a range rivalled only by the English centre of Spitalfields in London. The production of these two centres covered everything from plain satin and taffeta weaves in self colours to the very elaborate polychrome and metallic brocaded silks used for furnishings and dress. Unlike Lyons other French centres tended to specialise in one of the many types of fabrics. Tours was renowned for the ribbed silk which carried its name *gros de*

Tours. Nîmes, Avignon and Paris concentrated on plain silks, a useful, less fashion-conscious staple, suitable for middle-class demand and for the periods of mourning which caused upheaval in the novelty branches of the industry. In the course of the eighteenth century silk fabrics from centres outside France also entered the French repertoire. Italy contributed high-quality cut velvets, especially from the 1730s, and England passed on watered, or moiré, silks, from the early 1750s. Novelty in design and good taste were two factors which contributed to the success of the French industry.

From 1667 guild regulations were detailed with regard to the fabrics and expanded to encompass new fabrics as the eighteenth century progressed. They emphasised quality and the need to differentiate pure silks from silk mixes. They listed each type by name and defined its width, content in terms of metallic threads, silk and other fibres, and also the density of the warp and weft. Despite guild restrictions, there was a constant undercurrent of experimentation and change in the silk industry, although, overall, change in fabrics was cosmetic rather than technological.

Writing in the 1770s, Jean Paulet, designer and manufacturer, indicated the importance of design, suggesting that difficulties in identifying different fabrics arose partly because small changes in design sometimes led to new names for a fabric already in existence. In the two parts of his treatise Paulet dealt with some twenty fabrics, drawing attention to three different weaves which were incorporated into different fabrics in varying combinations – satin, taffeta and twill. These three weaves corresponded to different seasons. Satin was popular in winter, taffeta in summer, and twill in autumn and spring. Paulet's own invention of a new fabric called *musulmane* combined all three weaves to produce a fabric popular all the year round.

Throughout the century a hierarchy of fabrics and prices existed (see table), although the use of different fabrics altered with time and fashionable demand. At the beginning of the century, for example, it was not unusual for the most expensive metallic categories to be used for formal dress in aristocratic circles as well as for some more excessive furnishing projects. By the end of the century, however, although silk was still in use, and the very elaborate silks still in production, their appeal was limited. They had become the prerogative of the Catholic Church and were used for ecclesiastical vestments rather than fashionable dress. Taste in dress silks had simplified, as even formal portraits of Marie Antoinette (1755–93) by her court painter, Elisabeth Vigée-Le Brun (1755–1842), demonstrate. In full dress she preferred plain silks or plain velvet to the elaborate gowns worn by preceding queens. In Lyons the proportion of looms working on brocade and plain silks reflected the shift in fashion.

The fabric hierarchy did not change during the century, but taste in designs changed regularly and in the type of patterning gradually. Rothstein has identified eight phases in design

clusively for furnishing rather than dress fabric. The informality of comber repeats suited the increasing naturalism in silk design which developed in the second quarter of the century and continued until the end of the period.

Motifs changed and different combinations of colours appeared from decade to decade. In the early years (until the 1730s) manufacturers offered a choice of formal lace-patterned silks and 'bizarre' silks to fashionable society. Both types specialised in large patterns with as much as a metre (3 ft) drop, and presented stylised shapes and abstract forms, sometimes recognisable as flowers or fruits. Both came in differing degrees of richness, using metallic threads either in

FRENCH SILK PRICES

Taken from a memorial addressed to De Gournay in 1751, cited in Godart 1899 (p. 390)

Fabric type		Retail price per ell (livres/sols)	Piece rate per ell/ payment to weaver (livres/sols)
Silks brocaded in gold and silver:	very rich	180–350/400l	
	rich	36–180l	
	less rich	13–36l	3–36l
Worked velvets		16–70l	3–18l
Plain velvet		17–26l	50s–4l 10s
Silks brocaded in pure silk (chiné also belonged to this category)		4–30l	20s–16l
Plain silks		2–14l	8–22s
Mixed fabrics (silk and wool or linen)		4–8l	8–30s

NB The cost of weaving is an indication of the complexity of the weave. Brocades with metallic threads are divided into categories according to the weight of gold or silver in each fabric. The greater the weight, the greater the end price. Weaving with gold and silver was also difficult in comparison with ordinary silk because of the brittle quality of the threads. Velvet was more complex than ordinary brocades and plain silks because rods had to be slotted between threads and the pile cut after weaving. Mixed fabrics contained cheaper fibres such as wool and linen, hence their relatively low price. Weaving progressed at the incredibly slow rate of one-eighth of an ell to three ells per day, according to the complexity of the pattern and the weave.

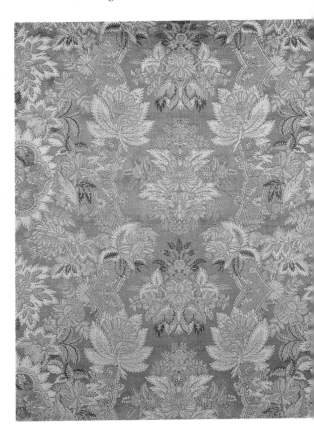

ABOVE RIGHT 209 Lace-patterned, brocaded lampas with green ground and beige and green pattern. The very long repeat length (34.5 cm, 13.6 in) is typical of the early 18th century, when this type of pattern was used in both dress and furnishings.

between 1700 and 1795 alone, with each phase representing roughly a ten-year period (Rothstein 1990). In the eighteenth century, however, contemporaries were probably able to detect changes in patterns and colours by the year in which they were sold. This was quite possible as silk manufacturers produced new collections at least twice yearly in the early years, and quarterly by the end of the period.

Two types of designs coexisted throughout the century – point repeats and comber repeats. Point repeats were symmetrical about a vertical axis, whilst comber repeats were asymmetrical. Point repeats were more formal than comber repeats and by the 1730s were used almost ex-

profusion or in moderation. Fashion favoured very heavy, rich effects, hence the apparent formality. The effects differed, however, with bizarre patterns relying on a very pronounced diagonal emphasis and lace patterns on perfect symmetry. The fashionable cut of dress responded to the immense proportions of such lace patterns by spreading women's skirts into a bell shape supported by wide panniers, and apartments in palaces and mansions clad their suitably immense walls in these large repeats.

Bizarre silks, like lace-patterned silks, did not remain unaltered during their years of popularity. Small pavilions and archways, diagonal screens and balustrades took the place of purely

210 Chasuble made of 'bizarre' silk, from the early 18th century. c. 1707–8.

because of their dramatic impact, but simpler stylised floral patterns coexisted with them from the late seventeenth century. In the early eighteenth century the small rows of flowers became more naturalistic, being woven in colour rather than in metallic threads and thus becoming almost three-dimensional. By the 1720s such flowers were integrated with broad stripes to create a suppler, less formal effect.

The 1730s, however, marked a watershed in silk design, and each decade thereafter is fairly well documented in terms of design progression. This decade coincided with the career of the first well-known Lyonnais silk designer, Jean Revel (?1684–1751). His name has since become synonymous with the distinctive style which consisted of heavy three-dimensional fruits and flowers. These motifs dwarfed both human figures and architectural features which strayed into the composition. In these figures and architectural features an interest in the Orient was apparent, but an Orient subservient to the central design of natural motifs. In technical terms the superlative shading of these motifs resulted from the use of *points rentrés*, supposedly an invention of Revel's, which consisted of the interlocking of different shades of colour so that the division between them was less severe.

The scale of flowers and fruits decreased noticeably in the following decade and continued gradually to diminish for the next forty years until the plain ground of the silk dominated the tiny, separate bouquets of flowers or individual scattered flowers. The 1740s and 50s were characterised by meanders of flowers across a plain or diaper ground. Unlike their English counterparts, French flowers did not develop in terms of naturalism but remained somewhat stylised. Sometimes there were secondary meanders of lace, ribbon or fur accompanying floral meanders, or a shadow pattern in the colour of the ground which echoed the main string. The designs of the 1750s tended to be stiffer than those of the preceding decade, with the meanders becoming geometric in nature – a zigzag rather than a meander – or lying on a geometric diaper ground. Fur and lace patterns were popular particularly in the late 1750s and 60s. In fact, the 'giant' of French silk design, Philippe Lasalle (1723–1804), claimed retrospectively to have been the first to incorporate fur as a decorative element into his fabrics in 1758 or so. This 'invention' marked the beginning of a long and successful career in the Lyons silk industry.

By the end of the 1760s, under the influence of neo-classicism, the curling rococo shapes of plants and foliage gave way to stripes, around which meanders curled for a while but which

abstract forms from about 1707, and small semi-naturalistic flowers began to appear from 1705, gradually gaining in importance and impact from 1712 onwards. Throughout their lifespan, however, bizarre motifs were exotic and strangely shaped, oriental in origin. In colour they were very striking, marrying together the most diverse and brilliant combinations – pink with green and brown, red with gold and brown, and so on. So strange were these colour combinations that contemporaries dubbed them 'bizarre', two centuries before Vilhelm Slomann popularised this label (*Bizarre Designs in Silks*, Copenhagen, 1953). In the 1730s Hamonet advised his merchant partners De Vitry et Gayet of changes in colour for the coming season, 'bizarre' shades of 'brownish wine colour', cherry, cinnamon, brown, violet-grey and green.

Lace-patterned and bizarre silks stand out

RIGHT 212 Brocaded *gros de
Tours* with a meandering
pattern on a lemon ground.
Metallic and polychrome silk
are used in the brocading of
these silks, which have
typically rococo swirls.
c. 1740–60.

ABOVE 211 Weft-patterned,
brocaded satin with the
luxuriant foliage and
decoration associated with
Jean Revel and typical of the
late 1730s and early 1740s.

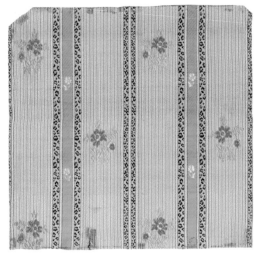

RIGHT 213 Silk with salmon-
pink, white and leopard-skin
stripes. The flowers have
chenille centres. Philippe
Lasalle claimed to have been
the originator of the first fur
motifs in the late 1750s.

came to dominate and regulate the patterning
into straight lines. These columns varied in
width and in texture. Insects and single flowers
were scattered across them in the 1770s, but by
the 80s single flowers or simple stripes often
adorned different silks.

By this stage in the century painting and
embroidery provided delicate alternatives to
brocading on fashion silks. Their popularity
dated to about mid-century and originated in
the growing interest in imported printed cottons
and the setting up of print-works in France (see
II, 26). Painting and embroidery were typical of
innovations in textiles during the century:
neither required profound changes in weaving
technology as they could both be applied to
fabric weaves already in existence. Painted and
embroidered silks cost as much as brocaded
silks: even in the middle of the century Nicholas

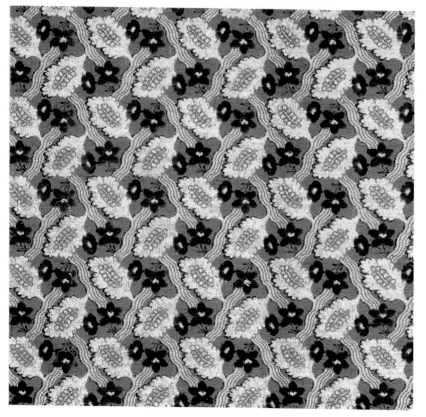

Joubert de l'Hiberderie (b. 1729), author of a treatise on silk design (1765) and a designer himself, considered *chiné* (warp-painted silk) an expensive form of patterning, comparable with brocading.

The silks used for men's clothing were often similar to women's dress fabrics, but there was also a range of fabrics especially for men's suiting, often carrying a small lozenge-shaped repeat pattern. Such fabric was heavier in weight than most of the brocaded silks used in ladies' dresses, because the patterning was close and heavily textured across the width of the fabric. Suiting frequently contained woollen yarn to give added strength and durability. The colours could be very bright, and the motifs were often floral.

On the whole furnishing fabrics seem to have developed parallel with but separate from dress silks. They continued to use large patterns in keeping with the walls they adorned, introducing new motifs of suitable dimensions to fit the changing mood of the times. Thus, in the 1760s, neo-classical features began to flourish, and medallions, garlands, trophies, musical instruments and wildfowl replaced the more traditional point repeats of the early years of the century. Furnishing design was not as transient as dress-silk patterns, and red, yellow and green damask remained popular throughout the period. Even elaborate silks had fairly long lives as furnishings. For example, the 1730 commission for Versailles was not hung until 1775, and the order for Marie Antoinette's bedchamber was hung during the first Empire. The copyright law of 1787 underlined the difference in lifespan between furnishings and dress, patenting furnishings for fifteen years and dress fabrics for only six years.

Changes in the designs on silks were the result of changes in taste rather than changes in technology, and of consumer demand for novelty – a demand which delighted and encouraged designers, manufacturers and retailers.

ABOVE LEFT **214** *Chiné* taffeta with a pattern of lozenges filled with vases of flowers and fleurs-de-lys. *Chiné* patterns were governed by the same copyright legislation as brocaded patterns from 1766 onwards – the period at which they were particularly fashionable.

LEFT **215** Cut velvet with a lamé ground. The small lozenge pattern in red and gold is typical of some of the luxurious silks used for men's suiting in the middle of the 18th century.

22   Figured linen damasks

Figured damasks produced in and around The Netherlands between the sixteenth and eighteenth centuries are interesting historical documents for a number of reasons. Firstly, several commemorate events such as battle victories and coronations; some were commissioned by kings, bishops and other influential holders of office. Heraldic crests, mottoes and dates are invariably incorporated. Inscriptions sometimes identify the person for whom the piece was woven, the weaver and the town in which the cloth was made, the action of the event, and occasionally include lines of appropriate verse. These prized, fine linens were handed down through generations and were often presented as gifts – for example, on the occasion of marriage. Made in sets and used as table-linen, they were objects of ritual belonging to a privileged sector of society, because they were extremely expensive to produce and because they required meticulous care and attention by household servants.

Although the name of Holland is synonymous with linen cloth, and Haarlem in particular was an eminent centre of linen damask production during the golden age of the seventeenth century, the centres of production did shift, in response to politico-religious circumstances and the rise and fall of Dutch commerce. The Irish linen-damask industry was much encouraged by Louis Crommelin, a French Huguenot weaver who fled from Picardy following the revocation of the Edict of Nantes in 1685. In the eighteenth century Gross-Schönau in Saxony also became an important centre of damask production.

By the sixteenth century fine damask weaving was a professional activity, located in strictly organised urban workshops. Coexistent was the plain weaving of linen and hemp in a cottage industry which produced yarn and cloth at a subsistence level, mostly for domestic consumption. Figured linen damasks were woven on drawlooms, often imitating the floral designs of Italian silk damasks. The predecessors of these cloths were woven with little all-over goose-eye and chevron patterns, generally known as diapers. The simplest of these could be woven on a four-shaft loom, though some were much more complicated. Indeed, the linen table-cloths associated with Perugia in Italy were often of this diaper type but were additionally embellished with striking horizontal bands of figures, created by a supplementary weft of indigo-dyed cotton. One such table-cloth is depicted by Domenico Ghirlandaio (1449–94) in his *Last Supper*, dated 1480 (Florence, Ognissanti).

Designs were drawn from the repertoire of, on the one hand, figured medieval silks featuring the 'Tree of Life', paired birds and animals, and, on the other, Renaissance vegetal and floral forms developed in late fifteenth- and early sixteenth-century Italy. Italian damasks and velvets would have arrived in Flanders via the port of Bruges; and it was in nearby Courtrai (Kortrijk) that the first workshops for linen-damask weaving were set up. However, owing to the religious intolerance of Spain in the south Netherlands from around 1580, the weavers – Protestants – fled northwards to the United Dutch Provinces.

In the early seventeenth century plant forms continued to dominate the designs, though sometimes figures and animals interact: peacocks and cockerels strut about, birds peck at fruit, and the ancient 'Tree of Life' device provides a focal point towards which confronted

216 White linen damask napkin designed by Pasquier Lammertijn, 1602.

185

pairs of human figures and birds are turned. By the second half of the century, however, figures play the prominent role. In the central panel of a table-cloth there may be as many as six different scenes, arranged in horizontal bands and repeated up the length of the cloth. Delicate

217 Detail from a large cover depicting the seasons. The roses and pomegranates, reflect a mixture of north European and Mediterranean motifs. 3rd quarter of the 17th century.

borders include pomegranates, grapes, tulips and other flowers taken from herbals, which also featured in embroidery of the same period. Some feature simple, meandering tendrils; others have more sophisticated arabesque or grotesque arrangements.

Graphic scenes include mythical characters such as Orpheus and Old Testament favourites, including Cain and Abel, Samson and Solomon. They are framed by vines or other formalised plants sometimes growing from urns; alternatively, figures may be placed in an architectural setting. The subject-matter is historicised by the presence of oriental- or Roman-looking costumed figures, closely resembling those which appear in Brussels tapestries of the same date, or a little earlier.

In the eighteenth century the architectural and outdoor scenes look more panoramic; designs tend to be less cramped. Plant and architectural devices are not so much used as a framework for the design motif but repeat across the whole width of the central panel, giving an illusion of movement across the cloth. This arrangement is especially effective in processional scenes or souvenir cloths of Amsterdam, London, Paris and Venice depicting the river or canal frontages with bird's-eye views of the city behind.

At the same time much more attention is paid to wider, symmetrical borders, with motifs carefully angled into the corners. In napkins and cloths of square format floral designs and emblems are arranged concentrically, sometimes with a centrally placed medallion encasing a key motif or inscription. Many designs reflect the evolution of French silk design from lace patterns to Philippe Lasalle (see II, 21). Similarly, in the first half of the nineteenth century linen damasks adopt the neo-classical themes found in the other decorative arts. However, although linen and silk damasks – in Holland at least – were woven in the same workshops (the common element being the figure harness), designs in linen often lagged behind fashions for silk.

The sources of design, though often related to contemporary silks, were not exclusively imitative of Italian (and later French) woven textiles. For example, one very large table-cloth commemorating the coronation of George II (1683–1760) in 1727 (discovered in Winchester Cathedral in 1981) is based on popular woodcut prints published in a booklet which explained the order of ceremony and significance of the ancient crowning ritual in Westminster Abbey. Made in Waringstown, County Down, Ireland, the cloth was woven in one piece, measuring 3.4 × 2.7 m (11 × 9 ft). The workshop would not have had time to set up the loom afresh for such a large commission if the complex work was to be completed in time. Therefore all the figures – even their identities – were taken from visual records of the coronation of George I (1660–1727) thirteen years earlier. Only the date and George II's name have been added.

Damask cloths were always made in sets.

Each set typically comprised a large table-cloth, twelve napkins, a cupboard cloth and a long towel for a servant to carry over an arm or shoulder or to present to a guest for drying his hands when the washing bowl was passed round. Some literary references and diaries give

adequate sets of table-linen to see the top table of the household through to the end of the week.

In Holland extensive fields were devoted to 'grassing' (laying out) newly woven cloth, for exposure to sun, air and dew. In this way the lye (water alkalised with fern, wood ash or kelp)

218 Historical events are featured on much table-linen to have survived from the 18th century. This is a detail of a linen damask table-cloth depicting the coronation of George II, though the image is based on woodcut illustrations of his predecessor's coronation procession. Irish, early 18th century.

an idea of how the cloths were used. For example, Erasmus of Rotterdam (1466–1536), in his *De civilitate morum puerilium* of 1530, noted the function of the napkin in a period when forks were not used, and, although spoons were provided, the guest might have to bring his own knife: 'If a serviette is given, lay it on your left shoulder or arm. . . . If you are offered something liquid taste it and return the spoon, but first wipe it on your serviette. To lick greasy fingers or wipe them on your coat is impolite. It is better to use the tablecloth or the serviette.'

Initial bleaching and subsequent laundering were essential processes in the art of damask and, along with the design, one of the reasons why these cloths were so highly treasured. Their figured patterns could not be read without a play of light on the warp- and weft-faced surfaces. This meant treating the linen to a smooth finish. These damasks distinguished the upper classes. The luxury of pristine cleanliness at each time of use necessitated wealth – to afford servants skilled in this specialised task – and

was left to activate on the cloth for up to two weeks, before the cloth was 'soured' in a weak solution of acid to neutralise it. The cloth was then beetled, or pounded, to bring out the surface shine. Laundering linen – the only aspect of household duties entirely controlled by female servants – involved the same processes as the final stages of finishing – and, in addition, they starched the cloth to help it resist dirt.

During the eighteenth century the Dutch damask industry declined, owing to the success of foreign weaving centres and consequent reduction in exports, the reduced commercial activity and fortunes of Dutch traders, and perhaps also the competition from cotton which was gathering momentum. In particular, Saxony enjoyed the recognition which had once been Holland's. The linen-damask industry was one of the last to adapt to modern methods of chemical processing and power-driven production; but now that it has, it is enjoying a renaissance – though not so much in table-cloths as in designer fashion and furnishings.

23 Tapestry

RIGHT 219 'The Month of
January' from *Les très riches
heures du duc de Berry*.
Illumination, *c*. 1415. The
walls of the banqueting
chamber are hung with a
large pictorial tapestry.

The need for the collaboration of skilled weavers and the high cost of wages and materials have ensured that large-scale tapestry production has traditionally depended upon organised workshops, either subsidised by rich patrons, or funded by wealthy merchants who could afford to wait several years for a return on their investment. Consequently, although tapestry is an ancient craft, the turbulent social and economic conditions of the early medieval period probably account for the fact that, with the exception of isolated production in monasteries, no significant industry developed in Europe until the early fourteenth century.

From around 1300 archival records show that tapestries with simple emblematic and decorative motifs were being woven in Paris and Arras. Initially this industry was small, but under the enthusiastic patronage of the French and Burgundian nobility it seems to have expanded rapidly after 1350, and surviving inventories indicate that from this date tapestries were mostly pictorial. Some doubt has existed as to the relative importance of Paris and Arras because several of the most important tapestry merchants lived in Paris, but it is clear that by the end of the century Arras had become the main centre of production, specialising in high-quality tapestries which often included gold and silver thread. As this unfamiliar luxury product was exported around Europe, the name of the town became synonymous with the article. In Britain high-quality tapestry was called 'arras' well into the seventeenth century, irrespective of its origin, and in Italy tapestries are still called *arazzi*.

OPPOSITE TOP 220 Detail of 'The Otter and Swan Hunt', one of the four so-called *Devonshire Hunting Tapestries*. Arras, *c*. 1450, wool. Whole: 4.24 × 11.18 m (13.9 × 36.7 ft).

Late fourteenth- and early fifteenth-century accounts record the huge sums that the Burgundian and French nobility spent on this art form, and their enthusiasm is easy to understand. Part of the appeal was practical. Tapestries were easily portable and therefore well suited to the peripatetic life-style of the northern courts, providing a means for insulating and decorating the coldest and gloomiest castle. In addition, tapestry was a potent vehicle of propaganda, both because it was expensive and therefore impressive, and because of the opportunity it provided for political display in an age in which the pictorial image was rare. Perhaps most importantly tapestry was appreciated as an art form in its own right. It was an expensive equivalent to fresco, which was inappropriate to the damp

OPPOSITE 221 'St Michael fighting the Dragon', detail from the third panel of the so-called *Angers Apocalypse*. Arras (?), *c*. 1375–80, wool. Detail: 1.7 × 2.5 m (5.6 × 8.2 ft).

northern climate anyway, and the size of the collections amassed by the nobility of the day, which far exceeded their practical needs, reflects their love of the art.

Very few of these early tapestries survive, their raw materials having made them extremely vulnerable to the ravages of time in the form of wear and tear, light, mould, rats and moths. In addition, tapestries which included gold thread were frequently burnt in later periods in order to extract their precious metal. Those that have survived, such as the vast fragments of the Angers *Apocalypse* (woven *c*.1373–80), indicate the sophistication which the industry had already attained by the end of the fourteenth century. Like the manuscript illuminations of the day the earliest tapestry designs were unconcerned with realism, instead placing large stylised figures against decorative backgrounds. However, in line with contemporary artistic developments tapestry design reflects an increasing interest in narrative and naturalistic detail from the end of the century. Tapestries from the first third of the fifteenth century are characterised by the way in which pockets of narrative are arranged all over the tapestry surface, separated by areas of stylised foliage and rocks, in an arrangement which ensured that the whole of the tapestry was of decorative interest.

During the second third of the fifteenth century Arras was replaced by Tournai as the main centre of production and trade, although with-

out archival evidence it is practically impossible to distinguish between their products, or those of other new centres like Lille, Bruges and Brussels. Philip the Good (1396–1467), Duke of Burgundy, was one of the most influential patrons of the Tournai ateliers, and it is apparent from contemporary chronicles that tapestry was an integral element of the display and propaganda for which his court was notorious. For example, he had a huge tapestry of the *History of Gideon*, patron saint of his chivalric order, woven between 1449 and 1453 for use on ceremonial occasions, and when he visited Paris in 1461 we are told that the Parisians queued night and day to see the *Gideon* and *Alexander* tapestries, which were hung on the façade of the Hôtel d'Artois were he was staying.

The tapestry production of Arras, Tournai and other contemporary centres was controlled by a handful of extremely wealthy merchants who were equally involved in the trade of wine and cloth and in civil administration. One of the most important Tournai merchants of the second half of the fifteenth century was one Pasquier Grenier (active 1447, d. 1493). Typically, Grenier did not have any workshops of his own. Rather, he owned tapestry cartoons, in

222 *Scenes from the War of Troy*, originally the ninth of a set of eleven tapestries. Tournai, *c.* 1480, wool and silk. 4.16 × 7.37 m (13.65 × 24.18 ft).

effect the copyright of a design, which he would farm out to independent workshops with advances for wages and materials as and when he received commissions. The most famous of his cartoons were those for a *History of the Trojan War*, of which sets were owned by many of the leading rulers of the day, including Charles the Bold (1433–77), Duke of Burgundy, Henry VII (1457–1509), King of England, and Federigo Montefeltro, Duke of Urbino. These tapestries illustrate the crowded compositions which characterise tapestry design in the second half of the fifteenth century, with static court scenes interspersed with violent battles.

During the second half of the fifteenth century Brussels became the focus of Burgundian court life with the consequence that the town became

a centre of artistic talent and patronage. A separate tapestry guild had been established in the town in 1447, and with these advantages the Brussels industry was to dominate the high-quality tapestry market by the end of the century. Strong guild restrictions guaranteed the high material quality of Brussels tapestries, whilst that of the designs was ensured by the fact that in 1476 the painters' guild of St Luke obtained a monopoly over the production of new cartoons. During the next forty years Brussels weavers became increasingly sophisticated and specialised in order to embody the pictorial standards of the cartoons from which they were working. Yet, despite the artistic developments which were being made in Italy during this period, tapestry design retained a

conservative character in which the emphasis continued to be decorative, with scenes arranged all over the tapestry surface, and with static figures in elaborate costumes arranged close to the picture plane. It was, after all, an expensive, traditional art form, and style was dictated by the tastes and requirements of the wealthy patrons.

A revolution in tapestry design was precipitated between 1516 and 1530 by the execution of several series of cartoons painted by or after designs by Raphael (1483–1520) and his pupils, which were sent to the leading Brussels atelier of the day by order of Pope Leo X (1475–1521) and his successor, Clement VII (1523–34). These cartoons, of which the first and most famous were Raphael's *Acts of the Apostles* (designed 1515–17, woven 1516–21), introduced northern patrons and tapestry designers to the developments of the Italian Renaissance. During the 1530s this influence encouraged the leading Brussels designers, of whom the most important was Bernard van Orley (*c.*1491–1542), to develop a style in which the traditional Flemish interest in narrative and detail was combined with Italianate interests in spatial and aerial perspective, and dramatic monumental figures. The combination was well suited to the medium and resulted in a period of extra-

ABOVE RIGHT **223** *The Triumph of Christ*, Brussels, *c.* 1500, wool, silk, gold and silver thread. Whole: 3.3 × 4.07 m (10.8 × 13.4 ft). A detail (RIGHT) shows one of the angels.

ordinarily varied tapestry design, which ranged between the parameters of extreme conservatism, Italianate mannerism and northern realism.

This revolution in tapestry design coincided with a period of unprecedented demand for tapestries. Via the annual fairs at Antwerp and Bergen-op-Zoom expensive Brussels tapestries and cheaper pieces from Enghien, Oudenarde and other centres were exported all over Europe. The most important patronage continued to come from the northern sovereigns for whom tapestry remained one of the principal elements in the competitive court display of the day, as well as a much-prized art form. Charles V (1500–58), the Holy Roman Emperor, owned tapestry series commemorating the great military campaigns of his reign, such as the *Battle of Pavia* (fought 1525, woven *c*.1530), at which his forces defeated those of the French king, and a vast twelve-piece set of his crusade against the Sultan Khair-ed-Din Barbarossa, known as the *Conquest of Tunis* (woven 1548–53). The French king François I (1494–1547) bought Brussels tapestries designed by the leading Italian artists of the age, including a twenty-two piece *Hannibal and Scipio* partially designed by Giulio Romano (*c*.1492–1546). In Britain Henry VIII (1491–1547) was just as enthusiastic a connoisseur; when he died the Crown collection included over 2,000 tapestries.

The remarkable number of high-quality tapestries produced in Brussels during these years depended upon an economic climate in which patrons and merchants felt secure to invest large sums in projects which might take years to produce. This security was entirely disrupted by the religious persecution and civil war into which The Netherlands were plunged in the last four decades of the sixteenth century. Apart from direct consequences, such as the sacking and looting of the Antwerp tapestry market by Spanish troops in 1576, the long-term effects were profound. Many skilled weavers left the southern Netherlands to re-establish themselves in Holland and Germany, or further afield. This both depleted the pool of skill on which the Brussels industry had depended and diverted to other centres much of the patronage which had previously been channelled to Brussels.

The consequence of this disruption was that whilst the history of high-quality production in the sixteenth century was dominated by the Brussels industry it thenceforth became much more diverse. By the end of the century new centres in Holland, particularly that of Delft, were already vying with Brussels for commissions from British and Dutch patrons. An entirely new source of competition emerged in the opening years of the seventeenth century when the French king, Henri IV (1533–1610), established an industry in Paris staffed almost entirely with Flemish weavers whom he had at-

tracted to the city with the promise of generous rewards. By the founding contract of 1607 the directors of this manufactory, Marc Comans and Frans van der Plancken, undertook to maintain an industry of eighty looms, sixty in Paris and twenty in Amiens, in return for various privileges, including a ban on the import of all Flemish tapestries for fifteen years. Inspired by this example the British king, James I (1566–1625), and his son Charles, Prince of Wales (1600–49), also established a manufactory at Mortlake near London in 1619. This too was staffed by Flemish weavers, and it was to produce some of the finest tapestries of the day before Charles's execution removed the source of funding on which its quality production depended.

Faced with this competition the Flemish tapestry guilds introduced strict laws to prevent further emigration, and the Regents of The Netherlands, Albert (1559–1621) and Isabella, provided the leading ateliers with financial aid and numerous commissions. Although Brussels had lost the lead in the high-quality market, these allowances, combined with the strong tradition which the town commanded in this field, ensured that it continued to dominate the commercial market for medium-quality tapestries. During the 1630s, 40s and 50s cartoons by Rubens (1577–1640), Jordaens (1593–1678) and their pupils provided the industry with dramatic and fashionable designs which by limiting the details and atmospheric affects they required,

226 'The Enemy Sortie from La Goleta', one of twelve *Conquest of Tunis* tapestries depicting Charles V's campaign of 1535, designed by Jan Cornelisz Vermeyen. Brussels, workshop of Willem de Pannemaker, 1546–54, wool, silk, and silver and gold thread. 5.24 × 9.37 m (17.19 × 30.74 ft).

OPPOSITE ABOVE 224 'The Miraculous Draught of Fishes' from the *Acts of the Apostles*, designed by Raphael for the Sistine Chapel. Brussels, workshop of Pieter van Aelst, *c.* 1517–20, wool and silk. 4.92 × 5.12 m (16.14 × 16.80 ft).

OPPOSITE BELOW 225 'The Month of March', one of the twelve tapestries known as the *Hunts of Maximilian*, designed by Bernard van Orley. Brussels, workshop of Jan Ghieteels (?) *c.* 1530–5, wool, silk, and silver and gold thread.
4.4 × 7.5 m (14.4 × 24.6 ft).

and by having large borders and restricted landscapes, could be produced on a successful commercial basis.

The greatest products of the day, however, came from the Paris workshops. The generous conditions granted by Henri IV and his successor, Louis XIII (1601–43), combined with the popularity of designs by Rubens, Simon Vouet (1590–1649) and other leading artists, had already ensured the industry's success during the first half of the century. In 1662–3 Jean-Baptiste Colbert (1619–83), Louis XIV's finance minister, amalgamated the existing Parisian ateliers at the Gobelins site, where they were joined in 1667 by

227 'The Battle of Milvian Bridge', one of a set of twelve tapestries of *The History of Constantine*, designed by Peter Paul Rubens. Paris, Saint Marcel workshop, *c.* 1623–5, wool, silk, and silver and gold thread. 3.25 × 5.35 m (10.66 × 17.55 ft).

the best of Parisian craftsmen from other industries. Overall direction of these workshops was placed in the hands of Charles Le Brun (1619–90) and their product was reserved exclusively for Louis XIV (1638–1715), in order to provide suitable furnishing for the sumptuous palaces in which he staged his court. Working with a team of artists and specialist cartoonists, much in the way that the great sixteenth-century cartoon workshops must have operated, Le Brun produced designs for several series of tapestries which featured either Louis XIV in person, such as the *L'Histoire du Roi* series (first weaving begun 1665), or mythological and historical figures with whom Louis wished to be identified. Colbert also set up workshops at Beauvais in 1664 to provide tapestries for the commercial market, and in 1665 existing ateliers at Aubusson received official support to promote the production of cheaper tapestries.

The example being set by the French court ensured that the use of tapestry remained fashionable throughout Europe. Baroque taste called for new or antique 'large-figure' tapestries

in state and formal apartments, whilst 'small-figure', light-hearted tapestries were considered suitable for more private apartments. In France tapestries for the commercial market came from Beauvais and Aubusson. The rest of Europe could buy medium-quality or cheap tapestries from centres such as Antwerp and Oudenarde, and high-quality tapestries were once again being produced for the commercial market by the Brussels workshops. Indeed, during the 1690–1740 period the Brussels workshops seem to have enjoyed something of a second renaissance. The historical and mythological designs of cartoonists such as Lambert de Hondt (*op.*1679) and Jan van Orley (1665–1735) were exactly suited to the grandiose taste of the late baroque period, whilst genre designs derived from the paintings of David Teniers the Younger (1610–90) were extremely popular for more informal settings.

During the first half of the eighteenth century the Gobelins provided the inspiration, and in some cases the weavers, for new workshops in Madrid, Munich, Naples, Rome and St Petersburg, although it should be noted that the product of these was largely reserved for the founding patrons. In Britain the Mortlake works, which had never really recovered from the effects of the Civil War, was officially closed in 1703, but independent workshops in London enjoyed a moderate success in the first half of the century, providing decorative hangings for the domestic market.

In France the tapestry industry adapted with ease to the change of taste which accompanied the accession of Louis XV (1710–74). Tapestry was entirely appropriate for the light and decorative interiors of the rococo style, and the Beauvais works enjoyed great commercial success with the pastoral designs of Jean-Baptise Oudry (1686–1755) and François Boucher (1703–70). The popularity of Boucher's work led to his appointment in 1755 as Inspector of Works at the Gobelins, where his most important design was a collaborative venture known as *Boucher aux Alentours* (design completed 1764). This involved *en suite trompe l'oeil* tapestry furnishings for walls and furniture, and several series were subsequently exported to England for use in houses designed by Robert Adam (1728–92). Examples survive at both Osterley Park and Newby.

Generally speaking the demand for tapestry began to decline during the second third of the eighteenth century. In Britain tapestry had been well suited to Palladian interiors but from the 1730s it faced increasing competition from the display of painting collections and the new fashion for Chinese wallpaper. Besides, the practical appeal of tapestry was no longer rele-

228 'King Louis XIV visiting the Gobelins Manufactories' (15 October 1667), one of a set of fourteen tapestries of *The History of Louis XIV*, designed by Charles Le Brun. Gobelins (Paris), 1673–9, wool, silk and gold thread. 4.9 × 6.88 m (16 × 22.6 ft).

vant in the comfortable and well-heated interiors of eighteenth-century houses, and tapestry production was an increasingly expensive option. Whilst the decoration of very large houses such as Holkham and Houghton still led to commissions for several suites of tapestries, many lesser houses relegated their tapestries to one or two rooms, leading to the concept of the tapestry room, now a familiar feature in many British country houses. The consequence of declining demand was that the last weaving ateliers in London closed in the 1780s. On the Continent the effect of changing fashions was similar, and the last Brussels atelier also closed in the 1780s.

Continuing court patronage allowed both the Gobelins and the Beauvais works to produce a number of designs adapted to the neo-classical taste of the reign of Louis XVI (1754–93) but the French Revolution destroyed the clientele upon which the workshops depended. Whilst scaled-down versions of both works were subsequently maintained during the nineteenth century and continue to this day, their limited production

has largely been reserved for use in government buildings. The Aubusson industry was equally affected by the Revolution and during the last quarter of the eighteenth century converted almost entirely to the production of tapestry carpets.

Thus, by the early nineteenth century tapestry had, in effect, become an art form of the past, of which the surviving examples were subject to the whims and taste of those who inherited them, and it was between 1790 and 1850 that many of the most appalling acts of vandalism and neglect were perpetrated against surviving masterpieces. In 1797, for example, twenty-six of the greatest antique sets in the French State Collection were burnt to extract their gold thread, whilst a similar disdain for tapestry is indicated by the fate of the Angers *Apocalypse*, which was cut up and used as insulation in an orangerie.

Interest in tapestry revived, however, in the second half of the nineteenth century. Antiquarian research began to draw attention to the historical importance of the art, whilst apprecia-

ABOVE **229** 'The Charlatan and the Peep
Show', one of eight tapestries in the
Fêtes Italiens series, designed by
François Boucher, 1734–46, and
a detail (LEFT). Beauvais, *c.* 1762,
wool and silk. Whole: 3.24 × 4.17 m
(10.63 × 13.68 ft).

tion of its aesthetic potential was spurred by various attempts to revive the industry. The first of these was the workshop established under royal patronage at Windsor (1876–90), with French weavers who had left France at the time of the Franco–Prussian war. The Windsor works were not a commercial success but they were significant in that they promoted interest in the art on both sides of the Atlantic. The display of

Windsor tapestries at the Chicago World Fair in 1893 provided the furnishing entrepreneur William Baumgarten with the inspiration to set up his own manufactory (established New York, 1893; subsequently moved to Williamsbridge; closed 1912), which was partially staffed by ex-Windsor weavers.

The revival of interest in tapestry was also fuelled by the attentions of the Arts and Crafts

to the simplicity of palette and design of gothic tapestries. His theories were embodied in the beautiful designs of Edward Burne-Jones (1833–98), such as the *Holy Grail* series, of which the first set was completed in 1894 for Stanmore Hall, home of the industrialist William Knox D'Arcy. The expense of the weaving process largely limited Merton Abbey production to commissioned work, but if its output was restricted its influence was considerable, and during the first decades of the twentieth century it provided the inspiration for the establishment of several new ateliers, including the Herter workshops (established New York, 1908) and the Dovecot Studios in Edinburgh (established 1912, still producing tapestries for the commercial market).

Since then changing tastes and changing living spaces have restricted demand for tapestries, but there has been enough to maintain a steady market in both antique and modern tapestries. During the 1930s and 40s a second tapestry revival was championed at Aubusson by the French artist Jean Lurçat (1892–1966), who rejected pictorial weaving in favour of abstract and decorative motifs. Lurçat's work, primarily executed at the Aubusson workshops, inspired a generation of weavers, and in the last thirty years respect has continued to grow for independent weavers producing one-off works of tapestry art.

ABOVE 231 The dining room at Stanmore Hall, Middlesex, photographed in 1899 and showing 'The Beckoning' from *The Holy Grail* series, designed by Edward Burne-Jones and woven at the Merton Abbey workshops, 1890–6, wool and silk (the tapestries have since been dispersed).

Movement. Along with carpet weaving and embroidery tapestry was one of the textile crafts which captured the attention of William Morris (1834–96), and after various experiments in the late 1870s the Merton Abbey Tapestry Workshop was founded in 1881. Rejecting the sophisticated pictorial and illusionistic effects of the Gobelins and Windsor manufactories, which took pains to reproduce a painted cartoon as accurately as possible, Morris sought to return

RIGHT 232 General view of the *Song of the World* tapestry sequence, designed by Jean Lurçat. Aubusson, Tabard workshop, 1957–66, wool, nine panels with a total of 500 square m (5,382 square ft) and an average height of 4.35 m (14.27 ft).

OPPOSITE 230 The tapestry room at Osterley Park, Middlesex, hung with Gobelins tapestries from the so-called *Boucher aux Alentours* series, designed by François Boucher in collaboration with other artists, 1758–63. Gobelins, 1775–6 (this weaving), wool and silk.

24 Embroidery

Two details from the Creation hanging (OPPOSITE), depicting Christ as Ruler of the World (TOP), and the creatures of the sea and the birds that fly (ABOVE).

Circa 1000–1500

It is clear from the quality of the few surviving examples that European embroidery was highly developed before the close of the first millennium AD, although the evidence on which to build a comprehensive picture of its development before 1500 is patchy. None the less, some general points can be made. The importance of embroidery as a decorative technique was ensured by the rarity and high cost of patterned woven silks, which until the thirteenth century were largely imported from the Byzantine Empire and the Islamic Near East. The richest embroidery materials also had to be imported, and their use in any country indicated a certain degree of wealth. Throughout Europe most embroideries were made from wool and linen in a variety of techniques, some now represented by a single chance survival – for example, the Bayeux Tapestry. The more routine pieces seldom survive, although some groups have been preserved within the static convent communities in which they were made.

Noble households and convents played an important part in the production of embroideries, although it is not true that they were the main source of professional pieces. Secular workshops, employing both men and women, existed from the beginning of the period and became increasingly important as towns grew, the guild system became established, and international trade developed. Professional embroideries were made within communities of craftsmen, and the designs were often the work of artists working in other disciplines. They reflected the steady evolution of styles from Byzantine to Romanesque, from Gothic to Renaissance.

Embroidery was used for furnishings and for dress, for ceremonial and domestic purposes, and in the service of the Church and the State. Yet, with few exceptions, what survives is ecclesiastical or, if secular, owes its survival to having been given to the Church. This is true of some of the earliest and most spectacular pieces, all embroidered on silk grounds with silk and metal threads. They include the Star Mantle of the Holy Roman Emperors, which was given to Bamberg Cathedral by Henry II (1002–24) or his wife, St Kunigund, two of whose mantles are also in the Cathedral, and the coronation mantle of the Hungarian kings which, in a reversal of the normal practice, was made from a chasuble

given to the church of Székesfehérvár by King Stephen and Queen Gisela in 1031. Whether worked, like the Bamberg pieces, in southern Germany or in Hungary, it is a splendid example of Germanic Romanesque art with Byzantine overtones (National Museum, Budapest).

Byzantine influence was much stronger in those parts of Europe which had been, or still were, part of the Byzantine or Islamic Empires. The so-called chasuble of Thomas à Becket (Fermo Cathedral) is decorated with a pattern common in Byzantine and Near Eastern woven silks and, according to the Kufic inscription embroidered on it, was worked in Almería in Islamic Spain in 1116. The spectacular coronation mantle of the Holy Roman Emperors (Schatzkammer, Vienna) similarly has a Kufic inscription stating that it was made in the royal workshops of Palermo in 1133/34 for the Norman, Roger II (1095–1154), who was made King of Sicily in 1130 (see II, 5 and II, 17). Despite their daunting cost, woven silks and metal threads were not confined to southern Europe; English embroidery (*opus Anglicanum*) of the eleventh to thirteenth centuries was worked almost entirely in gold thread on a silk twill. The patterns often incorporated foliate scrolls and small animals reminiscent of those on the woven silks, although the stiff hieratic figures are purely Romanesque. These highly prized gold embroideries were traded throughout Europe.

The impression that all early medieval embroideries were so rich is corrected by the few pieces made of plainer materials, including the Bayeux Tapestry. This vigorous account of the Norman Conquest of England in 1066 is worked on a linen ground with wool in laid and couched work, chain, stem and split stitches. The scenes stand out against the plain linen ground, unlike those on another eleventh-century embroidery, the Creation hanging in Gerona Cathedral, Spain. This magnificent Catalan embroidery has a wool twill ground entirely covered with couched wool and a little linen thread. Although now unique, both objects have affinities, if not direct links, with other pieces: the form of laid and couched work on the Bayeux Tapestry also features in Scandinavian and Icelandic wall-hangings of the fourteenth to sixteenth centuries, although their woollen grounds are entirely hidden, as in the Gerona hanging.

This is also the case with the linen-based hangings which have survived in Germany, in-

233 The Creation hanging from Gerona Cathedral. Catalonia, 11th century. Woollen twill embroidered with wools in couched work, stem, chain and a little satin stitch.
3.65 × 4.6 m (12 × 15 ft).
In the centre, Christ as Ruler of the World (see top detail OPPOSITE) is surrounded by scenes of the Creation, the rivers of Paradise and, in the border, Annus, the four Seasons, the Months, the Sun and the Moon. In the damaged area at the bottom is depicted the Finding of the True Cross. (See details OPPOSITE.)

cluding a group spanning the fourteenth and fifteenth centuries in the Convent of Wienhausen in Lower Saxony. Although predominantly ecclesiastical, the group includes one piece of about 1300 which tells the story of Tristram. All pieces are embroidered with coloured wools in a form of couched work, understandably called *klosterstich* (convent stitch), which was used throughout Germany, Austria and Switzerland, although not always for religious pieces. Distinctly secular, for example, are two hangings of which one, embroidered in Bavaria in about 1370 (Regensburg Museum), is decorated with roundels containing pairs of lovers, and the other, probably worked in Franconia, about 1470 (Nuremberg Museum), shows lovers and musicians beneath trees.

Convent stitch was one of the wide range of stitches employed in working the white linen embroideries that also survive in Lower Saxony.

Drawn-thread work was sometimes used for substantial areas, as on a thirteenth-century altar frontal from Heiningen. Although now appearing all white, details and outlines were often embroidered with coloured silks and occasionally wool, but these frailer materials have tended to drop out or fade. That white linen embroidery was common throughout Europe is clear from the inventories and the survival of one or two pieces in almost every country. Ecclesiastical subjects dominate, but some, such as the late twelfth-century cover from Lombardy in the Vatican Museum, have geometric or purely ornamental designs. Others, like the fourteenth-century Swiss table-cover from the convent of Feldberg, have more fanciful secular subjects.

Surviving mainly in Germany, Austria and Switzerland are linen-based embroideries in which the ground is entirely covered with silk and a little metal thread, mainly in long-armed

201

ABOVE **234** Detail of a linen table-cover, embroidered with linen thread and a little coloured silk in satin, brick, eyelet and plait stitches. Switzerland, 14th century. The motifs include fanciful figures, mythical beasts and other animals. From the Convent of Feldberg in Switzerland, but probably originally made for secular use. Whole: 105 × 308 cm (41.3 × 121 in).

ABOVE **235** Detail of a woollen cover in inlaid patchwork and appliqué, with details in couched leather strip. Sweden, early 15th century. From Dalhem Church, Småland, but originally made for secular use.

ing. The linen grounds were entirely covered, usually with silver-gilt threads couched in diaper or more elaborate patterns.

Although rightly famed, *opus Anglicanum* was not alone; the French embroiderers, also working with silks and metal threads in split and underside couching, produced masterpieces of Gothic art. By 1300 the city-states of Italy were thriving, and in Rome, Florence, Venice and Milan the fruitful co-operation of embroiderers and other craftsmen resulted in embroideries like the frontal, signed and dated by the embroiderer 'Jacopo di Cambi 1336', in the style of Bernardo Daddi (*c.*1290–1350), a follower of Giotto (1267–1337). Later Florentine embroideries were to illustrate the growth of naturalism, which was one aspect of the developing

cross, stem, brick and satin stitches. All are ecclesiastical and include the set of vestments (now in Vienna) made for the Convent of Göss in Austria under the direction of the Abbess Kunigund (1239–69). In addition to the main figurative subjects they are decorated in part with geometric patterns not unlike those on some fourteenth- and fifteenth-century cushions from Westphalia. Worked on linen canvas in brick and long-armed cross stitches, they mark an early stage in the long history of canvaswork embroidery.

Other techniques employing wool and linen are represented only by token pieces, one of the most spectacular being the huge linen cover made in Sicily about 1400 (divided between the Victoria and Albert Museum, London, and the Palazzo Davanzati, Florence). It tells the story of Tristram with pictures and inscriptions, both in heavily padded quilting. The Tristram legend is also the subject of a north German hanging of the late fourteenth century (Victoria and Albert Museum, London) of dark blue wool with applied decoration in coloured wools and gilt strip. Other examples of woollen patchwork include a seal bag of 1280 in Westminster Abbey, London, and several large pieces made in Scandinavia from the fifteenth to seventeenth centuries in the inlaid or intarsia technique.

Linen was the foundation for some of the most beautiful of all medieval embroideries – those worked in the professional workshops with coloured silks, gold and silver threads, pearls, stones and metal ornaments in a variety of techniques and styles. All surviving examples are ecclesiastical, and chief amongst them are the great *opus Anglicanum* vestments. By the late thirteenth century the silk twill ground of earlier pieces had been replaced by a fine linen that made easier the drawing and working of detailed figurative subjects with coloured silks and metal threads in split stitch and underside couch-

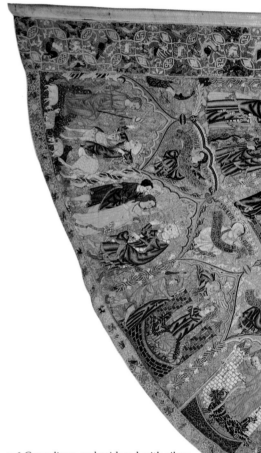

236 Cope; linen embroidered with silver and silver-gilt thread and silks in underside couching, split, tent, satin and overcast stitches, and originally ornamented with pearls. England, 1315–35. The silver-gilt thread is couched in decorative patterns including foliate scrolls and heraldic beasts. Arcades, arranged in concentric semi-circles, contain scenes from the lives of the Virgin, St Margaret and St Catherine. At the centre back is the Coronation of the Virgin. The cope was given to Pienza Cathedral in 1462 by Pope Pius II. 133.5 × 340.5 cm (52.5 × 134 in).

Detail of an altar frontal showing the 'Coronation of the Virgin', signed and dated 'Jacopo di Cambi, 1336'. Italy (Florence). Linen embroidered with silver-gilt thread and coloured silks in laid and couched work, with details in split and chain stitches and raised work. To either side of the central panel are seven saints and apostles, and on the super-frontal are scenes from the life of the Virgin. Whole: 105 × 425 cm (41.3 × 167.3 in).

the designs were based on the work of such artists as the Master of Flémalle (c.1378–1444), Rogier van der Weyden (c.1400–64) and Hugo van der Goes (active c.1467–82). The close links between The Netherlands and Spain resulted in *or nué* being taken up in the already flourishing workshops of Barcelona, Toledo, Seville and Valencia. It was to be employed on many of the superb embroideries produced during Spain's period of greatness following the unification of the country under Ferdinand (1479–1516) and Isabella (1475–1505).

Some of the most expressive of all ecclesiastical embroideries were those produced in Bohemia in the late fourteenth and early fifteenth centuries in which some small details were embroidered in raised work. This technique was developed in the later fifteenth century as realism became an aim, and three-dimensional embroideries were worked throughout Europe but most spectacularly in southern Germany, Bohemia, Hungary and Austria.

Plain velvet woven in Italy and Spain began to be used as a ground fabric in the later thirteenth century for both ecclesiastical and secular embroideries. Some idea of its richness is conveyed by a fragment of a pouch from the second half of the fourteenth century in the Musée des Tissus, Lyons, which depicts the return of the hunter to

ABOVE 238 Detail of an altar frontal showing the 'Mystical Marriage of St Catherine'. Netherlands (Brussels), mid-15th century. Linen embroidered with gold thread and coloured silks in *or nué*, split and satin stitches and with applied velvet, gold braid, pearls, topazes and sapphires. From the set of frontals and vestments given to the Order of the Golden Fleece by Philip the Good of Burgundy (1396–1467).

Renaissance style. It may have been due to the influence of the Dukes of Burgundy, who patronised both Italian and Flemish workshops, that the Flemish technique of *or nué* was introduced into Italy during the second half of the fifteenth century. Laid gold thread was couched with coloured silks to create naturalistic shaded effects and it was used, in conjunction with sharp perspective, in embroideries designed by artists such as Antonio del Pollaiuolo (c.1431–98), Sandro Botticelli (1440–1510) and Andrea del Sarto (1486–1530).

The *or nué* technique had been perfected early in the fifteenth century in the southern Netherlands under the patronage of the Dukes of Burgundy and it was used to spectacular effect on the set of vestments, worked during the second and third quarters of the century, which Philip the Good (1396–1467) presented to the Order of the Golden Fleece which he had founded in 1429. Almost certainly embroidered in Brussels,

240 Fragment of a velvet pouch, with applied linen embroidered with silver and silver-gilt thread and silks in couched work, satin, stem and split stitches, and ornamented with cabochons and spangles. France (possibly Paris), second half of the 14th century. Illustrated on the front is the return of the hunter to his lady, and on the back is a falconer. 21 × 20 cm (8.3 × 7.9 in).

ABOVE **241** Linen border embroidered with blue and yellow silk, the ground in tent stitch and the details of the voided pattern in back stitch. Putti are shown playing amongst the Renaissance foliage. Italy, late 16th century. 22 × 72 cm (8.7 × 28.3 in).

OPPOSITE **239** Orphrey; linen embroidered in high relief with applied gold brocade, gold thread and silks in couched work, stem and satin stitches, and ornamented with pearls. Austria, c. 1470. Depicted are the Virgin and Child with Saints Barbara, Dorothy, Catherine and Ursula. H (orphrey): 129 cm (50.8 in).

his lady. To achieve the fine detail the gold and silk embroidery was worked through a layer of linen laid on top of the velvet and subsequently cut away round the figures. By the mid-fifteenth century patterned velvet and brocaded silks from Spain and Italy were replacing embroidery in many areas. In England, which had also suffered from the Black Death and civil war, embroidery underwent a marked decline, but elsewhere in Europe the developing spirit of the Renaissance and the changing patterns of wealth ensured its continuing success.

Circa 1450–1715

From the mid-fifteenth century the number of surviving embroideries increases; the range is wide and includes secular clothing and furnishings, both made professionally and within the home. It is clear that the traditions of the medieval period continued in the more isolated areas such as Scandinavia and Iceland where, for example, inlaid patchwork and woollen hangings in couched work and long-armed cross stitch kept medieval designs alive well into the seventeenth century. In Germany and Switzerland wool and whitework embroideries made within convents and conservative secular communities remained based on late Gothic ornament throughout the sixteenth century, even though the clothes of the figures changed in line with contemporary fashions.

In Italy the professional workshops continued to use *or nué* to work pictorial embroideries that reflected developments in Renaissance paintings. Such work was also produced, largely for ecclesiastical use, in The Netherlands, Spain and France. During the early sixteenth century, however, smaller pictorial panels, enclosed within increasingly elaborate, gold-embroidered frames and separated by ornamental patterns, came to replace the continuous, story-telling scenes of the medieval period.

Renaissance ornament design also had an impact on embroidery; the exploration by Raphael (1483–1520) and other artists of the excavated art of ancient Rome included both the naturalistic carvings and the fanciful images of the wall-paintings on which the grotesque style was based. In addition, flat, stylised floral forms and interlaces (arabesques) were introduced from the Islamic world. The fruits of this rich mixture were spread with the help of printed sheets of ornament designs and pattern-books, some of which were aimed specifically at the amateur embroiderer. The earliest known was printed in Germany in 1524, closely followed by the first of the Italian books.

The influence of the printed designs is most clearly seen in the fine linen embroideries of the mid-sixteenth century onwards. They were worked both for dress and for furnishings, usually with border patterns varying from simple, geometric interlaces to complex designs of swirling, naturalistic foliage or fanciful combinations including grotesque figures. The embroidery was worked in silk in monochrome or in two colours, such as red and yellow or yellow and blue, in a wide range of techniques. Linear patterns like those on the garments shown in Holbein's portraits were sometimes worked in double-running or Holbein stitch, although back, stem and tiny cross stitches were also common. The more complex pieces employed more than one stitch, and in some instances the pattern was left void, except for the fine details, and the ground entirely covered in long-armed or other form of cross stitch. In other cases the ground was decorated with drawn-thread work, and those pieces embroidered solely in white were increasingly elaborated with tiny cutwork holes in a technique that was to evolve into needle lace. The same designs were also used on grounds of hand-made net (*lacis* or *filet*) and a coarse woven gauze which the Italians called *burato*.

Strapwork, a form of ornament drawn as if constructed of strips of leather, was also widely popular and, one of its earliest uses was at Fontainebleau, the great Renaissance palace built by Francis I (1515–47) with the help of Italian artists. Interlace patterns, sometimes in the strapwork style, replaced pictorial embroidery on vestments and furnishings before the end of the sixteenth century. The designs were worked with flat, laid gold threads on grounds of plain satin, and although raised details continued to be added in Spain and Austria, this flatter style prevailed elsewhere. Very delicate appliqué was sometimes used as an alternative to the laid gold thread.

When worked on a large scale and shaded with silk embroidery or paint to achieve three-dimensional effects, appliqué was also a popular means of decorating secular and ecclesiastical furnishings, especially in Spain and Italy, throughout the later sixteenth and seventeenth centuries. The bold patterns, which were at first based on Renaissance scrollwork, later echoed

ABOVE 243 Red velvet chasuble with an applied orphrey of linen embroidered with silver and silver-gilt thread in laid and couched work, heavily padded, and ornamented with stones and pearls. The Netherlands, second half of the 17th century. 112 × 73 cm (44 × 28.7 in).

ABOVE 242 Detail of a satin bed tester, decorated with satin appliqué edged with couched threads and embroidered with silks in satin, stem, back and chain stitches, in a Renaissance design of strapwork and grotesques. France (possibly Fontainebleau), c. 1550.

RIGHT 244 Silk cover embroidered with gold and silver thread and silks in laid and couched work, split, satin and long and short stitches. Italy (possibly Rome), early 17th century. The cover was probably made as a christening mantle. 192 × 99 cm (75.5 × 39 in).

the designs of large-patterned woven silks. They were usually worked with plain satins or velvets in a limited range of basic colours; the more elaborate pieces combined velvet, satin and cloth of gold or silver, and the designs were outlined with couched cord. In the related technique of inlaid patchwork it was possible to make, for example, a pair of hangings with the pattern in gold on a red ground in one and with the colours and fabrics reversed in the other.

Bold effects and heavily padded gold embroidery continued to be popular in Spain and Austria into the seventeenth century, but elsewhere France led the way in combining the flat gold embroidery with flowers worked with coloured silks. This rich but delicate style is well illustrated by the clothes and furnishings embroidered in France for the Swedish kings in the first quarter of the seventeenth century, now

245 Hanging entitled 'Summer', from a set of the Seasons. France (Paris), *c.* 1685. Linen embroidered with coloured silks and wools in tent stitch, the ground covered with spirals of couched silver-gilt thread. The set was probably designed by Charles Le Brun and worked in the School of St Joseph de la Providence, Paris. 442 × 279 cm (174 × 110 in).

preserved in the Royal Armoury in Stockholm. Lighter floral embroideries in silk and gold were also produced in Italy, where the art of naturalistic needle-painting was becoming important for floral and pictorial pieces.

There was no country in which flowers were not a feature of embroidery during the seventeenth century. In England, for example, rather stiff coiling stems enclosed recognisable flowers on the linen-based dress and furnishing pieces of the first half of the century, while in Holland some beautiful flower pictures were embroidered during the 1650s in a needle-painting

technique that captured the spirit of the contemporary still-life paintings. A Netherlandish table-carpet in the Metropolitan Museum, New York, is representative of another form of floral embroidery and also of the canvaswork technique which was used throughout Europe for the production of wall-hangings, cushions, valances and a variety of covers. Although some pieces were in an international style, including the universally popular flame-stitch technique, more, as in this example, reflected the tastes of their own country.

Flowers featured, often prominently, in baroque embroidery. This style, which had started in Italy in the late sixteenth century, was at its most influential during the two middle quarters of the seventeenth century and it was the dominant style of the Counter Reformation. The many baroque churches built throughout Catholic Europe in the seventeenth and early eighteenth centuries were equipped with furnishings and vestments designed to contribute to the overall grandeur of the interiors. Some were of woven silk, but many were decorated with lavish gold embroidery, often mixed with coloured silks, in exuberant designs combining flowers and scrolling foliage.

The baroque style spread throughout Europe, although it was expressed differently in different countries; in France, under the direction of Charles Le Brun (1619–90), it was combined with a more formal classicism in a unifying style that encompassed all the arts. It was consciously dedicated to the glorification of Louis XIV (1638–1715). By the 1690s, however, French designers were experimenting with lighter, more fanciful

ABOVE **246** Panel from a state coach, cloth of gold and silver with applied painted silk and embroidery in silk thread in satin, stem, overcast and long and short stitches. France and Sweden, 1699. Designed by Jean Bérain for Charles XI of Sweden and amended for Charles XII. The applied silk was painted by Jacques Fourcquet and the embroidery was worked in Sweden by Tobias Leuw. The design, which illustrates the lighter style introduced in the late 17th century, is in the National Museum, Stockholm. 138 × 134 cm (54 × 53 in).

many Renaissance and baroque embroideries, but they often used other devices, such as the Indian 'Tree of Life' design, which features in English crewel-work hangings. These sometimes tentative or experimental developments were all to be taken further in the eighteenth century.

Circa 1700–1815

During the eighteenth century the artistic domination of France and its hold on the loyalties of fashionable society imposed a certain uniformity on the output of the professional workshops that can sometimes make it difficult to pinpoint the provenance of a particular embroidery. Yet at the same time the difference that had always existed between the embroideries made for the very highest level of society and those available to people of lower rank appears more marked, as does the difference between professional and amateur work. Distinct traditions had also developed within peasant communities in many countries, and surviving embroideries therefore exhibit a great variety of styles which can reflect their social as much as their geographical origin.

Embroidery remained a means of decorating large-scale furnishings during the first half of the century, although it lost ground to the fashionable wall-coverings of silk and wallpaper and to the light, decorative tapestries being woven at the Gobelins and Beauvais factories and elsewhere. Large hangings, usually in the style of contemporary tapestries, were professionally embroidered in several countries, as were fitted wall panels, usually of canvaswork. Later, however, such large items were worked either in more conservative areas or by dedicated amateurs. This was also true of canvaswork screens and seat furniture, where professional production dropped sharply from the mid-century onwards. Carpets were made until the very end of the century but in relatively small numbers. None the less, for use on lighter furnishings embroidery withstood better than the patterned silks the effects of the neo-classical style. It remained commercially viable to embroider the discrete, mainly border patterns that were important in creating the overall effect, while, at the very highest level and in contrast to the general trend, some exceptionally elaborate embroideries in the extreme neo-classical style were created for the court of Napoléon (1769–1821) in the opening years of the nineteenth century.

The same general trend was also apparent in dress, where floral-patterned silks came to dominate the clothing of the leaders of fashion during the two middle quarters of the century, although here, too, embroidery held its own at

247 Detail of the centre of a linen coverlet, flat-quilted in back stitch and embroidered with silk in chain, satin and stem stitches. England, early 18th century. Both the design and the technique show a mix of English and Indian influences. 117 square cm (18.14 square in).

designs based both upon Renaissance grotesques and arabesques and on more novel images drawn from the textiles and other objects imported in increasing quantity from the Far East. The new style was epitomised by the work of Jean Bérain (1640–1711).

Although velvets and heavy fabrics were still employed for more formal furnishings, like the grand beds and window drapes designed by Daniel Marot (1663–1752), and canvaswork continued to be used for wall panels and seat furniture, many hangings and covers (as well as vestments and items of dress) were embroidered with silk on lighter linen and silk grounds. In France and England, in particular, crewel wools and lengths of knotted threads of silk and wool were popular embroidery materials. These lighter pieces were often decorated with delicate floral patterns that lacked the controlling ornamental structures present in so

RIGHT **249** Detail from the train of a court dress. Satin decorated with applied velvet, padded silk and oval ornaments and swansdown, embroidered with chenille thread and silks in satin and stem stitches and couched work. France, late 18th century.

BELOW **248** Silk wall panel decorated with silk appliqué, painted details and embroidery with chenille and silks in satin and tamboured chain stitches. France (Lyons), *c.* 1800–05. This panel, featuring the goddess Athena, is one of a set of neo-classical panels which formed part of a complete room setting. A related design by J.-D. Dugourac (1749–1825) is in the archive of the silk firm of Tassinari & Châtel, Lyons. 251.5 × 88.9 cm (99 × 35 in).

the highest level. It was also used for informal dress and for the dress of lower social classes until the 1770s when it tended to be replaced by printed cottons. Men's formal dress was an important outlet for the skills of the professional embroiderer throughout the century, and men's court dress of the neo-classical period was as spectacularly embroidered as that of the women. Ceremonial and ecclesiastical furnishings, notably the vestments required for the Catholic Church, provided another stable outlet that was to be largely responsible for carrying the basic skills through into the nineteenth century.

The eighteenth century saw the fanciful elements present in some late baroque designs transformed into the light-hearted, asymmetrical rococo style, before being confined once more within the formal structures of neo-classical design. These fanciful images included grotesques, *commedia dell'arte* figures and the chinoiserie motifs that feature on many fashionable embroideries of the first half of the century, notably those worked in France, England and Germany. Many were in the form of canvaswork screens, wall panels and seat furniture, although they also appear on silk and crewelwork curtains and muslin dress accessories. More unusually, there survives (Österreichisches Museum für Angewandte Kunst, Vienna) a complete set of bed and wall panels with chinoiserie designs cut from Indian chintz and applied to grounds of white cotton, which was made, probably in Vienna, for Prince Eugène of Savoy (1663–1736) in the 1720s.

The classical ornaments and architectural devices of the seventeenth century did not reappear until the 1760s, but figurative subjects, worked as pictures and large hangings, and as centre-pieces within floral surrounds on seat furniture and screens, often had classical

250 Sofa seat or back. Linen embroidered with silks and wools in tent stitch. Probably England, second quarter of the 18th century. The chinoiserie buildings and Indian trees in the centre are taken from unidentified printed sources. The lower border, with its flowery hillocks, suggests that the panel is English rather than French. 76 × 191.3 cm (30 × 75.3 in).

251 Detail of a silk pallium embroidered with a variety of silver and silver-gilt threads, metal strip and silks in laid and couched work, partially padded, satin, stem and long and short stitches. Italy (Bologna), mid-18th century. The detail shows the rococo ornament to the side of the central medallion, which is painted with the Martyrdom of St Bartholomew. Whole: 90 × 294 cm (35.4 × 115.75 in).

themes. During the first half of the century other popular subjects included pastoral scenes and illustrations from literature, as for example, scenes from Gay's *Fables*, which decorate a set of chair seats in the Victoria and Albert Museum, London. During the last quarter of the century a new type of pictorial embroidery became popular, particularly in England: crewel wools were worked in irregular long and short stitches on a coarse canvas in a needle-painting technique to produce copies of oil-paintings. Some exponents of the art – Mrs Knowles, Miss Morritt and Miss Linwood – achieved considerable fame. Possibly more attractive to modern eyes are the contemporary pictures worked both in silk and

wool on silk taffeta grounds, in which such details as the sky and the faces of the figures are painted in water-colour. These, too, were based on paintings or engravings by artists such as George Morland (1763–1804). Commemorative mourning pictures worked in this technique were particularly popular in America.

Naturalistic flowers played a prominent role in almost every eighteenth-century embroidery, whether worked with wool on canvas, skilfully shaded with silks on silk, or tamboured with polychrome silks or white cotton on the light fabrics of the last quarter of the century. The most beautiful floral embroidery was that worked with silks and metal thread on silk or, early in the century, on fine linen. It was a technique employed in the professional workshops throughout Europe to decorate wall panels, bed sets and other furnishings, vestments and items of dress. In some instances the flowers predominate, as on the English court dresses of the 1740s and men's court dress from later in the century; in others – for example, some German furnishings and Italian ecclesiastical pieces – it was the rococo ornament that was emphasised.

These pieces were worked mainly in satin, long and short and stem stitches, with raised laid and couched metal threads, but when embroidered on other fabrics, different stitches were employed. The fine linen pieces with delicate floral trails or sprig motifs, which were embroidered in England during the first quarter of the century, were often worked with silk or crewel wool in chain stitch, in imitation of the effect of some Indian embroideries. Chain stitch was also popular in the last quarter of the century, when it was worked with a tambour needle

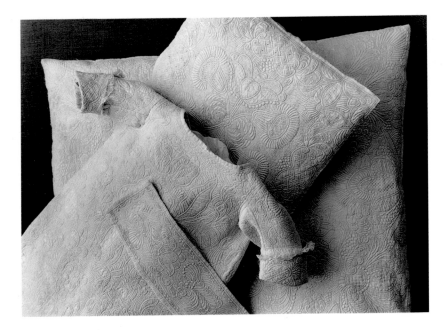

TOP **252** Baby's layette. Linen, Italian-quilted with linen thread. Possibly Denmark, 1740–60. Dense, complicated patterns were easily visible due to the raised outlines of Italian quilting.

ABOVE **253** Detail of a sofa back. Cream satin embroidered with coloured silks in tamboured chain stitch. France, late 18th century. The design is in the style of Philippe Lasalle (1723–1804).

ferent, made professionally and domestically in every country. Quilting was another widely made form of whitework, especially during the first half of the century. Linen, backed with coarser linen or fustian, and sometimes interlined, was either simply quilted through the layers or more elaborately worked in Italian quilting and other techniques. It was applied to a wide range of furnishings and to items of dress from baby clothes to men's waistcoats, the latter being particularly fashionable from the 1730s to 50s.

Women of all classes wore quilted garments, often of plain coloured wool or silk, and from the 1730s to 80s quilted silk petticoats and even complete dresses were acceptable for fashionable wear; they can be seen in a number of portraits. Many of the elaborate, polychrome bed sets had grounds flat-quilted in cream or yellow silk, and other monochrome furnishings of silk and linen were similarly worked with yellow silk in both padded and flat quilting.

Another technique that grew in importance during this period was patchwork. Although applied and inlaid decoration had long been part of the embroiderer's repertoire, the joining together of small scraps of fabric in all-over patterns seems to have been an innovation of the eighteenth century. English covers exist patched together from oblong pieces of silk which date from the late seventeenth to mid-eighteenth centuries, and contemporary accounts bear witness to the craze for patchwork at the end of the century when new printed cottons were bought to be cut up, and centre-pieces and borders were specially printed in response to the demand.

Increasingly during the later part of the century, as furnishings and dress became plainer, the most decorative forms of embroidery were concentrated on accessories such as belts, purses, shoes, and so on. The embroidery materials included silks and chenille thread, metal threads, spangles, straw, feathers and beads. France, in particular, produced beadwork of exceptional fineness including a group of purses and shoes decorated with motifs commemorating the first successful launch of a hot-air balloon in 1783.

Circa 1800–1915

The development of embroidery during the nineteenth century can be summed up by the contrasting images of Berlin woolwork and the designs of William Morris (1834–96), although the reality was more complex. The printing of designs on squared paper, which formed the basis of the Berlin woolwork technique, was started by a Berlin print-seller as early as 1804, and until the 1840s the soft, beautifully shaded

to decorate high-quality French furnishings, as well as home-made muslin dresses and accessories.

Whitework was important throughout the century, particularly in the opening and closing decades, when simply decorated muslin often replaced lace, and from the mid-1730s to 60s, when the richest effects of fashionable Flemish bobbin lace were imitated with muslin embroidered with shadow work and a variety of fillings in drawn-thread and pulled-fabric work. The finest pieces were produced in Saxony and exported to the rest of Europe via Dresden, and the name 'Dresden work' was frequently misapplied to whitework, some good, some indif-

254 Cotton canvas panel for a cushion or fire screen, embroidered with Berlin wools in cross and plush stitches. England, 1850s. The finer canvas grounds of the 1840s and 50s were often left unworked, as in this example, Amateur embroiderers usually sent their panels away for the plush stitch pile to be cut and shaped. 80 × 62 cm (31.5 × 24.4 in).

embroidery wools were also produced in Germany. At that early period, however, most canvaswork was still of high quality including, for example, the still-life pictures professionally embroidered in Vienna in fine silk tent stitch. Floral patterns dominated early Berlin woolwork, although figurative subjects, many based on famous paintings, were popular in the 1840s and 50s, when the technique was also elaborated by the addition of beads and new stitches, including three-dimensional plush stitch. The best pieces exhibited a certain panache, but it was also at this time that the designs became debased and the technique coarsened as it was taken up by growing numbers of middle-class women to wile away their time. The sheer quantity of their surviving work has tended to overshadow that of the more skilled amateurs, who continued the traditions of the eighteenth century into the 1840s.

These amateurs embroidered wool and silk pictures on painted silk grounds and others, worked with black silk, known as 'print' or 'engraved' work. They also worked dress borders and small accessories in silk and wool, as well as many whitework accessories of fine lawn, muslin and machine net. The delicate techniques of the 1820s to 40s were largely ousted in the 1850s and 60s by the bolder, simpler methods of *broderie anglaise* and cut-out Richelieu work, which were taken up with enthusiasm by less skilful needlewomen. Other interests of the amateur included quilting and patchwork, but here the size of many of the projects seems to have weeded out many of the less able, and these techniques were used to work pieces of great technical skill and beauty.

The image of the amateur embroiderer is so strong that it is difficult to see past it to the professionals who existed throughout the century working, most importantly, on ceremonial embroideries including military and court-dress uniforms, robes and trains for women's court dress, and vestments for the Catholic and, later, the Protestant Churches. These were worked mainly with metal threads in a variety of techniques, including one developed in Austria as early as the 1720s in which the metal threads were laid over strips of leather or card to create a flat, sharply delineated effect. Patterns varied, but the more conservative pieces, notably the vestments, were in rather watered-down versions of baroque and rococo styles, while neo-classical motifs still featured on some court embroideries, and in England court trains of the 1820s and 30s reflected the curving floral sprays popular in contemporary lace. From the mid-century the metal-thread embroideries, often combined with coloured silks, became more elaborate reflecting, for example, the eighteenth-century revival style favoured by Napoléon III (1808–73) and the Empress Eugénie (1826–1920).

The interiors of the first half of the century, although growing steadily more crowded and heavily draped, offered little scope for embroidery. Bed sets, valances and table-covers were sometimes decorated with appliqué, but the often elaborate window drapes were of plain fabric trimmed with *passementerie*. Only the secondary, muslin curtains that hung at most windows had embroidered borders and, as patterns returned to favour in the second quarter of the century, these became more heavily decorated. Despite the introduction of the embroidery machine and of machine-made lace curtains, tamboured muslin drapes continued to be worked by hand, notably at Tarare, near Lyons, into the early twentieth century.

Canvaswork carpets were embroidered in decreasing numbers during the first half of the century, whilst canvaswork upholstery increased in importance during the second and third quarters. In the second half of the century embroidery, mostly worked with silks on silk or velvet, was more extensively applied to table-covers, *portières* and the borders of curtains; complete bed sets were worked in a debased eighteenth-century style, and in England imitations of the crewel-work curtains of around 1700 were worked with wools on linen.

The simple dresses of the 1810s and early 20s were sometimes professionally embroidered with floral borders in coloured silks, wool and chenille, but in the later 20s the more prominent decoration round the hems and sleeve tops was more often in self-coloured appliqué. More elaborate effects, worked with beads, shaded china ribbon and aerophane (a form of fine silk gauze), were concentrated on accessories. In the 1830s and 40s printed cottons and patterned silks were favoured above embroidery, except for the large whitework collars, veils and handkerchiefs, which were often finely embroidered with drawn-thread and other openwork techniques.

More professionals are likely to have been engaged on whitework than on any other form of embroidery. Much that was produced was of a very high standard, including the delicate work, elaborated with needle-lace fillings, which was a speciality of France and which was introduced into the Ayrshire region of Scotland after 1815 and taken subsequently to Ireland. There was no country in which whitework embroidery and fine, plain sewing were not practised, and some industries survived into the twentieth century, despite the introduction of coarser techniques and of the embroidery machine. This was invented by Josué Heilmann of Mulhouse in 1828 and was developed in Germany, Switzerland and England. By the 1860s the machines could reproduce most of the effects of hand embroidery, including scalloped edges, pierced work and needle-lace fillings.

Coloured silk embroidery was also copied by the machines, and an early example was shown by Henry Holdsworth of Manchester at the Dublin Exhibition of 1853 (Victoria and Albert Museum, London). It was not until the 1870s, however, that silk machine embroidery became important, as women's clothes became more heavily decorated. Embroidery, both machine- and hand-worked, was then in great demand for use on accessories, details such as collars, cuffs and revers, and sometimes complete garments. Much was in monochrome, but evening dresses were often multicoloured and the satin and stem stitches that formed the basis of most work were relieved by couched cords and a growing quantity of beads. Sometimes the whole decorative scheme was in beads, most typically in jet. The opulent clothes made for the leaders of fashion from the 1870s to the 1910s by Charles Frederick Worth (1825–98) and other French couturiers were decorated with a mix of fabrics and techniques that sometimes included, on the same garment, both hand- and machine-made lace and embroidery.

These elaborate confections were created long after William Morris and other reformers had begun their campaigns for greater honesty in design and simplicity of method. One of the first to do battle had been A. W. N. Pugin (1812–52) who in his search for embroiderers capable of carrying out his designs in an appropriate technique had had to turn to the military uniform embroiderers. The important role played by the avant-garde ecclesiastical architects in the revival of embroidery skills during the second half of the nineteenth century has been rather overshadowed by the understandable concentration on the work of William Morris and the followers of the Arts and Crafts Movement, which spread throughout Europe and America from the 1880s onwards.

The upsurge of interest in crafts did not in fact take place within a unified movement, although certain beliefs were held in common by many of its proponents. Sometimes the efforts of individual artist-craftsmen coincided with those of governments struggling to deal with rural poverty, and, for example, in the Austro-Hungarian Empire, Italy, parts of Scandinavia and Ireland State-backed lace and embroidery industries were, fortuitously, linked with some of the more avant-garde schools of art and design. The embroideries worked during this period have no common style or technical reper-

BELOW 255 Evening dress; satin embroidered with brilliants and beads, decorated with machine-made lace. France (Paris), Jean-Philippe Worth, 1900.

RIGHT 256 Velvet cope hood embroidered with gold thread, worked over strips of card. England, designed by A.W.N. Pugin, 1841.
In the centre is a raised shield bearing the arms of St Chad. The cope is part of a set of vestments designed by Pugin for use at the consecration of the Roman Catholic Cathedral of St Chad, Birmingham, in 1841. The silk ground was woven at Spitalfields and the embroidery was worked by Lonsdale and Tyler of Covent Garden, 'Gold and silver Lacemen & embroiderers to her Majesty . . . Army Accoutrement makers'. Cope: 150 × 284.5 cm (59 × 112 in).

toire; they range from near-perfect reproductions of sixteenth- and seventeenth-century linen embroideries to William Morris's innovatory designs worked in a technique loosely based on that of late seventeenth-century crewel-work and to bold appliqué work, by artists such as Godfrey Blount (1859–1937) and Ann Macbeth (1875–1948), that owes little to any earlier style.

All are distinguishable from contemporary commercial products, however, by the quality of their designs and the links with other crafts that they often demonstrate. Thus, C. R. Ashbee (1863–1942), who worked mainly in wood and silver, designed altar frontals decorated in appliqué with slender stylised plants that echo those on his silver. In Belgium Henri van de Velde (1863–1957), who had also started as an architect and designer, experimented with the use of appliqué in working (with the aid of his aunt) the figurative hanging *La Veillée des Anges* of 1893 (Kunstgewerbemuseum, Zurich) which in its use of bold, flat areas of colour is reminiscent of the work of artists such as Gauguin (1848–1903). It also shows the influence of the art nouveau style, of which van de Velde was a leading exponent in Belgium. Embroidery was a particularly sympathetic medium for art nouveau designs, and a list of those who used it contains the names of many of the movement's leading artists and designers, from A. H. Mackmurdo (1851–1942) and Walter Crane (1845–1915) to Herman Obrist (1863–1927) and Hector Guimard (1867–1942). The work of several of the

ABOVE **257** Detail of a linen table-cloth decorated with linen appliqué and embroidered with silk in satin stitch. Scotland (Glasgow), designed and embroidered by Ann Macbeth, *c.* 1900.

258 Sample panel of dress embroidery; silk with appliqué of tulle, cut and embroidered with silk in stem, padded satin and overcast stitches. France, designed by Hector Guimard, 1906–7. Guimard was the designer of the art nouveau entrances to the Paris Métro. H: 68 cm (26.75 in).

Arts and Crafts and art nouveau designers fore-shadowed developments of the twentieth century, and in the field of embroidery the teaching of such artists as Jessie Newbery (1864–1948) and Ann Macbeth at the Glasgow School of Art established principles for, and an approach to, the craft that have had a lasting influence.

Circa 1915–1990

Embroidery has been practised during the twentieth century against a background of technological, economic and social change. The success of mass-produced machine embroidery has seemed at times to threaten the viability of hand work yet, despite periods of stagnation, it has survived. As in the nineteenth century, the amateur embroiderer played a major part in maintaining interest in the craft; increased leisure time has enabled many women and some men to turn to it as a pastime. Although the great majority have made use of ready-prepared designs and instructions on the choice of materials and techniques, from the beginning of the century the teaching of creative embroidery, along lines laid down by Ann Macbeth and others, continued in some schools and colleges. It was a movement that bore fruit after 1950 as an increasing number of colleges developed embroidery courses, and painters and graphic artists within the colleges turned to embroidery as an exciting medium for new ideas.

The avant-garde embroiderers of the late twentieth century were following in the footsteps of the much smaller number of individuals who in the early part of the century had ensured that embroidery was part of such experimental ventures as the Wiener Werkstätte (established 1903), the Omega Workshops (1913) and the Bauhaus (1919). Throughout Europe embroideries reflected trends in modern art from cubism to abstract art and free expression. Increasingly, and particularly after the 1960s, the emphasis on design as opposed to technique resulted in a marked divide between the proponents of embroidery as art and those concerned with its traditional uses and techniques. Efforts to bridge the gap were made by such societies as The Embroiderers' Guild in Britain and by the promotion of magazines, exhibitions and competitions. Many were sponsored by thread manufacturers such as D.M.C. (Dollfus, Mieg et Cie) in France and J. P. Coats in Britain who in 1934 started the influential Needlework Development Scheme.

One of the first advisers to the Needlework Development Scheme was Rebecca Crompton (1895–1947), who taught the use of simple materials and simple stitches to create lively and imaginative pieces. She was also one of the first teachers to promote the use of the domestic

259 *The Magic Garden*. Cotton appliqué and free surface stitches. England, Rebecca Crompton, 1937. 51.5 × 35.5 cm (20.3 × 14 in).

ABOVE **260** *Blau–Rot*. Canvas panel embroidered with red and blue wool in cross stitch. Switzerland, Elsi Giauque, 1925. 245 × 200 cm (96.5 × 78.75 in).

ABOVE **261** *Virgin and Child*. Machine embroidery in grey-greens, black and grey. England, Margaret Traherne, 1952. 66 × 49.5 cm (26 × 19.5 in).

sewing-machine as a useful tool in the embroiderer's repertoire, and, despite initial opposition, various types of machine were soon used either in conjunction with hand embroidery or alone. Community projects were another means of drawing together embroiderers of different persuasions to work, for example, a set of kneelers for a local church or a commemorative hanging for a village hall.

As in the nineteenth century, countries sought to promote their traditional skills – for example, the whitework embroideries of Scandinavia and in England the Rural Industries Bureau tried unsuccessfully to revive north of

England quilting on a semi-commercial basis. Quilting and patchwork were techniques revived by amateur embroiderers and in the late 1970s were taken up by the professionals and developed as an art form.

During the early part of the century and again

262 *Harlequin*, from a set of four panels entitled *Quatres Arlequins sur l'herbe*. England, designed and embroidered by Alice Kettle, 1990. Felt stitched with cotton, silk, metal and rayon threads. 76 × 58.5 cm (30 × 23 in).

from the 1960s public institutions and commercial companies patronised embroiderers by commissioning large hangings for foyers, boardrooms and public spaces. But even more important to the survival of the individual professional embroiderer was the patronage of the churches. As in the nineteenth century, the opportunity to preserve the skills of hand embroidery was provided by commissions for altar frontals and vestments which, in Britain in particular but also elsewhere, became a vehicle for avant-garde work. The effectiveness of embroidery as a medium was appreciated by artists such as Henri Matisse (1869–1954) and John Piper (1903–92). Despite the importance of such commissions, however, a far greater quantity of ecclesiastical embroidery came, particularly during the first half of the century, from such professional workshops as those of Louis Grossé in Belgium and of G. Dutel, Bouvard and Feige in France. They maintained the traditions of the nineteenth century, both in technique and style, and this was also true of the ceremonial and military embroiderers who continued in operation, although in dwindling numbers.

During the first half of the century some

machine-embroidered vestments were made in St Gallen in Switzerland, which was (and still is) the leading centre for high-quality machine embroidery. Well-designed fabrics in imaginative colour combinations and mixed with openwork details in the burnt-out technique, or decorated with three-dimensional details, beads or jewels, were supplied to the couture dress industry. These products were a far cry from the mass-produced embroidered fabrics, trimmings and appliqué motifs that were manufactured elsewhere for the decoration of lower-quality clothing.

The *haute couture* trade also patronised the hand-embroidery industry; during the first half of the century the Paris fashion houses supported the workshops of Fleury in Lyons and of Lallemant, Rébé and, above all, Lessage in Paris. The 1910s and 20s were particularly fruitful with designers such as Callot Soeurs producing sumptuously decorated clothes. Costume embroideries were designed by such artists as Raoul Dufy (1877–1953) and Sonia Delaunay (1885–1979), and almost every evening dress was liberally decorated with beads. During the 1930s, when the emphasis on cut favoured the use of plain fabrics, embroidery retained its importance for evening wear, and designers like Schiaparelli (1896–1973) used embroidered details to offset the severity of their day clothes. World War II and the years of restriction that followed were not good for embroidery, nor were the revolutionary 1960s, when such designers as Ungaro (b. 1933) and Courrèges (b. 1923) concentrated on shape and colour rather than on decoration. Even then, however, Norman Hartnell (1901–79) among others designed lavishly embroidered dresses, and in the 1970s, with the return of more fluid styles, younger designers made use of embroidery too. They also reflected street fashion with the introduction of such items as embroidered jeans and appliqué motifs, and drew upon the concurrent interest in ethnic embroidery. In the 1980s more formal styles returned, and embroidery, both hand and machine, was again popular.

There have been ups and downs for both hand and machine embroidery during the twentieth century, but since the late 1960s there has been an explosion of experimental activity. Embroidery now encompasses a range of techniques from meticulous counted-thread work to glued and machined pieces. Felting, painting, dyeing and photography are now part of the embroiderer's repertoire, and materials range from traditional fibres to lurex, plastic, leather, wood, paper, plaster and metal. The finished objects may be worn, hung as a picture, or displayed as free-standing sculpture. Without a doubt embroidery has survived as a living craft.

216

25 Lace

263 Bobbin lace edging attached to a cutwork border. Italian, third quarter of the 16th century. The plaited bobbin lace of linen thread resembles patterns published in R.M. *Nüw Modelbuch*, Zurich, *c.* 1561.

BELOW **264** Standing collar of cutwork. Italian, *c.* 1610. This spectacular collar has been cut from the man's shirt of which it formed an integral part. H: 35 cm (13.8 in).

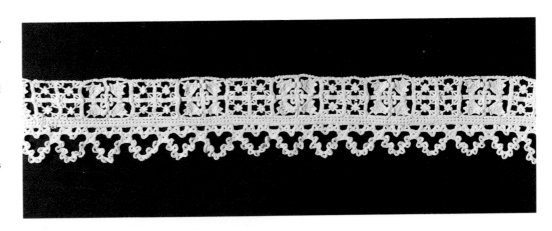

Throughout its history lace-making has been practised both by professionals and by amateurs to make a wide range of goods from costly accessories to cheap trimmings. High-quality lace has constantly changed, technically and stylistically, in response to fashionable demand, and these changes have filtered down to the more conservative secondary and domestic laces. To chart their development is, therefore, to provide a framework for the craft as a whole.

The two main forms of lace date back only to the late fifteenth and early sixteenth centuries. The first to emerge was bobbin lace which evolved out of braiding, probably in Italy – a centre both for *passementerie* and for the silk and metal threads of which much early bobbin lace was made. In its early, plaited form it was laid down on the surface of clothes and furnishings or, when made of linen thread, was used as insertions and edgings for linen covers and garments. It was in this form that it began its association with needle lace, a technique which had quite different origins.

The increasingly visible use of linen in fashionable dress during the first half of the sixteenth century stimulated its decoration with fine embroidery including whitework, which was elaborated with lines of openwork and tiny cutwork holes. From the 1550s onwards more and more fabric was cut away to create a geometric grid dependent on the underlying woven linen – a technique known in England as cutwork and in France as *point coupé*. The finest was made in Flanders and in Italy, where the rosette patterns were described as *reticella*. Amongst other areas, it decorated the frilled collars of men's shirts and women's shifts, which gradually developed into the great ruffs of the

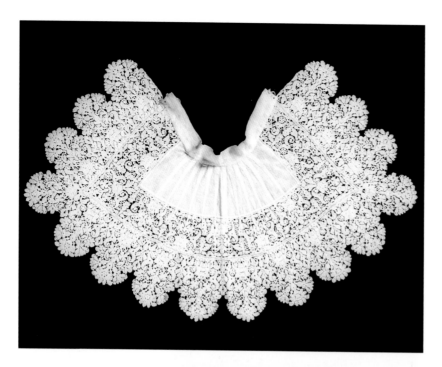

using the part-lace technique. These developments were taken further when fashions changed during the 1620s and falling collars trimmed with soft, opaque bobbin lace came into favour. Although decorated with Italian designs, it was Flemish bobbin lace that dominated the market, for the Flemish merchants not only had access to a skilled workforce and the finest linen thread but were also practised in anticipating the needs of their clients, notably the French nobility. Between the 1630s and the 60s the deeply scalloped borders of Flemish lace became straight-edged, and mesh grounds and simple fillings were introduced as patterns changed in line with Italian silk designs.

Needle lace altered even more spectacularly as cutwork was replaced by freely formed needle lace, which the Venetian lace-makers transformed into a three-dimensional fabric in keeping with the baroque style of the later seventeenth century. Under the leadership of Louis XIV (1638–1715) it was used with the elaborate clothes of the 1660s to 80s, which also

ABOVE **265** Falling collar of bobbin lace. Flemish, 1635–40. Such collars feature in the portraits of Van Dyck and other artists of the 1630s and 40s. The soft Flemish bobbin lace is worked in cloth stitch and the pattern pieces are hooked together where they touch. There is no mesh ground.

266 Man's bib-fronted needle-lace collar. Italian (Venice), 1665–75. Three-dimensional Venetian needle lace dominated fashion during the second half of the 17th century. Its bold, baroque patterns, worked in smooth, creamy button hole stitches with sculptured raised outlines, rival carved ivory in their sharp detail.

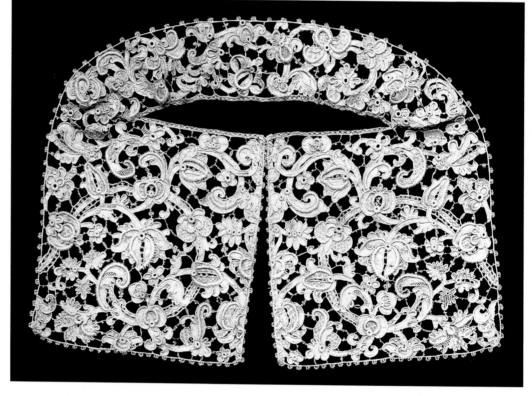

1580s and 90s, although it was, perhaps, displayed to even greater effect in the standing collars of the 1610s.

Linen bobbin lace was often used for the spiky edgings of the ruffs, or as a cheap means of making imitation cutwork, but by about 1600 Italian furnishing laces were being made with flowing patterns worked in cloth stitch and

favoured gold and silver bobbin lace and silk gimp. It was to stop the import of costly Venetian needle and Flemish bobbin laces that the French government established in 1665 a sponsored company to develop local needle and bobbin laces, of which the most successful was the needle-lace industry based on Alençon and Argentan. French needle lace (*point de France*)

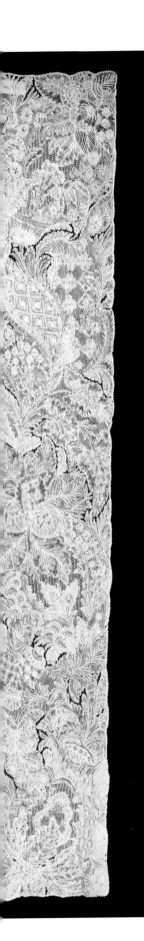

soon equalled that of Venice and in the closing years of the century developed a distinctive form with patterns in the style of Jean Bérain (1640–1711). However, neither French nor Italian needle lace retained its hold on the market: from about 1700 to 1715 the fashionable world preferred accessories of plain muslin, and although the rejection of lace was never total, the slump was sufficiently severe to destroy several centres, including Venice.

The revival was led by the Flemish industry which had perfected a bobbin lace with all the softness of muslin but combined with rich patterns based on those of contemporary French silks. The link with the silks was to continue throughout the century and was to result in further technical changes, notably the return of mesh grounds in the 1740s when the silk designs became more open. By that time bobbin and needle laces matched one another closely in weight and texture, although basic differences were acknowledged, as in the designation of Mechlin as a summer lace. Laces had been named after the main centres of production since the late seventeenth century, but the distinctive technical features, notably their mesh grounds by which they are now distinguished, were not fully developed until the 1750s.

Eighteenth-century laces reflected not only silk patterns but also elements of design common to all the decorative arts – chinoiserie birds and figures, rococo scrollwork, fountains and flowers, trophies of war and love were meticulously reproduced in Brussels, Alençon, Argentan, Mechlin and Valenciennes lace. Debased versions of these designs were used in many secondary centres, which with some major ones, also made lace in an archaic style for the peasant and colonial markets. Metal-thread and silk bobbin laces also remained relatively unaffected by contemporary designs. Among these was *blonde*, a simple lace of undyed silk with geometric patterns and a coarse mesh ground which was made in the environs of Paris and from the 1750s gained widespread fashionable popularity. This was a development in keeping with the move away from heavy patterned silks to lighter fabrics – gauze, muslin and cotton – which, coupled with a reduction in ornament, marked the decline of the rococo and the rise of the neo-classical style.

LEFT **267** Bobbin lace lappet. Brussels, 1715–25. The complex pattern based on contemporary French silks was made in small sections.

RIGHT **268** Bobbin lace lappet. Valenciennes, *c.* 1760. Clarity of image has become more important than complex details of design or technique. The lace was worked all in one, cloth-stitch pattern and plaited-mesh ground together.

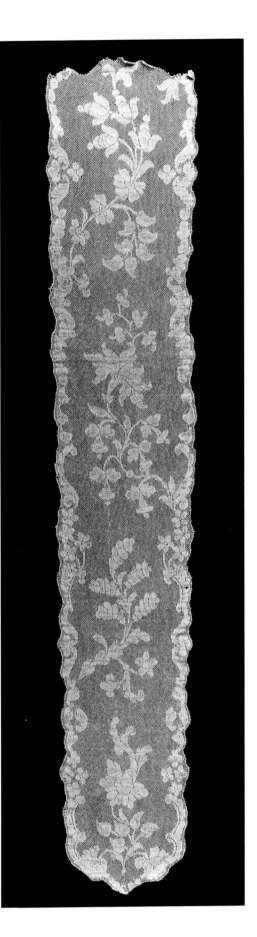

269 Detail of Apollo from a bobbin lace panel illustrating the 'Metamorphosis of Daphne'. Flanders (Brussels), *c.* 1800. The delicate net ground is made with the bobbins in strips 1 cm (0.4 in) wide, invisibly joined. The smaller details are applied to the surface. The panel reflects neo-classical taste in its subject matter.

OPPOSITE **271** Machine-lace shawl of black wool and silk thread. Probably French, 1860s. The shawl is a fine example of Pusher lace and its skilful design suggests that it was made in France rather than England. It is a stylish imitation of hand-made Chantilly bobbin lace. 141.7 × 278 cm (55.8 × 109.4 in).

ABOVE **270** Fichu of *blonde* silk bobbin lace. French, 1825–35. The lace was made in straight strips, delicate net ground and glossy pattern together, and invisibly joined. It was shaped in the making to form a concave curve along the central fold.

The lace-makers could produce plain or slightly patterned nets, and some superb examples of Brussels lace were made in the neo-classical style; but large accessories like shawls, veils and aprons could as effectively be made of gauze, muslin or point net. This delicate silk net was made on an adaptation of the stocking-frame first patented in 1778 and improved in 1786. It was commercially important until the invention by John Heathcoat (1783–1861) of the bobbin-net machine in 1809. This produced a superior net identical with the twist-net grounds of Lille and Buckinghamshire bobbin lace. It also broke the link with the stocking-frame and by having each thread on a separate bobbin paved the way for their individual control and the eventual production of patterned machine lace. Initially, however, all machine nets were plain, and any ornamentation had to be embroidered (or run) by hand. Lace-running was to be an important industry throughout the nineteenth century.

Gradually, from about 1810, the neo-classical style lost its dominance and such historical fashions as vandyked ruffs encouraged the use of lace. Patterns re-emerged, and the tiny border sprigs grew into large curved sprays that filled the scalloped edges of the accessories of the 1820s and 30s. Many were made of embroidered net, but Brussels, Lille, Mechlin, Buckinghamshire and, above all, *blonde* were also popular. The latter was now made with a fine twist-net ground that contrasted with the solid floral motifs worked with a glossy silk thread. In the 1840s *blonde* gave way to a matt black silk lace with delicate floral patterns which was made at Chantilly. It dominated fashion until the 1860s and was copied in several centres and by the machines.

Efforts to make patterned lace had centred on the Pusher machine, invented in 1812, and on John Leavers's machine of 1813, and they came to fruition with the application of the Jacquard to the Pusher in 1839 and to the Leavers in 1841.

Also important was John Livesey's curtain-net machine of 1846, which was to form the basis of the most stable section of the Nottingham lace industry. By the time of the Great Exhibition in 1851 the machines were, according to the jury, 'making admirable imitations of the beautiful black lace of Caen and Chantilly, the patterns of which are most correctly copied, while the difference in price is seventy-five per cent'. Despite this, the sale of hand-made lace continued to increase as the market for all qualities of lace grew with the rise of the middle classes, the increase in population and the opening up of world-wide trade.

The industry was led by large, international companies, like that of Auguste Lefébure at Bayeux and Verdé, Delisle et Cie of Paris and Brussels, who made quality lace for such leaders of fashion as the Empress Eugénie (1826–1920). They were prominent at the international exhibitions where they exhibited increasingly elaborate and technically accomplished pieces; the spindly patterns of the 1840s were replaced in the 1850s by delicate arrangements of naturalistic flowers and these gave way in the 1860s to more structured designs controlled by scroll-work and hard-edged ribbons. The major firms made more mundane laces for the mass market, which was also served by centres such as Le Puy in France, Pellestrina and Cantu in Italy and Erzgebirge in Saxony.

The lace of the second half of the nineteenth century may be divided into three main groups. The first contained such quality laces as Chantilly, Alençon, *point de gaze*, Valenciennes and Brussels application lace. The second group was made up of heavier, mainly bobbin-made laces

272 Fanleaf of needle lace. Austrian and German, *c.* 1900. The fanleaf was designed by Professor Hrdlicka of the Vienna Lace School and worked by W. Horner of Gassengrun. Traditional techniques were used in a new way to create a delicate design in the art nouveau style.

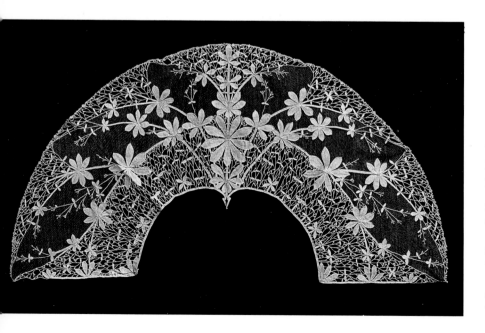

like Maltese, Cluny and Torchon. Related to this group were such imitation laces as crochet, tape lace and decorated nets. In the final group were the reproduction laces. Some quality lace, notably Alençon, was made with watered-down eighteenth-century designs from the 1860s, but it was the interest in earlier lace, particularly seventeenth-century Venetian needle lace, that stimulated the production of increasingly accurate copies. These were made both by major producers like Lefébure and in new centres such as Innishmacsaint and New Ross in Ireland and Burano in Italy, which had been created as a means of fighting rural poverty, although their development also fitted in with the general enthusiasm for handcrafts which from the 1880s stimulated the revival of lace industries throughout Europe.

The machines sought to imitate all these laces, and their capabilities were increased by the invention in 1883 of the chemical or burnt-out

273 Needle-lace flounce. French (Bayeux), 1867. This technical and stylistic *tour de force* was designed by Alcide Roussel and made by the lace firm of Lefébure et fils of Bayeux. It was shown at the Paris International Exhibition of 1867, where it was considered the finest piece of lace on display.

technique. This turned machine-embroidered patterns into lace by removing the ground fabric, and it was an excellent means of reproducing needle lace, including the raised Venetian laces. St Gallen in Switzerland was the main centre of production, and its manufacturers used the technique for both reproduction and avant-garde laces, including some in the art nouveau style. Although this style worked particularly well with lace, its use was largely confined to workshops associated with such lace schools as those at Vienna, Halas in Hungary and Apeldoorn in Holland. The major producers, both of hand and machine lace, continued with more established styles during the lace boom of the 1890s and 1900s.

The boom ended shortly before World War I, which accelerated the social and economic changes that underlaid the collapse of the hand-lace industry. Tremendous efforts were made to keep it alive; some superb lace was made in

Belgium during and immediately after the War, and the Italian industry, based on Burano, Cantu and the coast region near Genoa, managed to maintain a market, mostly for lace-trimmed linen, until after World War II. In the end, however, the cost of hand-made lace, coupled with the lack of scope for its use (something that also affected the machine industry), prevented its survival as a commercial proposition.

Instead, the twentieth century has seen the conversion of lace into a medium for the production of one-off pieces by artist-craftsmen. This development, which had its roots in the more avant-garde lace schools, developed in eastern Europe and Germany and spread, mainly after World War II, to Belgium, Holland and the United States of America. More recently it has begun to find adherents among the amateur lace-makers who have kept alive the more traditional aspects of the craft.

26   Printed textiles

often seem to derive from those found in Byzantine, Italian and Sicilian silk textiles.

With the setting up of the Dutch (1597), English (1600) and French (1664) East India Companies the technically far superior painted and dyed Indian cloths found their way into Europe, where their bright, fast colours were greatly admired. Light in weight, washable and with bright and exotic patterns, they were instantly in demand for both furnishings and clothing, particularly informal wear such as dressing- and morning-gowns. Their enormous commercial success inevitably prompted imitation by European printers, although the earliest attempts were very poor substitutes for the brilliantly dyed and patterned fabrics from the East. It was not until the 1670s that a successful industry was established, almost simultaneously, in England, France and Holland, although it was England and France which eventually became the foremost producers of printed textiles in Europe.

In France manufacturers of *indiennes*, as the imitation Indian cloths were known, seem to have been operating soon after the middle of the seventeenth century, whilst in Holland a printing works was set up at Amersfoort in 1678. A William Sherwin took out the first English patent in 1676, claiming to have found 'the only true way of East Indian printing and stayning . . . never till now performed in this kingdom'; and by 1700 the English industry was well established around London along the tributaries of the River Thames, wherever copious supplies of fresh, clear water were available for the dyeing and clearing (washing) processes. As with the Indian imports, the basic dyestuff used was madder which was capable of producing a whole range of colours including pinks, reds, purples and black depending on the mordants or fixing agents, with which the cloth was first printed. However, the European copies were made by printing with woodblocks rather than painting by hand, which was much too slow a process to be economically viable. Extra colours, such as blue and yellow, were added afterwards by hand, a technique known as 'pencilling'.

The growing popularity of printed cotton meant that before long fear of competition amongst the much longer-established silk and wool manufacturers caused them to put pressure on government to stifle the fledgling industry. First in France in 1686, then in England in 1700 and 1720 legislation was passed prohibiting

274 Block-printed linen fragment with a design taken from a contemporary Lucchese woven silk. Italy, probably 14th century.

Printing remained a relatively primitive method of decorating textiles in Europe until the second half of the seventeenth century, when the technical problems involved in fixing colours on cloth began at last to be overcome. Some textile printing had been carried on earlier, from the twelfth to the fifteenth centuries, and isolated pieces are known from Holland, Italy and north Germany. A detailed description in Cennino Cennini's *Trattato della pittura*, written in Florence around 1400, testifies to the practice of the craft in medieval Italy. However, doubt has been cast on the view which assigns a large number of early printed fragments to the lower Rhineland region of Germany (King 1962).

The technique was closely related to woodcut: carved wooden blocks were smeared with some kind of pigment mixed with a binding agent such as linseed oil. Most of the paint stayed on the surface of the fabric, which only barely absorbed the paint. Needless to say, printed fabrics of this kind were not fast to washing and were thus unsuitable for use as clothing. They were probably seen as a cheap alternative to woven silks and velvets, since their patterns

275 The earliest dated copperplate-printed textile incorporates both the name of the printer, Robert Jones of Old Ford, Poplar, and the date of production, 1761. A complete repeat (not shown) measures a little under 2 m (6.5 ft) in length and would have required two plates to print. The detail (BELOW) testifies to the very high standards of design, engraving and printing achieved in these early prints.

not only the import of Indian painted cloths but also the production of the printed imitations. Prohibition in France, which lasted until 1759, seriously stymied the development of the industry, even though infringement of the regulations and smuggling were rife. In England, on the other hand, where the legislation remained in force for even longer (until 1774), various loopholes still allowed cotton to be printed for export, particularly to the rapidly expanding American colonies, and printed fustian (a linen and cotton mix cloth) to be produced for the home market. As a result, new and improved dyeing techniques continued to be developed there, and by the 1730s printed cotton was competing seriously in the market for fashionable materials.

The earliest European designs were florals in the Indian manner, although by the mid-eighteenth century they tended to imitate the designs of contemporary fashionable silk brocades, with more naturalistically drawn flowers on a white ground being the most popular. At about the same time the industry was transformed and the design repertoire greatly extended by the introduction of printing from engraved copperplates. Although the initial engraving of the plates was time-consuming and therefore expensive, the technique did make possible the printing of designs with repeats up to a metre in length, whereas with block printing the size of motifs was governed by the size of block which could be easily manipulated by hand.

The technique was related to intaglio printing on paper and its appearance similar, in that much finer detail and more subtle effects of light and shade could be achieved than with block printing. It was, therefore, to paintings, prints and book illustrations that the designers turned as their main source of inspiration; details would be copied, sometimes from a variety of sources, then the motifs reassembled to form new compositions. The main limitation of copperplate prints was that they could be produced only in monochrome, since the fine engraving made it difficult to overprint with a second colour, but this characteristic has tended to enhance their attraction. They were printed usually in purple, red or sepia, which all derived from madder, or in 'China blue', which required a laborious and chemically sophisticated series of dyeing operations using indigo.

Copperplate printing was first carried out successfully by Francis Nixon (d. 1765; printing at Merton, Surrey, 1757–65) at the Drumcondra print-works outside Dublin in 1752 and was soon after brought over to England. By the early 1760s several factories in the London area were producing top-quality copperplate prints,

ABOVE **276** Block-printed *indienne*. Jouy, France, late 18th century.

ABOVE RIGHT **277** Copperplate-printed cotton depicting scenes from the novel *Paul et Virginie* by Bernardin de St Pierre, first published in 1788. Manufactured by Petitpierre et Cie of Nantes, *c.* 1795.

which count amongst the finest of all surviving English printed textiles. Their repertoire included a wide range of floral and bird patterns, exotic designs, especially chinoiseries, pastoral and theatrical scenes, and episodes from classical mythology or recent history. Surviving pattern-books containing paper impressions taken from English eighteenth-century calico printers' copperplates show that the Dublin and London printers enjoyed a virtual monopoly of copperplate printing for almost a quarter of a century, until the technique was adopted by C. P. Oberkampf in the 1770s at his factory at Jouy-en-Josas outside Paris.

French calico printing blossomed after the lifting of the ban in 1759, and many factories were set up. The Rouen region in Normandy, Nantes in Brittany and the Île de France around Paris were all important centres for printed textile production in the second half of the eighteenth century. In Alsace, which was not part of France until 1798 and to which the ban thus did not apply, the first factory had opened in 1746 in Mulhouse, and the area soon had the largest number of print-works in France. Not surprisingly, after almost three-quarters of a century of prohibition, there were few French craftsmen with the knowledge and skills required to develop the industry, and in the early years French manufacturers used the expertise of foreign printers, from Germany, Holland and, especially, Switzerland.

Cristoph Philipp Oberkampf (1738–1815) was a German national living and working in Switzerland when in 1758, just before the lifting

of the ban, he was invited to Paris to assist with setting up a new print-works there. Two years later, in 1760, he opened his own factory at Jouy, near Versailles, which within a short period of time became the most famous and one of the most commercially successful print-works in France. At the beginning Oberkampf employed skilled foreign workers to train his own printers, whilst he himself travelled widely to research new machinery and to absorb new developments in dye chemistry. He made his first trip to London, for example, in 1773, visiting many of the major manufactories and carefully noting down everything he observed. In 1783 Louis XVI (1754–93) granted the Jouy works the title of Manufacture Royale, and in 1806 Oberkampf was invested with the Légion d'honneur by Napoléon I (1769–1821).

As far as the designs were concerned toiles de Jouy were as varied as the production of any other leading manufactory, and by no means confined to the monochrome copperplate prints for which the factory became so famous. The staff designers were engaged mainly in producing floral designs for woodblock printing; these *indiennes*, as they continued to be called, are not well known today but in fact represented much the largest part of the factory's output. Oriental textiles, especially Indian and Persian, remained a rich source of designs for them, though these might be combined with native birds and flowers or with rococo motifs such as fluttering ribbons or garlands.

Copperplate printing was introduced to Jouy in 1770, probably reaching the pinnacle of

278 Corner of a cotton kerchief, dyed Turkey red and block-printed and 'pinned'. Mulhouse, Alsace, *c.* 1840. Turkey-red dyeing was one of the specialities of the Alsace industry.

achievement in the craft after 1783 when Jean-Baptiste Huet (1745–1811) became chief designer. His fine drawing and the high quality of the engraving in the many pictorial designs he produced for Oberkampf set new standards in printed textiles. Huet's style was widely imitated in France and abroad, and the term 'toile de Jouy' has come to be universally applied to monochrome figurative designs wherever and by whomsoever they were produced. Popular subjects, as in England, included classical mythology, ancient and modern history, genre scenes and episodes from popular literary works such as *Robinson Crusoe*, *Don Quixote* or *Paul et Virginie*. Major events of the day also gave rise to fleetingly popular patterns – the first balloon ascent by the Montgolfier brothers in 1783, the American War of Independence, or the festivals of the French Revolution such as the Fête de la Fédération of 1790.

After the death of Oberkampf in 1815, the factory came under the control of his son, Émile, and the firm's chemist, Samuel Widmer, but the unstable economic climate in France after the Napoleonic wars, coupled with the competition from the rapidly developing textile printing centres in Alsace and Normandy, created problem after problem for the new managers. The Jouy factory eventually closed down in 1843, and many other French printing firms folded about the same time.

In contrast, the printing industries of Alsace and Rouen in Normandy both experienced a phenomenal rise in production during the nineteenth century, when the Rouen printers tended to specialise in styles for the rural population (as did the local weavers), leaving the Alsatian printers to concentrate on urban customers. The emphasis on good design and quality goods also enabled the Alsatian printing firms to compete successfully with the English manufacturers, whose standards dropped as they catered for an ever-widening market. The Normandy and Alsatian industries were particularly noted for their *mouchoirs*, a term applied not only to small pocket handkerchiefs, often plate-printed with commemorative scenes, but also to much larger headsquares. Several print-works in both centres specialised in the production of scarves and handkerchiefs, which achieved an unrivalled position in European textile markets.

The geographical centre of the printing industry had also shifted in England, from London to the north. The Lancashire printers benefited from cheaper labour and, more particularly, from their proximity to the weaving mills which had been producing English cotton since the mid-eighteenth century. By 1820 the bulk of textile printing had moved to Lancashire and Carlisle, leaving a small number of London printers virtually limited to specialities such as the printing of handkerchiefs. Very little copperplate printing was done by the Lancashire firms, who concentrated instead on polychrome woodblock prints for both furnishings and dress and, increasingly after 1815, on the new technique of rotary printing from engraved metal rollers.

Although engraved copperplates had made a difference to the appearance of printed textiles,

in allowing more detail and larger patterns with each impression, they had made little difference to the organisation of labour. With roller printing, however, it became possible to print an entire length of cotton continuously in a single mechanical process. The initial patent had been taken out by a Scotsman, Thomas Bell, in 1783, and roller printing was already being done in the Preston area of Lancashire by 1790, although it was at first limited to small dress patterns in single colours. It was soon adapted to accommodate the larger patterns appropriate to furnishing fabrics, but even then the difficulties of registering successive colours with several rollers were such that it was used at first mainly for monochrome figurative designs which imitated copperplate pictorial prints. Many of the pictorial designs produced at Jouy after 1800 were printed in this way, indicated by a finely patterned ground or a greatly reduced vertical repeat. The latter was necessary because of the limited circumference of the rollers, producing repeats about 30 cm (1 ft) in length as opposed to the 1 m (3 ft) possible with a copperplate.

These mechanical developments also went hand in hand with advances in dye chemistry, which radically transformed the traditional chintz palette during the first thirty years of the nineteenth century. Up until then most printing was done with vegetable dyes, principally madder, indigo and weld or quercitron bark for yellow. The first fast 'single green' was patented in 1809, replacing the traditional but rich 'double green' which had required the overprinting of blue and yellow; it was followed, before 1830, by

ABOVE **279** Roller-printed cotton known as *Les Monuments de Paris*, after a design by Hypolite Le Bas. Jouy, France, 1816.

280 Pattern-book of block-printed furnishing cottons. English, 1830s. The various colourway samples are typical of the rather garish and unusual colour combinations popular at the period.

281 Block-printed furnishing cotton in chinoiserie style. English, 1800–10.

a whole new range of colours from mineral sources, including manganese bronze (a dark brown colour), chrome yellow and antimony orange. The new dyestuffs were taken up enthusiastically by the industry, with the result that the fine drawing and engraving which characterised many of the designs of this period were often combined with garish colouring.

Chemical and mechanical developments in printing, coupled with the almost contemporaneous advances in the spinning, weaving and finishing of cloth by machine, amounted to no less than a revolution, but one which was as much social as technological. Greater mechanical ease of production led inexorably to a wider market and to a greater volume of production. The new consumers were the middle and skilled working classes, and even quite modest houses would now contain decorative fabrics, used on beds, tables and at windows. Printed cotton also allowed all classes of society, from domestic servants upwards, to dress fashionably. The repeal of the excise duty on printed textiles in 1831 had an even greater impact,

making goods for home consumption thirty to forty per cent cheaper. The period thus saw not so much a lowering of standards in the design and production of printed textiles, as is so often claimed, as the development of a much wider market with differing requirements.

The increased volume of production fed the growing demand for new patterns. After 1800 fashions in printed cotton changed routinely from season to season for dress patterns and every two to three years for furnishing fabrics. The relatively low cost of printed textiles compared with woven silks and velvets facilitated, in particular, the more rapid turnover of furnishing styles. In 1841 it was estimated that in Manchester alone 500 people were working as pattern drawers for printed cottons, and, in addition, many printers went to Paris three or four times a year to buy designs and to see what the French were doing.

The designs themselves were eclectic. Inspiration was sought, as it had been earlier, in Indian and Chinese textiles and other artefacts, but there was added a new interest in classical and

283 Corner of a cotton kerchief, printed to achieve a 'rainbowing' effect. Alsace, c. 1830.

standard of engraving and led at first to improved draughtsmanship and more careful block cutting since the woodblock printers were forced to raise their standards in order to compete. Until about 1840, when the mechanical and chemical difficulties hindering the printing of two or three colours consecutively were at last removed, most polychrome roller prints had the ground and basic design printed by engraved roller, then the extra colours added by woodblock or by relief printing with wooden surface rollers. These combination machines were known as 'union' or 'mule' machines. They allowed the fine line engraving of fancy machine grounds to be contrasted with the rich areas of overlapping colours provided by relief printing. Another novelty of the 1820s was 'rainbowing', the creation of stripes in bright colours which blended at the edges.

Because mechanisation greatly increased the quantity of cloth that could be printed from a single pattern, it made a successful design far more valuable than was the case with handblock or plate printing. It is not surprising, therefore, that it was in the 1830s and 40s, when rotary printing began to expand rapidly, that manufacturers first became concerned to protect ownership of their designs and to campaign for the copyright laws to be extended to cover designs for printed cottons.

The technological revolution of the late eighteenth and early nineteenth centuries enabled British manufacturers of printed textiles to turn out thousands of metres of cheap designs in the same time as, and often at less cost than, one length produced by hand. In the end it was the profit motive which brought about a lowering of standards in design. Design costs were reduced by copying foreign or earlier designs, and by using the quickest methods of cutting or engraving. Examples are known where to save time and money a copied pattern has not been adapted to a new width of cloth but has been simply cut away, thus destroying the repeat. Similarly, in order to satisfy the demand for new patterns all too often after 1840 incongruous ornament was added to, or spaces filled haphazardly in, existing patterns rather than new ones commissioned. In giving evidence to the Parliamentary Select Committee on Arts and Manufactures, set up in 1835 to look into the causes of the apparent inferiority of British design, J. C. Robertson, editor of the *Mechanics' Magazine*, attributed it to the 'talents of our artisans being employed in a more profitable direction than to any inferiority of taste in them. The great object with every English manufacturer', he explained, 'is quantity; with him, that is always the best article to manufacture of which the largest supply is required; he prefers

Egyptian motifs, particularly in the first decade of the century, whilst patterns borrowed from Kashmir shawls proved a long-lasting influence. The period from 1820 to 1850 saw many printed 'shams', or *trompe l'oeil* devices, which imitated, for example, the appearance of woven silks or needlework, even stained-glass windows, architectural details, swagged drapery or *passementerie*. And when new ideas were not forthcoming, the pattern drawer could always resort to revamping old patterns. Revivals of past styles were a recurrent feature of the period after 1820, encouraged by the prevailing taste for revived styles of furniture and interior decoration generally.

The new technology first began to be applied in earnest after 1825 and engendered a period of prolific experimentation. Cheap labour and raw materials further encouraged an uninhibited approach to design, and one cannot help but admire the flair, complexity and startling colour combinations which characterised the more expensive printed textiles of the second quarter of the century. Early roller prints show a high

much a large supply at a low rate to a small supply at a higher . . .'. Thus did industrialisation become linked in the artist and craftsman's mind with utility, with ugliness and with profit.

William Morris (1834–96) is generally regarded as the most influential figure in the movement which sought to reform standards of design in the second half of the nineteenth century, and in no field perhaps was his influence greater or longer-lasting than in that of printed textiles. When Morris set up his decorating firm in 1861, standards of design and printing in the English textile industry were at a low ebb. The larger Lancashire manufacturers depended on the sale of vast quantities of cheap printed cottons made especially for export to keep the industry afloat, while the high-class print-works merely copied the latest fashions sent over from France.

Most of Morris's designs for printed textiles were produced between 1875 and 1885. Working first in collaboration with Thomas Wardle (1831–1909), an established authority on silk cultivation and dyeing, at the latter's dyeworks at Leek in Staffordshire, Morris experimented during that period with various methods by then regarded as commercially obsolete. To achieve the effects he wanted Morris eschewed

roller printing in favour of a return to block printing. He hated the garish and unnatural colours of the aniline dyes which flooded the market from the later 1850s, and since the colours and shades of fading that he so admired in historical textiles were all produced by natural dyestuffs, he studied and revived for commercial purposes the use of vegetable dyes. The technique which most interested him, that of indigo discharge, eluded him until he set up his own print-works at Merton Abbey, just outside London, in 1881, but after that a large number of patterns were printed in this way.

Morris's earlier patterns were inspired, above all, by his knowledge of and interest in horticulture and botany; the later patterns, however, designed after the move to Merton Abbey, combine naturalism with a formality of organisation that Morris learned from his study of historical textiles at the South Kensington Museum in London (now the Victoria and Albert Museum). He was particularly influenced by Persian and Turkish textiles and by Italian woven silks of the thirteenth and fourteenth centuries (see II, 18), whence he borrowed the idea of showing pairs of birds and animals confronted or addorsed in mirror repeat. Indeed, many of his later designs use the so-called 'turnover', or mirror repeat,

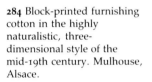

284 Block-printed furnishing cotton in the highly naturalistic, three-dimensional style of the mid-19th century. Mulhouse, Alsace.

ABOVE **286** William Morris, 'Honeysuckle', block-printed furnishing cotton, 1876. This was the first of Morris's printed textile designs to employ the 'turn-over' or mirror repeat.

RIGHT **287** A. H. Mackmurdo, 'Cromer Bird', block-printed cotton manufactured by Simpson & Godlee, Manchester, for the Century Guild, *c.* 1884. The sinuous, curving forms of Mackmurdo's designs later influenced the development of continental art nouveau in the years around 1900.

OPPOSITE **285** William Morris, 'Strawberry Thief', indigo discharge and block-printed furnishing cotton, 1883. The pairs of confronted and addorsed birds are inspired by the design of late medieval Italian woven silks.

rather than a straight or half-drop, and thus his patterns often exploited the whole width of the fabric from selvage to selvage. It is a method of pattern-making borrowed from weaving.

From the start Morris's designs made a great impact, although the hand methods used in their production made them inaccessible to those outside middle-class circles. Yet Morris's real influence lay not in his pattern-making *per se* but in the realm of ideas and in the impact which his theories had on the work of younger architects and designers such as A. H. Mackmurdo (1851–1942), Walter Crane (1845–1915) or C. F. A. Voysey (1857–1941). Indeed, the whole Arts and Crafts Movement in Britain and the United States of America owed a great deal to Morris's pioneering and liberating example. The revolutionary breakaway from traditional pattern-making, which is to be found especially in the designs of Mackmurdo and Voysey, clearly prefigures the developments which came to be identified as the art nouveau style. By the turn of the century the influence of Morris and the British Arts and Crafts Movement had spread to Europe – in particular to France, Germany and Holland – and Morris is justifiably regarded as one of the founder figures of the modern movement in the European decorative arts.

Britain continued to dominate world production of printed textiles into the early years of the twentieth century, both in terms of design innovation and manufacturing strength. The two were not unrelated: a sound manufacturing base in cheap, printed textiles largely produced for export emboldened manufacturers to experiment with more innovative designs. However, as the bread-and-butter industry began to contract dramatically between the two World Wars, so too did confidence generally in British design.

The beginnings of the decline were already evident by the end of the nineteenth century, when the industry's initial response was to amalgamate, with the aim of discouraging internal competition and controlling prices. The calico printers, a consortium of forty-six printworks which represented, in all, about eighty-five per cent of the printing trade in Great Britain, formed the Calico Printers' Association in 1899, a body which lasted into the 1960s. However, increasing competition for world markets from the United States of America and Japan in particular meant that the decline could not be reversed. British exports of printed textiles reached their nadir in the early 1930s, when they represented only one-tenth of their 1900 total. During the second half of the twentieth century European production of cheap, basic cloths has been entirely superseded by that of India and the countries of the Far East, where labour costs have remained low.

288 Two roller-printed designs manufactured by Turnbull & Stockdale, Lancashire, in the early 1930s. In spite of the growing popularity of abstract designs during the 1920s and 30s, there remained a steady market for floral patterns of all kinds.

An emphasis on good design and technical excellence has remained, however, an important feature of European printed textiles. In the years between the two World Wars Germany had the most forward-looking manufacturers, designers and studios, of which the Bauhaus (established 1919) was but one. Although it produced no printed textiles, the design philosophy of the Bauhaus had a significant influence on European printed textile designers during the 1920s and 30s, whilst the more widespread interest in abstract pattern which developed after 1950 also owed a great deal to the teachings of the Bauhaus. In its encouragement to students to form guilds of craftsmen similar to those which had existed in the Middle Ages, the Bauhaus borrowed from the ideas of William Morris and other British Arts and Crafts designers but diverged from them in its promotion of a machine aesthetic.

During the 1920s French design reigned supreme, with the 1925 Paris Exhibition acting as a showcase for what became known as art deco, in reality an eclectic mix of influences borrowed from cubism, the Bauhaus, the Orient, ancient Egyptian art, and the sets and costumes from Diaghilev's Ballets Russes, which toured Europe throughout the 1910s and

20s. World War II and its immediate aftermath restricted new developments in the Western European textile industries. During the 1950s it was the Scandinavian countries of Denmark, Finland, Norway and Sweden which were responsible for introducing a new, bright colour palette together with bold, geometric shapes on to a European market only slowly recovering from wartime restrictions, an influence which prevailed for several decades.

Stylistically, variations on the stylised floral patterns of art nouveau continued to sell until well into the second decade of this century, but the period from 1913 onwards saw a growing revolt against traditional pattern-making in favour of abstract and geometric designs. However, the floral tradition in printed textile design has never been fully abandoned, and the century has been characterised by a continuous tension between modernity and tradition. The move towards abstraction has meant that textile design in the twentieth century has often been closely aligned to contemporary developments in architecture and the fine arts. Architectural designs were particularly prominent in the 1950s and 60s, whilst artists themselves have, from time to time, been commissioned to produce designs for printed textiles. From 1912 to

234

*c.*1928 Raoul Dufy (1877–1953) had a contract with the Lyons silk manufacturer Bianchini-Ferrier and produced a large number of designs for them; in Britain many leading artists – Henry Moore (1898–1986), Ben Nicholson (1894–1982), Graham Sutherland (1903–80), John Piper (1903–92) to name a few – put their talents at the services of the printed textile industry between 1930 and 1960.

The adoption of screen printing fairly early in the twentieth century helped to make such de-

289 Sven Markelius, 'Pythagoras', screen-printed furnishing cotton manufactured by AB Nordiska Kompaniet, Stockholm, Sweden, 1956. Scandinavian design was highly influential in Europe during the decade or so following World War II.

sign experiments feasible. Because screens were relatively inexpensive to initiate and designs need not be restricted in scale nor in the number of colours employed, the technique allowed the designer great freedom and made it possible for manufacturers to print modern designs in limited runs without tying up large amounts of capital. Screen printing had begun on a commercial scale in France by the mid-1920s and by the beginning of the next decade its use was also well established in England and other parts of Europe. A hand process until the mid-1950s, it could not at first compete with roller printing for speed and thus was not appropriate for long runs of a particular design.

Screen printing has revolutionised the industry and encouraged a more rapid turnover of fashions in printed textiles since a relatively short gap can now be achieved between the production of a new design, the preparation of the screens and the appearance of the cloth in the shops. By the end of the 1960s rotary screen printing had taken over almost entirely from roller printing. In other sectors of the market, such as polyester bedding or printed т-shirts, heat-transfer printing is an alternative to screen printing. The technique is an industrial version of that which has been used for a long time to transfer embroidery patterns to cloth. Block printing, meanwhile, has become a craft technique in the twentieth century. Phyllis Barron (1890–1964) and Dorothy Larcher (1884–1952) were major proponents of the craft in England in the 1920s and 30s, making use also of discharge and resist techniques that had fallen into disuse since William Morris rediscovered them in the 1870s and 80s.

Another factor influencing the design of printed textiles in the twentieth century has been the introduction of numerous synthetic fibres. The industry was well established in Europe by the 1920s. Viscose and acetate were in use before World War II, with nylon and polyester following soon after; indeed, shortages of natural fibres during the War encouraged further experimentation with synthetics. The early synthetics had several disadvantages which prevented their being used in many markets: they draped badly and yellowed quickly, for example. By the mid-1960s, however, most of these problems had been eradicated so that, with the added advantage of new finishes such as drip-dry and pre-shrunk, they became much more desirable. The introduction of synthetic fibres has also encouraged extensive research into new dyes and dyeing techniques, as colour absorption using traditional dyes is sometimes problematic with synthetics. Post-war colour trends have naturally reflected these innovations and improvements in dye chemistry.

In Britain in the 1970s and 80s there has been a return to natural fibres and a revival of traditional crafts, reflecting perhaps a deep-seated nostalgia for the pre-industrial past. By 1980 many manufacturers of printed furnishings were producing 'document' (historical) styles, taken or adapted from museum and company archives, to the exclusion of almost all else. Meanwhile, ironically perhaps, the focus of both design and technological innovation has tended to shift from Europe to Japan, bringing the story of printed textiles full circle as Europe looks to the East for inspiration once more, some three centuries after the establishment of its own industries.

Central and eastern Europe

27 Eastern Europe

Textiles from central and eastern Europe fall naturally into two distinct categories – a small number, dating from before 1800, which were the products of professional workshops, and a much larger number, mainly embroidered, which were produced by women within the home for their own use; most of these date from about the 1820s to the 1920s.

In the first category the oldest-surviving textiles, some from the twelfth century, are exquisitely worked embroideries intended for use within the Orthodox Church, either as hierarchical vestments to be worn by the clergy, as liturgical cloths to be used during services, or as church furnishings. Such items were usually produced in the schools and workshops which were attached to most convents. Designs followed Orthodox principles, the more complex ones being drawn by the same artists who illuminated manuscripts with, it should be noted, more movement and expression than is found in contemporary Greek or Byzantine embroideries. Most were embroidered with invocations and verses from hymns in Slavonic, and sometimes with the name of the donor and with

the date. Probably the most numerous embroideries to have survived are large panels decorated with the body of the crucified Christ attended by angels which were carried in procession on Good Friday; whereas some of the most dramatic are tomb-covers (intended to cover the tombstone) which are decorated with life-sized portraits of patron saints or with a funerary portrait of the dead person.

Although nuns continued to make all the important vestments and cloths until the seventeenth century, skill with a needle was highly prized, and from the sixteenth century onwards the large houses and palaces of the nobles always included a workroom in which women would make and embroider cloths for the Church (as well as household linen and clothes). The most costly materials which could be obtained were used – coloured silks, metal threads, jewels, spangles and oriental pearls. By the seventeenth century each regional capital also had commercial workshops for church embroidery. These tended to specialise in the extensive use of metal threads, working with gold and silver and emphasising details by contrast-

290 Detail of a bed valance. Linen embroidery and drawn thread work on a linen ground edged with bobbin lace. Russian, late 18th century. 83.8 × 182.9 cm (33 × 72 in). This is typical of the quality of domestic embroidery produced in the workrooms which were attached to very prosperous households.

extensively on garments and on accessories, especially as deep fringes on the most important of all accessories, the head-dress. Some of the finest examples date from the eighteenth century and were bequeathed from mother to daughter as the most precious item in her wardrobe. There was great regional variation, not only in Russia but throughout eastern and central Europe, where it was *de rigueur* for married women to conceal their hair. While special headdresses of varying complexity were used on feast days and festivals, simple caps or scarves would be used during the week, usually decorated with embroidered borders. Such embroidery was of great significance to those who could 'read' it: often the depth or number of borders indicated the age of the wearer – certainly the motifs used and their disposition indicated the region or even the village from which the wearer came. The head-dress was often the most traditional and distinctive part of an outfit, its style seldom changed, and even when all other regional garments had been dis-

ABOVE 291 Velvet panel, probably for a cushion, embroidered with metal threads and silk. Russian, 1865–6. 71.1 × 63.5 cm (28 × 25 in). This panel was worked for the Paris Exhibition of 1867 and, although of late date, illustrates the skilled use of metal thread which for centuries was typical of the best professional workshops in Russia.

292 Man's sash, compound tabby woven with silk and metal threads. Polish, late 18th century. 487.7 × 38.1 cm (192 × 15 in). There is a woven inscription at one end showing that this sash was the product of Franciscus Masłowski's workshop in Cracow, which was founded in 1786. This design seems to have been copied from ones then in production in other workshops in Sluck.

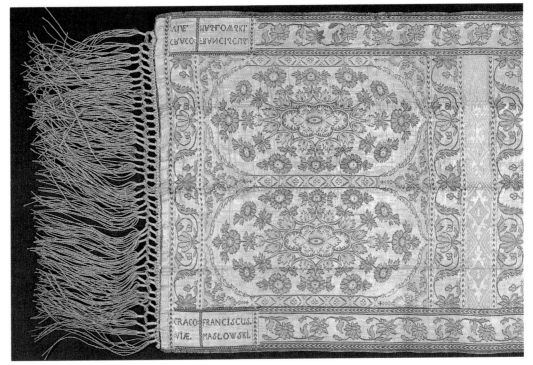

ing textures and, later in the century, with raised work.

Such lavish and formalised use of metal thread and applied ornaments was not confined to the Church. Seed pearls, in particular, were a popular form of decoration in the northern Russian provinces of Archangel, Novgorod and Olonetz, as they were readily available from the large rivers flowing north into the Arctic Ocean and were reasonably cheap. They were used

carded in favour of more fashionable dress, the local type of head-dress would still be worn on important occasions.

Another distinctive and indispensable accessory, this time for men and limited in use to the Polish aristocracy, was a sash of woven silk which would have been wound several times around the waist and then tied loosely. In the sixteenth and seventeenth centuries such sashes were imported with other textiles from Persia, but this trade was abruptly ended when Persia was invaded by Afghans in 1722. By the 1740s Armenian weavers had established workshops in many areas of Poland to produce local versions of Persian designs, and some Polish weavers added to their number. Often the sashes were designed in such a way that they could be folded along their length to reveal two different patterns or two different colour schemes and so make them more versatile. After Poland was partitioned in 1795 and its land was divided up between Prussia, Russia and Austria, the tradition of wearing such sashes was gradually abandoned in favour of more cosmopolitan fashions.

Cultural identity is not easily defined or destroyed by changing political borders, which are drawn with more regard to defensible terrain than to divisions of language, religion or race, and so it is necessary to understand the map of central and eastern Europe at the beginning of the nineteenth century. In 1815 central Europe was a patchwork of small principalities and kingdoms which were gradually and sometimes forcibly united – those south of Switzerland to form the Kingdom of Italy in 1870 and those to the north to form the German Empire in 1871. Each small unit tended to retain its characteristic and often unique textile traditions, fiercely guarding such distinctive cultural markers and continuing to call themselves Bavarian or

Genoese instead of German or Italian. In contrast, eastern Europe was dominated by three long-established empires – those of Austria, Russia and the Ottoman Turks. Many different cultural groups existed within these vast domains, and they were as determined as their contemporaries in central Europe to resist total cultural assimilation. Traditional garments and furnishings not only emphasised separate regional identities but some were even adopted by the intelligentsia and the ruling classes to represent their nationalistic aspirations.

In eastern Europe political independence could not erase 300 years of Austrian, Russian or Turkish culture, and their textile traditions – whether in design or in technique – are still inextricably mixed with more localised traditions. It is said that the art of the furrier, the appliqué decoration of garments made from sheepskin, was introduced to Hungary by the Ottoman Turks who ruled the area until the end of the seventeenth century. It has become one of the most distinctive forms of Hungarian art, and its Turkish origins are reflected not only in the techniques used but also in some of the favourite motifs – the rose (also said to have been introduced to Hungary by the Turks), the tulip and the pomegranate. In the middle of the nineteenth century brightly coloured woollen embroidery replaced appliqué, and the designs became more detailed. The furriers did every-

ABOVE 293 Tobacco pouch, leather embroidered with silks. Hungarian, 1850s or 60s. L. (excluding tassels): 99 cm (39 in). These pouches were used on feast days and festivals and were worn against the leg, with the point thrust into the top of the boot so that the embroidery and tassels hung down towards the ground.

Map 7 Central and eastern Europe in 1815.

294 Festival costume: blouse, skirt, apron, waistcoat, head-dress and boots. Hungarian (Transylvania), late 19th century. The most precious items in this outfit would have been the machine-embroidered boots and the embroidered sheepskin waistcoat, both made professionally. Although the sleeves of the blouse and parts of the apron are also embroidered, the greatest visual impact is created by the extensive use of beads and ribbons and by lifting part of the skirt to reveal an orange lining.

Russia, serfs. The second category of textiles to be discussed – home-produced costume and furnishings – were made by the peasants for their own use, not for sale. Such families would have owned or rented smallholdings on which they worked together to grow crops and raise animals. It was a hard existence, and only a large and united family would survive; marriages, births and deaths were therefore important events for the family, and each was marked in a formal manner which included the correct textiles and garment for the occasion.

The most important celebration was a wedding, at which the bride and groom would be attired in new garments which reflected the village's traditions. Not only was this a restatement of the identity of the village but it made practical sense for hard-working and provident couples to eschew fashion in favour of tradition: the clothes in which they were married had to last the rest of their lives, to be worn again on Sundays, feast days and festivals. The most lavishly decorated garments, usually the head-dress or a leather jacket, would be bequeathed to the next generation, and in some traditions the plain shirt and the chemise worn at the wedding were put on one side to be used later as the couple's shrouds. Everything was important and nothing was wasted; even decoration was applied only to the parts of the garment which would show – to the sleeves of a blouse but not to those areas which would be hidden under a waistcoat, or to the hem and side seams of a skirt but not to the central area over which an apron would be worn. The motifs and colours used were usually significant, with bright colours often indicating the youth of the wearer or the fact they were Roman Catholic, and with more sober shades worn by older people and by Protestants. However, it must be emphasised that any significance was normally localised to small areas and could be meaningless elsewhere. In the second half of the nineteenth century, when manufactured goods were made readily available from pedlars or from markets, embroidery was used less and visual impact was achieved with the lavish use of brightly coloured ribbons and braids, glass beads, paste and spangles.

For months, if not years, before the wedding the female members of the bride's household would have concentrated on making everything she would need for her dowry. Garments, especially those for the actual ceremony, were important, but greater status was attached to household furnishings – covers, sheets, curtains, towels, flat-woven rugs and cushions. These would be paraded through the streets of the village on the day before the wedding and would indicate the wealth and status of the girl. Most houses were built with two rooms, one for

thing: they prepared the hide, tailored the garment and completed the decoration. The finished garment (waistcoats, jackets and cloak-like *subas*) could be bought from their workshops and was usually the most valuable item in anyone's wardrobe, sometimes bought or given as part of a dowry settlement.

Not everyone could afford professionally made textiles – nor, in fact, was everyone entitled to wear them. There were sumptuary laws in most countries which decreed what class of person could wear what sort of garment, and there were many unwritten laws correlating the style and decoration of dress with the social status of the wearer. At the beginning of the nineteenth century five per cent of the population of central and eastern Europe belonged to the nobility, a further two per cent lived in large towns, and the rest were either peasants or, in

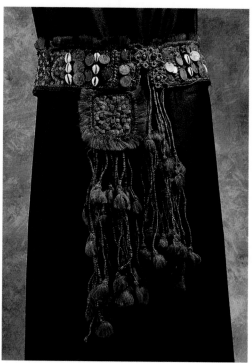

LEFT **295** Apron, indigo-dyed and glazed cotton embroidered with cotton and edged with bobbin lace. Czechoslovakia (Moravia), 1920s. L.: 61 cm (24 in). The use of colourful embroidery and lace on fabric already laboriously printed with a design illustrates the time and energy which was frequently devoted to the creation of regional costumes.

BELOW **296** Belt, wool embroidered with wool and decorated with applied ornaments including cowrie shells, beads, metal plaques, Austrian coins and tufts of dyed animal hair. 53.3 × 88.9 cm (21 × 35 in), including tassels.

livestock and one for the family. Even if more than one room was available, it was customary for the bed to be in the main room, on view to all. It was the most important item of furniture, and the greater the number of decorated cushions and pillows piled on to it, the wealthier the household. In order not to waste effort and materials it was normal for the cushions at the bottom of the pile to be undecorated or to have a simple border on the edge which would be seen, whereas the ones on top would have been embroidered all over. Curtains around the bed could provide warmth but were frequently used only in the period around childbirth to offer privacy and were often embroidered with whatever were thought to be 'lucky' motifs to ward off evil and to protect the mother and child.

LEFT **297** Interior of a 19th-century peasant house in Transylvania. This shows how the bed was one of the features of the main room and was piled high with richly decorated pillows.

Most designs, especially geometric ones worked in counted thread stitches, were traditional to particular areas and distinguished the textiles of one region or even of one village from another. The embroideress had more artistic freedom when working with other stitches so that traditional motifs such as vases and sprays of flowers, hearts, stags and birds could be combined in a variety of ways. There was always one person in each village who could draw well-balanced designs directly on to fabric for others to embroider. Homespun woollen threads coloured with natural dyes and strong, undyed linen fabric were used for both dress and furnishings until they were replaced in the later nineteenth century by synthetically dyed cotton threads and commercially woven cotton.

The economic, political and social changes hastened by World War I caused the creation and the use of traditional textiles to decline: in some countries small communities were forced out of their isolation, and in most the younger people began to migrate to towns and cities, moving away from subsistence agriculture into manufacturing industries. Sadly, the decorated furnishings and garments made in central and eastern Europe since the 1950s are part of an artificially revived 'folk art' intended to satisfy tourists' desire for souvenirs, and they have inherited very little of the exuberance and charm of the genuine article.

28 Greece, the Greek Islands and Albania

Greek embroidery from the Aegean and Ionian Islands is a splendid example of how a particular set of historical and social circumstances can affect the existing traditions of embroidery – in this instance by creating not one new style but a number of them, one for each of many small and sparsely populated communities that are not likely to have generated such individual styles of their own.

The whole Greek world came under the influence of the great artistic flowering of classical Greece which persisted for many centuries, though this pure stream was later muddied by a succession of powerful external influences. The first was Byzantium, the natural inheritor of the classical tradition, which brought in ideas and techniques from Sassanian Persia, the Arab world and China, and which imposed the new Christianity throughout the region. From the beginning of the thirteenth century the mainland of Greece and the islands were invaded or occupied by a succession of culturally diverse people: the Frankish invasion brought Crusaders from France, Italians arrived from the city-states of Genoa and Venice, Normans came

from Sicily, Arabs attacked from Mamluk Egypt, Catalan mercenaries occupied Athens for a while, and finally the Ottoman Turks conquered Greece and the Balkans as far as the walls of Vienna. During the long period of Ottoman rule the mainland and some of the islands of Greece were partly repopulated by Slavs and Albanians from the north as part of a political reorganisation of the country, and Greece was continuously under attack from the European powers of France, Venice, England and Russia. It was only in 1947 that Rhodes and the last of the Dodecanese were ceded to Greece creating the country it is today.

All these foreigners brought with them new technologies and new fashions that were gradually absorbed into the native culture to create many different local embroidery styles in which the various imported elements could still be distinguished. The main areas of distinctive traditions are the island embroideries: Aegean work which has some commonality can be subdivided into the four main subgroups of the Dodecanese, the Cyclades, the Sporades and Crete; the Ionian group embraces the work of

Map 8 Traditional textile-producing areas of mainland Greece and the islands.

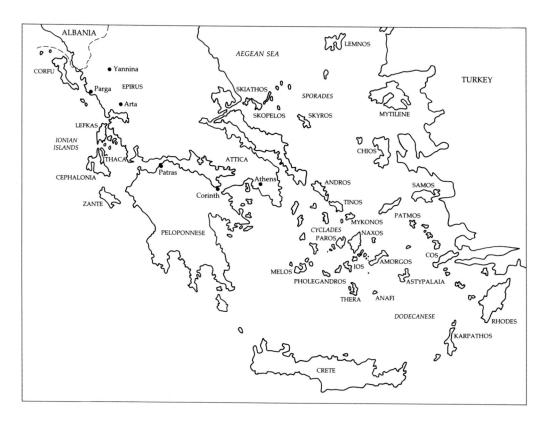

Corfu and the other islands lying south of it. The important groups of mainland embroideries are those from Epirus, Macedonia and Thrace, Attica, the Peloponnese and Rumeli; most of the mainland styles have more in common with the larger Balkan tradition than with the exotic world of the islands.

There are two great differences between island and mainland work: one is that mainland embroidery developed as a decoration for costume, particularly women's dresses, whereas in the islands decorative embroidery was used for a wide range of domestic textiles including dresses; the second is that the Ottoman occupation of the mainland was more oppressive and attempted, by persecution and the enforced immigration of foreigners, to suppress the individual spirit and to destroy the local style. In addition to this the introduction of cheap machine-made cloth and industrial dyes and the generally impoverished condition of the villages meant that the local textile and embroidery crafts were abandoned and a debased uniform style was adopted. In the more inaccessible islands, however, the hand of the occupier was lighter, and so the islanders, through their commercial enterprise and independent natures, remained relatively richer and their local traditions survived longer, although by the beginning of the twentieth century even they had lost most of their own distinctive traditions of embroidery.

The most commonly embroidered article throughout Greece is the woman's dress, the *poukamiso*, which is found throughout the Near and Middle East, as well as the Balkans, and which has been worn in this form for at least 2,000 years. It is a simply cut, full-length shift with long sleeves that was universally worn both as the standard daily costume and, in a decorated form, as a festive, ceremonial dress. It is made of straight lengths of a standard-width cotton or linen weave sewn selvage to selvage; the two outer panels of the skirt are cut diagonally to form a flare, and sleeves are either joined on at the shoulder or added as boxes or inset at the yoke. The *poukamiso* was usually worn as part of a layered arrangement of clothing and so only those portions that were likely to be seen were decorated: these are usually the base of the skirt, the area around the straight-cut neck opening and that portion of the sleeve that the local version of the costume allowed to be seen.

The simplest version of the embroidered decoration has a wide border around the base of the skirt, the same pattern in a narrower band around the lower edge of the sleeve and a very simple edging around the neck opening. It is usually worked in a monochrome dark red, dark blue or black in a clotted geometric pattern that becomes a solid block of colour with a barely discernible pattern. More elaborate versions have narrow vertical columns of the pattern

FAR RIGHT **301** Detail of the skirt of a *poukamiso* from Astypalaia. Polychrome silk on cotton. The border is filled, alternately, with ships manned by three sailors and mounted horsemen.

RIGHT **300** *Poukamiso* from Argos, showing the more conventional geometric decoration that is a feature of much mainland embroidery.

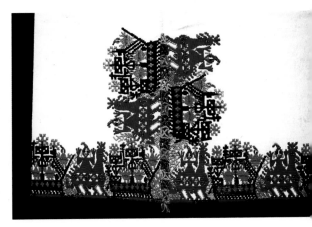

rising up the skirt from the border; there can be from two to eight of these columns which occasionally reach as high as the waist. Sometimes isolated architectural motifs are set above the broad band to form a turreted pattern. The sleeves in some costumes become very full and can be embroidered all over, even covering the shoulders. The strict geometric pattern elsewhere becomes more fluid and elaborate: in Crete, for example, it develops into a rich frieze of flowers and figures, and in Attica small floral

ABOVE **302** Detail of a skirt from Crete, decorated with a frieze of stylised motifs derived from Venetian originals. Signed 'Maria Papadopoula, 1757'. Blue silk on linen/cotton.

303 Bed tent (*sperveri*) from Rhodes, complete with its 'cap'. Each panel is covered with versions of a coat of arms and a broad leaf pattern.

or architectural motifs are set out in repeats to form dense blocks of pattern that cover the skirt, back and front, for three-quarters of its total length. Elsewhere skirts are additionally embroidered with metal thread and festooned with coins and ribbons. The range of colours used also varies, particularly in the skirts from Attica and Crete where the whole spectrum of polychrome silks is used.

Although skirts are also embroidered in the islands (there are some very spectacular dresses from Karpathos in the Dodecanese), embroidery was more commonly used there for decorating a large range of domestic textiles. Home in the islands was usually a single room separated into an area for cooking and living, with another for sleeping. Privacy, such as it was, was achieved by curtains. These curtains and the coloured plates and copper utensils which were hung about the walls were the only decoration to be found in the house. The bed was the most important piece of furniture in the house: it was often the only permanent fixture and always occupied a dominant position, placed on a platform or in a niche and hidden behind a hanging. The embroideries associated with the bed are those most commonly found in the islands and are the most magnificent of all Greek embroideries.

In the Dodecanese a large bed tent, the *sperveri*, had been introduced into the islands by the patrician families of Italy and the Knights Hospitaller who owned Rhodes until 1522, and was similar to bed furnishings found in the noble houses of Europe. The tents were imposing structures and their lavishness was used to make a statement about the importance and wealth of the family that owned them. The most elaborate of these tents were made by professional ateliers in Rhodes and the neighbouring islands, and must have represented a very considerable expense to the family that had them made.

The tent was made of linen panels which taper from bottom to top forming an elongated bell shape about 3.5 m (11.5 ft) in length and which could measure up to 8 m (26 ft) around the bottom; it was hung from a wooden disc suspended from a hook set in the ceiling. The tent is usually composed of ten front panels that are embroidered all over on the outside and four back panels that are only lightly embroidered on the inside. A double panel, split up the centre and worked in a different pattern and style, is set in the front to form an easily recognised entrance door. The patterns of the tent panels are usually large single motifs which are either simplified versions of heraldic coats of arms or stylised urns of flowers. The same motif can be repeated throughout, or a number of different

304 Large bolster cover (*maxillari*) from Naxos. Polychrome silk on linen. The design is composed of broad green lattice filled with a quartered medallion.

305 One strip from a set of bed curtains from Melos. Polychrome silk on linen. The design has three columns of alternating broadleaf and *spitha* patterns.

motifs can be worked together on each tent, either in monochrome or in two alternate colours. In all cases the scale of the motif is adapted to fit the tapered shape of the panels.

In contrast, the door panels are worked with a large range of different motifs which reflect the past of the island. The side jamb panels of the door are usually filled with a combination of two major patterns. Called the King and Queen patterns by an early collector, these are not the local names, which are the broadleaf and the *spitha*. *Spitha* is the word for a spark, which is an acceptable description of the shape. The area above the gable of the door is filled with motifs which reflect the history of the islands; it is locally called the *mostra* and can contain Mamluk stars from Egypt, Christian emblems of crosses and double-headed eagles from Orthodox Byzantium, heraldic castles and towers from medieval Europe, galleons, sailing ships and sailors from the contemporary world, and a menagerie of lions, leopards, dogs, deer, peacocks and parrots from local folklore.

In the other islands of the Cyclades such as

Naxos, Melos and Pholegandros and in the northern Dodecanese islands of Cos and Patmos the bed was set into an alcove, and instead of having a tent hung around it was screened by curtains rather like the box beds of northern Europe. These curtains were made of straight panels of linen weave and were much shorter than the bed-tent panels. In this case the curtains were composed of two leaves, each of four panels sewn selvage to selvage.

The most widely recognised of all Aegean embroideries are the curtains and bolster-covers made in Naxos. The whole surface of these curtains is covered in a complicated geometric pattern which in its elaborateness and its many variations is very reminiscent of Islamic ornament. The curtains are worked in satin stitch in a monochrome red floss silk which is laid in two directions, giving the appearance of having been worked in two tones of the same colour. In Melos and Pholegandros a stylised pattern of candelabra and animals is worked in elaborate columns vertically within each panel.

The version of the curtains that is attributed to

306 Curtain to enclose a bed alcove, from Cos. Silk on linen. Each panel has a vertical row of the *spitha* pattern with a simple border of isolated stars.

Patmos is worked only in a combined broadleaf and *spitha* pattern, although modern research suggests that these curtains were also made in the Cyclades. In Cos and the other Dodecanese islands the curtains and tents are invariably embroidered with a pattern called the *dixos*, which is a stylised development of a medallion very similar to those found in Eastern textiles, Turkish carpets and in the silks and damasks woven in Renaissance Europe. Some fifty named versions of this pattern have been identified. The *dixos* are set as isolated repeated motifs in columns up the centre of the panels, bordered by a small repeated cruciform motif. They are usually embroidered in cross stitch in a monochrome red, blue or green floss silk and occasionally in two of these colours used as contrast within each motif.

A number of other articles were also decorated to match and accompany the bed furnishings – long valances that were stretched along the front of the bed, innumerable long bolster cushions (*maxillaria*) and small, square cushion-covers. These were either piled on the bed or were stacked in columns alongside it. In many islands only one face of the cushion is covered

with embroidery; in others the embroidery is confined to just the edges, sometimes the edges on both faces of the cushion. In islands such as Anafi and Astypalaia which did not develop special bed furnishings these cushions and bolsters form the largest category of all embroidered pieces.

The large covers, called *sendonia*, were worked around all four edges with broad borders, with a separate motif, usually an urn of flowers, set inside the border at the four corners. In the Sporades this solid border is replaced by an open arrangement of large, isolated, floral, curvilinear motifs. Although *sendoni* means 'sheet', it is unlikely that they were ever used as bed sheets, and far more probable that they were hung on the walls behind the bed, particularly in Naxos, or draped over the banisters of the low parapet surrounding the bed platform as part of the room decoration.

In Skyros and the Sporades embroidery was used mainly for costume, most particularly for the women's blouses which were made of fine silk in bright colours and decorated at the sleeve ends and shoulders with embroidery in metal thread. The patterns were those elaborate flower and leaf forms that are found throughout the Near East. Many small, occasional, commemorative pieces such as cushion-covers and hand-towels were also decorated to celebrate weddings and christenings. These pieces depict a jolly, carefree life: engaged couples hold hands amid wreaths of flowers, the wedding guests carry candles and bunches of flowers, smoke pipes and play violins, hunters ride their horses in the hunt, armed with rifles and swords, and ships with sailors standing in their rigging sail in seas full of fish. These islands also produced one of the most powerful of all island images, the strutting multicoloured cockerel, the embodiment of the independent, anarchic spirit of the islander.

Crete was the jewel of the Venetian Empire in the east, and Venetian fashion and the whole repertoire of Renaissance European design were introduced very early into the folk crafts of the island. Embroidery in Crete is invariably associated with the skirts of the Cretan *poukamiso*, which is usually decorated with a deep multicoloured frieze depicting mermaids, crowned kings, snakes and dragons, urns of flowers ornamented with little manikins in the branches, or portraits of villagers dancing and playing musical instruments. There are a few pieces which were worked as betrothal cushions and even a few pieces intended for use in the Church as chalice-covers or bishops' copes. Crete produced a unique stitch worked like the grains on a corn stalk called corn stitch or Cretan feather stitch.

The Ionian Islands were also influenced by Venice from an early date, and Ionian embroideries reflect this influence, though in a quite different way from that of Crete. Ionian embroidery has none of the exuberance and gaiety of Cretan work; the same repertoire of motifs and stitches is used, but they are set out in a structured and formal way that makes the pieces more like Italian work of the same period than the more spontaneous island work. The Venetians also controlled a number of towns on the Adriatic coast of Epirus, such as Arta and Parga, and the embroideries attributed to these towns are part of the Epirote tradition.

The most exciting and diverse of all the mainland embroideries come from the province of Epirus. After the Frankish Conquest of Greece

ABOVE 307 Ceremonial Skyros cushion cover, most probably from a wedding, portraying guests, thirteen men and eight boys, carrying candlesticks, rifles, swords and flowers.

ABOVE RIGHT 308 Border of a sheet, from the Ionian Islands.

RIGHT 309 A cockerel from Skyros, a popular symbol of the island, representing its anarchic, independent spirit.

in 1208 Epirus remained part of the Byzantine Empire, and when the Ottomans conquered the Balkans after the fall of Constantinople in 1453 Epirus remained partly independent; by the middle of the eighteenth century it had become one of the richest manufacturing centres in the Ottoman Empire. Yannina, the capital of Epirus, was the centre of a flourishing textile and embroidery industry and provided uniforms and formal costumes for the Empire in Europe and the Mediterranean.

As well as the semi-mechanised industry which concentrated on embroidery in precious metals there was a very strong professional industry that produced embroideries for the Church and the home. In addition, there were a number of local domestic traditions that produced women's costume and domestic textiles which were an amalgam of both the Greek and Turkish traditions and provided the models for costumes in the Balkans and central Europe. This was based on loose-fitting caftans worn over baggy trousers and shirts and held in by belts and sashes.

Weddings were the most important social occasion in village life; they strengthened the community by creating alliances and consolidating ties, and the ceremony was recorded by the making of a number of special objects, separate from the dowry on which the new bride had worked from childhood. In Epirus there were betrothal cushions, showing the couple and their sponsors and relations, and special large cloths to be used on the wedding bed. These large embroideries were part of the Islamic tradi-

tion but were also used by non-Muslims; their broad borders are covered with the emblems of good luck and prosperity – tall cypresses, ewers of water, abundant flowers and the parrots that carry messages between parted lovers. These sheets were used, traditionally, on the wedding night and were displayed stained with blood the next morning to prove that the bride had been a virgin. They were also treasured and preserved, which accounts for the pristine condition of so many of them.

As elsewhere in the islands, the Roman Catholic Church existed alongside the native Greek Orthodox Church, and in Epirus altar cloths were made that must have been for the Roman churches. They are very rare textiles and the few that have survived portray a stylised angel that is not greatly dissimilar to the *peri* found on Persian carpets and Syrian silks. These winged creatures are set in designs composed of all the motifs from the common repertoire of Middle Eastern design, together with a number of local motifs which may include the double-headed eagle, the human-headed harpie and castle towers.

Embroidery in Greece was primarily a domestic craft and part of the daily household ritual. Every household had a loom, and both linen and cotton cloth were woven on it. Any surplus material was sold locally. All clothes were made at home and when they were decorated it was by embroidery. Silk was cultivated in many of the islands and was one of the most valuable commodities exported, either as a raw material or knitted into stockings. It was this locally produced silk, dyed at home, that was used for embroidery and which gives Greek island work its richness and quality. Because such an expensive material as silk was used, special stitches were developed to ensure that as much silk as possible was visible on the outer surface. The most common stitches were darning, stem and cross stitch; a particular version of the last was developed in the Dodecanese, the Rhodian cross stitch, in which the second arm of the cross is anchored not to the ground fabric but to the first arm, producing a raised surface unlike any other in European embroidery. Braided and twisted silk was also couched into patterns secured with small stem stitches, again to ensure that as much silk as possible was visible and that the desired bulky quality was achieved.

The embroidery of Albania is very much part of the Balkan Turkish tradition and virtually all of it is for clothing, though in this case for men and children as well as for women. In addition to the universal *poukamiso* dress tabular aprons and supplementary skirts are also embroidered, as well as many forms of headsquares used by both men and women. The jackets, made of sheep-

310 Wedding pillow from Epirus, showing the bride and groom standing on either side of a ewer representing both purity and future abundance. Polychrome silk on linen.

skin with the fleece on the inside, are embroidered on the outside. The motifs used are all part of the Balkan Turkish repertoire, mainly stylised flowers with a very occasional small bird. Unlike Greek work it is worked for the most part in harshly dyed wool in a variety of stem and darning stitches.

The gold embroidered surcoat, the *pirpiri*, which is usually called the Albanian coat, was produced mainly in the professional ateliers of Yannina, although some were made in Elbasan in southern Albania. It is an extravagant example of couched metal-cord or -braid work in gold or silver, where as much as ninety per cent of the surface broadcloth is covered with floral and geometric patterns related to those found on textiles from India and Persia. The version worn by men as uniform and as a ceremonial coat was heavily flared and had vestigial sleeves attached to it. It was worn over embroidered trousers, a white shirt and an embroidered waistcoat, together with multicoloured sashes and belts. It would have been hung about with a metal encrusted belt and holster, a scabbard with sword and dagger, pistols, a powder horn and an ammunition holder, creating an image of strength and power. The women's version, which was more lightly embroidered and not so flared, was worn over light baggy trousers and a billowing shirt. Albanian costume also included headscarves, sashes and large veils but they are all part of the same larger tradition, and it is now very difficult to be categorical about where particular pieces were made and who wore them.

ABOVE **311** Detail of one panel from a long altar frontal from Epirus. The complete piece shows a series of angels amidst flowers, above a border filled with ships, horses, castles and people.

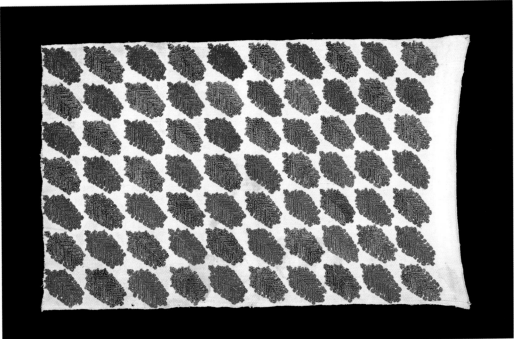

312 Cushion cover from Rhodes, with repeats of a feathered leaf design in two colours. Thick floss silk on linen.

29 Colonial North America (1700–1990s)

The North American population (its growth *and* its composition), climate, soil and sheer land mass resulted in a textile tradition different from that of the European nations, even though much in the way of technology and design was initially drawn from them. To have a substantial amount of indigenous textile manufacture, whether hand-crafted or industrially made, a country needs people – to provide both consumers and labourers – as well as the necessary raw materials, technology and (although essential to a lesser degree) design skills. The extent to which these elements were present or lacking in North America could not help but influence the character of textile manufacturing as it developed there during the eighteenth, nineteenth and twentieth centuries.

Labour shortages initially exerted an inhibiting force but by about 1800 encouraged industrialisation. It was not until the middle of the nineteenth century that America finally overcame its labour shortage and just equalled Britain's population, surpassing it by eight and a half million in 1870. Even then the forty million Americans were to be found scattered mainly over rural areas, for the rapid acquisition of land between 1840 and 1870 had increased the number of states to thirty-seven, enlarged the land mass from 1,750,000 to 2,970,000 square miles (essentially the size it remained until Alaska and

Hawaii became states in 1959), and shifted thousands of settlers to new, westward communities, leaving behind new immigrants – mainly Irish and French-Canadian – to work in the mills. The 1870s also marked the beginning of a forty-year period of more extensive immigration, during which time another forty million people, mainly from central and eastern Europe, arrived on the Atlantic seaboard. Providing labour essential to the continued growth of the textile industry, few could afford to emulate their predecessors and escape by homesteading or claim-staking. So while two-thirds of the late nineteenth-century population lived in rural areas and were supplied with textiles by the extensive railway network, those who tended the mill machines remained instead in densely populated pockets, contributing to the growing numbers of urban poor. The response to these conditions, both within and outside the textile industry, drove America – often uneasily and unevenly – towards social legislation, labour laws and more technology.

In 1990 the United States of America's Census Bureau recorded just under 250 million Americans, the rough equivalent of 1,000 people for every single resident recorded in 1700. No other Western textile-producing nation experienced such dramatic growth. It can be argued that population shifts and growth were the critical

313 Yarn-hooked rug with a burlap ground, made in the eastern United States in the early 20th century. The making of textiles in the homes of North America has continued throughout its history.

factors in the dominance of the United States of America's production over Canada's (hardly settled in 1770 and with twenty-six and a half million residents in 1990) and, indeed, in shaping a history of North American textiles that contrasts sharply with European textile development, which was stylistically, technically and economically far in advance until the mid-nineteenth century. This was particularly true of Britain which, by virtue of its Empire, commanded an enormous market; but North American experience differed also from that of France, where the population barely increased between 1870 and 1918 (a boom period for both North American textile production and population). As both the French and British Empires began to disintegrate in the twentieth century, North America continued to increase its population. With ever more and wealthier citizens the North American economy supported the rise of giant textile corporations and at the same time subsidised a significant proportion of the finest European textile manufacture.

The eighteenth century

Today it is difficult to set aside what we know of the present-day North American continent and imagine it as it was at the beginning of the eighteenth century – a vast wilderness divided by foreign sovereigns into territories largely uncharted, sparsely populated and with boundaries that were to be constantly disputed during the eighteenth century. In 1700 France believed itself proprietor of virtually all of the continent, save the southernmost regions stretching from present-day Florida through Texas to California (which were claimed by the Spanish Crown) and the British-held colonies around Hudson Bay and hugging the Atlantic coast. French claims were abandoned to the British and Spanish in 1763. Whatever their affiliation, however, the North American settlements, all ranged within striking distance of the eastern seaboard, were still firmly annexed to their European masters until the latter part of the eighteenth century.

Their occupants and the foreign governments and investors prized America for its natural resources. Both the French and English took substantial catches from the sea; furs came from the northern interior, as did timber; and tobacco from Virginia was so prized in London that it could be used as currency by tobacco growers. The future of North America seemed destined to rest on its exports of raw materials. Returning ships were laden with manufactured goods, including textiles. Among the many simple textiles imported – for America needed canvas for ships' sails, jute sacking, ropes, cords and other utilitarian cloths – the most numerous until the Revolution were wool fabrics, essential as protection from the winter climate in northern settlements, as vividly evoked by the name of an imported stout woollen cloth, fearnought. Some, such as the plain (tabby-woven) camlets, were for both clothing and furnishings. These sometimes included other fibres (typically silk or goat's hair) combined with wool, or were made entirely from worsted yarns. Worsted camlets, when stamped with damask-like patterns or watered, became the harateens, moreens and cheneys so often listed in eighteenth-century American inventories.

The preponderance of wool cloths was not solely due to climate (they were anyway less significant numerically in the south, where linen, silk and cotton were a better match for the humidity and heat); they also represented Britain's most well-established and therefore most fiercely defended textile industry. Protection for the woollen trade – although not created specifically for it – was offered by a series of British Acts passed between 1650 and 1696, which stipulated (and later gave teeth to the initial formula) that all but specially licensed foreign ships were barred from the colonies and that goods must arrive in England in ships belonging either to Britain or the country of origin. One of these Acts, the Navigation Act of 1660, also proved the importance of North American raw materials to the British textile trade for, with tobacco, sugar and ginger, it ensured that indigo, fustic and cotton were not to be transported out of the Empire.

Although trade to North America was largely controlled by Britain throughout the eighteenth century, fabrics from other countries were still available; for despite the regulations Dutch and, in particular, French merchandise was

ABOVE **314** Few documented American-made textiles survive from the 18th century, but this type of 'resist-blue' (or resist and direct indigo block-printed) cotton of about 1740–70 is found only in America. It is still disputed whether they were imports or of local manufacture.

FAR RIGHT **315** Whole-cloth coverlets such as this were typical of many early American textiles, with the decoration provided by stitching. Dated 1746, it was a wedding gift from Jonathan Misflin of Philadelphia to his daughter, Sarah Misflin Jones. The silk top-cloth (quilted on to a linen back) would have been imported from England or China.

316 These 18th-century linen checks were found in Pennsylvania and are typical of the patterns associated with German weaves, which were widely copied in America as they employed coarse yarns.

radically since the early seventeenth century, when James I (1566–1625) sponsored the planting of mulberry trees in Jamestown. Virginia continued to be a source of silk in the eighteenth century but produced less than Georgia (made a separate colony in 1732) and the Carolinas, where refugee Huguenots established in the 1680s were said to be the first to weave mixed silk goods, and in 1730 settlers were granted free land for planting 100 mulberry trees for every ten acres cleared. However, of the southern colonies it was Georgia that most actively pursued silkworm raising, bringing sericulturists from Italy and England in 1732. In Pennsylvania the rearing of silkworms began in the 1720s, and by the 1730s Pennsylvania cocoons were said to produce a cloth equal to that of the French and Italian looms. The best results, though, were obtained only by sending the silk to England for weaving. After 1749, when Britain removed the import duty on colonial silks, reeling mills (to draw the silk from the cocoon) were to be found in Philadelphia as well as Savannah, the latter site probably responsible for the 4,536 kg (10,000 lb) of silk fibre sent from Georgia to England in 1759. In the next year Connecticut began silkworm rearing and quickly established a lead that it held until the 1830s.

In the second half of the eighteenth century cotton slowly replaced silk as the fibre crop of the south; until the 1790s it was more time-consuming to prepare than flax or silk. Flocks of sheep, already part of the North American rural landscape by 1700, provided both food and wool. However, because cloth could be imported and food could not, wool was typically regarded as a secondary product from sheep until the early 1800s, when merinos were introduced especially for their fine-quality fleece.

With so much available raw material it was impossible for Britain to stop textile manufacture, despite such measures as disincentives placed on Virginian manufacture in 1628, the ban on exports of woollen cloth (including to other colonies) in 1699, and the outlawing of weaving in the Carolinas in 1719. As the earlier of these measures indicates, even in the seventeenth century textiles were being made by the European settlers of North America. The Philadelphia area in the same period had a good number of wool weavers and, judging by the fact that in the 1760s it had twelve fulling (wool-finishing) mills, continued to do so. There were sufficient silk weavers to warrant the construction of another silk-reeling mill in 1770, treating cocoons raised in Pennsylvania, Delaware, Maryland and New Jersey. Linen weaving also increased dramatically, for in 1752 Benjamin Franklin (1706–90) reported to the English Parliament that the flax represented by 70,000

smuggled into American ports. Since Britain did not make a full range of cloths, her own merchants imported foreign textiles which could be re-exported to the colonies. So while America's fine imported floral-brocaded dress silks undoubtedly originated in Spitalfields, and vividly coloured, striped and brocaded worsted calamancoes (also for clothing) were most probably from Norwich, imported furnishing silks, although uncommon until the second half of the century, were likely to be from Italy, a primary source of the silk damasks then used by English upholsterers themselves. India provided the world's most finely spun and vividly patterned washable cottons until the 1770s, both to Britain and, via British ships, to North America. All arrived in small quantities, relative to the number of wealthy North Americans.

The coronation in 1714 of the Hanoverian King George I (1660–1727) caused an increased British trade in Prussian and German textiles such as the sturdy, coarse linen or hempen cloths known after their original source as *osnaburg* and *ticklenburg*. These came to America too, together with fine linens from Holland and northern France, as it was only in the mid-eighteenth century that Ireland began to re-develop its industry based on this particular fibre. Ireland's increased interest in flax-growing was, in fact, partly responsible for the widespread cultivation of this crop in North America, where both flax and jute were indigenous plants; in the middle of the century Americans were annually sending tens of thousands of bushels of flax-seed to Ireland.

Indeed, the variety in soil types and climate meant that North America was better able than Britain to supply a full range of raw materials. In recognition of this sericulture was also encouraged by colonial governors, as it had been spo-

bushels of exported Pennsylvania flax-seed had all been made into coarse linen. (Fine linen thread was by now associated with Londonderry, New Hampshire.) By 1760 Philadelphia was the largest and wealthiest North American community (with 22,000 residents). As the principal North American port and mercantile centre, the area held the greatest concentration of textile manufacture on the continent.

Wherever there were concentrations of permanent residents, there were also professional wool carders and combers, fullers, spinners, weavers and dyers. Printing was also undertaken: newspapers – which began to appear in the 1710s – contained advertisements for block printers (as early as 1712 in Boston) and occasionally (after about 1760) copperplate printers. All this was done on what was essentially an *ad hoc* basis; farming families often completed a proportion – and sometimes all – of the processes. The rigid controls of the guild system, so essential to the development of European textiles, were never instituted.

Because so few documented examples have survived, little is known of the appearance of colonial cloths, although some impression can be gained from government reports, inventories and advertisements. As yet, nothing has conclusively proven the use of drawlooms, meaning that to create patterns weavers had to exploit the many possibilities of textural weaves and different yarn colours, resulting in twills and herringbones, or stripes, checks and the more elaborate interplay of these that became known as overshot designs. The bold effect of many overshot and checked patterns owed much to the German tradition which, as in America, relied heavily on linen and coarse wool (as op-

ABOVE **317** The Landis pattern-book, containing drafts for multi-shaft damask and coverlet weaving, dates from the 18th century and was probably brought to Pennsylvania by an immigrant German weaver, as the notations are in German.

318 Woven on a four-shaft loom in white cotton and dark blue and red wool, this overshot coverlet was made in Tennessee. Dated examples of this type of coverlet survive from as early as 1773, though this example dates from some fifty years later.

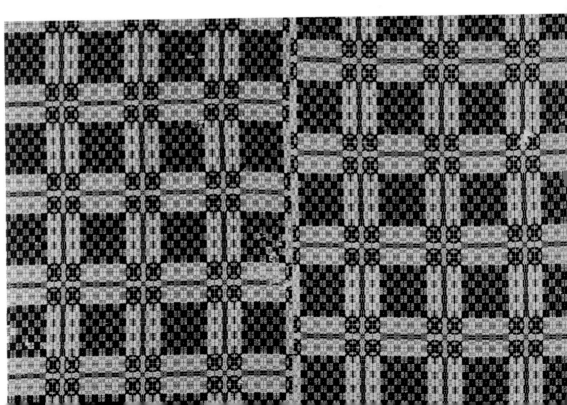

319 The fashionable patterns on this patchwork coverlet were block-printed by John Hewson between 1790 and 1810. His Philadelphia printing works was established in 1774; interrupted by the Revolution, it continued in his son's hands after 1810.

posed to England's finer wools and worsteds). Using the same materials, sturdy, striped, narrow-width carpets were also made. For designs that broke away from the geometry imposed by the multiple-shaft loom, patterns were printed or, more commonly in home manufacture, embroidered in brightly coloured crewels.

The Revolutionary period (1765–1800)

Since agriculture – both to establish ownership of land and to provide food and raw materials

for export – was foremost among North American occupations during the eighteenth century, manufacturing was not seen as the way of the future until the events of the 1760s. Then, as patriotic fever increased in response to taxation by Britain (especially after the Stamp Act of 1765), local cloth-making began to be seen – although not by everyone – as another means to independence. Until 1775, and again after the Revolution, many patriotic, philanthropic and philosophical societies sponsored attempts to establish more efficient textile manufacture, and several inventions for multiple spindle and reeling machines were patented.

Despite these measures, three elements combined to suspend development for another twenty years. The first was Britain's dramatic surge forward in the mass production of cotton yarns, with a consequent increase in their export to the colonies, together with British mixed cotton cloths, which had appeared in North America in ever greater quantities since the 1750s. The second was the Revolution itself, for while it interrupted the supply of British textiles from 1775 to 1783, it also hindered the attempts to mechanise in America and served, if anything, to reinforce the value of home production. Finally, although the estimated population had increased to over two million by 1770 and was confirmed as just under four million in the first official census of 1790, labour was not plentiful enough to provide low-cost workers, essential to compete with imported textiles. Giving infant North American textile manufacturers no time to recover, in 1784 British manufacturers flooded the North American market, most notably with their newly perfected all-cotton cloths printed with fashionable patterns.

The situation can be summarised by looking at Philadelphia and to Phineas Bond, British Consul, who in 1789 wrote to the Duke of Leeds that America would long need to import vast quantities of manufactured goods, particularly cottons, because British cottons were far better in quality and cheaper, since the credit allowed by English merchants was extremely liberal. Manchester-printed and -woven cotton cloths were sold at three-quarters the price of those made in Philadelphia and, he noted, this had given a sensible check to the progress of cotton manufacturing in America. So weaving continued in the hands of individual professional weavers, about 170 of whom were listed in the Philadelphia street indexes of 1785–1800, with about a third making stockings and a handful specialising in lace (braid), fringe, silk or carpet weaving. There were fewer than ten printers, among whom was John Hewson, whose printworks had existed briefly before the Revolution and survived into the next century. Like John Hewson, many who contributed to the growing understanding of cotton cloth-making and printing were English, although French, Scottish, Irish and German immigrants remained important, particularly to the hand-weaving trade.

The Philadelphia pattern was duplicated on a smaller scale in other growing communities, most notably in and around Boston. By the end of the century textile manufacture was still not industrialised, but the groundwork had been laid: in Beverly, Massachusetts, a completely integrated mill (combining hand-carding, -spinning and -weaving) was founded by George Cabot in 1787 and until the early 1800s made a wide variety of cotton cloths including corduroy, jean, denim, marseilles (double cloth) quilting, muslin and dimity; in 1790 Samuel Slater, an Englishman working for Almy and Brown, succeeded in establishing the first water-powered cotton-spinning mill in Providence, Rhode Island; and in 1793 Eli Whitney (1765–1825) perfected the cotton gin (which stripped the fibres from the seeds), setting in motion the development of vast plantations of upland cotton (more suitable to the southern climate than the finer sea-island cotton and more in need of the gin). There is also evidence that the appearance of North American textiles was coming into line with that of European textiles: a handful of surviving prints carry fashionable floral patterns, and North American weavers more often used imported fine worsted yarns and machine-spun cotton yarns, creating more supple and more durable cloths respectively.

1800–1860

In the first half of the nineteenth century progress was both dramatic and erratic. For example, Slater's water-powered spinning mill soon spawned others (seven by 1800, 213 by 1815) clustered along rivers in Connecticut, New Hampshire and, especially, Rhode Island and southern Massachusetts, where agriculture was limited by the rocky terrain. Nevertheless, since weaving was still done by hand – typically on an 'outworker' basis – the final appearance of North American woven cotton fabrics remained unchanged. The first efficient power looms came into use in 1815, but these machines initially made only plain cloth; even in the 1820s relatively simple cotton fabrics (such as gingham) were still hand-woven. The great number of independent weavers preserved the making of a variety of good-quality fabrics, a feature of the 'Rhode Island system', as it became known.

The installation of power looms coincided with one of a number of 'boom' periods, in this case the war of 1812–15, which increased demand for locally made cloths and alleviated some of the problems surrounding the Embargo and subsequent trade restriction Acts which from 1807 had plunged American merchants into financial losses. It was this interference with America's export trade that made some, such as the Boston Associates, a group of merchants headed by Francis Cabot Lowell, consider manufacturing as an alternative investment.

Nephew of the founder of the first American textile factory, Lowell had toured England in 1810–12 and observed power looms in operation, using this information to construct his

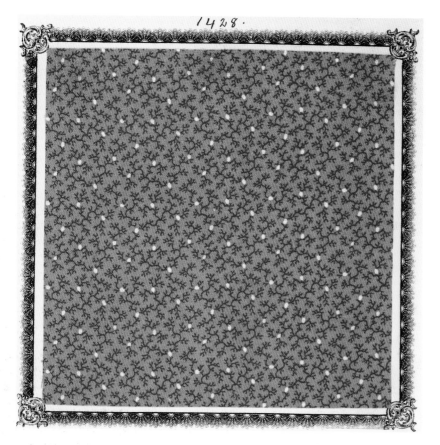

1428.

320 Discharge and semi-discharge madder prints were produced in large quantities after about 1835. This example of *c.* 1880 was roller-printed by Allen Print Works, founded in Providence, Rhode Island, in 1830–1. Such clothing cottons with small patterns became known as 'calicoes'.

cultivation extended to central Alabama, central Tennessee and the lower Mississippi River region, nearly four million bales by 1860. Most was exported to the United Kingdom; by the 1840s European ports annually welcomed some 4,000 ships carrying American cotton and Canadian timber (still its principal product).

The New England and Philadelphia mills began to machine-print cotton in earnest in the 1820s. Once more the effect was dramatic: in 1810 *Niles' Weekly Register* claimed that the greatest concentration of cloth printing occurred in the eight factories around Philadelphia, a fact not at all surprising, since one firm, Thorp, Siddel and Company, had just installed the first printing machines (one surface, or raised wooden roller, the other engraved copper roller). In 1812 they produced 1 million m (1.4 million yds). By 1832 the same district in north-east Philadelphia County had twelve such print-works, but by this time their competitors in New England were also well established. Within a few years even the tiny state of Rhode Island had a greater number of printers, among them Allen Print Works and Clyde Bleachery and Print Works, from which later samples of shirtings and dress fabrics survive in the Museum of American Textile History in North Andover, Massachusetts. The same collection holds samples from other New England firms set up as machine printers in the 1820s and important manufacturers into the twentieth century – Merrimack Manufactory Company, printing at Lowell from 1824; Dover Manufacturing Company in New Hampshire, from about 1827 (later Cocheco Manufacturing Company); and Hamilton Print Works at Lowell, from 1828. No pre-1860 samples have yet been identified from any of these firms.

We know little of the appearance of the early roller prints, save enough to refute the once widely held view that a cloth could be considered American only if it was crudely patterned. Some engraved rollers were imported and after 1825 increasingly made in America. These carried small all-over patterns (which became known in America as calicoes) and scenic designs, both of which remained popular for several decades thereafter. In the middle decades of the century the majority of designers were English, some hired in England by American mill owners, but the *patterns* were closely modelled on French designs. In the 1840s, for example, J. Briggs and Company (in Frankfort, six miles north of Philadelphia) used patterns supplied by John and William Ashton, designers lately from England, to supply their two four-colour and four six-colour machines. The Ashton designs followed French silks, vestings and prints (especially lightweight wools or delaines, which were

own version by 1815. The full integration of his mill at Waltham, Massachusetts – together with a corporate structure's enormous investment potential, a professional manager in place of an owner-manager and the use of subcontracted selling agents – all set this venture apart from the 'Rhode Island system'. In 1822, five years after Lowell's death, his associates began development of a new location north of Boston where the water-power was capable of running dozens of mills; named Lowell, it was to become one of America's largest textile-manufacturing cities and a model for much of its industrialisation.

Rapid factory development took place between 1820 and 1860. By 1850 there were 896 power-driven mills in New England, almost 500 of them in northern Massachusetts and based on the 'Waltham system'. This growth reflected the threefold increase in both population and wealth in the United States since the early 1800s, and occurred despite the serious depressions which followed the end of the war of 1812 (when British textile manufacturers again flooded North American markets) and which recurred in the seventh or eighth year of each succeeding decade during that period. It was also supported by the huge increase in cotton production in the Southern States, which counted 100,000 bales or approximately 230 kg (500 lb) in 1801, over 400,000 per annum in the early 1820s and, with

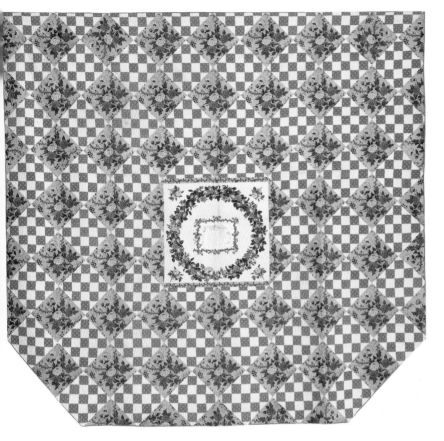

321 The roller-printed cottons in this nine-patch bridal quilt, signed and dated 'Philada May, 1841', were probably made in America. The zinnia print is found on other Philadelphia quilts, and is like those printed by Briggs & Co. in nearby Frankfort.

floral prints could easily be purchased (rather than salvaged). Such choice meant that different regional, ethnic or religious groups could more readily express their own aesthetic. While the Amish maintained into the twentieth century their use of plain fabric pieces in non-figurative patterns, the Pennsylvania Germans, equally enthusiastic and expert quilters, gradually introduced calicoes into their vividly coloured patchworks composed of stylised tulips, feathers, birds, hearts, sunbursts and other patterns that originally had symbolic meaning within their culture. Snowflake-like cut paperwork provided templates for a number of mid-nineteenth-century appliqué coverlets made – using red calico on a white ground – by Anglo-Americans in Delaware County, Pennsylvania, while the Anglo-French heritage in Maryland and Charleston, South Carolina, favoured the use of central flower-filled baskets.

The persistence of regional and ethnic preferences remained a feature of North American textile consumption; 'cheap and showy' prints were, for example, said to suit the western market in the years following the gold rush of 1849. Tastes also echoed the racial and ethnic origins of successive waves of immigrants as well as reinforcing the pre-Revolutionary, multicultural, non-integrated nature of society. As in the eighteenth century, the wealthy purchased imported cloths. Other elements from the eighteenth century also continued into the nineteenth. These include the persistence of handweaving, both by 'amateurs' at home and by professional weavers. In particular, the hand-weaving of wool was given impetus by the early nineteenth-century craze for merino and Saxony sheep breeding as well as the introduction of the hand-powered Jacquard mechanism, first used in Philadelphia in 1824 by the German-born, French-trained silk weaver W. H. Horstmann. The Jacquard added large, elaborately flowered and figured coverlets to the thriving production of linen-warp, woollen-weft coverlets with geometric double cloth and overshot patterns (and their variant, made by Pennsylvania German weavers without the long floats and known as 'Summer and Winter' coverlets). Until the 1860s Jacquards were otherwise used only in the linen-damask, coach-trimming and, after 1842, the carpet-making trades. So although by the 1840s basic factory-made woollens were being produced, the elaborate hand-woven coverlets continued to be made in Pennsylvania until about 1870 and eastern Canada thereafter (otherwise from the 1840s hand manufacture gradually moved west, as did the rearing of sheep).

highly fashionable), and their patterns had French names, with the result that many thought they were foreign. Despite the enormous increase in cotton-growing, printing and weaving, textiles of all types still accounted for the greatest proportion of imports in the decades before the Civil War; most came from the United Kingdom and typically were of the most expensive and fashionable sort, for since 1816 tariffs on cottons and woollens had protected American manufacture of stout, practical cloths. Thus, however up to date American patterned cottons may have been, the cloth itself was typically less fine than foreign versions.

Coverlets

The mechanisation of cotton printing coincided with the period during which patchwork and appliqué superseded the making of embroidered or whitework coverlets, as well as quilted whole-cloth or pieced (but plain fabric) coverlets, which had been well established in the eighteenth century, and typically used home-woven linsey-woolsey (a mixture of linen and wool). Appliqué and patchwork, already a sophisticated American art in the last quarter of the eighteenth century, relied 'for best' on imported cottons and this remained true into the 1820s. Thereafter with, for example, Merrimack prints dropping in price from 23 cents a yard in 1825 to 12 cents in 1840, small calico and larger

The Civil War to World War I

The Civil War had both an immediate and long-term effect on textiles. In the short term it disrupted trade and, in particular, the supply of cotton. The ensuing shortage harmed cotton mills in Europe and America but gave a boost to the production of woollen cloths – both printed and woven – as well as waste yarn spinning and the use of hemp, linen and silk. These fibres were often combined with cotton, with the result that for several decades many of America's cloths had a slubbed, textured or 'fuzzy' surface, particularly when waste yarns were used.

Sericulture, which had collapsed in 1840, was again attempted in California to no avail, and in 1860 only the Cheney Brothers' silk-processing firm in Manchester, Connecticut, survived from among the numerous mills established in the 'boom' years of the 1830s. Nevertheless, silk processing and weaving were by now well understood (a narrow-width power loom had, for example, been perfected in 1837–8 by William, son of the Horstmann already mentioned in connection with the Jacquard). Manufacturers returned to using European supplies during the Civil War, but in 1867 the Pacific Mail Steamship Company opened a direct service to China, and a new American silk industry began to develop, with New York becoming one of the largest silk markets in the world. By World War I America had far outdistanced France in its consumption of silk, mainly for stockings, and the industry also provided the firm base on which the man-made fibre industry was to develop.

The cotton shortage also forced many firms to streamline, and where once there were many multi-fibre and multi-process mills, these were far less numerous after the Civil War. Large factory complexes continued to expand in the north but were increasingly associated with one fibre or product. The Boston–Providence area dominated throughout this period: Fall River became the leading cotton-cloth producers, with fine cotton weaving dominated by New Bedford; Lawrence was the centre for worsted cloths, and Lowell, the site of the Hamilton and Cocheco mills, for printed fabrics. Paterson, New Jersey, aided by the influx of skilled French workers, became America's silk centre (producing fifty million dollars' worth of goods in 1909), while Philadelphia grew dominant in the use of wool for hosiery, knitted goods, carpets and upholstery cloths. The heart of this trade was New York, which dominated clothing manufacture and distribution, the latter from Worth Street.

The Southern States were slow to recover after the Civil War, and cotton production returned to pre-war levels only gradually. At the outbreak of war they produced only one-tenth of America's manufactured goods and hardly seemed placed to threaten the north's lead, but were gradually able to do so for a number of reasons. After the Civil War, and still counting on the north for technology and skilled workers and technicians, southern mills were often quicker to implement new ideas, such as Sawyer's high-speed ring-spinning machines, perfected in 1871 and well suited to coarse cotton yarns. One such enterprise based initially on this technology was the Cannon Mills of Concord, North Carolina, founded in 1887 by J. W. Cannon; within sixty years it was the world's largest supplier of household textiles and furnishing fabrics. Such firms were slowly able to take advantage of steam-power, the proximity of cotton (and coal for fuel) and the labour surplus created by the Reconstruction. These were poor whites, willing to work long hours for low pay. By the 1880s labour was a major factor, for while the ten-hour day was becoming a reality in northern mills and the minimum age rose to thirteen, neither of these practices, nor night-work for women and children (gone from the north by about 1900), was banned in the south until 1933.

In the decades before World War I the northern workers rebelled against their worsening living and working conditions. There were some 24,000 strikes between 1880 and 1900, but the most crucial were still to come. The Fall River strike of 1904 shut eighty-five mills for six months; almost half the workforce left the city. Eight years later a strike closed all the mills in Lawrence (where American Woolen [sic] in 1905 had built the world's largest cloth factory, covering thirty acres). The workers won higher wages, and their victory boosted organised labour throughout industry. The War created a temporary boom, but in the depression which followed its conclusion Lawrence was stricken by a further five-month strike in 1919, a year after the widespread United Textile Workers' strike, and in 1922 further wage cuts brought out workers in Rhode Island, then New Hampshire, Massachusetts and Maine.

Throughout this period southern production quietly and steadily grew. By the turn of the century there were well over fifty southern cotton mills, among them Dan River Mills (founded in 1882 in Danville, Virginia) and seven in Spray and Draper (North Carolina) that in 1902 began producing for Marshall Field and Company and subsequently, in the mid-1930s, became Fieldcrest Mills. Initially their product was cotton towels, sheeting and print-cloth or the cotton 'plaids' long made in northern factories for the southern and western markets. Northern mills continued to supply higher-quality goods; prints of all types ranged from lightweight cottons dotted with bicycles to sturdy cretonnes with patterns influenced by William Morris's designs; in Philadelphia mills were employing

322 In about 1885 Martyn Brothers of Jamestown, New York, made this lounge, upholstered in a carpet-weight Jacquard-woven 'tapestry' (weft-faced flat weave). Together with plush and moquette, wool and linen 'tapestry' was a principal product of Philadelphia mills.

new machines to make elaborate furnishing moquettes and plushes in deep, glowing shades. French patterns remained the most influential and imported fabrics the most desirable.

However, the dependence on foreign tastes was beginning to pale. The Lowell School of Design was established in 1872, and within a few years Charles Kastner (a Frenchman and former print designer for Pacific Mills in Lawrence) was training designers of prints and weaves; typical of many of the early schools, its origins lay within the industry. The Philadelphia Centennial Exhibition in 1876 inspired the foundation of a School of Industrial Art; by the 1880s there were also two design schools in New York, where its distributors, agents and garment-makers increasingly influenced design decisions. To improve public taste art education for schoolchildren was widely mooted. In matters of taste the Centennial had revived the colonial style, restoring with it the fashion for home weaving and patchwork quilting (neither of which had disappeared). Out of the discussion surrounding appropriate industrial design and an independent American style came a

lively arts and crafts movement, which set in motion a number of decorative art societies from New York (1877, co-founded by Candice Wheeler (1827–1923), who from 1883 to 1907 designed and produced textiles through Associated Artists) to California (where the Women Artists' Association in the 1900s was largely composed of weavers) and back to Montreal (where the Canadian Handicrafts Guild was founded in 1905). Members of such organisations were offered contact with firms such as Cheney Brothers and Marshall Field through the joint efforts of *Women's Wear (Daily)* and the American Museum of Natural History, which from 1916 sponsored a series of competitions and educational programmes. By 1919 a member of the museum's staff recorded that American-designed goods were selling in the discriminating markets of Paris and London.

1920 to today

In the wake of industrial strife many New England mills slipped into bankruptcy and those that remained found themselves gathered into consolidation plans (which often led to liquidation).

323 'Trees with Leaves', hand-screen-printed in c. 1948, was designed by Stanley Cosgrove and produced by Canadart Print Company for Henry Morgan and Company, a Montreal firm that in 1947 launched a collection of avant-garde products. It also sold at Robert Simpson Company in Toronto.

Although many mills continued to operate, they suffered by generally ignoring two significant changes in the industry – the increasingly rapid change in fashions, not just of designs but in fabric structure, and the introduction of man-made and synthetic fibres. The south, in contrast, embraced these changes and by the 1950s had become the centre from which both North American and world-wide textile empires were run. Two of these are Dupont and Celanese, which in Canada are two of that country's three largest textile companies (with home-owned Dominion Textiles second in Canadian sales and first in employment) and with Monsanto are the world's largest synthetic fibre and yarn producers.

The most striking feature of this period, however, is the development of an independence in design. Building on the gradual developments of the previous decades, both American and Canadian weavers extended their understanding of both modern and 'rustic' weaves. The depression of the 1930s hastened the need for handcraft industries. European *émigrés* to Canada created small influential studios such as Canada Homespun, founded in 1929 by the Dane Karen Bulow, who trained weavers who then reproduced her designs from home. As a result of government sponsorship and with the help of a French specialist, hooked tapestries from designs by Quebec artists were made during the 1940s and 50s, by which time the École de

Meuble had a textile department. Firms such as Canadart Print Company began, after World War II, to produce Canadian-designed screen-printed cottons; at the same time there were an estimated 70,000 handlooms in Quebec alone.

In America the pace was similar, and the turning-point was 1929, when the first Swedish weaver arrived to produce furnishings for Cranbrook Academy of Art, near Chicago. Other Europeans were influential: among them were the ex-Bauhaus weaver Anni Albers (b. 1899, at Black Mountain College from 1933 to 1949) and the Finnish-born, Swedish-trained weaver Marianne Strengell (b. 1909, at Cranbrook from 1937). On the eve of World War II hand-weavers such as Dorothy Liebes (1899–1972) and Boris Kroll (1913–91) became well established and began to influence the appearance of power-woven fabrics. Many such weavers existed, although few became household names, and they occupied positions in firms as diverse as Forstmann Inc. (which after the War employed Margaret Swanson to hand-trial their tweeds) and Virginia Mills, whose furnishing-fabrics division was run in the 1960s by Henning Waterson, a weaver and designer who trained with Frank Lloyd Wright (1869–1959).

Diversity, in fact, came to be recognised as the strength of the American textile tradition; as early as 1930 some machine printers were using modern designs by Donald Deskey (1894–1989) and Henriette Reiss (b. 1890), while others remained faithful to calicoes, by now the equivalent of the French provincial prints. By the late 1930s independent hand-screen printers could compete successfully with larger firms. With a significant proportion of mill production diverted to War use, hand prints provided much of the style leadership of the mid-century years and were produced by Laverne Originals, Elenhank Designers Inc., Dan Cooper (b. 1926), Adler-Schnee, Schiffer Prints and Angelo Testa (1921–84), the latter an articulate spokesman for

contemporary American textile design. Immigrants were also crucial to prints: it was George Neumann's upbringing in his family's Hungarian print-works that ensured the success of Vera (his wife and the name used by their firm Printex, founded in 1946 as hand-printers and said to be the first in America to install Buser automatic screen-printing machines); and it was the presence of ex-Bauhaus directors Walter Gropius (1883–1969) and Ludwig Mies van der Rohe (1886–1969) at the Institute of Design in

324 'Manhattan', by Ruth Reeves, was one of a series of designs commissioned by the New York firm W. & J. Sloane in about 1928. Block-printed on a wide range of cloth types and weights, the imagery typifies the increased confidence in American post-World War I design.

ABOVE **325** Innovation in off-loom structures has characterised the work of many American fibre artists, with results ranging from the exuberant to the authoritative, as here, in Ferne Jacobs' coiled and twined waxed-linen thread 'Red Bird Totem', 1991.

Since World War I, America has developed its own style, characterised by strong imagery as seen in a 1920s Stehli Silk 'Manhattan' (**326:** RIGHT), and bold colours, as epitomised by the fall/winter cover of *American Fabrics*, 1963 (**327:** OPPOSITE TOP). The vitality of post-World War II American art has also contributed to a unique style. 'Worried Man', 1974 (**328:** OPPOSITE BOTTOM), was designed by Frances Butler as a two-layer calendar and printed on cotton by Goodstuffs Handprinted Fabrics, her screen-printing firm, which operated in Emeryville, California, between 1972 and 1979. A graphic artist, Butler began printing on cloth in the late 1960s, and was influential in creating the taste for more sophisticated visual imagery which superseded fabric designs in the pop art idiom. The Fabric Workshop, founded in 1977 in Philadelphia, screen-printed Kim MacConnel's 'Bamboo Curtain' in 1978 (**329:** FAR RIGHT) – seen here with 1975 painted chair as shown at the ICA, London, 1987 – and remains the principal source of American artist-designed fabrics.

Chicago that influenced designers such as Ben Rose (1916–80) and Testa. In the 1950s Testa's designs were also roller-printed by other firms, including Knoll Associates who, together with Herman Miller Inc. (with designs by Alexander Girard, b. 1907), were furniture manufacturers who also promoted modern textiles.

Geographical diversity also continued to influence textiles. By the mid-1930s, for example, California's distinct style had aroused national interest, and its burgeoning clothing industry, soon to be second only to New York's, helped to support small enterprises such as California Handprints, Eric Hand Prints, Maria Kipp, the small hand-weaving firm operating in Los Angeles since World War II, and, in the 1960s and 70s, Frances Butler's Goodstuffs, as well as larger firms such as Elza of Hollywood, which produced influential, informal fruit and flower prints in the 1940s and 50s. New England's

tastes still support the use of stencil and quilt-like patterns. There remained, also, a taste for European designs, but by 1963 when, for example, one-third of all Marimekko production was sold in the United States, the American print producers no longer felt threatened but rather welcomed comparison with their own fabrics with confidence. This confidence barely diminished in the 1970s, since the textile-trade depression was far more severe in Europe and Japan.

Today the American market still supports the range of designs typical of the 1950s and 60s – textural and Jacquard-figured weaves and prints with abstract designs, document florals, scenic toiles, printed stripes and plaids, 'conversational' motifs and artist designs, the latter a reflection of the independent American school of art. Fibre-art textiles, grown up from the revival of hand-weaving, are also well estab-

lished, many deriving their inspiration from American Indian basket-making techniques. Patchwork, too, remains an important vehicle for the expression of the 'new' American tradition. Side by side with these highly visual accomplishments are the less glamorous products which form the backbone of the industry: synthetic yarns, vastly improved by texturing and blending; stretch fabrics, first made in America in 1954; laminates and layered fabrics, among which is the space suit; and an endless variety of industrial fabrics, from canal linings to cleaning cloths. Bolstered by perpetual growth in population and stimulated by successive waves of immigration (accounting, for example, for one-fifth of the total American population increase in the 1980s), the North American textile manufacturers have come to expect growth and diversity as a natural feature of their industry, both at home and abroad.

30 Native North America

In considering textiles produced amongst the North American Indians one automatically thinks of the Navajo and their colourful and much sought-after blankets and rugs, which are produced on the vertical blanket loom, a 'true-loom' introduced in the south-west some time during the Great Pueblo period (AD 1050–1300). However, true-loom weaving was confined to the south-west and is relatively recent compared with the tradition of finger-weaving.

Tribes from all over North America have produced a variety of objects for thousands of years by various techniques of finger-weaving. Using materials such as grasses, plant fibres, bark, human and animal hair, everyday articles such as mats, bags, sashes, aprons, sandals and blankets were produced by numerous, ingenious methods; twining, plaiting, crocheting, netting, braiding, looping, coiling and knitting have all been described. The complexity of these finger-weaving techniques varied greatly, the simplest perhaps being the suspension of warp threads from a loop of string, used by the Anasazi Indians of the south-west around AD 400–600, for making remarkably good sandals, vital protection in a hostile terrain of cactus, rocks and scrub. In contrast, some of the bast-fibre bags made in the early historic period by the Indians of the Great Lakes region were fabricated from an unusual and complicated weft-twining technique (described in Whiteford 1977, p. 59). To distinguish between some of these finger-woven textiles and some forms of basketry is often impossible as both use not only similar techniques but also similar materials.

Woven materials are naturally susceptible to climatic conditions, and most archaic and pre-historic examples have decayed. However, among specimens which have survived are fragments of ponchos and mats and even small items like sandals and belts, made by the Anasazi basket-makers of north-eastern Arizona and their Mogollon contemporaries in south-western New Mexico around AD 100–600. A notable collection, in the Arizona State Museum in Tucson, reveals a surprising variety of design layouts, although not as varied and numerous as those used on ceramics of the same period. In addition, imprints in clay can sometimes indicate a prehistoric textile technique, or a design on a piece of pottery, such as the depiction on a Mimbres (prehistoric south-west, c.1200) bowl which shows details of belts worn by two figures, can give an insight into the culture of this early period. Weaving in one form or another was produced, and in a few places is still produced, in many of the cultural areas, and some of the most prolific, unique, or interesting achievements are outlined below.

The Northwest coast

The tribes of the Northwest coast produced some of the most exciting artwork in North America, the Chilkat blanket being a prime example. These superb blankets, although not woven on a true-loom, equalled – some would say surpassed – the finest work produced in the south-west. Worn as ceremonial regalia and only by chiefs, the blankets are bold and instantly recognised by their long fringes and their

RIGHT **330** Reconstruction showing how the Anasazi blanket (FAR RIGHT) would have appeared in its original state.

FAR RIGHT **331** Detail from an Anasazi (prehistoric) loom-woven cotton blanket from Painted Cave, north-east Arizona.

332 Chilkat blanket, 19th century. These distinctive blankets, worn as ceremonial regalia and only by chiefs, were made by the Tlingit Indians of southern Alaska using a finger-weaving technique.

distinctive and dramatic designs. Representing usually stylised eagles, bears and sea monsters, possibly hereditary crests, the designs were first outlined on boards by the men and then copied by the women who did the actual weaving, the two almost certainly co-operating with each other during the long weaving process.

The band of Tlingit Indians from southern Alaska, who in the late eighteenth and nineteenth centuries produced these remarkably

Map 9 Approximate location of North American Indian tribes mentioned in the text.

complex blankets, used a finger-weaving technique where the warps, made of the inner bark of cedar shredded finely and mixed with the wool from the mountain goat, were hung from a horizontal bar; the double woollen wefts were then twined across and one blanket would require the hair from at least three goatskins. Sea-otter fur was also used.

One of the most intriguing aspects of the Chilkat blanket is the formation of perfect circles which are woven into the design and which are not found in other weaving styles. The designs were worked in three colours – black (obtained from hemlock bark), yellow (from tree mosses) and the distinctive blue-green from soaking copper in urine. It is interesting to note that members of James Cook's expedition to the area in 1778 likened these patterned, twined textiles to the New Zealand Ahoo and remarked upon several similarities in culture between the west coast Indians and the New Zealand Maoris (Samwell 1967, pp. 1099–1100).

Chilkat textiles are rare. However, a number of specimens do survive in museums, not only in North America and Russia (St Petersburg, where there are a number of early specimens in the Academy of Science) but also in Europe, in the Vienna Museum of Anthropology, in the Perth Art Gallery and Museum, Scotland, and in the Museum of Mankind, London, where there are several examples of Chilkat blankets, includ-

333 Clal-lum woman (Coast Salish Indian) weaving a unique style of white blanket, which incorporated the hair of a small, tame, white dog, now extinct (shown in the painting, by Paul Kane, 1847).

ing an unusual specimen which incorporates a painted design and is said to be from the Cook expedition, though it is possibly of a later date.

The Chilkat blanket was not the only textile produced on the Northwest coast. The Salish Indians, the largest tribe, were also weavers and made a unique style of blanket. Using a distinctive twill-plaiting technique, the Salish women produced a fine off-white blanket using the wool from mountain goats, cat-tail fluff and, uniquely, the hair (much finer than that of goats) of a small, tame white dog specially bred for this purpose and now extinct.

Later, after contact with whites, commercial yarns became obtainable and a few, very beautiful, coloured blankets were woven, before trade goods such as the famous Hudson Bay blankets (then, as now, manufactured in England in Witney, Oxfordshire, and traded throughout Canada) pushed Salish weaving in the 1860s–70s into a rapid decline. Examples of the coloured blankets are to be found, but only a few of

the rare off-white blankets exist today in isolated collections. However, in the 1970s there was a revival of Salish weaving, and using natural dyes from alder, cedar and hemlock bark, lichen and Oregon grape, attractive blankets with geometric designs were once again being produced (Ashwell 1978, p. 62).

The Plateau

Moving south from British Columbia, across the state of Washington into the Columbia Plateau, one encounters the Nez Perce, a tribe who practised the art of weaving quite considerably (in contrast to the neighbouring tribes of the Plains), although they did not make blankets. They produced various other articles, however, amongst them mats and women's hats, but a bag partly made from cornhusk was the craft for which the tribe was best known. Measuring anything from 15 × 30 cm (6 × 12 in) to 51 × 91 cm (20 × 36 in), these bags are well represented in many ethnographical museums.

Made in the plain-twined weaving technique, they were overlaid by false embroidery in coloured wool. The overlap with basketry is clearly evident, and sometimes these bags are included under that heading in general literature on native American art.

The warp threads were usually suspended from a horizontal rod and, working from the bottom of the bag to the top, the wefts were woven in pairs, one thread passing over a warp and the other under, these then crossing before repeating at the next warp. The embroidery is not an addition, as with true embroidery, but is twisted over the exterior of the bag. Many of the later (twentieth-century) bags used cornhusk for producing the false embroidery threads, but the earlier bags were made with bear grass (also known as squaw grass), collected by the women in the late summer from the Bitterroot Mountains, with Indian hemp for the warps and wefts. Colours were produced from the roots of the Oregon grape (also used by the Salish Indians for their blankets) and from variegated clays which made red, yellow and orange. Slime from rocks on the river beds gave green. Recently made bags, however, exhibit bright colours produced by aniline dyes and have commercial cotton replacing the native Indian hemp. The work was time-consuming.

Simple geometric patterns which appeared on both sides of the bag and which were usually different from each other formed the designs, some influence for which may have come from neighbouring groups. As a semi-nomadic people highly dependent on trade, the Nez Perce obviously came into contact with other cultures, and a design similar to that on a Northwest coast basket, for example, may appear on one bag and a more complex framed design from the Plains region on another. The popular star symbol used by this tribe may have been inspired by the American flag, given to various Plateau groups by the explorers Merryweather Lewis (1774–1809) and William Clark (1770–1838) in 1805–6. The bags were used for carrying and storing a variety of items, including the camas bulb (a food root and important part of the Nez Perce diet), and were also widely traded.

The Woodlands, Great Lakes and Prairie

Moving eastwards across the Plains some 1,200 miles, one encounters an entirely different terrain – a land of lakes, forests and, to the south, wide expanses of treeless grasslands. The Indians from this large area, of whom the Chippewa and the Iroquois were the most numerous and the best known, were adept at weaving the everyday articles that most suited their needs: bags, mats, sashes and garters were their main products, and a good cross-section of types may be found in museum collections today.

Small bags for storage of sacred objects as well as large bags up to 46 × 51 cm (18 × 20 in) or so for carrying food and other domestic everyday items were produced from bast fibre – particularly basswood – nettle fibre, mulberry and cedar bark, and moose, buffalo and opossum hair; they were fabricated using different techniques of finger-weaving, simple plaiting and twining being the most common. Decorative, final results were achieved with geometric patterns dividing figures such as thunderbirds, water monsters and humans. Coloured yarn was in-

RIGHT **334** Late 19th-century cornhusk bag, woven by the Nez Perce Indians of Idaho, a semi-nomadic tribe whose contacts with other cultural groups probably influenced the designs.

FAR RIGHT **335** Reverse side of the cornhusk bag.

ABOVE **336** Chippewa woman weaving a yarn sash.

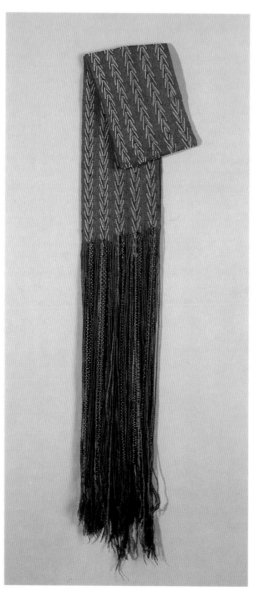

337 Iroquois finger-woven yarn sash. L. 1.5 m (4.9 ft).

troduced with the later bags, after about 1850, and using a twining technique the designs developed to include conventionalised floral motifs with geometric bands, the two faces of the bags presenting different patterns. As trade goods became more abundant, the bags used for ceremonial purposes were woven in loom beadwork.

Sashes, with long fringes, and garters were woven from commercial yarn using a simple finger-weaving technique where the threads were wound and interlaced around parallel rows of short sticks, the same strands being used for both warps and wefts. As with the bags, the weaving progressed downwards. Occasionally netting and braiding (diagonal plaiting) were also used. Both sashes and garters were worn by men and women. Normally the sashes, sometimes with small white beads woven in them, were worn as belts around the waist and, together with a native-made silver brooch, were more decorative than practical; they could also be worn over the shoulder, bandolier style, be used as turbans by the men, and, on occasions, be wrapped around a medicine bundle for transportation. Garters were made for fastening buckskin leggings and worn just below the knee, again by both sexes. Belts, highly symbolic and frequently exchanged at peace treaties, were woven, especially by the Iroquois, of wampum (purple and white cylindrical beads manufactured from clam shells).

Mats were an important feature of the wigwam and those made of bulrushes were the finest and the most common. Apart from their obvious use as floor-covering, they sometimes served as 'table-cloths', especially at feasts. The rushes were collected in early summer (if scarce, bast from red cedar would be substituted for a similar type of mat) and prepared for use with basswood which would serve as the weft; again the weaving went from top to bottom, and designs were geometric, although not all mats were coloured – for example, those made by the Huron from the north-eastern woodlands. Sometimes a smaller mat was made to serve a more sacred purpose – the wrapping for a war bundle, for example, and then the thunderbird motif could be used to promote power and/or protection. Mats sewn with a long bone needle were made from cat tail which was collected in the autumn. The primary function of this type of mat was to serve as a covering for the wigwam; they were of particular importance to the Prairie groups who needed to cover their entire wigwams with them. Unlike the woodland tribes, who could also use birch and elm bark, they had little access to these trees and in consequence made mats sometimes twice the size of their forest neighbours. Rushes and reeds were particularly useful plants to these people and were also used for making basketry utensils.

The textile arts of the woodlands people were diverse, and silk appliqué, or 'ribbon work', was another important technique which was practised possibly as early as 1750 in the Great Lakes area. As one progressed northwards in the region, this particular craft became less sophisticated. Patterns, mostly floral but sometimes geometric and frequently elaborate, were cut from silk obtained in trade and then sewn on to clothing. This elaboration was not solely confined to women's dresses but can be found on men's leggings, moccasins and cradle boards, although it is rarely found on buckskin. Before the advent of the sewing-machine, during the last quarter of the nineteenth century, the women sewed a design cut from one colour of silk on to a panel of a contrasting colour, using cross or herringbone stitch in yet another colour for more impact. Unfortunately, as is so often the case, silk appliqué has now almost disappeared as a craft in this region.

The south-west

Fifteen hundred miles south-west of the woodlands and Prairies, straddling the Mexican border, is the most famous weaving area of North America. The twenty-five or so settlements that comprise the Pueblos are strung out through New Mexico and north-eastern Arizona in a rugged and sometimes hostile terrain, a land of deserts and mountains where the climate varies from extremely hot summers to very cold winters. This colourful, magnetic landscape is home to the Pueblo Indians, once North America's most sophisticated weavers.

As with the other cultural areas, various techniques of finger-weaving were practised and in use in the south-west amongst the forerunners of the Pueblos about 1000 BC, during what is termed the 'Cochise Culture'. However, by around AD 100 the south-western groups had access to the belt or waist loom (which has been classified as a 'true-loom'), which probably filtered up, along with cotton, from Mexico. True-loom weaving progressed with the vertical blanket loom which was known to be in use during the Great Pueblo period (AD 1050–1300) and on which, before the arrival of the Spanish, some extremely intricate weaves were produced. Nevertheless, the belt loom – one of the oldest forms of loom in the world – was still being used in some areas into the early twentieth century – for example, at Isleta and San Felipe Pueblos.

The early finger-woven textiles, which included aprons, sashes, belts and blankets, were made – as was always the case – from what the local environment could supply – in this instance various plant fibres, mainly yucca, human and animal hair, and particularly rabbit skins. Then, with the arrival of cotton and the belt loom the weaving tradition expanded with cotton being continually harvested by most of the Pueblos until early this century. With the introduction of sheep by the Spaniards in the late sixteenth century a further expansion occurred, and the techniques used for weaving cotton were gradually transferred to include wool.

Traditional clothing, little changed, is still often worn at the fiestas and ceremonies which play an important role in Pueblo life. Unmarried girls wear large white cotton shawls woven in a diagonal twill technique with broad red and blue wool borders; women wear the classic *manta* (a rectangle of finely woven black or brown wool generally wider than it is long), made also in diagonal twill and worn off the left shoulder and pinned over the right. The men wear sashes and kilts, notable for their symbolic embroidery decoration, which has survived as a craft over several hundred years and which peaked during the Spanish period.

Different Pueblos had distinguishing elements. The Hopi, for example, the largest of the Pueblos situated in the middle of the Navajo Reservation in Arizona, bordered their dresses with dark blue diamond twill, whilst the men's sashes had distinctive cornhusk-covered knobs above the fringe. The Hopi men also decorated their ceremonial sashes and kilts with a unique brocading technique where strands of coloured yarn are wrapped around the warp, whilst only a very thin weft is used. This contrasts with the 'false embroidery' of the Nez Perce of the Plateau region, where the threads are wrapped around the wefts during weaving. The traditional *manta* is elaborated on by the Zuni, with the addition of silver brooches and a lace apron; and whereas the Zuni used blue to decorate their dresses, the Acoma, for example, preferred red.

The largest piece of cotton fabric woven is the Hopi wedding dress or robe and, as is usual with the Hopi, was woven by the men, in this instance relatives of the bridegroom. This plain-weave dress, whitened with chalk, has long tassels symbolising fertility hanging from the corners. Later, for use at important ceremonies, the wedding robe was enlivened by the addition of coloured-yarn embroidery, the designs including motifs of birds, butterflies, dragon-flies and rain clouds.

Blankets, which were once woven at most of the Pueblos (by the men, with the exception of the Zuni), are now produced only on a limited scale by the Hopi. Blankets were not only used for bed-coverings but were also worn over the

338 The manta, a black dress worn by the Pueblo women, is woven in diagonal twill and is generally wider than it is long. The decoration varies between the individual Pueblos: the Zuni, for example, embroider in blue, while at the Acoma Pueblo red is preferred.

339 Transitional old-style Ganado Navajo rug, dating from the first quarter of the 20th century. The cross design element was used extensively in the Ganado area prior to the 1930s.

and a few women from the New Mexico Pueblos make belts, but the modern materials used, including acrylic yarn, are mostly of an inferior quality.

Navajo blankets and rugs

When Washington Matthews undertook the first study of Navajo weaving in the late nineteenth century, he surmised 'that with no other tribe in America, north of the Mexico boundary, has the art of weaving been carried to greater perfection than among the Navajos' (Matthews 1884, p. 371), and so stimulated an interest that has resulted in the production of more literature in this field than in any other aspect of North American Indian art studies. However, although we know today that Chilkat weaving can be put in the same class (see p. 264), the quality, quantity and decorative appeal of Navajo rugs have made them much sought after, not only in North America but in other parts of the world, especially in Europe.

The Navajo, the largest tribe in North America, occupy an area in Arizona and New Mexico which extends over fifteen million acres, a majestic landscape of mountains, deserts and canyons, where it is unusual if the sky is not a startling, deep blue. The women learned the art of weaving from the Pueblo Indians around 1700, and the original blankets and dresses they made for themselves, woven from the wool of the *churro* sheep introduced by the Spaniards, were naturally similar to those of the Pueblo – quiet colours and simple, striped designs. The 'Chief' blankets made during what is termed the Classic period (*c.*1850–70) evolved from this simple, striped style and are extremely valuable and rare. These blankets were trade items and bought and worn by chiefs of other tribes, as far away as the Sioux and Blackfeet of the northern Plains. Sitting in front of a large vertical blanket loom, often for many tedious hours, the weavers progressed with the aid of 'weaving songs', which established a rhythm to work by.

After the 1860s (when they were imprisoned at Fort Sumner, also known as the Bosque Redondo), the Navajo broke with the early traditions, and with the acquisition of trade cloth and new ideas received from outside contacts they began also to weave rugs. Some of the main influences on the developments in Navajo weaving at the end of the nineteenth and early twentieth centuries came from Indian traders, the best known probably being Lorenzo Hubbell, who opened his trading-post on the Reservation at Ganado in the late 1880s (the trading-post is still in existence and has a wide range of Navajo weaving for sale). John Lorenzo Hubbell (?1855–1930), and others, suggested that the decline of Navajo weaving might be halted if

shoulders by the men. Different styles of blankets were woven for different purposes, and in general they were more loosely woven than those made by the Navajo. One of the oldest styles is the 'Moki', woven with deep blue or black stripes; a contrasting style was made from white or cream wool with stripes in blue, brown or black. Men's shoulder-blankets are boldly checked in black, white or grey 'tartan' style, and a few, brightly coloured examples, not traditional, have been produced for the tourist trade in recent years.

The fact that the Pueblo historically wove most of their textiles for their own needs and not for sale to outsiders is one of the main reasons why their weaving skills are less well known than those of the Navajos, even though the latter learned the craft from their Pueblo neighbours. Weaving today amongst the Pueblo is carried out on a very limited scale: a few Hopi men weave and embroider traditional items,

340 A group of Brule Sioux young men wearing Navajo chief blankets. These blankets were sold and traded to other tribes throughout North America and are today rare and highly prized by collectors.

341 Navajo women spinning and weaving.

and 1910, mostly very finely woven, have become known as 'eye-dazzlers', the bright colours and bold, geometric patterns making them easily recognisable. Various breeds of sheep were experimented with for wool varieties at the turn of the century, and today the most common to be found on the Reservation is the *rambouillet* (the French merino).

From that period Navajo weaving has constantly changed, and with the variety of imaginative designs it is often possible to identify from which of the thirteen weaving regions on the Reservation (which give their names to a particular style) a rug originates. For example, most of the Yei rugs (the elongated religious figures seen in sand paintings but which have no sacred significance in the rugs) are made in the Shiprock area in the north-east corner of the Reservation. A geometric-style rug, known as 'Two Gray Hills', comes from the area south of Shiprock and north of Gallup and is woven in black, white, grey and brown; it is considered to be 'the finest rug that has come – and continues to come – from the post-Classic Navajo loom' (Maxwell 1963, p. 25). The typical 'Teec Nos Pos' rug is distinctive for the zigzag designs of diamonds, bands and squares usually in red, black, white and grey, outlined with a vibrant array of colours which can include yellows, greens, purples, oranges and fluorescent pinks. It has been suggested that a trader showed pictures of rugs from northern Persia to the women of this area – close to Four Corners – in the early 1900s, whence originated this style (Maxwell 1963, p. 24). 'Wide Ruins', south of Chinle Valley and

rugs were produced for 'Anglo' homes, made heavier than the blankets, and, to suit 'Anglo' taste, given a central design with a border all round.

Also around this time a commercial yarn, mostly four-ply, called Germantown (named after a large textile centre now in Philadelphia) was introduced, and dyed with anilines was available in a range of brilliant colours which greatly attracted the Navajo women. In consequence, Germantown rugs made between 1880

342 'Yei' rug from the Shiprock area of the Navajo reservation, New Mexico. The Yei (elongated figures) traditionally appear in Navajo religious sand-paintings but do not have any religious significance in the rugs.

in a higher elevation, is the centre for vegetal-dye rugs and the colours are subtle: amongst the shrubs used are rabbit-brush for yellow, sumac for black and mountain mahogany for a dullish red (for a comprehensive discussion of dyes see Amsden 1934, pp. 67–93). However, the most traditional and 'familiar' deep red, black, white and grey rug, with bold simple designs, is the 'Ganado' – home of the famous Hubbell trading-post referred to above. The largest Navajo rug woven, 7.3 × 11 m (24 × 36 ft), came from here in the 1920s and took four weavers four years to produce (on average a good 1 × 1.5 m (3 × 5 ft)

rug will take about 240 hours of straight weaving, and in consequence most weaving is done in the women's spare time and is not the main source of family income).

Needless to say, many other types and styles of rugs are produced, including a 'two-faced' weave, where both sides of the rug present quite different patterns, and 'pictorial rugs', which come mainly from the Lukachukai Mountains area. However, when looking at Navajo rugs it should be borne in mind that there are variations and sometimes overlaps between the different weaving areas.

31 Latin America

Pre-Hispanic textiles in Mesoamerica and South America

Few parts of the globe are as geographically diverse as this region, which includes high mountain ranges, parched deserts, fertile plains and tropical forests. Over time many distinctive cultures evolved, with no proven outside influence until Spanish and Portuguese colonisation in the sixteenth century. Pre-Hispanic art has left its most conspicuous remains in Mesoamerica and in the north and central Andes, where civilisations such as the Aztec, the Maya and the Inca reached high levels of organisation and developed complex religions. Their élite dressed with increasing splendour and the textile arts flourished. Meanwhile cloth production persisted in smaller-scale societies. Equally creative and well adapted to often harsh surroundings, they made skilful use of meagre resources.

Mesoamerica

The term 'Mesoamerica' is applied to the cultural area which extends into northern Mexico and reaches in the south-east into Honduras and El Salvador. Archaeological examples of Mexican basketry, twining and netting have been dated to around 5000 BC; loom weaving (linked with the spread of agricultural settlements) followed after 1800 BC. Unfortunately for the study of early Mesoamerican textiles relatively few cloth samples have survived the heat and damp of centuries. Some 600 carbonised textile fragments, encased and preserved by thick mud, have been dredged from the sacred well at Chichén Itzá in the Mexican state of Yucatán. Additional specimens recovered from dry caves, and pottery remains bearing textile imprints, offer further information about pre-Conquest materials and methods.

Weavers worked with white cotton and with a toffee-brown strain known to botanists as *Gossypium mexicanum*. For warmth cotton could be interspun with downy feathers or with fur from the soft underbelly of rabbits and hares. Smooth and flexible cloth was also woven from agave, yucca and similar fibres. Vegetable colourants included indigo, brazilwood, logwood and annatto, while the animal world provided cochineal and shellfish dye; chemical analyses have also revealed the role played by iron oxide and other mineral substances. Although yarns may sometimes have been hand-twisted, most were spun with the aid of a spindle.

Textiles were intricately patterned on the backstrap loom. So far the following constructions have been identified – plain weaving with warp and weft stripes or checks, tapestry, end-to-end warp locking, double cloth, twill, gauze, weft-wrap openwork, and the superstructural devices of brocading and looped-weft weaving. (In the north of Mexico a different type of loom evolved: horizontal and stationary, it was built close to the ground from four logs.) Finished cloth was sometimes decorated with embroidery, free-hand painting or onlay work using feathers, shells, small bells and other ornaments. Textiles may also have been printed with pottery stamps and cylinders, while a single cloth fragment from Mayapán in Yucatán suggests that batik methods were understood. Blankets and garments often featured fringes and tassels.

Pre-Conquest design motifs and clothing styles are evoked by a multitude of clay figurines, stone carvings, polychrome pottery vessels, mural paintings and codices. Women wore wraparound skirts, waist-sashes, capes and head-decorations. Some, according to region, wore a sleeveless tunic called a *huipil*, or a closed shoulder-cape called a *quechquemitl*. Male garments included loincloths, hip-cloths, kilts, sashes, aprons, woven or netted capes, tunics and often spectacular head-dresses.

Spanish observers have left us several descriptions of native textiles and their uses. Fine weavings served as dowry payments and as wrappings for the dead; they were also offered to the gods and used to adorn the inner chambers of temples. In central Mexico lengths of cloth were an intrinsic feature of the Aztec economy, which operated according to a barter system; subjugated peoples were also required to provide the Aztec with tributary textiles. Valuable information is similarly provided for the ancient Mixtec, the Zapotec, the Otomí, the Totonac, the Huastec and the Michoaque (Purépecha) of Mexico. The Maya, whose territories included Tabasco, Chiapas and the Yucatán Peninsula in Mexico, together with Belize, Guatemala and parts of Honduras and El Salvador, were much praised by Spanish chroniclers for their textile achievements. In highly stratified societies like those of the Aztec and the Maya, dress served to reinforce the status of priests, nobles and warriors, while that of the lower class was controlled by strict rulings.

Pre-Hispanic South America

People have lived in South America for at least 10,000–15,000 years. At the time of the Spanish Conquest there were over fifteen million people. Most were subsistence farmers, with many relying to a greater or lesser extent on hunting and gathering. In the Andes a number of states and empires emerged and disappeared during the course of the past 2,000–3,000 years.

Weaving and other textile crafts were widespread throughout most of South America in the pre-Hispanic period. Sixteenth-century Spanish conquistadors recorded the sophistication of the finely woven fabrics of the Colombian highland communities, such as the Chibcha (c. eleventh to sixteenth centuries), decorated with complementary warp-faced patterns and painted designs. Used in burials, religious rituals and as ceremonial gifts, the value of these fabrics was considerable, and even a few hundred years after the Spanish Conquest a cotton *manta*, or shawl, given in tribute was worth two woollen ones.

On the east coast of Brazil in the sixteenth century the Tupinamba used hammocks of cotton and vegetable-fibre yarn. Made and used all over tropical South America, these became one of the first indigenous inventions borrowed by Europeans. Spun cotton yarn was used in the tropical forests for anything from binding feathers on arrow shafts to woven slings for carrying babies. Early European paintings show the feather head-dresses and ornaments of many Brazilian groups, fixed to cotton twined, knotted or woven backings.

Most of the existing pre-Hispanic textiles of South America come from the coast of Peru where they have been preserved by the hot desert conditions. Cotton was cultivated and used for textiles in Peru as early as 3000 BC, but it was probably domesticated and used for making textiles at an earlier date in Ecuador. The first Peruvian cotton textiles were twined and looped, with a few fragments of plain weave. These were techniques originally developed to produce baskets and fabrics of vegetable fibre, the earliest known dating from the fourth to fifth millennia BC. Some of the cotton fabrics had dyed as well as natural coloured yarns, interworked to create geometric designs, and figures already with stylistic features common in later Peruvian textiles.

With the use of camelid 'wool' from llamas and alpacas, domesticated in the pre-ceramic period, and wild vicuña and guanaco, a revolution in textile production occurred. Some of the most outstanding pre-Hispanic textiles come from hundreds of burials in the Paracas Peninsula (last part of the first millennium BC). They were wrapped around mummies to form bundles, some containing several hundred textiles. These cloths are notable for their vivid colours, owing to the use of camelid wool which takes dyes far more readily than cotton. Over 120 colour hues in these textiles have been identified from three main dyes: indigo, an unknown yellow-brown plant dye, and red, possibly from a species of *relbunium*, achiote (*Bixa orellana*), or from cochineal. Cochineal has been found in south-coast Nazca textiles (c. 200 BC–AD 200) and later eleventh-century textiles of the north coast. It was also widely used during the Inca period.

For all the sophistication of pre-Hispanic Andean textiles the equipment used was relatively simple. For making cotton yarn a spindle with or without a whorl was rotated in the fingers of one hand, while the cotton was pulled from a roll with the other. Camelid fibre was spun efficiently with a drop spindle. Still the most popular method of spinning and plying in the Andes, it can be done while walking, tending animals, or carrying out other work.

Pre-Hispanic cloth was woven to size, with four uncut selvages, on a loom using a continuous warp. Looms consisted of lengths of wood for breast and warp beams, shed sticks, sword beaters and bobbins. One of the early and most important developments was the introduction of the heddle (at some time between 1400 and 400 BC) for opening sheds more efficiently. Backstrap looms have been found in pre-Hispanic burials. They are effective only for weaving fabrics the width of the weaver's reach. For wider textiles and techniques requiring a fixed tension on the warp an upright loom was probably used, as shown on a pot from the north-coast Chimu culture (c. AD 1000–1500).

Every known weaving technique was used in pre-Hispanic Peru. By 400 BC all the processes were fully developed. During the late Paracas/early Nazca period on the south Peruvian coast embroidery was extensively used. Huge cloths, some several square metres in size, have wide borders and sections covered in stem stitch that completely obscures the ground weave. Others are fringed by three-dimensional figures of people, animals, birds and patterns worked in a cross-knit loop stitch that resembles knitting. Braids, fringes and cloths woven in sprang, double and even treble weave are also common among Paracas and Nazca textiles.

Tapestry began to replace embroidery as the dominant technique in the late Nazca period, and by the seventh century AD the most notable textiles were the large shirts woven in interlocking tapestry developed by the Tiahuanaco and Huari cultures which were spreading their influence over much of southern and central Peru. Possibly originating in the highlands, this tech-

ABOVE 343 Detail of a painted cotton textile, with characteristic Chibcha motifs including stylised human figures. It is the largest of a group of textiles said to have been grave wrappings from Gachansipá, near Bogotá, Colombia, c. 11th–16th century AD. Whole: 120 × 135 cm (47.2 × 53.1 in).

344 Huari-style textile fragment in interlocking tapestry, with camelid fibre wefts. The motif is a highly stylised winged figure which commonly appears in both Tiahuanaco and Huari iconography. Peru, c. AD 500–700. 29 × 26.7 cm (11.4 × 10.5 in).

made knotted textiles and delicate cotton gauzes, edged with heavy brocade borders, so fine that it is doubtful if they were ever used for any practical purpose. Coastal artists also produced cotton textiles and elaborate head-dresses covered with featherwork.

A technique unique to pre-Hispanic Peruvian weavers was the weaving of textiles with both discontinuous warp and weft. This required a scaffold of threads set up on a frame to keep the weaving in place while working and was pulled out on completion. The result, although resembling double weave or tapestry, is a much lighter, thinner fabric. Known from the Middle Horizon period (seventh to eleventh centuries AD), this technique is used by the Qeros of the southern Peruvian Andes today to weave small *mantas*.

There are tie-dyed and batik textiles beginning *c.* 900–200 BC onwards and a few examples of ikat. Some of the first painted textiles are cotton 'masks' stitched on to mummy bundles dating from around 300 to 200 BC. Large, unmordanted pieces from the Nazca period, painted with fertility and warrior images, were used as mummy wrappings but were probably also wall-hangings, altar cloths or banners.

Many pre-Hispanic textiles are decorated with images of mythical beings as well as naturalistic pictures of animals, plants and humans. The complex iconography hints at sophisticated religions and world-views. Some subjects recur

345 Detail of a fragment of a Paracas fabric, from the south coast of Peru, *c.* 400–100 BC. Camelid fibre. It might have been part of the border of a larger textile. The base and three-dimensional human figures are embroidered in cross-knit looping. The fabric is reversible, with figures holding staffs and fan-like objects edged in buttonhole stitch. H. (of human figures without border): approx. 2.5–2.7 cm (1–1.06 in).

nique was still being used 500 years later by the Inca to create their most prestigious textiles, called *qompi*, reserved for the Inca nobility.

On the north coast of Peru the Moche (*c.*AD 200–600) produced fine slit tapestries which continued to be popular among the later Chimu and the central-coast Chancay. Chimu weavers also produced brocades and elaborate textiles decorated with fringes, gold and silver ornaments, beads and shells. The Chancay

346 Tapestry from the north or central coast of Peru, with camelid fibre wefts. *c.* AD 1300–1500. 68 × 71 cm (26.8 × 28 in).

347 Inca tunic of a luxury type called *qompi*, reserved for the nobility. Possibly from the south coast of Peru, *c,* late 15th–early 16th century AD. Camelid fibre weft and cotton warp. Tapestry weave, entirely covered with complex geometrical designs called *t'oqapu*. Similar tunics with overall *t'oqapu* are shown worn by Inca rulers in an early 17th-century manuscript of Inca history, and may have been reserved solely for them.
91.5 × 77 cm (36 × 30.3 in).

over a long period of time, such as trophy heads (related both to war and agriculture) on Nazca textiles, but also in later cultures such as the north-coast Chimu; while others have become indicators of particular periods or cultures – for instance, the distinctive crescent head-dress depicted on many Chimu pieces.

Many of the burial textiles are clothes. Some show signs of wear; others seem to have been made for burial or as offerings since they are unused; and others are miniature garments. Peruvian clothing was untailored. A man's outfit consisted of a shirt, loincloth, mantle, belt, woven bag and head-dress. The latter could be a band, or type of hat, conical or square, denoting the wearer's cultural origins and role in society. A woman's dress was usually a wraparound garment, a belt, a mantle and a band or cloth for the head, again indicating her identity.

Only during the late Inca period does a clear picture emerge of the role of textiles in pre-Hispanic Peruvian society. They were used to mark different passages in a person's life from birth to death; they were used ritually, especially in ceremonies connected with animal fertility; they indicated a person's status in society, with the finest cloth reserved for the Inca emperor; and they also denoted regional origins. The camelid wool, and much of the cotton, was owned by the emperor and distributed among the population who were obliged to produce cloth as tribute. Hundreds of warehouses of cloth were stored all over the empire for distribution to the emperor's armies, conscripted labour force or for use as gifts.

Women in each household spun and wove cloth for their family's needs and for the tribute required by the Inca emperor. Luxury cloth was produced by specialist male weavers and 'chosen' women living in special enclosed societies. It is estimated that one weaver working a thirty-five-hour week would have taken over ten years to produce the cloth for one Paracas mummy bundle. It is the sheer scale of this human labour and the time and skill devoted to textile production that indicate the central role of textiles in these pre-Hispanic societies.

Post-Conquest and contemporary textiles in Central and South America

Mexico and Guatemala

Although Mexico and Guatemala have large non-Indian populations, they are still inhabited by more than fifteen million Indians speaking over seventy languages. In remote regions many groups lead a surprisingly marginal existence; others, in more accessible areas, have joined the national culture while retaining a number of their own traditions. Continuity with the past is reflected in the material culture of many communities where house-building, basketry, potting and weaving remain essential arts.

Although some Indian households use home-produced blankets and all-purpose cloths, textile skills centre chiefly on the creation of clothing. Under colonial rule new materials, techniques and costume styles were introduced. Spain's cultural heritage was shared in part with her European neighbours but it also owed much to Moorish occupation. The scope of these outside influences was further enlarged after 1565 when the Philippines came under Spanish domination. Contemporary textiles derive their vigour from the fusion over centuries of Old and New World traditions.

In many Indian villages women still dress much as they did before the Conquest. Wraparound skirts and waist-sashes are often worn with long or short *huipiles*. The *quechquemitl*, too, has survived in parts of Mexico; today, however, it is combined with the blouse – Spain's most significant contribution to female dress. Rectangular shawls are favoured in both Mexico and Guatemala. Women in some regions also use headcloths and carrying-cloths, and intertwine their hair with ribbons or cords.

Since the Conquest male dress has undergone more changes than female dress. Although the Lacandón in Chiapas still retain sleeveless tunics, men in most places have adopted shirts and trousers; often these are used with waist-sashes. In some Guatemalan villages a rectangular cloth is worn like a wraparound skirt over trousers. To make up for the lack of pockets in Indian dress men usually carry their belongings

RIGHT **348** Two-web single-faced *huipil* of cotton yarn with brocaded designs. Nacahuil, Guatemala. 152 × 109 cm (60 × 43 in).

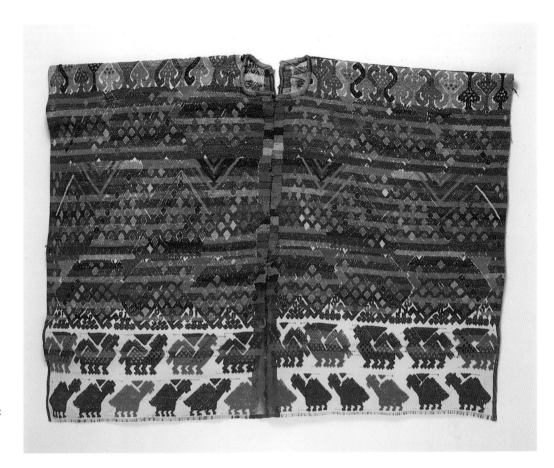

BELOW **349** Weaver holding up a two-web *tzute*. When in use, it covers the head and hangs down behind. Designs are brocaded with silk thread. Santa María de Jesús, Sacatepéquez, Guatemala.

BELOW RIGHT **350** Nahua woman wearing a wraparound skirt, warp-patterned sash, blouse embroidered in running stitch, and a gauze-woven *quechquemitl*. On feast days, woollen cords are twisted into the hair to form a turban; this may be topped by a second *quechquemitl*. Cuetzalan, Puebla, Mexico.

rectangles or squares of fabric. The elegance of Indian garments depends less on construction than on the texture and decoration of the cloth itself. White cotton is the fibre most used by weavers; brown cotton is rare and highly prized. Agave yarn is still used in Mexico to weave durable bags and carrying-cloths; in Guatemala agave fibres may be used in conjunction with cotton or wool to provide stiffening for sashes and ribbons. Sheep's wool and Asiatic silk, introduced during the colonial period, found wide popularity. Today, however, they are being increasingly supplanted by synthetic fibres such as acrylic and rayon.

Although the European spinning-wheel has been adopted in most wool-weaving centres, yarns of all types are still spun with a spindle in countless villages. Fibres are fed on to the tip of the spindle shaft with the left hand, while the right hand whirls the stick-and-whorl in a dish or half-gourd, or on smooth ground. Sometimes factory threads are respun by this method. Yarns, whether locally or commercially produced, are often dyed at home. Synthetic agents are popular, but fruits, flowers, leaves, barks and woods still serve as rural colourants; of these indigo has the widest distribution. Red and lilac shades are obtained, albeit rarely, with ground cochineal insects and with the secretion of shellfish. Iron oxide, gypsum and ochres occasionally furnish stable pigments when mixed with other elements; old iron, left to decompose in water, sometimes provides the basis for a powerful black dye. It is not known whether ikat dyeing was current before the Conquest. Today tie-dyed yarns are incorporated into shawls, sashes, skirts and shirts. Rarely figurative in modern Mexico, patterning in Guatemala includes tree and doll motifs and lettering.

The backstrap loom allows weavers in Mexico and Guatemala to achieve a vast range of textures and designs. Plain-woven cloth is often patterned with stripes for shawls and skirts; it can also feature raised bands created with thick or additional weft threads. In Mexico double weaving is a speciality with some Otomí, Cora and Huichol weavers, who produce handsome sashes and bags. Twill techniques may be used to pattern woollen skirts and small blankets. Gauze-patterned *huipiles* are worn by Kekchi women from Cobán in Guatemala; *quechquemitl* of figured gauze, featuring double-headed birds and human figures on horseback, are woven by Nahua women in Xolotla, Mexico. Weft-wrap openwork, like gauze, demands great skill; until recently Zapotec weavers from Santiago Choapan in Mexico made gala *huipiles* with bird, animal, flower and human designs using both weft-wrap and plain-weaving methods.

351 Tapestry-patterned *sarape* with cotton warp and wool weft. Woven in two webs on a treadle loom during the first half of the 19th century, it displays geometric motifs grouped round a central lozenge. Saltillo, Coahuila, Mexico. 238.7 × 157.5 cm (94 × 62 in).

in shoulder-bags. During cold weather many Mexicans don a woollen *sarape*, or blanket, with an opening for the head. Like the rectangular shawl this garment evolved under Spanish rule. Alternatively over-tunics or jackets may be used in Guatemala and the Chiapas highlands. Further elements include hats and headcloths.

Costume differences reveal the wearer's cultural group and place of origin; sometimes they indicate honorary status within the community. As in pre-Hispanic times, most garments are assembled without tailoring from

The versatility of the backstrap loom is further demonstrated with curved weaving: by converting a group of adjacent warp threads to weft threads some Otomí, Totonac and Nahua weavers in Mexico create cloth webs which are shaped at one corner of each end; these are joined to make gently rounded *quechquemitl*. With warp patterning raised designs are formed. Mexican sashes are embellished in this fashion in many regions; alternatively they may display areas of warp brocading. The most widespread form of woven decoration, however, is weft brocading. Textiles can be either single-faced or double-faced, but in Guatemala, where weavers use a range of brocading methods, double-faced cloth from villages such as Sololá carries an identical pattern on both sides. Closely related to brocading is weft-loop weaving; in Mexico the Otomí of San Pablito create double-headed eagles and eight-pointed stars

ABOVE **352** Trique villagers in San Andrés Chicahuaxtla, Oaxaca. The weaver uses a backstrap loom. She and her female companions wear everyday clothing, consisting of a wraparound skirt, sash and a long weft-brocaded *huipil* of wool, acrylic and cotton. Mexico.

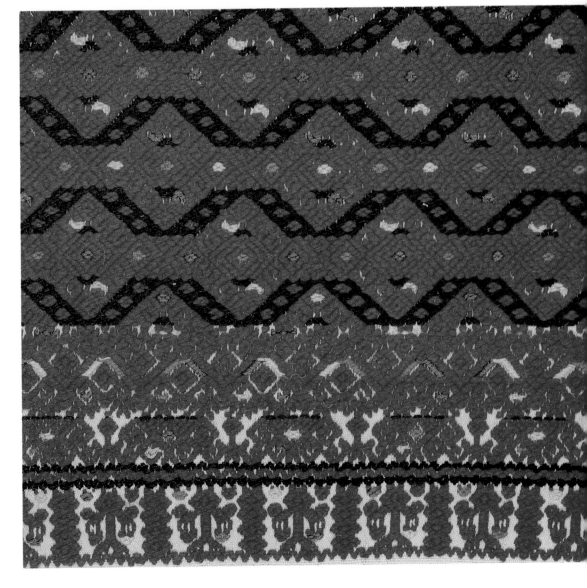

353 Detail from a Tzotzil woman's *huipil*. Woven on a backstrap loom with cotton yarn, it is richly brocaded with geometric patterning. San Andrés Larrainzar, Chiapas, Mexico.

by pulling up supplementary-weft threads to form a pattern of loops.

The rigid log loom is still used in northern Mexico by the Tarahumara, the northern Tepehuan and the Mayo. Square or rectangular in shape, it lends itself to the weaving of heavy woollen blankets and sashes. Techniques include plain and tapestry weaving, warp patterning and, on occasion, warp brocading. Weaving with native looms remains an almost exclusively female pursuit, but the Spanish treadle loom, or shaft loom, is generally worked by men. Output includes skirt lengths, shawls and blankets, patterned to meet local demand. Tapestry and twill are a speciality with many weavers. In Guatemala treadle looms have undergone many modifications of design. Drawlooms, with extra pattern harnesses, produce cloth with repetitive supplementary-weft designs for *huipiles*. Ribbon looms are constructed in a variety of ways. In San Miguel Totonicapán, for example, the loom resembles a small rectangular table; in the centre a raised structure supports four harnesses. Here head ribbons are tapestry-woven by men and women.

Spanish rule brought a new emphasis on embroidery. Fine work is achieved with cotton, silk, artificial silk, wool and acrylic yarns. Satin, running and crossed stitches are popular in many regions, while some garments combine hand and machine embroidery. Drawn-thread work, lace-making, crochet and knitting are post-Conquest skills. In Mexico small glass beads are sometimes sewn individually on to cloth, or netted to form bags and belts. Fringing is used, as in pre-Hispanic times, to embellish blankets and some garments. Further decorative techniques include appliqué, pleating, the onlay of sequins and the inclusion of ribbons, tassels and pompoms.

Indian costume has never been static. In recent years a love of ornamentation has led many Indians, who perpetuate ancient textile techniques, to adopt, simultaneously, day-glo colours in startling combinations, factory braid or lurex thread. Ancient motifs, too, have been joined by designs from printed pattern-books. Purists may regret these changes, yet one can only admire the tenacity of people who continue to take pride in their traditions and their clothing, when faced with such problems as economic hardship in Mexico and political turmoil in Guatemala.

The Cuna Indians of Panama

Little is known of the early history of the Cuna Indians. With an estimated population of 22,296 in 1970 the majority now live on the islands of the San Blas Archipelago; here Cuna culture is safeguarded by a strong internal autonomy. Past attempts by the Panamanian government

ABOVE **354** Two-web double-faced *huipil*, or woman's tunic. Woven on a backstrap loom with cotton yarn, it features brocaded patterning worked with cotton and artificial silk thread. It is edged with factory-made velvet. Santa María de Jesús, Sacatepéquez, Guatemala. 60 × 58 cm (23.6 × 22.8 in).

355 Tarahumara man's warp-patterned sash of hand-spun undyed wool. Woven on a rigid log loom, it has braided warp fringing at both ends. Norogachic, Chihuahua, Mexico. 203.2 × 9.5 cm (80 × 3.75 in).

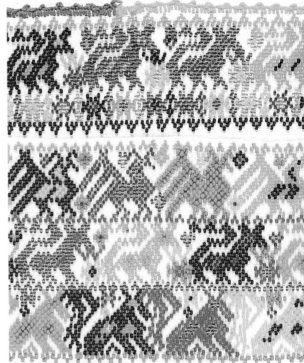

ABOVE 356 Tehuana gala costume. The velvet *huipil* and skirt are hand-embroidered with satin-stitched flowers. Isthmus of Tehuantepec, Oaxaca, Mexico.

ABOVE RIGHT 358 Decorative panel from a Cuna woman's *mola* blouse. San Blas Islands, off the Atlantic coast of Panama. 43 × 48 cm (16.9 × 18.9 in).

to modernise and integrate the island Cuna, and to prohibit the wearing of women's traditional clothing, have proved unsuccessful.

Today most Cuna women wear a wraparound skirt of printed trade cloth; after marriage they adopt a printed headscarf. In recent decades the Cuna have become famous outside Panama for the beauty and complexity of their *mola* blouses. *Mola* is the Cuna word for cloth. Each blouse comprises two sleeve panels, a yoke with a slit for the head, and two decorative panels which form the front and back of the garment. These

should be similar but not identical. The cloth is obtained from Colón, Panama City, or from island shops. *Mola*-makers are usually women, although there are some skilled male practitioners. Designs, achieved through a complicated and highly developed form of appliqué, are drawn on paper or directly on to cloth. In its simplest form *mola* appliqué requires a cloth base and a covering layer of a contrasting colour; this top layer is partially cut away to reveal shapes and colour beneath. Additional layers or sections of cloth may be inserted beneath the top layer; small patches of cloth may be superimposed on the top layer and on visible areas of these lower layers. Sewing is by hand and machine. Lines of running and chain stitch often decorate uncut areas of cloth.

Complex designs can defy interpretation by outsiders. They may reflect Cuna beliefs, daily life and the environment. Plants, birds, animals and marine creatures are frequently portrayed, together with themes from Cuna religion and the Bible. It has been suggested that symbols used long ago in body-painting and tattooing, or in picture-writing on balsa-wood, may have transferred themselves to the *mola*. Lettering and popular elements from mainland advertising campaigns and comic books have also been adopted in recent years. The often remarkable intricacy and the continued inventiveness of contemporary *molas* remain a source of pride for their creators and ensure much-needed revenue for the Cuna economy.

South America

After the Spanish Conquest the indigenous peoples of the Andes were decimated by war and disease. Many communities were forcibly moved nearer to Spanish centres for easier governing and conversion to Catholicism, and people were virtually enslaved to provide labour for Spanish overlords. It was only those in the remoter areas of the highlands or tropical lowlands who retained much of their traditional way of life.

The Spanish established local textile factories either worked by conscripted labourers or set up by villages to pay tribute. To increase demand textile imports from Spain were discouraged. As in Mexico, sheep and new types of equipment such as treadle looms were introduced. Indigenous techniques and styles disappeared as

359 Detail of a large colonial-period tapestry with Inca-style designs and European motifs. Inca nobles are shown in indigenous dress with European additions such as knee breeches. Peru, *c.* 17th century. Whole: 230 × 210 cm (90.5 × 82.7 in).

many spinners, weavers and dyers were fully employed producing European-style cloth. For a short while the luxury *qompi* cloth of the Inca survived, but European and oriental as well as pre-Hispanic designs were incorporated in the weave.

Indigenous dress changed dramatically. In the sixteenth century Indians (other than the Inca nobility) were forbidden to wear European-style clothing while at the same time forced to adopt more 'modest' attire – for instance, women sewed up the sides of their wraparound dresses. Then in the late eighteenth century, after a series of unsuccessful revolts against Spanish rule, the Indians were forbidden to wear 'native' dress and expected to adopt Spanish peasant clothing. As a result much 'Indian' clothing in Peru and Bolivia today is an adapted form of late eighteenth-century European dress plus survivals from the pre-Hispanic period –

360 A Quechua family in the region of Calca, Peru, in 1982. The shawls and ponchos of their local dress were woven on backstrap looms similar to the one used by the woman in the foreground. Their skirts and trousers were woven locally on European-style treadle looms.

the woman's shawl or *manta*, carrying-cloth, men and women's belts, woven shoulder-bags and cloths for carrying coca leaves. These are worn mainly by people in rural areas.

Indigenous textiles are still spun using the drop spindle and woven for the most part on backstrap looms. They are warp-faced, the only technique that has survived throughout the whole of Peruvian weaving history from the third millennium BC, perhaps always being the principal method for village textiles in the highlands. Patterns in complementary weave and double cloth decorate the edges and central panels. Many are identical with patterns found on pre-Hispanic pieces.

Much of the significance of textiles and clothing has remained the same, being used, for instance, to mark births, first hair-cuttings and deaths. In some communities, in southern Peru and Bolivia, textiles have been carefully pre-

served since the colonial period and are still an essential part of community ceremonies.

Conservatism is tempered with innovation. New patterns are constantly being added to the weaver's repertoire. Sheep's wool has largely replaced alpaca, and chemical dyes have almost completely supplanted natural dyes. Many spinners and weavers are now buying synthetic yarns to save time and labour, although these must be respun to obtain the necessary tight yarn for weaving.

In southern Peru and Bolivia generally speaking it is women who weave on the backstrap or ground-staked loom, although in places such as Apurimac and around Santo Tomás men do too. Some of these are itinerant curers who take weaving commissions as a sideline. In most village communities there are men who produce a plain-weave wool cloth (*bayeta*) on European-style looms; and men are usually the ones who

caps for themselves and their children, while on a neighbouring island it is the women who do the knitting. Just as spinning is often done while walking, so is knitting, with the different-coloured wools kept in plastic bags tied to a belt at the waist. Slings are still used for hunting small game, scaring off birds from crops, or for dancing. These are braided by men who manipulate the yarns by hand without tools.

Fiestas are an important part of community life. In some towns there are many professional artists who make their living from creating festive costume, and many dancers who will spend a large part of their year's earnings to pay for them. In central Peru male embroiderers work in

ABOVE 361 A dancer in Oruro, Bolivia, 1985. He represents *Rey Diablo* ('King Devil'). His mask is built up with plaster and painted with enamel paints. The eyes are of light bulbs. The dancer's costume is made of heavily embroidered synthetic fabrics and decorated with sequins and braid.

ABOVE RIGHT 362 Detail of a knitted wool arm-warmer, from the Department of Huancavelica, Peru, made in the late 1970s. 40 × 14 cm (15.75 × 5.5 in).

use European sewing-machines for tailoring and machine embroidery.

True knitting was introduced from Europe and is highly popular all over southern Peru and Bolivia for making hats, bags, figurines, dance masks, socks and arm-warmers. As in the pre-Hispanic period, hats indicate a person's origins and position in society and only the most Westernised person goes hatless. Brightly coloured and patterned knitted hats are almost exclusively worn by men and children from the rural areas. Each region has its different shape, colours and patterns. On the Titicaca island of Taquile unmarried men wear predominantly white caps, and married men red. Here men knit

lurex and synthetic fibres to create sequin-encrusted aprons and back panels for dancers. Others embroider small, women's mantles, often choosing their themes from comic books and cartoons. In Oruro, Bolivia, devil masks of the most fantastic shapes top costumes that match them for colour, materials and imagination.

Only a few indigenous groups of the southern Andes and pampas have continued their weaving traditions into the twentieth century. One example is the Mapuche of Chile (and parts of western Argentina), who produce finely woven ikat-dyed textiles using imported indigo as well as local plant dyes. These are used for their clothing, bedclothes and as saddle-blankets.

Early sixteenth-century accounts record them using llama 'wool' for weaving, but by the nineteenth century sheep's wool had replaced camelid fibre. For the large rectangular cloths they use an upright loom attached to vertical poles, whereas belts and fillets are woven on a horizontal ground loom.

Mapuche and neighbouring peoples were wearing ponchos (with a slit for the neck and unsewn sides) as early as the mid-seventeenth century. Indeed, it has been suggested that they were the inventors of this garment which then spread all over Latin America and to Spain. The Mapuche had quickly adopted the use of horses soon after the Conquest, and the poncho might have been adapted from the Andean sleeveless shirt with sewn sides to make it more comfortable for riding.

Many tropical-forest groups still make clothing and household items from handspun

that time. Later, owing to missionary influence, the Panoans covered themselves more 'modestly' and consequently produced more cotton clothing. The common garments for men and women are long shirts, and women also have carrying-cloths and mantles. These are woven on a backstrap loom, while a small oval-shaped loom is used for weaving smaller items. Women produce the cotton yarn using spindles which they support in half-gourds or pots while spinning.

All the garments are painted with complicated geometric patterns in black, red and yellow from plants such as *urucú* and *genipa*. These designs decorate other media such as pottery and wood,

ABOVE 363 Detail of an ikat-dyed wool poncho, with indigo dyes. Mapuche, Chile. 118 × 126 cm (46.5 × 49.6 in).

ABOVE RIGHT 364 Shipibo man wearing a loose cotton tunic. Ucayali River, 1970s. The designs are hand-painted by women, without preliminary sketching, using a vegetable dye applied with a strip of bamboo.

and woven bast and cotton. In the Guianas (early to mid-twentieth century) women used a bow-shaped loom to weave cotton aprons elaborately interwoven with thousands of glass beads. The utilitarian hammocks common throughout the Amazon are in some instances works of art. In the Río Negro region some have borders covered in featherwork mosaic.

Along the lower Ucayali River of eastern Peru the Panoan-speaking peoples such as the Shipibo make mosquito netting, knitted bags, loincloths and cushion-covers out of bast and clothing out of cotton. There are seventeenth-century accounts of Panoans wearing cotton shirts, but generally little clothing was worn at

and are used for painted body decoration (for example, face and hands). They are said to have come from the spirit world, transmitted to the painter in dreams. Each artist's paintings are distinctive, but they all conform to the general group style. Today, although handspun and woven cotton is still being made, industrially produced cotton fabric is also bought and then locally painted, especially for items sold to Europeans.

Traditional textile arts are under threat throughout South America, but there is hope that, although change is inevitable, the creativity of the artists and craftspeople will not be suppressed and that their crafts will survive.

'domi mansit lanam fecit' (she stayed home and worked wool)

Thus reads the epitaph of a Roman woman of the Republican period from Mezdour near Monastir. It is not a bad summary of the indigenous textile tradition of North Africa, where wool, the dominant material, was largely worked by women. North Africa has a rich tradition of both weaving and embroidery, the former being the deeper-rooted and more consistent throughout the area. Not a great deal has survived from the early period, the climate except in Libya being less propitious than in Egypt. The earliest-known *tirāz* fragment, dating from the caliphate of Marwan II (eighth century) is, however, probably from Kairouan in Ifriqiya. The wide range of local traditions is basically the result of a Berber and Arab substratum with foreign admixtures – Spanish, Mauretanian, Turkish and Jewish – producing great variety in both cloth and dress.

The textiles may be very beautiful and skilfully executed but they belong essentially to a refined folk tradition rather than to a courtly tradition which has percolated down the economic scale. This is confined to the textiles of a few 'noble' cities like Fez, and their imitations, and to the obviously Turkish elements such as the gold-embroidered wedding caftan, which appears in very similar form throughout North Africa. Early last century these caftans began to usurp the place of regional marriage dress and are now in turn giving way to white nylon and tulle.

Traditional costume in North Africa divides into draped and sewn. The former is very archaic and tends to be the dress of the nomadic, oasis and mountain people. Existing with two or three major variations all over the region, it is associated with weaving in wool and cotton, and usually, though not always, consists of a plain length of cloth, decoration being reserved for the elaborate woven belts, head-dresses, veils and magnificent jewellery, and also for the under-chemise, where worn. Belts form part of the marriage gifts and are ritually knotted or unknotted at weddings, in childbirth, at circumcisions and in mourning, and it is therefore hardly surprising that some of the finest weaving and embroidery (as well as metalwork) are to be found on them. The sewn clothing is essentially urban, the decoration is often embroidered in silk and metal thread, and its production is frequently associated with Jewish settlements or, in the past, the presence of a Turkish garrison.

Traditionally every country or nomad girl capable of learning to weave was taught by her female relatives. Not to be able to produce carpets, bed-covers and clothing was shameful and reduced a woman's value; skills, on the other hand, brought admiration and prestige as well as money. Embroidery was learned by middle- and upper-class urban girls as a matter of course, and many others aspired to learn: it was a reliable source of income and a way of escaping drudgery. Interestingly it does not seem to have been such an outlet for the imagination and creative instincts as it was in Turkey, perhaps because the harem system was on the whole much less developed. Weaving was usually learned at home, embroidery from a teacher or *ma'allema*, some of whom were designers and famous as such. They might also teach reading and writing and the Koran, and enjoyed considerable status as well as financial independence.

Generally speaking men wove and embroidered for sale and belonged to guilds. Women worked for their families and sold the surplus, although some like the *ma'allema* had professional status. Embroidery on leather and gold embroidery were generally done by men, partly no doubt because they required more physical strength and partly because they were intended mostly for sale. The elaborate braiding, silk buttons and tassels which add so much elegance to the caftans, jellabas and so on are also, perhaps more surprisingly, done by men, and it is usually men who sew the appliquéd *hiti* (hangings) and tents typical of Morocco. Women embroider their own clothes and household linen – silk embroidery is thus largely their prerogative – and used to do certain types of metal embroidery – for example, the sequin work used on wedding clothes in Tunis.

Weaving is more complicated and depends very much on the region. Generally silk, particularly such splendid fabrics as those of Djerba and Fez, was worked by men, who also tended to make the knotted carpets and certain items specifically intended for sale and which were more or less mass-produced – *sefseri* (veiling), *haïk* (draped outer garments serving as both cloak and veil) and blankets. Women wove a large number of *kelims* and household items,

Map 10 North Africa.

selling the surplus when they had one or were short of money.

Gold embroidery

Gold embroidery is the type most commonly found from Libya to Morocco and owes a great deal to Turkish influence. Gold thread (usually gold-washed base-silver thread, now often tinsel) was couched in elaborate scrolls on to a background of silk or velvet, most commonly dark blue, black, dark green, garnet or violet, to make marriage caftans, horse-trappings, belts, *qabqab* (mules), slippers, bags and pouches – especially for the Koran – and *hiti*. The designs are said to derive from Ottoman military uniforms. Paler colours, especially blue and white,

were used to make circumcision costumes for little boys. Calligraphy appears on mosque hangings, banners and tomb-covers – the most magnificent example still made (although not in North Africa) being the *kiswa*, or covering for the *ka'aba* at Mecca.

The embroideries on the Moroccan Jewish bridal and festival dresses are similar in technique, but the shape of these costumes is strongly reminiscent of sixteenth-century European dress. The bell-shaped wrapover skirt is heavily embroidered in gold with an asymmetric 'rising sun' pattern. The Jewish communities were famous as jewellers and throughout North Africa made much of gold thread, beads and sequins. Their departure is often said to be responsible for the decline in materials available and the increasing use of tinsel and plastic.

Tunisia, in particular, has some very original types of gold embroidery. The marriage costumes of Tunis, for example, were worked in silver- or gold-washed sequins and tubular beads in a wide range of patterns, sometimes clearly inspired by the classical or palaeo-Christian motifs found on sarcophagi or mosaics. The techniques and effects are very similar to those on the *traje de luz* (suit of lights) worn by Spanish matadors and on robes for the statues of the Virgin, and there may well be a connection. The embroidery was generally done on satin, which might be of any colour, and the costume was extremely heavy because of the vast size of the pantaloons. It was common practice for a woman in middle age to burn these wedding clothes in order to retrieve the silver, keeping only a strip as a souvenir, with the result that complete sets are rare survivals.

Another type of gold embroidery which is a Tunisian speciality is that made with flat metal thread, which may be couched into solid panels of design – fish-scales, 'snakes', 'Hand of Fatima', fish (the great Tunisian good-luck symbol), as on the Mokhnine tunics, or even worked into robes of gold as at Monastir, or else pushed through the loose weave of wool or cotton gauze to form patterns, rather in the manner of *azute* stoles from Egypt. The black and gold dresses from Hammamet are a good example of this, and their heavy gold horseshoe-shaped collars

ABOVE **365** Tunisian wedding dress of black wool gauze with gold braid, gold sequins, gilded thread and purple silk. Possibly Hammamet, 20th century.

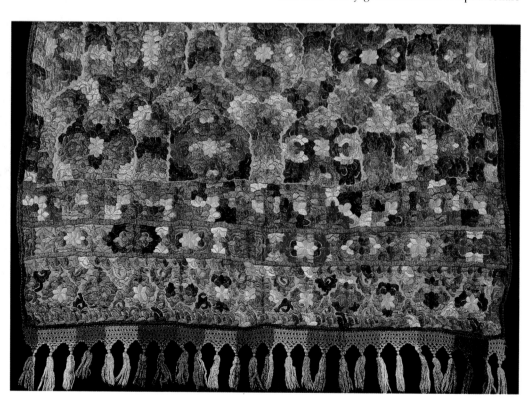

366 Embroidered silk shawl end from Morocco (Rabat), 19th century.

367 Silk embroidery on linen from Morocco (Chechaouen), 19th century.

are a particularly fine example of the *passementerie* which appears over and over again in traditional North African dress.

Silk embroidery

Silk embroidery exists in all the towns along the coast and in the central area. It becomes rare towards the south, among the tribes, in the mountains and in the deep countryside, all areas where weaving predominates and silk was probably expensive and hard to find.

Designs vary widely from the strictly geometric monochrome red, purple, blue or green tightly worked patterns of Fez, which seem almost east European, to the Turkish-looking stylised flowers and pomegranates of Tetouan, at their most classic embroidered on yellow satin in red, white, blue, black and green. In both Fez and Tetouan silk embroidery tends to be used for hangings, cushions and bed-covers rather than for clothing, and this is surprisingly often the case throughout North Africa, where women, although extremely fond of fine clothing, plied their needles for their homes rather than for themselves.

Rabat is an exception. There the beautiful satin-stitch embroidery seen at its finest in the marriage curtains, which might have forty or fifty shades of one or two colours in their designs suggesting great heaps of stylised flower petals, or perhaps clouds, was also used for the belts which held up the *sirwal* or pantaloons, or for the ends of head-coverings. Worked in soft floss silk on muslin (not infrequently already embroidered in whitework from India), the thread on Rabat pieces all too often wears away, leaving behind the pattern drawn by the *ma' allema*.

Although only a short distance away across the Bou Reg-Reg, Salé has a completely different style of embroidery, much more like that of Fez. Geometric and closely worked, it has none of the charm and individuality of the pieces from Rabat, but on the other hand it lasts very well. Today the Salé designs have tended to be swamped by those of Fez, and much Fez work is done there.

Other towns also have their own very distinctive traditions: Chechaouen with its densely worked polychrome veil-ends reminiscent of carpet patterns; Azemmour with its European-looking stylised scrolls and animals, usually in

368 Child's or young bride's chemise, embroidered in silk on fine linen. Morocco (Meknès), 19th century.

dark red or indigo on a natural ground; Meknès with its scattered geometric motifs worked on patterned muslin for veils, curtains or chemises (known locally as *yugoslavi*) has much in common with Tafilalet's veils; while the red and black embroidery on the Jewish men's shirts from the southern oases are again curiously reminiscent of those of southern Europe; and the blackwork of the northern towns is similar to that of parts of Tunisia, both allegedly having been introduced by refugees from al-Andalus.

Some of the oldest-surviving silk embroideries are from Algeria and they are often of very

fine quality, reminiscent of certain eighteenth-century European pieces, with their scrolling patterns worked like a chequer-board and dotted with small delicate flowers. Purple tends to be the predominant colour for these fine linen 'scarves', probably used as head-coverings, while the curtains are more often in blue and red, and the motifs, like those of Tetouan, derive ultimately from Turkey. Oddly enough there seems to have been relatively little domestic silk embroidery in Algeria, although gold embroidery of all kinds was highly developed.

Tunisia is a small country, and although the

fashions of the capital still have not completely swamped regional dress, certainly as far as silk embroidery is concerned, there is less local tradition than in Morocco. It may also be that with a smaller urban leisured class the emphasis remained on weaving rather than needlework. Gold-work is found in most urban centres, at least along the coast, as is the silk embroidery largely couched in thick thread or thin cord around the neck and sleeves and on the breast of men's robes.

The tunics of Raf-Raf provide one of the most striking examples of Tunisian rustic embroidery. The everyday dresses are of striped cotton with a plastron heavily embroidered in coloured wools or silks on a satin ground with the stylised good-luck motifs much loved all over Tunisia – flowers, fish, doves, and so on – picked out with gold beads and sequins. The 'tattooed' wedding tunic is even more richly embroidered, and the net sleeves are solidly worked in silk, wool and

369 Detail from a curtain panel of linen embroidered with silk. Algeria, 18th century.

gold thread, instead of with a sprinkling of flowers and stars. The very active Raf-Raf embroideresses, unlike those of much of the rest of North Africa, never seem to have decorated items for the home, only their own clothes.

Embroidery in black silk on linen, or more recently cotton, is a feature of women's tunics or chemises along the coastal strip between Hammamet and Mahdia. The embroidery may be more or less solid depending on local taste. In some places – Lemta, for example – the black-silk embroidery was traditionally done by pro-

fessionals and then decorated at home with sequins and gold thread. Here, as elsewhere, the trend has been away from fine silk embroidery towards a greater – and flashier – display of couched metal indicating wealth. As in Morocco, it is held that this blackwork originated in Spain, and it is not impossible, since not only were there many Andalusian settlers but Mahdia itself was a Spanish possession for a number of years.

Another surprisingly small town to have a very distinctive style of embroidery is El Djem, better known for its splendid Roman amphitheatre. Important as a centre of wool production, it is unusual in that the embroidery is done in silk on wool. The finest old pieces are the red draped dresses asymmetrically worked in brilliantly coloured silks with a round motif, the 'moon', 'pillars' and a variety of highly stylised animals. The edges are decorated with tassels, as are those of the veils, which were generally made at Ksour Es-Saf. Modern examples can be found, but as is so often the case, the fashion has veered towards velvet and rather tinselly gold, instead of fine wool and silk. Somewhat similar pieces are made in Gabès – always a great centre of textile production – for sale to neighbouring towns.

Other types of embroidery

Wool on wool embroidery is not particularly common since wool is decorated mostly with woven patterns. It is, however, sometimes added to a woven piece, as in the fine shawls from the mountains beyond Gabès in Tunisia, or on the draped dresses and veils, in use among the sedentary Berbers of the Moroccan Anti-Atlas, which are also splendidly tasselled. Interesting examples of wool on wool embroidery come from the Chenini district and the Gabès oasis, with motifs strongly suggesting sub-Saharan African rather than Mediterranean influence. The fine red-wool shawls from Kerkenna are also sometimes embroidered in wool rather than silk.

Spectacular examples of appliqué in North Africa are found on the hangings and tents made in Morocco, which are similar to those of Cairo. They are still made to order, green and red velvet being a favourite combination, and the arched pattern may be enriched with braid or embroidery. Fine appliqué also appears in unexpected places – for example, in the lining of men's robes, either a discreet formal pattern or, as in a black robe in the Dar Ben Abdallah, a nineteenth-century palace in Tunis housing a museum of Tunisian urban life, a riot of crimson, purple and yellow crazy patches in satin and damask.

Mirroring their seventeenth-century Euro-

pean counterparts, samplers were made all over urban North Africa, probably in order to graduate from a *ma'allema*. They serve as a pattern-book for motifs, largely geometric or very highly stylised, and for stitches. Unlike their European counterparts they very rarely include examples of calligraphy.

Weaving

North Africa was traditionally a weaving rather than an embroidering culture, and the weaving both of cloth and rugs is still a live art throughout the region, although silk production is very much in decline and the finest wool pieces are generally no longer made because commissioning them is too expensive.

Fine silk was woven especially at Tripoli and Kairouan, where during the Middle Ages there were official *tirāz* factories, and later at Fez, famous for its brocades, and Tunis. Djerba was known for its elaborately checked and striped silk cloths, generally woven by the Jews, and other production centres were the Gabès oasis, Tozeur and the Djerid, and the coastal cities of Algeria. Apart from a little plain silk, the industry has died, although it is claimed that there are still a few weavers, at least in Tunisia, who can make fine pieces if commissioned.

The great weaving tradition of North Africa is principally concerned, therefore, with different kinds of wool, often skilfully combined and

now, sometimes, mixed with cotton. Men's robes and cloaks might be woven of the finest cream-coloured camel wool – essentially a prerogative of the sheiks – or, as in the case of the men of the Rif, of several colours of natural wool worked in elaborate patterns into a cloth which is almost indestructible. At Nabeul, on the other hand, the plain woollen cloaks owe their beauty to natural dyes – terracotta, ochre and Roman purple – and the way in which their wearers drape them, reminiscent of classical statuary. In the Anti-Atlas the Berber men wore until recently spectacular black goat's-hair burnouses with a great orange half-moon at the back and patterned with delicate geometric designs. Analogous pieces were also made in the Kabili.

Some of the most elaborate pieces of weaving are women's veils – for example, the beautiful ones from Chenini and Douiret and the mountain area south of Gabès. White for girls, red for married women, blue for the elderly, they are patterned with finely worked, stylised motifs – combs, snakes, scorpions, and so on. When the veil is new, the design is hardly visible, but as the pile wears away it becomes clearer and clearer. Comparable pieces come from the El-Djem–Djebeniana region.

It is difficult to draw an exact line between woven carpets and other textiles in North Africa, for hangings, blankets, rugs to throw over seats, saddle-cloths, pieces made for grain

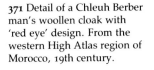

371 Detail of a Chleuh Berber man's woollen cloak with 'red eye' design. From the western High Atlas region of Morocco, 19th century.

sacks or saddle-bags are often of very similar pattern but of different weights depending on their intended use. Good examples come from numerous areas, especially the mountains, and have been the subject of several specialised studies. Much of the wool was woven by wo-

tent dividers and saddle-cloths, which are intended to 'reveal the fortune of the owner and the skill of the weaver'.

Like so much else in North Africa, knotted carpets raise complicated questions. From the variety of knots and types of pattern there seem

372 Wedding veil of fine wool dyed black, with decorative motifs in white cotton. Woven and worn by Berbers, from Tunisia (Medenine), 20th century.

men, although professionals produced certain items, particularly the large, elaborately patterned rugs.

Kelims are the form of North African weaving best known to the outside world and have been extensively documented. The finest ones are from Tripolitania and the areas of Tunisia around Gafsa and the mines of Sidi Bou Said, where there was immigration from Libya early this century. There is a tendency for the *kelims* to become more rustic as one moves west, although this is not true of city-made carpets. A number of these rugs/hangings are extremely interesting, however. There are, for example, those made by the Beni Mouild and the Beni Rached in Algeria and by the Zenmour in Morocco, which are essentially flat-woven in complicated geometric patterns but with bands of knots (often left uncut like a fringe), tassels, large sequins and even silk knots and glass beads as extra decoration, particularly on the

to be two basic types – the indigenous high-pile, simple Berber rugs, generally intended as bedding, and the urban, knotted carpets for which a relatively recent Turkish origin is generally given. The best known are probably those of Kairouan, where their manufacture is said to have originated with the daughter of the Turkish governor in the early nineteenth century. From there it moved to Bizerte, allegedly thanks to the widow of another Turkish official – in any case the patterns used today are very clearly from Asia Minor. The carpets from Kalaa in Algeria are again said to owe their existence to Turkish families who settled there. The pattern is repeated with the city-made, low-pile, knotted carpets of Morocco, which again claim a late eighteenth-century origin. Anomalies, of course, occur – for example, the very unusual Haouz rugs from Marrakesh which use an odd form of the Turkish knot and motifs that strongly suggest the Sudan.

33 Sub-Saharan Africa and the offshore islands

The mythology and oral traditions of sub-Saharan Africa are potent sources of discussion about the origins of textiles in particular regions. Many attribute the impetus that led to the development of distinctive styles of textile or technical innovation to well-known figures within the culture. Yet other traditions suggest that particular peoples have learnt their weaving skills from some foreign source, whether as the result of journeys undertaken by members of their own community or through the arrival of weavers from elsewhere. Some even portray the creation of the human world through imagery derived from weaving.

Of such tales those of the Dogon in Mali are among the most fully recorded and the richest (Griaule 1965, pp. 24–9). Weaving and related activities are frequently identified with the source of things. Spinning cotton, for instance, is one of the principal preoccupations of a woman who has just given birth, especially if the child is a girl (Griaule 1965, p. 157). The whole process and technology of weaving is also a primary reference in stories and speculations about the origins of the world:

> At sunrise on the appointed day the seventh ancestor Spirit spat out eighty threads of cotton; these he distributed between his upper teeth which acted as the teeth of a weaver's reed. In this way he made the uneven threads of a warp. He did the same with the lower teeth to make the even threads. By opening and shutting his jaws the Spirit caused the threads of the warp to make the movements required in weaving. His whole face took part in the work, his nose studs serving as the block, while the stud in his lower lip was the shuttle.
>
> As the threads crossed and uncrossed, the two tips of the Spirit's forked tongue pushed the thread of the weft to and fro, and the web took shape from his mouth in the breath of the second revealed Word (Griaule 1965, pp. 27–8).

Whatever else this snippet from the cycle of Dogon creation myth is about, it clearly uses the image of weaving as a metaphor for creation in general, and the image of the emerging cloth as an embodiment of distinctive, ordered human culture. Although only a mythic reference, it is at least suggestive of the longevity of textile production among the Dogon that its characteristic procedures should have been built into this fundamental narration.

There are also other indications of the antiquity of weaving traditions in this part of Africa. Coincidentally the Dogon happen nowadays to occupy an area where some of the oldest substantially intact textiles from sub-Saharan Africa have been found. These come from naturally occurring cave sites in the Bandiagara escarpment, an arid region where a large-scale series of burials has been found. The first use of the caves, dating from the eleventh century AD, is associated with predecessors of the Dogon, people they refer to under the name Tellem. The bodies of the Tellem dead were often clothed and sometimes wrapped in blankets, although the whole site has been substantially disturbed and it is difficult to associate the cloth with specific individuals (Bedaux and Bolland 1980/1). The cloth is in a variety of raw materials including wool, cotton and mixes of the two. It is also surprisingly uniform in style and technique up until the sixteenth century, a time when on other evidence the Dogon would seem to have begun to infiltrate the area.

Interestingly, and most importantly, these textiles are of two general types. One has a broad width and its configuration of pattern suggests a link to the textile traditions of the Berber in North Africa. That is not unexpected in a location on the fringes of the Sahara, at a period when it was already being extensively traversed by camel caravans. A second style of textile, however, is distinctive in having a much narrower web which does not exceed a maximum of about 25 cm (10 in) – these cloths, in other words, conform to a tradition of narrow-strip textile which is characteristic of men's weaving in West Africa right up to the present day, and whose origins remain a lively subject of enquiry and debate.

West Africa

There have been a number of attempts to classify the looms of Africa, and of West Africa in particular. The most comprehensive of early classifications was that of Ling Roth (1917). Of later discussions those of the Lambs are among the most accessible and detailed (1975, 1980a and b, 1982, 1984). The simplest division is that between the single-heddle loom, where the warp is mounted on two parallel bars, and the double-heddle loom, where the heddles are worked in pairs and manipulated by the use of foot peddles (Picton and Mack 1989, Chapters 4 and 5). In West Africa the former is associated with the

technology used by women, and the latter with men's weaving. The double-heddle loom is the source of the narrow strips of textile; these need to be sewn together selvage to selvage to yield a broader cloth.

Examples might be adduced from across West Africa to illustrate both the wide dispersal of the techniques of narrow-strip weaving and the varieties of cloth that are produced. In Sierra Leone in the west of the region some of the widest of textiles yielded by the West African double-heddle loom are woven; these are of similar dimensions to those discovered at the Bandiagara escarpment. They are usually associated with the Mende people, though not exclusive to them, and are distinctive in a number of ways (Easmon 1924; Lamb 1984). Firstly, the loom on which they are produced is technologically among the simplest of this variety. The double heddles are simply suspended on a tripod which, together with the weaver, moves along the warp as weaving proceeds. Several distinct types of cotton textile are produced. That with the widest web is the *kroikpoi*, a textile with a broad weft-faced pattern, usually in light and dark blue, light browns and the natural white of the cotton. The weavers are specialists, and the textiles are specifically commissioned for use in a variety of contexts – as wall-hangings on ceremonial occasions, for use in funerals, as payment of bride-wealth, and even as an item of

specialised trade, which in part accounts for their alternative name in English – 'country cloths' (meaning simply that they have been produced up-country and traded to urban centres).

The weaving traditions of Ghana provide a marked contrast to those of the Mende (Lamb 1975, Menzel 1972). Here the technology of weaving using the double-heddle system has achieved a much greater degree of complexity, which is also reflected in the elaboration of the textiles that are typically produced, especially among the Ewe and the Asante. The two heddles are here used in tandem, the one to produce weft-faced float patterns, the other to give the basic warp-faced ground weave. Supplementary heddles are also added to assist in producing further elaborations. The width of strips is considerably narrower than those woven by the Mende. Both silk and cotton cloths are woven in a wide variety of patterns and a rich array of colours by specialist weavers. Indeed, at Bonwire, the Asante weaving centre, the weavers form a separate professional group with their own chief producing cloths for the Asantehene (or King) and the royal court. The elaboration of textiles is related to the elaboration of the Asante political system. Some types of cloth are exclusive to particular individuals, such as *asasia* cloth, a silk woven with extra elaborations of pattern for the Asantehene alone. All the pat-

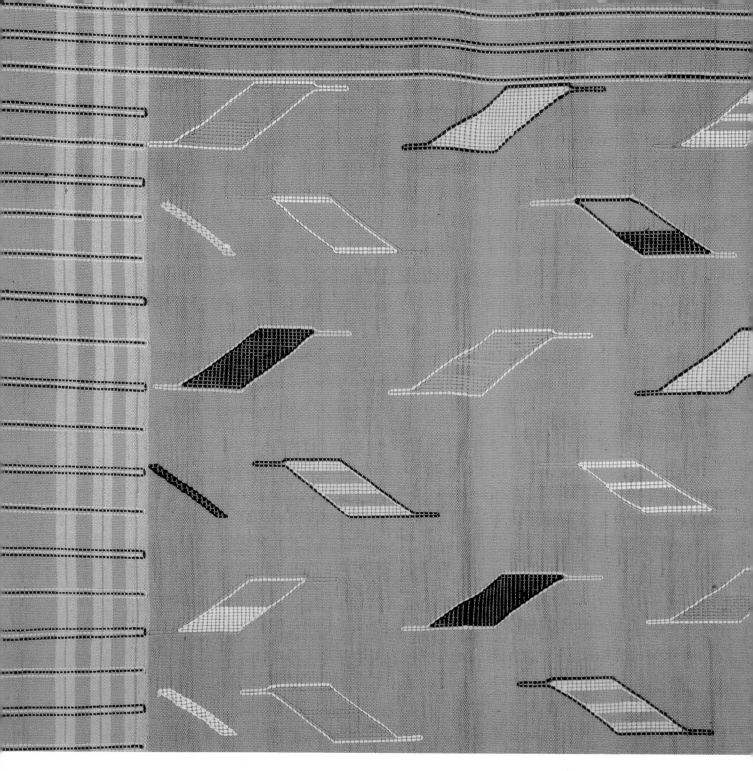

375 Cotton textile from
Akwete, an Igbo village,
Nigeria, 20th century.

terns are systematically named, one of the most
complex being known as *adwinasa*, often translated as 'my skill is exhausted'.

The alternative weaving system using the
single-heddle loom is in a West African context
principally associated with Nigeria and with
women. The cloth woven is generally the less
prestigious cotton and is of a much greater
width than that deriving from the double-
heddle loom – up to a maximum of about 125 cm
(50 in) compared with 25 cm (10 in) for the
widest of narrow-strip textiles. In contrast to

men's weaving traditions women characteristically weave individually or in families as
part of their regular domestic activities. The
cloth, as a result, is sometimes less elaborate
than it would be if it were being manufactured
on a commission basis or marketed systematically. An exception is the Igbo village of
Akwete in south-eastern Nigeria where a local
guild was established in the 1960s to allow women to sell their cloth in a more professional and
commercial manner (Aronson 1980).

There have been many speculative attempts

to explain the historical precedents for this complexity of technologies and cloths which characterise West African weaving. Apart from the evidence from the Bandiagara escarpment there are also reports of narrow-strip cloth from the ancient empire of Ghana. The Arab chronicler Al-Bakri describes such textiles in use by the eleventh century (Gilfoy 1988, p. 20). This evidence post-dates the spread of Islam into the Sahel, though of course it provides no surety of the ultimate date of the origins of narrow-strip weaving in West Africa. Even so some commentators have been tempted to associate the development of distinctive weaving technologies in West Africa with general cultural influences from across the Sahara. By at least the ninth

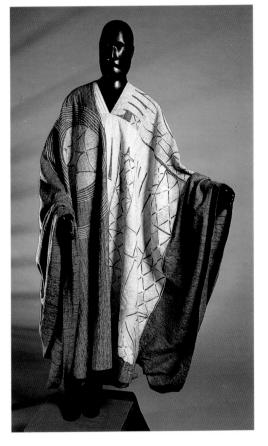

ABOVE RIGHT 376
Embroidered cotton gown. Hausa, Nigeria, early 20th century.

century AD Muslim traders and the Islamic faith had begun to penetrate the area of present-day Mali and neighbouring regions. Within several centuries the traditional annual *haj*, or pilgrimage, to Mecca would seem to have attracted West African converts. Some kind of link between the distribution of narrow-strip weaving and the routes taken by Islamic pilgrims is intriguingly suggested by an analysis of the distribution of cloth strips used as currency (Johnson 1980, p. 201).

There are, however, many problems in giving

proper weight to the influences of Islam and Islamic culture on West African practice in textile production. Just as an indigenous origin for West African metallurgy was for many years denied, so too an entirely local origin for many of the innovations in weaving technology is highly probable. Equally, for Islamic practice to have been influential does not necessarily imply conversion to Islam, nor, even among the African faithful, is an emphasis on Islamic styles and arts merely imitative. Indeed, the act of conversion is not necessarily destructive of other pre-Islamic characteristics of visual culture (Bravmann 1983).

Thus the emirates of northern Nigeria, for instance, are the source of a broad-sleeved style of man's gown associated in particular with the Hausa peoples though, even in the context of northern Nigeria, not exclusive to them nor necessarily made by them. It has a number of distinctive features. It is made of a series of narrow cotton strips sewn together at their edges to create the body of the gown. The neck is reinforced with a plaited band (*sharaba*). Triangular pieces (*linzami*) acquired separately from a specialist in their manufacture are fitted in around the neck at the front. A large pocket is added on the left of the gown as worn, and this is the focus of elaborate embroidered designs incorporating both interlacing motifs and angular or spiral elements often drawn for the guidance of the embroiderer by a Koranic scholar. It has been argued (Heathcote 1973) that the interlacing is derived from Islamic art, whereas the angles and spirals which recur in other local domestic arts are more likely to be indigenous.

Embroidery, more than any other aspect of West African textile production, is a technique generally associated with the spread of Islam, and embroidered gowns are found throughout the area. From the Hausa centre of Kano traders and craftsmen have themselves taken their products southwards into the rest of Nigeria, westwards to Manding country and beyond, and eastwards – there are even Hausa tailors established today in Mecca. Use of embroidered styles of gown is not, however, by any means an index of adherence to Islam. Thus many Yoruba in southern Nigeria have adopted the practice of wearing gowns which they now embroider themselves. A similar style of gown has even become emblematic of pan-Africanism and as such is now worn by many non-Islamic supporters of these separate political ideals – including many whose immediate origins and upbringing lie outside the continent of Africa.

All of this is not to undermine an emphasis on the originality of African textile production and design but to stress its vitality in eclecticism. There are many other examples that can be

ABOVE **377** Charm hat, incorporating claws and small packets containing Islamic texts. Ivory Coast.

mentioned of non-Islamic peoples adapting elements of the arts of Islam to a secular context. The common practice throughout North and Saharan Africa of attaching short texts as talismanic devices to costumes is copied, for instance, by hunters among the non-Islamic Bamana. Similarly, textiles collected among the Asante of Ghana sometimes have drawn and painted texts and designs intended to serve in magical contexts. The script, however, has not generally been applied by a professional Koranic scholar for it is only an approximation to Arabic and not even legible as such.

An equivalent situation occurs in certain resist-dyed textiles produced in Nigeria by the Yoruba. *Adire* is the general term the Yoruba use for a range of textiles which share in common the fact that, whether by tying or stitching them in appropriate ways or applying some resisting agent, pattern is created when they are dipped in a dye solution (Barbour and Simmonds 1971). Abeokuta and Ibadan are the two Yoruba centres of the techniques involved, though throughout West Africa tie and stitch dyeing, in particular, are widespread decorative techniques, and the deep blue of indigo is the common colour of the dye. Among the Yoruba more representational imagery is produced by painting or stencilling starch on to the base cloth before soaking it in the dye. The range of pat-

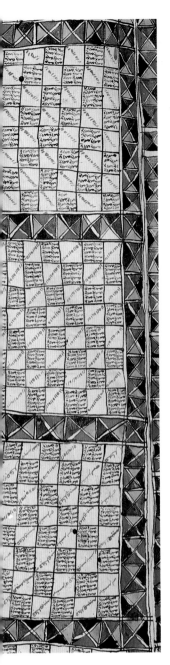

terns that are thus applied is very extensive. The favoured images include a popular Muslim devotional picture, that of the winged horse on which the prophet Muhammad flew from Mecca to Jerusalem. The particular image is copied from a print imported to Nigeria from Cairo and once widely available. Again the motif, though created in the first instance for an audience of the faithful, has been incorporated into textile design.

To complete its decontextualisation the winged horse generally appears beside another popular *adire* subject. This is King George V (1865–1936) and Queen Mary (1867–1953) whose regal appearance became familiar through the souvenirs disseminated in colonial territories in celebration of their Jubilee in 1935. Both these images have become stock figures in the repertoire of *adire* cloth design; but again they have been picked up and incorporated into a flamboyant range of local references rather than merely reproduced for their original significance. Similarly, appliqué banners from Ghana and the Republic of Benin have traditionally exploited a wide range of references in their choice of appropriate imagery. The Fante used flags to distinguish different military groupings (Ross 1979). From the nineteenth century they began to adopt the practice of attaching the Union Jack to one of the upper corners of flags in imitation of the ensigns flown by British naval ships. In picking out this foreign emblem, however, the

ABOVE **380** Flag with appliquéd motifs. Fante, Ghana, 19th or 20th century.

ABOVE **378** Imitation Arabic script applied to European cotton sheeting. Asante, Ghana.

ABOVE RIGHT **379** Modern resist-dyed *adire* cloth, Yoruba, Nigeria.

use of other more dramatic imagery developed locally continued undiminished. These situations provide a graphic illustration of a process that has continued for centuries.

In reviewing the most significant external influence on West African textile manufacture it is certainly to be found neither in the area of general technological refinement nor in the reproduction of specific design and pattern. Rather, the most important historical factor is an unwitting by-product of the long-term importation of textiles into the region. For centuries it appears that West African weavers have taken advantage of imported textiles as a source of new raw materials. The practice of unravelling imported cloth and reweaving the yarn is well established. Textiles acquired through the trans-Saharan trade or from European trading ships were treated alike.

The Equatorial forest

In contrast to the varieties of weaving technologies and textiles found in West Africa, those of the basin of the River Zaire (the former Congo) are relatively uniform. The loom in use is of a simple, upright, single-heddle variety, and the only raw material traditionally exploited is raffia, the stripped leaves of a type of palm. It is quite likely that a similar raffia loom was once in much more general use in Africa. Equivalent devices occur along the Cameroon/Nigeria borderlands today (Nicklin 1980), and historical examples are preserved from as far afield as Sierra Leone (Ling Roth 1917). Such a distribution suggests a much wider use of raffia as a raw material in the past, and, given its readily available vegetal source and the simplicity of its preparation for weaving, it raises the possibility that in many places raffia may have been the precursor of spun fibres.

However, in emphasising the technological simplicity that goes with a use of raffia in weaving it should not be assumed that the resulting textiles necessarily lack complex design. The use of supplementary heddles and shed sticks to create pattern is well established (Loir 1935). In Zaire float-weave patterns are characteristic of a number of regions, most notably those occupied by the Tetela who introduce dyed strands to contrast with the plain-coloured background of the raffia and emphasise the pattern. An example of the Tetela loom collected in 1908 has twenty-six supplementary shed sticks used in creating one half of a geometric pattern (Picton and Mack 1989, p. 91).

LEFT **381** Raffia cut-pile textile Kuba, Zaire, early 20th century.

The more unusual types of textile from Zaire include the so-called 'Kasai velvets'. These are best known among the Kuba, a long-established kingdom in an area to the south of the Kasai River, amongst whom a number of regional styles can be discerned. Technically the cloth is not a velvet but an example of cut pile, or Richelieu embroidery. Here different-coloured strands of raffia are introduced with a needle and taken under the cross-points of a plain-woven raffia square and up again on the top surface. The thread is pulled through until only a small amount of the loose end remains visible. The part taken through is then cut off at an equivalent height above the surface of the textile leaving a small U-shaped piece of embroidery in place. Blocks of colour are thereby built up.

The Kuba retain an oral tradition which re-

stance, the Sloane Collection, the founding collection of the British Museum, contains examples of Kongo embroidery, which though not technically identical with Kuba work are closely related. They also show an interest in the exploration and exploitation of geometric form which is also characteristic of Kuba embroidery and of Kuba design traditions in general.

Eastern Africa and the offshore islands

On the eastern side of the continent evidence of indigenous traditions of textile production is much more patchy than elsewhere in Africa. The site of Ingombe Ilede in Zambia has yielded fragments of cotton cloth used in burials dating to the fourteenth and fifteenth centuries AD.

382 Raffia cushion cover. Kongo, Zaire or Angola, 18th century. The patterns are directly comparable to later textiles associated with the Kuba in central Zaire.

cords that the arts of weaving and cut pile were introduced to them subsequent to a journey among peoples living to their west by Shyaam aMbul aNgoong, the founder of the ruling dynasty. Certainly in the opening decade of the century the Pende in the Kwilu River area also produced cut pile. Furthermore, at least up until the eighteenth century the Kongo, the once powerful kingdom on the Atlantic coast, produced textiles in a very similar style: for instance, the

Archaeological finds of textiles have also been made in Zimbabwe, including the site of Great Zimbabwe itself (Davison and Harries 1980, pp. 175–6). These are evidence of the historical distribution of a tradition of cotton weaving that has since been almost completely overtaken by the availability both of imports from India and latterly of industrially produced cloth from Europe. The ubiquitous product of local looms was a simple warp-striped textile. Only in a few

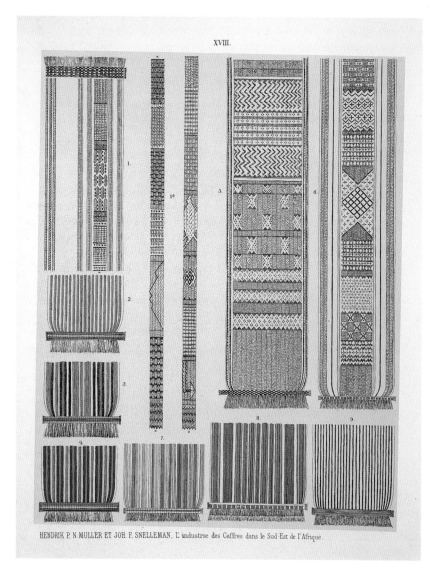

XVIII.

HENDRIK P. N. MULLER ET JOH. F. SNELLEMAN, L'industrie des Caffres dans le Sud-Est de l'Afrique.

383 Examples of south-east African textiles in a style which has since died out (Muller and Snelleman 1893, pl. 18). The link to textiles from Madagascar is apparent in the warp patterning and the band along the bottom.

produced in these centres themselves, possibly in some cases even by craftworkers from elsewhere around the Indian Ocean. Certainly until quite recently such cloth was being produced in places like Lamu, and some of the older printing blocks still exist.

This range of influences also stretched to the large island of Madagascar lying some 250 miles off the coast of south-east Africa. Here, however, an indigenous textile industry survived and continues using traditional hand-looms. Madagascar is unlike any of the other regions already considered. Its culture is an assemblage of the maritime influences a major trade route such as that which criss-crosses the Indian Ocean attracts. South-East Asian, Arabian and African elements are all evident, and its textile traditions are accordingly varied (Mack 1986 and 1989).

Thus all the raw materials that are found anywhere on the African continent are exploited by the Malagasy (the generic name for Madagascar's peoples as a whole). Some, though found elsewhere, are sufficiently characteristic that they are for ever associated with Madagascar. The term raffia, for instance, is derived from the Malagasy term *rofia*. The use of other raw materials appears to be virtually unique to Madagascar – such as the practice of extracting the longitudinal fibres from bark by a process of retting and weaving the resulting elements, as occurs among the Zafimaniry, a forest people to the south-east of the island's central plateau. The Zafimaniry also use the backstrap loom, a device otherwise found in Asia but not in Africa. Malagasy weavers, however, generally employ a type of fixed-heddle loom similar to that used in historical times in east Africa and in parts of the Arabian peninsula. A treadle loom was once common in eastern Madagascar.

Malagasy cloth in general is characterised by the extensive use of warp stripes. Since the 1830s, when British mission artisans (including weavers) were sent to Madagascar, aniline dyes have been in use, gradually replacing those derived from natural sources, especially in the centre of the island. In the nineteenth century this led – especially among the dominant group of the period, the Merina – to the production of cloth with vivid multicoloured stripes, all assembled on single textiles but somehow managing to escape incipient visual chaos. The use of supplementary heddles also enabled the introduction of complex floating weft patterns arranged in bands along the length of the cloth. The textiles were usually of silk and were reserved for aristocratic clans who wore them as a kind of shawl (*lamba*). With the dissolution of the Merina monarchy in the colonial period the use

places were more elaborately patterned cloths developed, as, for example, by the nineteenth century in the area of the Lower Zambezi (Muller and Snelleman 1893, pl. 18).

Clearly the importation of textiles of exotic origin was greatest along the east and south-east African littoral. Calico and printed cottons formed part of a highly complex pattern of trade that linked the coastal areas and the offshore islands to an extensive network of trading points around the Indian Ocean and into the Arabian Gulf. Much of the documented trade in textiles dates from the period of Portuguese exploitation of the Indian Ocean and east Africa trade, but even before that textiles were traded extensively principally for gold and ivory. Such trade took place at a variety of centres from Mogadishu (the present-day capital of Somalia) southwards to the Swahili settlements on the Lamu archipelago and beyond, and out to the Comores. Eventually printed textiles were also being

and manufacture of such cloths ceased (though there have been recent attempts to revive it). Today such patterns continue to be applied to cloth, only now the colour is white on white, whereas in the nineteenth century white was the colour of the shawls worn by the servant class.

Madagascar is perhaps best known for its production of burial shrouds. These are used to rewrap corpses in elaborate second-burial ceremonies similar to those that occur in parts of South-East Asia. They are known in Malagasy by the generic term *lamba mena*, literally red cloth. In practice shrouds are often in virtually any colour other than red, or they are plain. Ideally they should be silk, preferably the thick native silk of Madagascar rather than the introduced Chinese silk (*Bombyx mori*) that is used for shawls. Both these features – the verbal reference to redness and the preference for indigenous varieties of silk – are connected to the character of the rituals in which *lamba mena* are used. Exhuming and reshrouding the corpses of deceased relatives is a means by which the living ensure a continuing flow of blessings which are seen as deriving from well-disposed ancestors. The shroud must be appropriate. Red is a colour associated with power and authority; silk (*landy*) is seen as the finest of all materials – it was referred to in the nineteenth century under the alternative name *Andriamanitra* (literally, 'Fragrant Lord'), a word for God.

384 Silk textile. Merina, Madagascar, 19th century.

Further reading and sources cited

INTRODUCTION

Cammann, S., 1972. 'Symbolic meanings in Oriental rug patterns', parts I, II and III, *Textile Museum Journal*, Washington, DC, vol. III, no. 3

Gittinger, M., 1979. *Splendid Symbols: Textiles and Traditions in Indonesia*, Washington, DC

Gittinger, M. (ed.), 1989. *To Speak with Cloth: Studies in Indonesian Textiles*, Los Angeles

Hald, M., 1980. *Ancient Danish Textiles from Bogs and Burials*, Publications of the National Museum Archaeological–Historical Series XXI, Copenhagen

Rudenko, S. I., 1970. *Frozen Tombs of Siberia: The Pazyryk Burials of Iron-Age Horsemen*, London

Weiner, A. B. and Schneider, J. (eds), 1989. *Cloth and Human Experience*, Washington, DC and London

A Survey of Textile Techniques

Weaving, tapestry and general works

Beutlich, T., 1967. *The Techniques of Woven Tapestry*. Reprinted 1982, London

Birrell, V., 1959. *The Textile Arts*, New York

Bühler, K., 1948. 'Classification of basic textile techniques', *CIBA Review*, Basel, no. LXIII

Burnham, D.K., 1980. *Warp and Weft: A Textile Terminology*, London

CIETA, 1964. *Fabrics: A Vocabulary of Technical Terms*, Lyons

Emery, I., 1980. *The Primary Structures of Fabrics*, Washington, DC

Hecht, A., 1989. *The Art of the Loom: Weaving, Spinning and Dyeing across the World*, London

Schreus, T. and Braun-Ronsdorf, M., 1955. 'Damask', *CIBA Review*, Basel, no. CX

Seiler-Baldinger, A., 1979. *Classification of Textile Techniques*, Ahmedabad

'Velvet', 1953. *CIBA Review*, Basel, no. XCVI

Looms

Geijer, A., 1977. 'The loom representation on the Chiusi vase', *Studies in Textile History*, Toronto, pp. 52–5 (the warp-weighted loom)

Hoffmann, M., 1964. *The Warp-weighted Loom*, Oslo

Ling Roth, H., 1951. *Ancient Egyptian and Greek Looms*, Halifax. Reprinted 1978, Bedford

Ling Roth, H., 1955. *Studies in Primitive Looms*, Halifax. Reprinted 1977, Bedford

Rothstein, N., 1977. 'The introduction of the Jacquard loom to Great Britain', *Studies in Textile History*, Toronto, pp. 281–304

Schaefer, G., 1938. 'The loom', *CIBA Review*, Basel, no. XVI

Wild, J.-P., 1970. *Textile Manufacture in the Northern Roman Provinces*, Cambridge (for discussion of the warp-weighted loom)

Rug weaving

Denny, W.B., 1979. *Oriental Rugs*, Washington, DC

Tattersall, C. E. C., 1920. *Notes on Carpet-Knotting and Weaving*. Reprinted 1983, London

Embroidery

Christie, Mrs A., 1920. *Samplers and Stitches: A Handbook of the Embroiderer's Art*, London

Clabburn, P., 1976. *The Needleworker's Dictionary*, London

Thomas, M., 1934. *Mary Thomas's Dictionary of Embroidery Stitches*. Reprinted 1981, London

Lace

See bibliography to chapter II.25, 'Lace'

Dyeing and printing

Brunello, F., 1973. *The Art of Dyeing in the History of Mankind*, Vicenza

Bühler, A., 1954. 'Plangi: tie and dye work', *CIBA Review*, Basel, no. CIV

Bühler, A. and Steinmann, A., 1942. 'The ikat technique', 'Dyes and dyeing methods for ikat threads' and 'Origin and extent of the ikat technique', *CIBA Review*, Basel, no. CIV

Clark, H., 1985. *Textile Printing*, Aylesbury

Larsen, J.L., 1976. *The Dyer's Art: Ikat, Batik, Plangi*, London and New York (contains an excellent bibliography)

Ponting, K.G., 1980. *A Dictionary of Dyes and Dyeing*, London

Robinson, S., 1969. *A History of Dyed Textiles*, London

Storey, J., 1974. *The Thames and Hudson Manual of Textile Printing*, London

Knitting

Burnham, D.K., 1972. 'Coptic knitting: an ancient technique', *Textile History*, vol. III, no. 2, pp. 116–24

Collingwood, P., 1974. *The Techniques of Sprang*, London

Henson, G., 1831. *History of the Framework Knitters*. Reprinted 1970, Newton Abbot

Levey, S.M., 1969. 'Illustrations of the history of knitting selected from the collection of the Victoria & Albert Museum', *Textile History*, vol. I, no. 2, pp. 183–205

Palmer, M., 1984. *Framework Knitting*, Princes Risborough

Rutt, R., 1987. *A History of Hand Knitting*, London

Felt

Burkett, M.E., 1979. *The Art of the Felt Maker*, Kendal

'Felt', 1958. *CIBA Review*, Basel, no. CXXIX

Mellaart, J., 1966 (a). 'Excavations at Çatal Hüyük 1965', *Sonderdruck aus Archäologischer Anzeiger*, Berlin, Heft 1, pp. 1–15

Mellaart, J., 1966 (b). 'Excavations at Çatal Hüyük 1965', Fourth Preliminary Report, *Anatolian Studies*, vol. XVI, pp 165–91

Bark cloth

'Bark fabrics of the South Seas', 1940. *CIBA Review*, Basel, no. XXXIII

Brigham, W.T., 1911. 'Ka Hana Kapa: the story of the manufacture of kapa (Tapa), or bark-cloth, in Polynesia and elsewhere, but especially in the Hawaiian Islands', *Memoirs of the Bernice P. Bishop Museum*, Honolulu, vol. III, pp. 1–273

Koojiman, S., 1972. 'Tapa in Polynesia', *Bernice P. Bishop Museum Bulletin*, Honolulu, no. CCXXXIV

Koojiman, S., 1988. *Polynesian Barkcloth*, Princes Risborough

A Survey of World Textiles

THE ANCIENT WORLD

Introduction

Aldred, C., 1961. *The Egyptians*, London

Bowman, A.K., 1986. *Egypt After the Pharaohs 332 BC to AD 642*, London

Culican, W., 1966. *The First Merchant Venturers: The Ancient Levant in History and Commerce*, London

Herodotus, 1954. *Histories*, trans. A. de Selincourt, Harmondsworth

Mellaart, J., 1967. *Çatal Hüyük*, London

Miller, J. I., 1969. *The Spice Trade of the Roman Empire, 29 BC to AD 641*, Oxford

Woolley, L., 1982. *Ur of the Chaldees: The Final Account*, revised and updated by R. Moorey, London

Yadin, Y., 1966. *Masada*, London

The Mediterranean

Bourguet, P. du, 1964. *Catalogue des étoffes Coptes* (in the Louvre Museum), Paris

Forbes, R.J., 1964. *Studies in Ancient Technology*, vol. IV, Textiles, Leiden

Fujii, H. et al., 1983– . 'Textiles from At Tar Caves, Iraq', 'Al-Rafidan', Tokyo

Geijer, A., 1979. *A History of Textile Art*, London

Hall (Janssen), R., 1986. *Egyptian Textiles*, Aylesbury. New revised edition, 1991

McDowell, J. A., 1984. 'Kahun: the textile evidence', in David, A.R. (ed.), *The Pyramid Builders of Ancient Egypt*, London

McDowell, J. A., 1991. 'Autumn and Winter, two Roman embroideries from Egypt', *Hali*, London, vol. XIII, no. 3, pp. 114–22

McDowell, J. A., forthcoming. 'Ancient Egyptian textiles', in Harte, N.B. and Coleman, D.G.C. (eds) *The Cambridge History of Western Textiles*, Cambridge

Seagroatt, M., 1965. *Coptic Weaves* (in the Merseyside Museums), Liverpool

Thompson, D., 1971. *Coptic Textiles in the Brooklyn Museum*, New York

Vogelsang-Eastwood, G. M., 1987. 'A re-examination of the fibres from the Çatal Hüyük textiles', in Pinner, R. and Denny, W.B. (eds), *Oriental Carpet and Textile Studies*, London, pp. 15–19

Volbach, W.F., 1969. *Early Decorative Textiles*, London

Wessel, K., 1963. *Koptische Kunst*, Recklinghausen

Wessel, K., 1965. *Coptic Art* (English ed.), London

Yadin, Y., 1963. 'The finds from the Bar Kokhba period in the Cave of Letters', *Journal*, Israel Exploration Society, Jerusalem

Central and northern Europe

Hald, M., 1980. *Ancient Danish Textiles from Bogs and Burials*, Publications of the National Museum Archaeological–Historical Series XXI, Copenhagen

Bender Jørgensen, L., 1989. *Forhistoriske Textiler i Skandinavien* (Prehistoric Scandinavian Textiles), Nordiske Fortidsminder B9, Copenhagen

Schlabow, K., 1976. *Textilfunde der Eisenzeit in Norddeutschland*, Göttinger Schriften zur Vor- und Frühgeschichte XV, Neumünster

Vogt, E., 1937. *Geflechte und Gewebe der Steinzeit*, Basel

Walton, P. and Wild, J.P. (eds), 1990. *Textiles in Northern Archaeology, NESAT III: Textile Symposium in York 6–9 May 1987*, London

Wild, J.P., 1988. *Textiles in Archaeology*, Aylesbury

THE NEAR AND MIDDLE EAST

Sassanian textiles

Harper, P.O., 1978. *The Royal Hunter: Art of the Sasanian Empire*, New York

McDowell, J. A., forthcoming. 'Sassanian textiles', in Harte, N.B. and Coleman, D.G.C. (eds), *The Cambridge History of Western Textiles*, Cambridge

Early Islamic textiles

Arts Council of Great Britain, 1976. *The Arts of Islam*, London, pp. 73–7

Gabrieli, F., 1968. *Muhammad and the Conquests of Islam*, London

Golombek, L. and Gervers, V., 1977. 'Tiraz fabrics in the Royal Ontario Museum', in Gervers, V. (ed.), *Studies in Textile History in Memory of Harold B. Burnham*, Toronto, pp. 82–125

Grohmann, A., 1972– . 'Tirāz', in *Encyclopaedia of Islam*, second edition, Leiden

Kühnel, E. and Bellinger, L., 1952. *Catalogue of Dated Tirāz Fabrics: Umayyad, Abbasid, Fatimid*, Washington, DC

Lewis, B. (ed.), 1976. *The World of Islam: Faith, People, Culture*, London

Rice, D.T., 1965. *Islamic Art*, London. Revised ed. 1985

Sergeant, R.B., 1972. *Islamic Textiles: Material For a History up to the Mongol Conquest*, Beirut (quotes early Arab writers and gives a bibliography)

Shepherd, D.G., 1981. 'Zandanījī revisited', in Flury-Lemberg, M. and Stolleis, K. (eds), *Documenta Textilia: Festschrift für Sigrid Müller-Christensen*, Munich

Shepherd, D.G. and Henning, W., 1959. 'Zandaniji identified?', in Ettinghausen, R. (ed.), *Aus der Welt der islamischen Kunst, Festschrift für Ernst Kühnel*, Berlin, pp. 15–40

Spuhler, F., 1978. *Islamic Carpets and Textiles in the Keir Collection*, London

Woolley, L., 1988. 'A medieval treasury: the figured silks in the Victoria and Albert Museum', *Hali*, London, vol. xxxviii, pp. 21–7

Byzantine silks

Beckwith, J., 1971. 'Byzantine tissues', in *XIV Congrès International des Études Byzantines*, Bucharest

Duchesne, L. (ed.), 1892. *Liber Pontificalis*, Paris

Geijer, A., 1980. 'Bishop Gunther's shroud in Bamberg Cathedral', in Flury-Lemberg, M. and Stolleis, K. (eds), *Documenta Textilia: Festschrift für Sigrid Müller-Christensen*, Munich, pp. 156–62

Grabar, A., 1956. 'La Soie byzantine de l'évêque Gunther à la cathédrale de Bamberg', *Münchener Jahrbuch*, folge vii, pp. 7–24

Koder, J., 1991. *Das Eparchenbuch Leons des Weisen*, Vienna

Krüger, P., 1915. 'Codex Justinianus', in *Corpus Iuris Civilis II*, Berlin

Lopez, R. S., 1945. 'Silk trade in the Byzantine Empire', *Speculum*, vol. xxix, pp. 1–42

Moravcsik, G. and Jenkins, R.J.H., 1967. 'De Administrando Imperio', in *Constantine Porphyrogenitus*, i, Washington, DC

Müller-Christensen, S., 1960. *Das Grab des Papstes Clemen II im Dom zu Bamberg*, Munich

Müller-Christensen, S., 1966. 'Beobachtungen zum Bamberger Gunthertuch', *Münchener Jahrbuch*, vol. xvii, pp. 9–16

Muthesius, A.M., 1984. 'A practical approach to the history of Byzantine silk weaving', *Jahrbuch der Österreichischen Byzantinistik*, vol. xxxiv, pp. 235–54

Muthesius, A.M., 1990 (a). 'From seed to samite: aspects of Byzantine silk weaving', in 'Ancient and Medieval Textile Studies in Honour of Donald King', *Textile History*, vol. xx, no. 2, pp. 135–49

Muthesius, A.M., 1990 (b). 'The impact of the Mediterranean silk trade on Europe before 1200 AD', in *Textiles in Trade: Textile Society of America Biennial Symposium Proceedings*, Washington, DC, pp. 126–35

Muthesius, A.M., 1991. 'Crossing traditional boundaries: grub to glamour in Byzantine silk weaving', *Journal of Byzantine and Modern Greek Studies*, autumn

Muthesius, A.M., forthcoming (a). *History of Byzantine Silk Weaving*, Koder, J. and Kislinger, E. (eds), Byzantine Institute, Vienna. This expands on the author's 'Eastern silks in Western shrines and treasuries before 1200 AD' (Ph.D. thesis, Courtauld Institute of Art, University of London, 1982)

Muthesius, A.M., forthcoming (b). 'Lopez and beyond', in Harte, N.B. and Coleman, D.G.C. (eds), *The Cambridge History of Western Textiles*, Cambridge

Muthesius, A.M., forthcoming (c). 'Silken diplomacy', in *Proceedings: Spring International Byzantine Conference, Cambridge, 1990*

Pharr, C., 1952. 'The Theodosian Code', in *The Corpus of Roman Law*, i, Princeton

Reiske, I. I., 1829–31. 'De Caerimoniis aulae Byzantinae', in *Constantini Porphyrogentii Imperatoris*, Bonn

Wada, H., 1972. 'Prokops Rätselwort Serinda und die Verpflanzung des Seidenbaus von China nach dem

Oströmischen Reich' (Ph.D. thesis, Cologne University), pp. 63–70 (for Procopius and Theophanes of Byzantium). Discussed in Muthesius, 1990 (a) and forthcoming (b), cited above

Wentzel, H., 1972. 'Das Byzantinische Erbe der Ottonischen Kaiser: Hypothesen über den Brautschatz der Theophanou', *Aachener Kunstblätter*, vol. xliii, pp. 11–96

Safavid Iran (1499–1722)

Arts Council of Great Britain, 1976. *The Arts of Islam*, London, pp. 105–12

Bier, C. (ed.), 1987. *Woven From the Soul, Spun From the Heart: Textile Arts of Safavid and Qajar Iran, Sixteenth to Nineteenth Centuries*, Washington, DC

Chardin, J., 1927. *Sir John Chardin's Travels in Persia*, ed. P. Sykes, London

London, Victoria and Albert Museum, 1937. *Brief Guide to Persian Embroidery*, London

London, Victoria and Albert Museum, 1937. *Brief Guide to the Persian Woven Fabrics*, London

Los Angeles, County Museum, 1959. *Woven Treasures of Persian Art from the Sixth to the Nineteenth Century*, Los Angeles, pp. 33–64

McDowell, J. A., 1989. 'Safavid textiles', in Ferrier, R. (ed.), *The Arts of Persia*, New Haven and London, pp. 158–68

Pope, A. U. and Ackerman, P. (eds), 1938–9. *Survey of Persian Art*, Oxford. Reprinted 1981, New York, 'Textiles'

Reath, N. A. and Sachs, E. B., 1937. *Persian Textiles and Their Techniques From the Sixth to the Eighteenth Centuries*, New Haven

Spuhler, F., 1978. *Islamic Carpets and Textiles in the Keir Collection*, London

Welch, A., 1973. *Shah Abbas and the Arts of Isfahan*, London

Wulff, H. E., 1966. *The Traditional Crafts of Persia*, Cambridge, Mass.

The Ottoman Empire

Arts Council of Great Britain, 1976. *The Arts of Islam*, London, pp. 82–6

Aslanapa, O., 1971. *Turkish Art and Architecture*, London

Black, D. and Loveless, C. (eds), 1978. *Islemeler: Ottoman Domestic Embroideries*, London

Black, D. and Loveless, C. (eds), 1981. *Embroidered Flowers from Thrace to Tartary*, London

Colnaghi, P. & D., 1980. *An Exhibition of Imperial Ottoman Textiles*, text by D. King, London

Davis, F., 1970. *The Palace of Topkapi in Istanbul*, New York

Denny, W., 1974. 'A group of silk Islamic banners', *Textile Museum Journal*, Washington, DC, vol. iv, no. 1, pp. 67–81

Encyclopaedia of Islam, second edition, 1972– . 'Harir: the Ottoman Empire', Leiden, pp. 210–18

Esin, A., 1987. *The Age of Suleyman the Magnificent*, Washington, DC and New York

Johnstone, P., 1985. *Turkish Embroidery*, London

Lewis, R., 1971. *Everyday Life in Ottoman Turkey*, London

Mackie, L., 1974. *The Splendor of Turkish Weaving*, Washington, DC

Oz, T., 1950. *Turkish Textiles and Velvets, Fourteenth to Sixteenth Centuries*, Ankara

Petsopoulos, Y. (ed.), 1982. *Tulips,*

Arabesques and Turbans: Decorative Arts of the Ottoman Empire, London

Rogers, J.M. and Ward, R.M., 1988. *Suleyman the Magnificent*, London

Rogers, J.M., Tezcan, H. and Delibas, S., 1987. *The Topkapi Saray Museum: Costumes, Embroideries and Other Textiles*, London

Vienna, Historische Museen, 1983. *Die Turken von Wien: Europa und die Entscheidung an der Donau 1683*, Vienna

Wace, A.J.B., 1935. *Mediterranean and Near Eastern Embroideries*, 2 vols, London

Wearden, J., 1986. 'The saz style', *Hali*, London, vol. xxx, pp. 22–9

Central Asian textiles

Allgrove, J., 1973. 'Turcoman embroideries', *Embroidery*, summer, pp. 44–7

Browne, C.W., 1989. *Ikats*, London

Crafts Council, 1988. *Ikats: Woven Silks from Central Asia: The Rau Collection*, London

Kalter, J., 1984. *The Arts and Crafts of Turkestan*, London

Kendal, Abbot Hall Art Gallery, 1971. *The Turcoman of Iran*

Levinsteyn, Y., 1981. 'Unravelling Central Asian embroidery', *Hali*, London, vol. iv, no. 2, pp. 152–3

Palestinian embroidery

A comprehensive bibliography for Palestinian embroidery may be found in Weir, S., 1989. *Palestinian Costume*, London.

Crowfoot, G., 1936. 'Bethlehem embroidery', *Embroidery*, London, December

Crowfoot, G. and Sutton, P., 1935. 'Ramallah embroidery', *Embroidery*, London, March

Institut du Monde Arabe, 1988. *Memoire de Soie: Costumes et parures de Palestine et de Jourdanie: Catalogue de la Collection Widad Kamel Kawar*, Paris

Stillman, Y., 1979. *Palestinian Costume and Jewelry*, Albuquerque

Weir, S., 1970. *Palestinian Embroidery*, London

Weir, S., 1976. *The Bedouin: Aspects of the Material Culture of the Bedouin of Jordan*, London

Weir, S., 1989. *Palestinian Costume*, London

Weir, S. and Kawar, W., 1988. 'Costumes and wedding customs in Bayt Dajan', *Palestine Exploration Quarterly*, London

Weir, S. and Shahid, S., 1988. *Palestinian Embroidery: Cross-stitch Patterns from the Traditional Costumes of the Village Women of Palestine*, London

INDIA AND PAKISTAN
Historical development and trade

Adams, B.S., 1984. *Traditional Bhutanese Textiles*, Bangkok

Baden-Powell, B.S., 1872. *Handbook of the Manufactures and Arts of the Punjab*, forming vol. ii to the *Handbook of the Economic Products of the Punjab*, Lahore

Banerjei, N.N., 1897. 'Dyes and dyeing in Bengal', *Journal of Indian Art and Industry*, London, vol. vii, no. 59, pp. 11–20

Bhushan, J., 1958. *The Costumes and Textiles of India*, Bombay

Birdwood, Sir G., 1880. *The Industrial Arts of India*, London

Blochmann, H. and Jarrett, H., trans.,

1927–49. *The Ain-i-Akbari of Abu'l Fazl'Allami*, Bibliotheca Indica, 3 vols, Calcutta. Second edition (revised). The references to the *ains* relating the development of Mughal textiles under the Emperor Akbar are in vol. i, ain 21, and ains 31 and 32

Bühler, A. and Fischer, E., 1979. *The Patola of Gujarat*, 2 vols, Basel

Bühler, A., Fischer, E. and Nabholz, M.-L., 1980. *Indian Tie-dyed Fabrics*, Ahmedabad

Census of India. *Reports*, since the 1860s, *passim*, by area and district, and thence by town and village

Chandra, M., 1960. 'Indian costumes and textiles from the eighth to the twelfth century', *Journal of Indian Textile History*, Ahmedabad, vol. v, pp. 1–41

Culin, S., 1918. 'The story of the painted curtain', *Good Furniture*, Michigan, vol. xi, pp. 43–7

Gillow, J. and Barnard, N., 1991. *Traditional Indian Textiles*, London

Gittinger, M., 1982. *Master Dyers to the World: Early Indian Dyed Cotton Textiles*, Washington, DC

Guy, J. and Swallow, D. (eds), 1990. *Arts of India, 1550 to 1900*, London (the arts are discussed by period and by region; many historic textiles are illustrated in relation to the Indian arts of their time)

Irwin, J., 1949. 'The commercial embroidery of Gujerat in the seventeenth century', *Journal of the Indian Society of Oriental Art*, Calcutta, vol. xvii (issued 1952), pp. 51ff.

Irwin, J., 1952. 'Indo-Portuguese embroideries of Bengal', *Art and Letters: Journal of the Royal India and Pakistan Society*, London, vol. xxvi, no. 2, pp. 65–73

Irwin, J., 1959. 'Golconda cotton paintings of the early seventeenth century', *Lalit Kala* (Journal of the Indian Academy of Arts), New Delhi, no. v, pp. 8–48

Irwin, J., 1973. *Kashmir Shawls*, London

Irwin, J. and Brett, K., 1970. *The Origins of Chintz*, London and Toronto

Irwin, J. and Hall, M., 1971. *Indian Painted and Printed Fabrics*, Ahmedabad

Irwin, J. and Hall, M., 1973. *Indian Embroideries*, Ahmedabad

Krishna, R. A. and Krishna, V., 1966. *Banaras Brocades*, New Delhi

Lévi-Strauss, M., 1986. *The Romance of the Cashmere Shawl*, Milan. English translation, 1987, Ahmedabad

Mookerji, N.G., 1894. 'The silk industries of Moorshedabad', *Journal of Indian Art and Industry*, London, vol. v, no. 38, pp. 1–7 and plates 1–7

Murphy, V. and Crill, R., 1991. *Tie-dyed Textiles of India: Tradition and Trade*, London & Ahmedabad

Ramaswamy, V., 1985. *Textiles and Weavers in Mediaeval South India*, New Delhi

Schoff, W.H., 1912. *Periplus Maris Erythraei, The Periplus of the Erythraean Sea*, translated from the Greek and annotated, New York and London. Reprinted 1974, New Delhi

Taylor, J. (published anonymously), 1951. *A Descriptive and Historical Account of the Cotton Manufactures of Dacca in Bengal* (prepared for The Royal Society of Arts), London

Watt, Sir G., 1903. *Indian Art at Delhi: Official Catalogue of the Exhibition of 1903*, Calcutta

Yusuf Ali, A., 1900. *A Monograph on Silk Fabrics Produced in the North-western*

Provinces and Oudh, Allahabad. Reprinted 1974, Ahmedabad

Tribal textiles

Grayson, S., 1982. *The Living Arts of India: Craftsmen at Work*, London (catalogue of the travelling exhibition and demonstration by craftsmen and women from India, for the Festival of India, 1982)

Hutton, J.H., 1921. *The Angami Nagas: With some Notes on Neighbouring Tribes*, London

Konieczny, M.G., 1979. *Textiles of Baluchistan*, London

Kosambi, D.D., 1965. *The Culture and Civilisation of Ancient India in Historical Outline*, London (*passim*, and plates 3 to 36: costume; surviving tribal life, and traditions in village life)

Mills, J.P., 1922. *The Lhota Nagas*, London (pp. 8–11, dress; pp. 36–40, spinning, weaving and dyeing)

Mills, J.P., 1926. *The Ao Nagas*, London (pp. 34–41, dress; pp. 90–4, spinning, weaving, dyeing)

Naga Institute of Culture, 1968. *Arts and Crafts of Nagaland*, Kohima, Assam

Rivers, W.H.R., 1906. *The Todas* (with illustrations), London

Thurston, E., 1896. *Anthropology of the Todas and Kotas of the Nilgiri Hills*, Madras (Madras Government Museum Bulletin no. IV)

CARPETS

Arts Council of Great Britain, Hayward Gallery, eds D. King and D. Sylvester, 1983. *The Eastern Carpet in the Western World from the Fifteenth to the Seventeenth Century*, London

Arts Council of Great Britain, Hayward Gallery, ed. D. Sylvester, 1972. *Islamic Carpets from the Collection of Joseph V. McMullan*, London

Beattie, M.H., 1976. *Carpets of Central Persia*, London

Cammann, S., 1975. 'The systematic study of oriental rugs: techniques & patterns', *Journal of American Oriental Studies*, no. XCV, pp. 248–60

Edwards, A.C., 1953. *The Persian Carpet*, London. Reprinted 1975

Ellis, C.G., 1976. *Early Caucasian Rugs*, Washington, DC

Erdmann, K., 1970. *Seven Hundred Years of Oriental Carpets*, trans. M.H. Beattie, London

Ettinghausen, R. *et al.*, 1974. *Prayer Rugs*, Washington, DC

Hali, International Magazine of Fine Carpets & Textiles, London

Housego, J., 1978. *Tribal Rugs: An Introduction to the Weavings of the Tribes of Iran*, London

Landreau, A.N. (ed.), 1978. *Yörük: The Nomadic Weaving Tradition of the Middle East*, Pittsburgh

Mackie, L. and Thompson, J. (eds), 1980. *Turkmen: Tribal Carpets and Traditions*, Washington, DC

Petsopoulus, Y., 1979. *Kilims: The Art of Tapestry Weaving in Anatolia, the Caucasus & Persia*, London

THE FAR EAST

China

Becker, J. with the collaboration of D.B. Wagner, 1987. *Pattern and Loom: A Practical Study of the Development of Weaving Techniques in China, Western Asia and Europe*, Copenhagen

Burnham, H.B., 1959. *Chinese Velvets: A Technical Study*, Toronto

Huang Nengfu (ed.), 1985, 1986. *Zhongguo meishu quanji* (Complete Chinese Arts), *Gongyi meishu pian 6, 7* (Arts and Crafts 6, 7), *Yinran zhixiu (shang, xia)* (Textiles I, II), Peking

Kuhn, D., 1987. *Die Song-Dynastie (960 bis 1279): Eine neue Gesellschaft im Spiegel ihrer Kultur*, Weinheim

Riboud, K., 1974. 'A reappraisal of Han Dynasty monochrome figured silks', *CIETA Bulletin*, vol. XXXVIII, pp. 122–38

Riboud, K., 1977 (a). 'A closer view of early Chinese silks', in Gervers, V. (ed.), *Studies in Textile History in Memory of Harold Burnham*, Toronto

Riboud, K., 1977 (b). 'Some remarks on the face covers (*fu-mien*) discovered in the tombs of Astana', *Oriental Art*, vol. IV, pp. 48–64

Riboud, K. and Vial, G., 1970. *Tissus de Touen-Houang conservés au Musée Guimet et à la Bibliothèque Nationale*, Paris

Shih, H.-Y., 1977. 'Textile finds in the People's Republic of China', in Gervers, V. (ed.), *Studies in Textile History in Memory of Harold Burnham*, Toronto

Whitfield, R., 1985. *The Art of Central Asia: The Stein Collection in the British Museum*, vol. III, *Textiles, Sculpture and Other Arts*, Tokyo

Wilson, V., 1986. *Chinese Dress*, Victoria and Albert Museum Far Eastern Series, London

Japan

Egi, Y., 1988, 1989. *Kimono no bi* (The art of kimono), *The Sun*, Tokyo, special issue, winter

Fontein, J. (general ed.), 1983. *Living National Treasures of Japan*, trans. P. Massy, S. Kaneko and T. Shindo, Boston

Hirai, N. (ed.), 1987. *Tsutsugaki Textiles of Japan*, Kyoto

Ito, T., 1981. *Tsujigahana: The Flower of Japanese Textile Art*, trans. M. Bethe, Tokyo and New York

Japan Textile Color Design Center, 1980. *Textile Designs of Japan*, revised edition, 3 vols, Tokyo and New York

Kennedy, A., 1990. *Japanese Costume: History and Tradition*, Paris

Koren, L., 1983. *New Fashion Japan*. Tokyo, New York and San Francisco

Matsumoto, K., 1984. *Jodai Gire: Seventh and Eighth Century Textiles in Japan from the Shoso-in and Horyu-ji*, trans. S. Kaneko and R.L. Mellott, Tokyo

Minnich, H.B., with S. Nomura, 1963. *Japanese Costume and the Makers of its Elegant Tradition*, Rutland, Vermont, and Tokyo

Nakano, E. and Stephan, B.B., 1982. *Japanese Stencil Dyeing: Paste Resist Techniques*, New York and Tokyo

Noma, S., 1974. *Japanese Costume and Textile Arts*, trans. A. Nikovskis, Heibonsha Survey of Japanese Art, vol. XVI, New York and Tokyo

Stinchecum, A.M., 1984. *Kosode: Sixteenth–Seventeenth Century Textiles from the Nomura Collection*, Tokyo and New York

Takahashi, Y. (ed.), 1987. *Genji Monogatari no Iro* (Colours in the Tale of Genji), *The Sun*, Tokyo, special issue no. LX, winter

Tokyo, Tokugawa Art Museum, 1983. *The Shogun Age Exhibition*

Tomita, J. and Tomita, N., 1982. *Japanese Ikat Weaving: The Techniques of Kasuri*, London, Boston, Melbourne and Henley

Wada, Y., Rice, M.K. and Barton, J., 1983. *Shibori: The Inventive Art of Japanese Shaped Resist Dyeing*, Tokyo and New York

Yamaguchi, A. and Zentaro, K., 1984. *The Reproduction of Noh Costume*, Kyoto

Yamanaka, N., 1982. *The Book of Kimono*, Tokyo and New York

Yamanobe, T., 1979. *Meiji no moyo: senshoku* (Meiji patterns: textiles), Kyoto

Yang, S. and Narasin, R.M., 1989. *Textile Art of Japan*, Tokyo

South-East Asia

For a comprehensive bibliography of South-East Asian textiles see Fraser-Lu, S., 1988, *Handwoven Textiles of South-East Asia*, Singapore, and, for Indonesian textiles, Gittinger, M., 1979, *Splendid Symbols: Textiles and Traditions in Indonesia*, Washington, DC. The following works were either not cited in the above bibliographies or have been published more recently.

Arney, S., 1987. *Malaysian Batik: Creating New Traditions*, Kuala Lumpur

Barnes, R., 1989. *The Ikat Textiles of Lamalera*, Leiden

Cheesman, P., 1987. *Lan Na Textiles: Yuan, Lue, Lao*, Chiangmai

Cheesman, P., 1988. *Lao Textiles: Ancient Symbols – Living Art*, Bangkok

Gittinger, M. (ed.), 1980. *Indonesian Textiles: Irene Emory Roundtable on Museum Textiles, 1979 Proceedings*, Washington, DC

Gittinger, M. (ed.), 1989. *To Speak with Cloth: Studies in Indonesian Textiles*, Los Angeles

Hitchcock, M., 1991. *Indonesian Textiles*, London

Maxwell, R., 1990. *Tradition, Trade and Transformation: Textiles of Southeast Asia*, Melbourne

Selvanayagam, G.I., 1990. *Songket: Malaysia's Woven Treasure*, Singapore

WESTERN EUROPE

Sicilian silks

Grönwoldt, R., 1964. *Webereien und Stickereien des Mittelalters*, Hanover (catalogue)

Grönwoldt, R., 1977. 'Kaisergewänder und Paramente', in *Die Zeit der Staufer*, Stuttgart, pp. 607–44 (exhibition catalogue; contains an extensive further bibliography)

Guillou, A., 1974. 'La Soie sicilienne', in *Byzantino-Sicolo: Miscellanea . . . G. Rossi-Taibbi*, Palermo

Guillou, A., 1976. 'La Soie du Katepanat d'Italie', *Travaux et Mémoires*, Paris, vol. VI, pp. 69–84

Muthesius, A.M., 1982. 'Eastern silks in Western shrines and treasuries before 1200 A.D.', Ph.D. thesis, Courtauld Institute of Art, University of London, pp. 254–63

Siragusa, G.B. (ed.), 1897. *Liber de Regne Sicilie*, Rome, pp. 178–80

Weigand, E., 1935. *Die helladisch-Byzantinische Seidenweberei*, Athens

Italian silks (1300–1500)

Bini, T., 1883. *I Lucchesi a Venezia sopra i secoli XIII e XIV*, Lucca

Deuchler, F., 1963. *Die Burgundebeute: Inventar der Beutestücke aus den Schlachten von Grandson, Murten und Nancy 1476/77*, Berne

Falke, O. von, 1936. *Decorative Silks*, London

Flury-Lemberg, M., 1989. *Textile Conservation and Research*, Berne

Herald, J., 1981. *Renaissance Dress in Italy, 1400–1500*, London.

King, D., 1960. 'Sur la signification de "Diasprum"', *CIETA Bulletin*, vol. XI, pp. 42–7

King, D., 1969. 'Some unrecognised Venetian woven fabrics', *V & A Yearbook*, London, pp. 53–64

King, D. and King, M., 1988. 'Silk weaves of Lucca in 1376', in Estham, I. and Nockert, M. (eds), *Opera textilia variorum temporum – to Honour Agnes Geijer on her Ninetieth Birthday 26th October, 1988*, Stockholm, pp. 67–77

King, D. and King, M., 1990. *European Textiles in the Keir Collection 400 BC to 1800 AD*, London and Boston

Klesse, B., 1967. *Seidenstoffe in der italienischen Malerei des 14. Jahrhunderts*, Berne

Magagnato, L., 1983. *Le stoffe di Cangrande* (exhibition catalogue), Verona

Molinier, E., 1888. 'Inventaire du trésor du Saint Siège sous Boniface VIII (1295)', *Extrait de la Bibliothèque de l'École des Chartres*, Paris, 1882–8

Monnas, L., 1983. 'The vestments of Sixtus IV at Padua', *CIETA Bulletin*, vols LVII–LVIII, pp. 104–26

Monnas, L., 1986. 'Developments in figured velvet weaving in Italy during the 14th century', *CIETA Bulletin*, vols LXIII–LXIV, pp. 63–100

Monnas, L., 1987. 'Vestments of Henry VII at Stonyhurst College: cloth of gold woven to shape', *CIETA Bulletin*, vol. LXV, p. 69–80

Monnas, L., 1989 (a), 'New documents for the vestments of Henry VII at Stonyhurst College', *Burlington Magazine*, May

Monnas, L, 1989 (b), 'Silk cloths purchased for the Great Wardrobe of the Kings of England, 1325–1462', in Monnas, L. and Granger-Taylor, H. (eds), *Ancient and Medieval Textiles: Studies in Honour of Donald King*, Leeds

Muentz, E. and Frothingham, A. L. Jr., 1883. *Il tesoro della Basilica di S. Pietro in Vaticano dal XIII al XV secolo con una scelta d'inventarii inediti*, Rome

Peri, P., 1981. *Il parato di Niccolò V*, Florence

Podreider, F., 1928. *Storia dei tessuti d'arte in Italia*, Bergamo

Prato, Palazzo Pretorio, 1981. *Tessuti italiani del rinascimento, collezioni Franchetti Carrand* (exhibition catalogue), Florence

Santangelo, A., 1964. *The Development of Italian Textile Design from the Twelfth to the Eighteenth Century*, London

Smola, G., 1969. 'Das Grabgewand Herzog Ernst des Eisernen: Ein Samtbrokat des frühen 15. Jahrhunderts', *Joannea*, vol. II, pp. 335–55

Wardwell, A., 1976–7. 'The stylistic development of fourteenth and fifteenth century Italian silk design', *Aachener Kunstblätter*, vol. XLVII, pp. 177–226

Wardwell, A., 1988–9, 'Panni Tartarici: eastern Islamic silks woven with gold and silver (thirteenth and fourteenth centuries)', *Islamic Art*, vol. III, pp. 95–173

Italian silks (1500–1900)

Centro Italiano per lo Studio della Storia del Tessuto (CISST), 1984. *I tessili antichi e il loro uso*. Papers given at third conference, held in Turin

Devoti, D., 1974. *L'arte del tessuto in Europa*, Milan

Fennell Mazzaoui, M., 1981. *The Italian Cotton Industry in the Later Middle Ages 1100–1600*, Cambridge

Milan, Castello Sforzesco, 1983. *Tessuti serici italiani 1450–1530* (exhibition catalogue), Milan

Modena, Istituto per i Beni Artistici Culturali e Naturali della Regione Emilia–Romagna, 1985. *La Collezione Gandini del Museo Civico di Modena: i tessuti del XVIII e XIX secolo*, Bologna

Prato, Istituto Tecnico Industriale Statale Tullio Buzzi, 1975. *Il museo del tessuto a Prato* (exhibition catalogue), Florence

Prato, Palazzo Pretorio, 1981. *Tessuti italiani del rinascimento* (exhibition catalogue), Florence

Thornton, P., 1965. *Baroque and Rococo Silks*, London

Thornton, P., 1978. *Seventeenth-century Interior Decoration in England, France and Holland*, London

Thornton, P., 1984. *Authentic Decor: The Domestic Interior 1620–1920*, London

Spanish silks

Desrosiers, S. et al., 1990. 'Cloth of Aresta: a preliminary study', in Monnas, L. and Granger-Taylor, H. (eds), *Ancient and Medieval Textiles: Studies in Honour of Donald King*, Leeds, pp. 199–224

King, D. and King, M., 1990. *European Textiles in the Keir Collection 400 BC to 1800 AD*, London and Boston

May, F., 1957. *Silk Textiles of Spain, Eighth to Fifteenth Century*, New York

Tuscerer, J.M. (ed.), 1976. *Étoffes merveilleuses du Musée Historique des Tissus, Lyon*, vol. III, Tokyo

French silks (1650–1800)

Coural, J. and Gastinel-Coural, C., 1983. 'La Fabrique lyonnaise au XVIIIe siècle: la commande royale de 1730', *Revue de l'Art*, pp. LXII, pp. 49–64

Godart, J., 1899. *L'Ouvrier en soie.* Reprinted 1976, Geneva

Joubert de l'Hiberderie, N., 1765. *Le Dessinateur pour les étoffes d'or d'argent et de soie*, Paris

Léon, P., 1976. *Lyon et le grand commerce au XVIIIe siècle: Papiers d'industriels et de commerçants lyonnais*, Lyons

Miller, L., 1988. *Designers in the Lyon Silk Industry 1712–1787* (unpublished Ph.D. thesis, Brighton Polytechnic)

Paulet, J., 1779. 'L'Art du fabricant des étoffes de soie,' in *Dictionnaire des arts et métiers*, Paris

Peyrot, J., 1973. 'Les Techniques du commerce de soies au XVIIIe siècle à travers les documents commerciaux et comptables des fabricants de soieries', *Bulletin du Centre d'Histoire Économique et Sociale de la Région Lyonnaise*, no. 1, pp. 29–49

Rothstein, N., 1990. *Silk Designs of the Eighteenth Century*, London

Thornton, P., 1965. *Baroque and Rococo Silks*, London

Tuscerer, J.M. (ed.), 1976. *Étoffes merveilleuses du Musée Historique des Tissus, Lyon*, Tokyo

Figured linen damasks

Amsterdam, Stedelijk Museum, 1983–4. *Textiel voor tafel en keuken* (exhibition catalogue)

Baines, P., 1985. *Flax and Linen*, Princes Risborough

Burgers, C.A., 1981. 'Dutch damasks for

Denmark', in Flury-Lemberg, M. and Stolleis, K. (eds), *Documenta Textilia: Festschrift für Sigrid Müller-Christensen*, Munich, pp. 251–60

Durie, A.J., 1976. 'The fine linen industry in Scotland, 1707–1822', *Textile History*, vol. VII, pp. 173–85

Geijer, A., 1979. *A History of Textile Art*, London

Lewis, E., 1984. 'An eighteenth century linen damask tablecloth from Ireland', *Textile History*: vol. XV, no. 2, pp. 235–44

Mitchell, D. M., 1989. '"By your leave my masters": British taste in table linen in the fifteenth and sixteenth centuries', *Textile History*: vol. XX, no. 1, pp. 49–77

Prinet, M., 1982. *Le Damas de lin historié*, Berne

Thornton, P., 1978. *Seventeenth-century Interior Decoration in England, France and Holland*, London

Weiner, A.B. and Schneider, J. (eds), 1989. *Cloth and Human Experience*, Washington, DC and London: pp. 177–214, 'Rumpelstiltskin's bargain: folklore and the merchant capitalist intensification of linen manufacture in early modern Europe' by J. Schneider, and pp. 215–42, 'Spun virtue, the lacework of folly, and the world wound upside-down: seventeenth-century Dutch depictions of female handwork' by L. Stone-Ferrier

Ysselsteyn, G. T. van, 1962. *White Figured Linen Damask from the Fifteenth to the Beginning of the Nineteenth Century*, The Hague

Tapestry

Badin, J., 1909. *La Manufacture de tapisseries de Beauvais depuis ses origines jusqu'à nos jours*, Paris

Baldass, L., 1920. *Die Wiener Gobelinsammlung: Dreihundert Bildtafeln mit beschreibenden Text*, Vienna

Bertrand, P.-F. and Chevalier, D. and P. 1988. *Les Tapisseries d'Aubusson et de Felletin 1457–1791*, Paris

Brussels, Musées Royaux, 1976. *Tapisseries bruxelloises de la pré-Renaissance* (exhibition catalogue)

Brussels, Musées Royaux, 1977. *Tapisseries bruxelloises au siècle de Rubens* (exhibition catalogue)

Bury, A.R. and Stucky-Scheurer, M., 1990. *Zahm und Wild: Basler und Strassburger Bildteppiche des 15. Jahrhunderts*, Mainz am Rhein

Cavallo, A. S, 1967. *Tapestries of Europe and Colonial Peru in the Museum of Fine Arts, Boston*, 2 vols, Boston

Digby, G.W. 1980. *Victoria & Albert Museum: The Tapestry Collection. Medieval and Renaissance*, London

Fenaille, M., 1903–23. *État général des tapisseries de la Manufacture des Gobelins*, 6 vols, Paris

Göbel, H., 1923. *Wandteppiche I: Die Niederlande*, 2 vols, Leipzig

Göbel, H., 1928. *Wandteppiche II: Die Romanischen Länder*, 2 vols, Leipzig

Göbel, H., 1933–4. *Wandteppiche III: Die Germanischen und Slavischen Länder*, 2 vols, Leipzig

Heinz, D., 1963. *Europäische Wandteppiche I: Von den Anfangen der Bildwerkerei bis zum Ende des 16. Jahrhunderts*, Brunswick

d'Hulst, R.-A., 1967. *Flemish Tapestries from the Fifteenth to the Eighteenth Century*, Brussels

Junquera de Vega, P., 1986. *Catalogo de tapices del Patrimonio Nacional*, 2 vols, Madrid

Kurth, B., 1926. *Die Deutsche Bildteppiche des Mittelalters*, 3 vols, Vienna

Marillier, H. C., 1927. *History of the Merton Abbey Tapestry Works, Founded by William Morris*, London

Scottish Arts Council, 1980. *Master Weavers: Tapestry from the Dovecot Studios 1912–1980* (exhibition catalogue), Edinburgh

Standen, E.A., 1985. *European Post-medieval Tapestries and Related Hangings in the Metropolitan Museum of Art*, 2 vols, New York

Thomson, F.P., 1980. *Tapestry, Mirror of History*, Newton Abbot

Thomson, W.G., 1914. *Tapestry Weaving in England, from the Earliest Times to the end of the XVIIIth Century*, London

Thomson, W.G., 1973. *A History of Tapestry from the Earliest Times until the Present Day*, third edition revised by F.P. and E.S. Thomson, Wakefield

Weigert, R.-A., 1962. *French Tapestry*. London

Embroidery

Branting, A. and Lindblom, A., 1932. *Medieval Embroideries and Textiles in Sweden*, Stockholm

Brett, K.B., 1972. *English Embroidery in the Royal Ontario Museum: Sixteenth–Eighteenth Centuries*, Toronto

Bridgeman, H. and Drury, E., 1978. *Needlework: An Illustrated History*, London and New York

Carlano, M. and Salmon, L. (eds), 1985. *French Textiles from the Middle Ages through the Second Empire* (exhibition catalogue, Wadsworth Atheneum), Hartford, Conn.

Carmignani, M. (ed.), 1985. *Ricami e merletti nelle chiese e nei monasteri di Prato dal XVI al XIX secola* (exhibition catalogue), Prato

Cavallo, A.S., 1979. *Needlework*, Washington, DC

Christie, Mrs A., 1938. *English Medieval Embroidery*, Oxford

Clabburn, P., 1981. *Masterpieces of Embroidery*, Oxford

Dreger, M., 1904. *Die künstlerische Entwicklung der Weberei und Stickerei*, Vienna

Estham, I., 1971. *Figurbroderade mössshaker från reformationstidens och 1600-talets Sverige*, Stockholm

Estham, I., 1991. *Brigittinska Textilier*, Stockholm

Farcy, L. de, 1890–1900. *La Broderie du XIe siècle jusqu'à nos jours*, 3 vols, Paris and Amiens

Geijer, A., 1964. *Textile Treasures of Uppsala Cathedral*, Uppsala

Gonzales, M., 1974. *Catálogo de bordados del Instituto Valencia de Don Juan*, Madrid

Hackenbrock, Y., 1960. *English and Other Needlework, Tapestries and Textiles in the Irwin Untermeyer Collection*, Cambridge, Mass. and London

Howard, I., 1982–6. *Twentieth Century Embroidery in Great Britain*, 4 vols, London

Iklé, E., 1931. *La Broderie mécanique, 1828–1930*, Paris

Johnstone, P., 1986. *Three Hundred Years of Embroidery, 1600–1900* (exhibition catalogue), South Australia

Kendrick, A.F., 1967. *English Needlework*, London, second edition by P. Wardle

King, D., 1963. *Opus Anglicanum* (exhibition catalogue, Victoria and Albert Museum), London

Kroos, R., 1970. *Niedersächsische Bildstickereien des Mittelalters*, Berlin

Mayer-Thurman, C., 1975. *Raiment for the Lord's Service: A Thousand Years of Western Vestments* (exhibition catalogue, Art Institute of Chicago), Chicago

Morris, B., 1962. *Victorian Embroidery*, London

Nevinson, J.L., 1950. *Catalogue of English Domestic Embroideries of the 16th and 17th Centuries* (Victoria and Albert Museum), London, second edition

Palol, P. de, 1986. *El Tapís de la Creació de la Catedral de Girona*, Barcelona

Paludan, C., 1983. *Alverdens Broderier i Kunstindustrimuseet* (exhibition catalogue), Stockholm

Paris, Musée du Costume, 1964. *Dentelles et broderie dans la mode française du XVIe au XXe siècle* (exhibition catalogue)

Parry, L., 1983. *William Morris Textiles*, London

Parry, L., 1988. *Textiles of the Arts and Crafts Movement*, London

Ricci, E., 1925. *Ricami italiani*, Florence

Saint-Aubin, C. G. de, 1983. *The Art of Embroidery*, facsimile of *L'Art du brodeur*, 1770, trans. and annotated by N. Scheuer, Los Angeles

Schuette, M. and Müller-Christensen, S., 1963. *The Art of Embroidery*, London

Sonday, M. and Moss, G., 1978. *European Embroidery in the Collection of the Cooper-Hewitt Museum*, New York

Staniland, K., 1991. *Embroiderers*, Medieval Craftsmen series, London

Swain, M., 1955. *The Flowerers*, London and Edinburgh

Swain, M., 1970. *Historical Needlework: A Study of Influences in Scotland and Northern England*, London

Swain, M., 1982. *Ayrshire and other Whitework*, Princes Risborough

Symonds, M. and Preece, L., 1928. *Needlework Through the Ages*, London

Varju-Ember, M., 1980. *Old Textiles: Treasures of the Hungarian National Museum*, Budapest

Verkhovskaia, A.S., 1961. *Western European Embroidery in the Hermitage Museum*, Leningrad

Wardle, P., 1970. *A Guide to English Embroidery*, London

Wilson, D., 1985. *The Bayeux Tapestry*, London

Lace

For a comprehensive bibliography see Levey, S.M., 1983, *Lace: A History*, Leeds. The following works either were not cited in the above or have been published more recently.

Burkhard, C., 1986. *Fascinating Bobbin Lace*, Berne (facsimile of the pattern book *R. M. Nüw Modelbuch* of 1561, text in German, French and English)

Churchill Bath, V., 1974. *Lace*, Jersey City, NJ. Reprinted 1979, Harmondsworth

Earnshaw, P., 1986. *Lace Machines and Machine Laces*, London

Earnshaw, P., 1988. *Youghal and other Irish Laces*, Shamley Green

Faleyeva, V., 1986. *Russian Bobbin Lace*, Leningrad

Ferguson, S. & fils, 1862. *Histoire du tulle et des dentelles mécaniques en Angleterre et en France*, Paris (?)

Kraatz, A., 1989, *Lace: History & Fashion* London. First published in French, 1988, Paris

Levey, S.M. and Payne, P.L., 1983. *Le

Pompe, 1559: Patterns for Venetian Bobbin Lace, Carlton, Bedfordshire (facsimile of a 1559 pattern book, with introduction and practical instructions)

Longfield, A., 1978, *Irish Lace*, Dublin

Parma Armani, E., 1990. *Il Museo del Pizzo al Tombolo di Rapallo: La manifattura Mario Zennaro, 1908–1969*, Genoa

Pfannschmidt, E.-E., 1975. *Twentieth Century Lace*, London

Seguin, J., 1875. *La Dentelle*, Paris

Yefimova, L. and Belogorskaya, R., 1987. *Russian Embroidery and Lace*, London

The following exhibition catalogues contain substantial texts and/or good illustrations.

Antwerp, Koninklijke Museum, 1981. *Kant uit Belgie van de Zestiende Eeuw tot Heden* (exhibition of Belgian lace arranged by M. Coppens)

Brussels, 1990. *Les Dentelles royales* (exhibition of lace associated with the Belgian royal family arranged by M. Coppens)

Burano, Consorzio de Merletti, 1981. *Le Scuola dei Merletti di Burano* (exhibition illustrating the history of the Burano Lace School)

Burano, Consorzio de Merletti, 1982. *Diafano capriccio i merletti nella moda 1877–1922*

Burano, Consorzio de Merletti, 1984. *Cinque secoli di merletti europei: i capolavori* (important loan exhibition with sections on lace from throughout Europe, text in Italian, French, English and German)

Florence, Palazzo Davanzati, 1981. *Merletti a Palazzo Davanzati: manifatture europee dal XVI al XX secolo* (exhibition based on the Museum's collection by M. Carmignani)

Hamburg, Museum für Kunst und Gewerbe, 1987. *Spitzen* (exhibition based on the museum's collection by M. Gräfin Preysing)

Lyon, Musée Historique des Tissus, 1983. *Dentelles au Musée Historique des Tissus* (text by A. Kraatz and E. Gaudry)

Milan, Poldi Pezzoli Museum, 1977. *I Pizzi: modo e simbolo* (exhibition based on the museum's collection, text by A. M. Molfino and M.-T. Binaghi-Olivari)

New York, Cooper-Hewitt Museum, 1982. *Lace in the Collection of the Cooper-Hewitt Museum* (text by M. Sonday)

Paris, Musée de la Mode et du Costume, 1983. *Modes en dentelles, 1590–1983* (text by A. Kraatz and M. Delpierre)

Tokyo and Kyoto, Musée Nationale d'Art Moderne, 1987. *Dentelles européennes* (loan exhibition of lace from the Musée d'Art & d'Histoire, Brussels with text by M. Coppens)

Utrecht, Central Museum, 1985. *Lace in Fashion: Fashion in Lace, 1815–1914* (text by P. Wardle and M. de Jong)

Printed textiles

Albrecht-Mathey, E., 1968. *The Fabrics of Mulhouse and Alsace 1750–1800*, Leigh-on-Sea

Brédif, J., 1989. *Toiles de Jouy: Classic Printed Textiles from France 1760–1843*, London

Clouzot, H., 1928. *Histoire de la manufacture de Jouy et de la toile imprimée en France*, Paris and Brussels

Floud, P., 1960 (a). *English Printed Textiles*, London

Floud, P., 1960 (b). 'The origins of English calico printing', *Journal of the*

Society of Dyers and Colourists, vol. LXXVI, May, pp. 275–81

Floud, P. and Morris, B., 1957, six articles on English printed textiles of the late eighteenth and early nineteenth centuries in *Antiques*, vol. LXXI, March, April, May, June, September, October

Irwin, J. and Brett, K.B., 1970. *The Origins of Chintz*, London

Jacqué, J., 1978. *Chefs d'Oeuvre du Musée de l'Impression sur Étoffes*, Mulhouse, Tokyo

King, D., 1962. 'Textiles and the origins of printing in Europe', *Pantheon, Internationale Zeitschrift für Kunst*, Munich, vol. XX, pp. 23–30

Montgomery, F.M., 1970. *Printed Textiles: English and American Cottons and Linens 1700–1850*, London

Mulhouse, Musée de l'Impression sur Étoffes, 1977. *Toiles de Nantes* (exhibition catalogue)

Parry, L., 1983. *William Morris Textiles*, London

Parry, L., 1988. *Textiles of the Arts and Crafts Movement*, London

Robinson, S., 1969. *A History of Printed Textiles*, London

Schoeser, M., 1986. *Fabrics and Wallpapers*, London

Schoeser, M., 1991. *French Textiles from 1760 to the Present*, London

'Textile printing in eighteenth-century France', 1940. *CIBA Review*, Basel, no. XXXI

CENTRAL AND EASTERN EUROPE

Eastern Europe

Fel, E., 1976. *Peasant Embroidery*, Budapest (text in Hungarian)

Kress, M., 1979. *The Art of the Hungarian Furriers*, Budapest

Oprescu, G., 1929. *Peasant Art in Roumania*, Special issue of *The Studio*, London

Peasant Art in Austria and Hungary, 1911. Special issue of *The Studio*, London

Peasant Art in Russia, 1912. Special issue of *The Studio*, London

Snowden, J., 1979. *The Folk Dress of Europe*, London

Start, L. E., 1939. *The Durham Collection of Garments and Embroideries from Albania and Yugoslavia*, Halifax

Yefimova, L. and Belogorskaya, R., 1987. *Russian Embroidery and Lace*, London

Greece, the Greek Islands and Albania

Chatzimichali, A., 1925. *Skyros*, Greek Popular Art Series, Athens

Chatzimichali, A., 1930. *Epirus*, Greek Popular Art Series, Yanina

Chatzimichali, A., 1931. *Roumlouki, Trikeri and Icaria*, Greek Popular Art Series, Athens

Gentles, M., 1951. *Embroideries from the Burton Yost Berry Collection*, Chicago

Hennig, U., 1986. *Rhodos Stickerein*, Dresden

Johnstone, P., 1961. *Greek Island Embroidery*, London

Johnstone, P., 1972. *A Guide to Greek Island Embroidery*, London

Liverpool, Public Museum, 1956. *Mediterranean Embroideries from Professor Alan J. B. Wace* (exhibition catalogue, text by E. Tankard)

MacMillan, S.L., n.d. *Greek Islands Embroideries*, Boston

Montesanto, M., 1928. *L'isola dei Gigli*, Rome

Montesanto, M., 1928. *La città sacra*, Rome

Montesanto, M., 1930–31. 'Il ricamo nelle Sporadi', *Dedalo*, Rome, vol. XI

Pesel, L. F., 1906–7. 'Cretan embroidery', *Burlington Magazine*, vol. X

Pesel, L. F., 1907. 'Embroideries of the Aegean', *Burlington Magazine*, vol. X

Pesel, L. F., 1907. 'The so-called "Janina" embroideries', *Burlington Magazine*, vol. XI

Trilling, J., 1983. *Aegean Crossroads*, Washington, DC

Wace, A.J.B., 1914. *Catalogue of a Collection of Old Embroideries of the Greek Islands and Turkey*, London

Wace, A.J.B., 1935. *Mediterranean and Near East Embroideries from the Collection of Mrs F. H. Cook*, London

Wace, A.J.B., with Dawkins, R.M., 1914. 'Greek embroideries, 1 & 2. *Burlington Magazine*, vol. XXVI

THE AMERICAS

Colonial North America (1700–1990s)

A good recently published bibliography may be found in Sheridan, C.M. (ed.), 1987, 'Textile manufacturing in American history: a bibliography', *Textile History*, vol. XVIII, no. 1, pp. 59–86. References to specific details can be further studied in the following works.

Affleck, D.L.F., 1987. *Just New From the Mills: Printed Cottons in America*, North Andover, Mass.

Atwater, M.M., 1928. *The Shuttle-craft Book of American Handweaving*, New York, fifth ed. 1951 (for contemporary, not historical, accounts)

Bishop, J.L., 1861–4. *A History of American Manufactures from 1608–1860*, 2 vols, Philadelphia

Blum, D., 1989. 'Nineteenth-century appliqué quilts', *Bulletin*, Philadelphia Museum of Art, fall

Dunwell, S., 1978. *The Run of the Mill*, Boston

King, E.W., 1960. 'William Ashton and his collection of early American textiles', *American Fabrics*, vol. XLIX, Spring, pp. 92–3

Lesser, G., 1989. *École du Meuble 1930–1950: Interior Design and Decorative Art in Montreal*, Montreal

Lyle, D.S., 1976. *Modern Textiles*, New York

Mahon, R., 1984. *The Politics of Industrial Restructuring: Canadian Textiles*, Toronto

Schoeser, M., 1989. *English and American Textiles from 1790 to the Present*, London

Tryon, R.M., 1917. *Household Manufactures in the United States, 1640–1860*, Chicago

Wade's Fibre and Fabric, 1885– . Boston periodical

Walton, F.L., 1945. *The Thread of Victory*, New York

Young, T.M., 1903. *The American Cotton Industry*, New York

Native North America

Amsden, C.A., 1934. *Navaho Weaving: Its Technic and History*, Santa Ana, Cal.

Ashwell, R., 1978. *Coast Salish: Their Art, Culture and Legends*, Saanichton, BC, and Seattle

Berlant, A. and Kahlenberg, M.H., 1972. *The Navajo Blanket*, New York

Dockstader, F.J., 1987. *The Song of the Loom: New Traditions in Navajo Weaving*, New York

Holm, B., 1982. 'A wooling mantle neatly wrought: the early historic record of Northwest Coast pattern-twined textiles – 1774–1850', *American Indian Art Magazine*, Scottsdale, Ariz., vol. VIII, no. 1

Kent, K.P., 1981. 'Pueblo weaving', *American Indian Art Magazine*, Scottsdale, Ariz., vol. VII, no. 1 (textile issue)

Kent, K.P., 1983 (a). *Prehistoric Textiles of the Southwest*, Albuquerque

Kent, K.P., 1983 (b). *Pueblo Indian Textiles: A Living tradition*, Santa Fe

Matthews, W., 1884. *Navajo Weavers*, Third Annual Report of the Bureau of Ethnology to the Secretary of the Smithsonian Institution 1881–1882, Washington, DC, pp. 371–91

Maxwell, G. S., 1963. *Navajo Rugs – Past, Present & Future*, Palm Springs, Cal.

Ritzenthaler, R.E. and Peterson, F. A., 1956. *The Mexican Kickapoo Indians*, Milwaukee Public Museum Publications in Anthropology, no. II, Milwaukee

Rodee, M.E., 1987. *Weaving of the Southwest*, West Chester, Penn.

Rodee, M.E., 1989. 'Modern eye dazzlers: weaving of the Alamo Navajo', *American Indian Art Magazine*, Scottsdale, Ariz., vol. XIV, no. 3

Samuel, C., 1982. *The Chilkat Dancing Blanket*, Seattle

Samwell, D., 1967. *The Journals of Captain James Cook on his Voyages of Discovery: The Voyages of the 'Resolution' and 'Discovery', 1776–1779*, ed. J. C. Beaglehale, Cambridge, vol. II

Skinner, A., 1921. *Material Culture of the Menomini*, Museum of the American Indian, Heye Foundation, Notes and Monographs no. XX, New York

Spinden, H.J., 1908. 'The Nez Perce Indians', *Memoirs of the American Anthropological Association*, vol. II, pp. 165–274

Tanner, C.L., 1976. *Prehistoric Southwestern Craft Arts*, Tucson, Ariz.

Whiteford, A.H., 1977, 1978. 'Fiber bags of the Great Lakes Indians', parts I, II and III. *American Indian Art Magazine*, Scottsdale, Ariz., vol. III, no. 3, vol. III, no. 1 and vol. III, no. 2

Wyman, A., 1935. *Cornhusk Bags of the Nez Perce Indians*, Southwest Museum Leaflets, Los Angeles, vol. IX, no. 1, pp. 89–95

Latin America

Adelson, L. and Tracht, A., 1983. *Aymara Weavings: Ceremonial Textiles of Colonial and Nineteenth-century Bolivia*, Washington, DC

Anawalt, P.R., 1981. *Indian Clothing before Cortés: Mesoamerican Costumes from the Codices*, Norman, Oklahoma

Bird, J., 1973. *Fibres and Spinning Procedures in the Andean Area*, Washington, DC

Broadbent, S., 1985. 'Chibcha textiles in the British Museum', *Antiquity* (notes and news), Cambridge

Cordry, D. B. and Cordry, D.M., 1968. *Mexican Indian Costumes*, Austin

Deuss, K., 1981. *Indian Costumes from Guatemala*, London

Farabee, W.C., 1922. 'Indian tribes of Eastern Peru', *Papers of the Peabody Museum*, Cambridge, Mass., vol. x

Feltham, J., 1979. *Peruvian Textiles*, Aylesbury

Keatings, R. W., 1988. *Peruvian Pre-History*, Cambridge

Lechuga, R. D., 1982. *El traje indigena de México: su evolución dese la época prehispánica hasta la actualidad*, Mexico City

Le Count, C., 1990. *Andean Folk Knitting, Traditions and Techniques from Peru and Bolivia*, St Paul, Minn.

O'Neale, L. M., 1945. *Textiles of Highland Guatemala*, Washington, DC

Osborne, L. de J., 1965. *Indian Crafts of Guatemala and El Salvador*, Norman, Oklahoma

Pettersen, C. L., 1976. *The Maya of Guatemala*, Seattle and London

Puls, H., 1988. *Textiles of the Kuna Indians of Panama*, Aylesbury

Rowe, A. P., 1977. *Warp-Patterned Weaves of the Andes*, Washington, DC

Rowe, A. P., 1984. *Costumes and Featherwork of the Lords of Chimor*, Washington, DC

Sayer, C., 1988. *Mexican Textile Techniques*, Aylesbury

Sayer, C., 1990 (a). *Mexican Textiles*, London

Sayer, C., 1990 (b). *Mexican Patterns: A Design Source Book*, London

Steward, J. H. (ed.), 1946–59. *Handbook of South American Indians*, vols I–VII, Washington, DC

AFRICA

North Africa

Besancenot, J., 1942. *Costumes of Morocco*, trans. C. E. M. Stone. Aix-en-Provence. Reprinted 1990

Encyclopaedia of Islam, second edition, 1972– , under various headings (e.g. harir/silk, kattan/linen, kutn/cotton, libas/clothing, suf/wool, tiraz/embroidery), Leiden

Guérard, M., 1967, 1968, 1969, 1974, 1978–9. Articles in *Hespéris Tamuda*: vol. VIII, pp. 5–22 (Fès); vol. IX, pp. 123–56 (Fès–Aleuj et Rabat); vol. X, no. 1, pp. 191–216 (Tétouan et Alger); vol. XV, pp. 225–50 (Chéchaouan); vol. XVIII, pp. 211–32 (Salé)

Lombard, M., 1978. *Les Textiles dans le monde musulman VII–XIIe siècle*, Paris

London, Victoria and Albert Museum, 1935. *Catalogue of Algerian Embroideries*

Masmoudi, M., 1978. *Les Costumes traditionnels feminins de Tunisie*, Tunis

Reswick, I., 1985. *Traditional Textiles of Tunisia*, Los Angeles

Revault, J., 1960. 'Broderies tunisiennes', *Cahiers de Tunisie*, vol. VIII, pp. 137–57

Revault, J., with Poinssot, L., 1937–57. *Tapis Tunisiens*, 4 vols (with allied textiles), Paris

Ricard, P., 1923. *Corpus des tapis marocains*, 4 vols, Paris

Sergeant, R. B., 1972, *Islamic Textiles: Material for a History up to the Mongol Conquest*, Beirut

Stone, C., 1985. *The Embroideries of North Africa*, London

Sub-Saharan Africa and the offshore islands

Aronson, L., 1980. 'Patronage and Akwete weaving', *African Arts*, vol. XIII

Barbour, J. and Simmonds, D. (eds), 1971. *Adire Cloth in Nigeria*, Ibadan

Bedaux, R. M. A. and Bolland, R., 1980–1. 'Medieval textiles from the Tellem Caves in central Mali', *Textile Museum Journal*, Washington, DC, vols XIX–XX, pp. 65–74

Bravmann, R. E., 1983. *African Islam*, Washington, DC

Davison, P. and Harries, P., 1980. 'Cotton weaving in South-east Africa: its history and technology', in Idiens, D. and Ponting, K. (eds), *Textiles of Africa*, Bath

Easmon, M. C. F., 1924. *Sierra Leone Country Cloths*, London

Gilfoy, P. S., 1988. *Patterns of Life: West African Strip-Weaving Traditions*, Washington, DC

Griaule, M., 1965. *Conversations with Ogotemmeli*, Oxford

Heathcote, D., 1976. *The Arts of the Hausa*, London

Johnson, M., 1980. 'Cloth as money; the cloth strip currencies of Africa', in Idiens, D. and Ponting, K. (eds), *Textiles of Africa*, Bath

Lamb, V., 1975. *West African Weaving*, London

Lamb, V. and Holmes, J., 1980. *Nigerian Weaving*, Hertingfordbury

Lamb, V. and Lamb, A., 1980. 'The classification and distribution of horizontal treadle looms in sub-Saharan Africa', in Idiens, D. and Ponting, K. (eds), *Textiles of Africa*, Bath

Lamb, V. and Lamb, A., 1982. *Cameroun Weaving*, Hertingfordbury

Lamb, V. and Lamb, A., 1984. *Sierra Leone Weaving*, Hertingfordbury

Loir, H., 1935. 'Le Tissage du raphia au Congo Belge', *Annales du Musée du Congo Belge*, série III, vol. III, no. 1

Mack, J., 1986. *Madagascar, Island of the Ancestors*, London

Mack, J., 1989. *Malagasy Textiles*, Princes Risborough

Menzel, B., 1972. *Textilien aus Westafrika*, Berlin

Muller, H. P. N. and Snelleman, J. F., 1893. *Industrie des Cafres du sud-est de l'Afrique*, Leiden

Nicklin, K., 1980. 'Annang Ibibio raphia weaving', in Idiens, D. and Ponting, K. (eds), *Textiles of Africa*, Bath

Picton, J. and Mack, J., 1989. *African Textiles*, second impression, London

Ross, D., 1979. *Fighting with Art: Appliqued Flags of the Fante Asafo*, Los Angeles

Glossary

This is not intended to be a comprehensive vocabulary of technical terms for textiles. It contains only words which are used in the text but are not properly explained, either in Section I (Survey of Textile Techniques) or in the geographical survey (Section II). For embroidery stitches mentioned in the text, the reader is referred to the technical works listed in the bibliography under embroidery.

ANILINE DYES Aniline is a chemical base which yields many colours, though it is itself a colourless, oily, aromatic liquid. Now obtained from coal-tar, it was originally made by distilling indigo with caustic potash. The development of aniline dyestuffs was the high point of nineteenth-century dye research.

ANKH An ancient Egyptian life symbol, in the form of a cross with a looped top, it was later adopted by the Coptic Christian church.

APPLIQUÉ The application of fabrics cut to certain shapes, or of embroidered motifs, to the surface of a ground material to form a design.

AZUTE Stoles of coarse cotton tulle worked with patterns (generally geometric) of gold or silver by pushing strips of metal through the weave of the cloth. They were made in Egypt, especially in the 1920s, for the European market and were popular as souvenirs.

BANDHANA A tie-dyed silk or cotton cloth in which the design appears as tiny spots of white or light colour on a darker ground, caused by tying the spots tightly with a cotton thread before dyeing to resist the penetration of the dye. A *bandhana* may be made in two or three colours by dyeing the lightest colour first (usually yellow), then tying additional spots or areas for each successive colour.

BOBBIN NET Originally any form of mesh ground made with lace bobbins but, after the invention of John Heathcoat's bobbin-net machine in 1809 (see p. 220), the term was confined to machine-made net.

BROCATELLE A lampas-woven fabric with silk warps that is characterised by a marked relief of the warp-faced weave. This results from the use of coarse linen ground weft and silk pattern wefts, and from the appropriate tensions between warps and wefts (cf. LAMPAS).

BRODERIE ANGLAISE A type of CUTWORK embroidery which was developed in Britain in the mid-nineteenth century. It was worked with soft white MERCERISED cotton thread on fine cotton or linen and consists of a formalised pattern of round and oval holes. The edges of the holes are tightly overcast and the rest of the design is worked in padded satin stitch with a small amount of stem stitch. It was used particularly for decorating babies' and children's dresses and caps, the hems of nightgowns, etc.

BUNMEI KAIKA 'Civilisation and Enlightenment', a phrase coined to express the vogue for Western culture and customs during the early Meiji period in Japan.

BURATO From the Latin *bura*, meaning coarse cloth. An open gauze-weave fabric made in Italy and used like hand-made knotted net (LACIS) as a ground for embroidery.

BURNT-OUT (lace) A form of machine embroidery developed in the 1880s in which the pattern is worked in a vegetable fibre on a silk ground; the latter is then burnt out with caustic soda or chlorine. The technique is particularly effective in producing imitation needle lace and crochet. Burnt-out lace is also known as chemical lace.

BŪTĀ A conventional flowering plant, usually with a drooping bud or flower at the top, which traditionally appears as the main border-motif on Indian garment-cloths and other textiles.

BŪTĪ A miniature flowering plant or flowering sprig, used as a motif in the all-over pattern of the field in many Indian textiles.

CAFTAN A full-length outer robe worn in various Islamic countries. The Turkish version fastens in front and has short or long sleeves, the latter sometimes detachable.

CALENDERED A sub-pattern heat-stamped on to the ground of thin fabric such as TAFFETA.

CALICO The name derives from Calicut, a port on the west coast of India, south of Madras, where textiles were collected for shipment by the East India Company. The name was applied to Indian cotton cloth, whether coarse or fine, woven with coloured stripes or checks, painted or printed. In modern usage calico generally refers to cottons printed with small-scale patterns, especially dress goods.

CALIPH (Arabic: Khalifa) Originally a lieutenant of the Prophet, later the spiritual and temporal leader of Islam.

CARTOUCHE Oval medallion framing a pharaoh's regnal name.

CHINA RIBBON Very narrow coloured ribbon, no wider than 1.5 mm (0.16 inch), which was used as the thread in a type of embroidery fashionable during the nineteenth century.

CHINTZ From the Hindi word *chint*, meaning variegated, chintz was applied in the Indian trade either to printed or painted calicoes. In modern usage chintz generally refers to cotton printed with large-scale floral designs, usually glazed and especially suited to furnishings.

CLOTH STITCH (*toilé*) The solid areas of bobbin laces worked in a manner which gives the impression of a more or less even weave.

COPT From the Greek *Aigyptios*, and later Arabic *Qibt*, to designate native Egyptians, the term was later used to define Christians in Egypt.

CUTWORK Originally an APPLIQUÉ of cut-out shapes, the name was transferred to embroidery in which parts of the ground were cut away. From the mid-sixteenth century it became the generic name for all forms of needle lace based on a woven ground.

DIASPER From the Latin *diasprum*, derived from a family of adjectives found in documents dated between the ninth and twelfth centuries and perhaps indicating monochrome silks woven in two shades of a particular colour. By the late thirteenth century *diasprum* was being applied to a group of LAMPAS silks, often woven with a tabby pattern upon a tabby ground and with details brocaded in gold thread (cf. King, 1960, *passim*).

DIMITY A white cotton fabric in tabby weave, often with a slight corded self-stripe. At various times it has been thick or thin and could also be patterned with coloured satin stripes, or even flowered. Originally imported from India, from the eighteenth century it was also made in Lancashire and later the USA.

FILÉ THREAD Gold or silver thread formed by a narrow strip of gilt (or silvered) paper, parchment, membrane or metal, wrapped around a core thread of linen, cotton or silk.

FILET French name for LACIS, which it replaced in the late nineteenth century as the accepted international name for hand-made knotted net.

FIVE-SHAFT SATIN Satin weave in which the weft thread passes over four warp threads and under one.

FLOSS SILK Raw and untwisted silk thread made from the soft external covering of the silkworm's cocoon. As it is untwisted the threads lie closely and evenly together, making it suitable for long-and-short stitch where the shades must blend in evenly.

GAUZE A weave in which the binding is achieved by the displacement of warp ends. On the simplest looms, this is done by twisting the warp threads as weaving progresses. On more complex looms, warp ends called doup ends are made to cross over other warp ends called fixed ends. There are many variations, according to the complexity of the movements made by the doup ends in relation to the fixed ends. The resulting fabric is generally (but not always) an open weave.

GEISHA In Japan, a female entertainer trained in the arts of classical music and dance, aesthetic pastimes and witty conversation.

GIMP A silk- or metal-wrapped cord. Also, a baroque bobbin lace which incorporates such cords.

HEALD-STICK A very simple device for obtaining the shed on primitive looms, the heald-stick (sometimes called the sword-stick) is a flat stick, shaped to a curved point at one end. The threads are passed over and under the heald-stick; when turned on its side, a shed is obtained. The return-shed is obtained by taking out the heald-stick and re-threading it through the alternating threads. Patterns may be hand-picked or picked using the heald-stick.

INLAID/INTARSIA Carefully cut segments of fabric are set into identically shaped openings cut out of a ground fabric to form a design. Generally secured by stitching, the inlaid segments may also be secured to a lining fabric by means of adhesives.

ITALIAN QUILTING A design consisting of a pair of parallel lines is run or back-stitched through two layers of fabric, and then a soft cord is inserted between the two layers and the double lines in order to bring the design into relief.

JOK A Lao term for supplementary weft-patterning where the weft threads of the design are inserted by hand.

KA'ABA The square, embroidery-draped building at Mecca which marks the site of Abraham's sacrifice. The holiest place in Islam, it is the chief goal of the annual pilgrimage (hajj).

KABUKI A spectacular and flamboyant style of dance-drama in Japan, dating from the seventeenth century.

KALAMKĀRI Literally, 'pen-work' or 'brush-work', the painted and dyed cotton cloths of India. The process is complex, involving the painting of the mordants and then dyeing in an alizarin-based dye bath to obtain a range of reds, violets, browns and black. Where blue or dark green is required, the cloth is protected by coating it with wax to act as a resist, before a separate dyeing in indigo. Yellows and light greens are painted by hand with less fast local vegetable dyes; dark greens are achieved by over-painting

yellow on indigo, orange by over-painting yellow on pale red. The kalamkāri processes are aided by careful preparation of the cotton cloth to produce a smooth, firm surface, and by the use of the fruits and seeds of other plants as astringents in which the cloth is steeped before painting.

KAMISHIMO Formal male Japanese samurai attire comprising a kataginu, a wide-shouldered waistcoat, and Hakama-style trousers worn over a KOSODE.

KERMES From qirmiz, the Arabic name for the shield-louse which lives on a sub-tropical species of oak. The dried and ground bodies of pregnant females yield a brilliant and fast scarlet dye which has been known and used since ancient times.

KIMONO The principal Japanese garment worn by both male and female, the kimono is normally cut from a piece of fabric 12–13 m (39–42 ft) long and 36–7 cm (14–14.5 in) wide. All the seams are straight and the standardised pattern (see p. 150) varies only in the cut and length of the sleeve. With no fastenings, the kimono is wrapped around the body and secured with an obi (sash) in a variety of styles.

KOSODE A KIMONO with small wrist openings, the kosode was the principal Japanese outer garment from the Muromachi period and the ancestor of the modern kimono.

KUFIC A term deriving from an erroneous ascription to Kufa in Mesopotamia, it refers to the monumental script of the early Korans and other Muslim inscriptions – thick, compressed and angular, and often discontinuous.

LACIS An ancient technique in which hand-made knotted net is decorated with embroidery.

LAMPAS A figured textile whose pattern is created by a supplementary pattern or brocading weft, held in place by a binding warp, resting upon the ground weave produced by a main warp and ground weft. During the Middle Ages particular lampas weaves were denoted by specific historic terms (cf. DIASPER).

MAHABARATA A Hindu epic which chronicles the inter-familial feud between the Kurawas and the Pendawas.

MANDALA A visual representation of the universe, portraying Buddhist deities or their symbols in hierarchical order, which is made and used in acts of Buddhist worship.

MANTA Spanish term used in Latin America after the Conquest to describe Indian mantles and webs of cloth. Today it signifies unbleached cotton cloth or calico.

MERCERISED THREAD (perlé) A method of treating cotton thread with a solution of caustic soda which both strengthens it and gives it a silky lustre, discovered in 1844 by John Mercer (1791–1866), a dye chemist from Accrington in England.

MINAKĀRI Literally, 'enamelled work', the name given to a style of brocade weaving in Rajasthan and central India, where the pattern is brocaded in coloured silks on a field filled with weft of silver or silver-gilt thread. Minakāri is used chiefly for the borders and end-borders of garment-cloths such as SĀRĪS and orhnīs.

MOIRÉ Term used to describe textiles in which a rippled or watered effect is produced, by pressing certain warp rib fabrics in such a way as to flatten parts of the ribs and leave the rest in relief, so that the flattened and unflattened parts reflect the light differently.

MULHĀM Literally, 'permitted'. A mixed-fibre weave, with silk warp and cotton weft, it was worn in response to a prohibition against men wearing silk.

MUREX A species of shellfish yielding a purple dye used from antiquity up to the fifteenth century, when it was replaced by KERMES, cochineal and madder. Because of the enormous number of shellfish required – about 8000 to obtain 1g (0.035 oz) of dye – the dye was very costly and its use often signified political power and social status.

NOH An other-worldly, Zen-influenced style of Japanese dance-drama dating from the fourteenth century.

OGIVE/OGIVAL A nineteenth-century European term for a pointed architectural arch. In pattern design it refers to two arches joined, with points at each end, to form a single frame repeat.

ŌSODE A KIMONO with wide wrist openings in the style worn at the imperial court of Japan since the Heian period.

PAHLAVI The ancient Persian language.

PALMETTE A formalised plant form – flower, leaf, or fruit – cut longitudinally to reveal inner seeds.

PASSEMENTERIE A term used for trimmings of all descriptions – gold and silver lace, braids, GIMP, beaded edgings, tinsel, gold, silver and jet.

PATCHWORK The piecing together of fragments of material to make a pattern. The pieces may be regular or irregular shapes (as in crazy patchwork).

PATOLA A silk SĀRĪ woven in Gujarat by the double ikat technique. Traditionally, the patola is a marriage SĀRĪ in some communities of Gujarat.

POINT NET A patterned loop net made, from 1769, on the stocking frame.

RAMAYANA A Hindu epic which tells of the abduction of Sita by the demon Ravanna and her eventual recovery by her husband Rama and his brother Laksmana.

REPEAT The measurements in length and width according to which a pattern unit is repeated. A half-drop repeat is the repetition of a pattern unit by dropping it, in relation to its neighbour, by half the length of the unit. A mirror repeat is the repetition of a pattern unit by reversing it about an axis parallel to the warp.

RICHELIEU EMBROIDERY A type of whitework in which the design is first outlined in buttonhole stitch, the fabric is then cut away and the spaces joined with stitched bars.

SAMITE A medieval term denoting a kind of plain or figured silk, derived from the Latin (*examitum*, *samitum*) and from the Greek (*hexamitos*). The face and the reverse of the cloth are covered by weft floats bound in a 1:2 twill, by a binding warp, while the main warps lie concealed within the material. The warp sett comprises six threads, alternating one main with one binding warp.

SĀRĪ Long garment-cloth forming the dress of the women in many parts of India. The *sārī* is pleated around a tight waist-cord to form a long skirt falling to the ankles; the free end, which is usually decorated, is then draped up over the back to fall gracefully over the head or over one shoulder.

SA-SI-GYO Long ribbons used to bind sacred Buddhist texts in Burma. They are often patterned with the donor's titles and pious aspirations.

SATRAPY An Iranian province, whose governor was called a satrap.

SHADOW WORK An embroidery technique producing a muted effect of colour, it is always worked from the back in closed herringbone stitch in a strongly coloured thread on to a sheer fabric. From the front the design appears in outline as a row of back stitches with the colour of the closed herringbone stitch softly muted.

SHOGUN The head of a Japanese military dictatorship. Throughout the Edo period the Tokugawa family ruled Japan as shoguns, with only nominal subservience to the Emperor as head of state.

SLIP Literally, a 'plant cutting'. Slips illustrating sixteenth-century engraved books were adapted to embroidery, particularly in Elizabethan England.

SOUMAK(H) Named after the town of Sumakh (Shemakha) in the eastern Caucasus, the term refers to a construction with one warp and a weft that does not pass through a shed but is carried manually over a group of warp ends, then passed under and back around part of the group. The process is repeated with successive groups of warp ends across the width. On one face, the weft floats are at right angles to the warp, but on the other they cross obliquely. Soumak may be patterned using weft threads of different colours for different areas, and is sometimes used for brocading. In rug weaving, one or two tabby picks are usually beaten in after each or every other row of soumak weft.

SPANDREL Architectural term for the triangular space between the point of an arch and the nearest corner.

SPINDLE WHEEL The tool used for spinning thread.

SUPPLEMENTARY WARP-/WEFT-PATTERNING The use of the term supplementary in describing either warps or wefts indicates that they are non-structural elements added to create a pattern or enrich a ground weave.

TABLET WEAVING A method of weaving using a number of tablets or cards pierced with holes through which the warp ends are threaded. The sheds for the passage of the weft are made by rotating the cards. Depending upon the number of holes in the cards, the method of threading the warp ends and the method of rotating the cards, many types of weave may be produced. However, as the number of warp ends is limited by the number of tablets that can be operated conveniently, tablet weaving is normally used for braids, belts, etc.

TAFFETA Crisp, closely woven cloth of silk or silk-like fibres such as rayon.

TAMBOUR WORK A technique by which surface chain stitches are formed with the aid of a hooked needle, often used to decorate machine net.

TIRĀZ Textiles produced in government workshops, often with woven bands of calligraphy for presentation as official gifts.

TULIS Indonesian term for hand-drawn batik.

TURKIC Turkish-speaking peoples, not necessarily from Anatolia.

WARP-LOCKING (end-to-end) Short warp threads, generally of different colours, are linked together.

WATERED See MOIRÉ.

WEFT-WRAPPING A weave in which the weft does not pass through a shed but is carried around the warp ends in turn. Usually the weft wraps single warp ends, but the term is also used in a general sense to cover wrapping in groups, and in this sense it is synonymous with SOUMAK.

ZOROASTRIANISM The worship of the god Ahuramazda ('The Wise Lord') through the ancient Persian prophet Zoroaster. A central belief (dualism) is that humankind contains both good and evil as two equal sides.

Illustration acknowledgements

Illustrations are reproduced by courtesy and kind permission of the following. Abbreviations: BM (Trustees of the British Museum); BL (Trustees of the British Library Board); MISE, Mulhouse (Musée de l'Impression sur Etoffes); MMA (The Metropolitan Museum of Art, New York); PMA (Philadelphia Museum of Art); TM (The Textile Museum, Washington, DC); V&A (Board of Trustees of the V&A); WAG (The Whitworth Art Gallery, University of Manchester, photos Peter Burton/Michael Pollard). Figure artwork by Technical Art Services (fig. 18 after Larsen 1976; fig. 20 after D. K. Burnham 1980).

TITLE PAGES WAG (T.9260; T.11453; T.11910)
CONTENTS WAG (T.8223)
1 WAG (T.9508)
2 WAG (T.11810)
3 Manchester Museum, University of Manchester (382.1968)
4 WAG (T.18.1989)
5 Slovak National Museum, photo Velke Krtiš, courtesy Sheila Paine
6 Trustees of the Wallace Collection, London
7 Petrie Museum, University College London (UC.9547), photo courtesy Ann Hecht
8 Ashmolean Museum, Oxford (G249)
9 MMA (30.7.3), Anonymous Gift, 1930
10 Photo courtesy WAG
11 Eva Wilson (*Ancient Egyptian Designs*, London, 1986)
12 Master and Fellows of Trinity College Cambridge (MS.0.9.34, fol. 32v)
13 V&A (D.1656–1904)
14 BL (vol. I, pl. 9, fig. 513, p. 120)
15 WAG (T.11884)
16 WAG (T.11848)
17 WAG (T.8211)
18 WAG (T.93.1987)
19 WAG (T.254.1975)
20 WAG (T.19.1989)
21 WAG (T.11910)
22 BL (vol. 26, pl. IX, fig. 1)
23 Hermitage, St Petersburg
24 Photo courtesy WAG
25 Photo courtesy WAG
26 Michael & Jacqueline Franses
27 WAG (T.26.1986)
28 WAG (T.10036)
29 BL (*Recueil de Planches*, Brodeur, pl. I, figs 1–2)
30 WAG (T.10060)
31 WAG (T.13192)
32 WAG (T.8088)
33 WAG (T.8642)
34 BL (Supplement, pl. XII)
35 MISE, Mulhouse (954.504.2)
36 Photo WAG
37 Photo WAG
38 Stork Screens B.V., Boxmeer, Holland
39 WAG (T.11277)
40 WAG (T.9642)
41 WAG (T.11081)
42 WAG (T.9229)
43 V&A (IS.5440)
44 WAG (T.12398)
45 WAG (T.20.1987)

46 WAG
47 Manchester Museum, University of Manchester, photo Geoff Thompson
48 WAG (T.10.1989)
49 Photo Peter Wallum
50 Photo Ian Skelton, Crafts Council
51 WAG (T.12060)
52 WAG (T.9017)
53 Photo courtesy WAG
54 Egyptian Museum, Cairo (JE46526)
55 Griffith Institute, Ashmolean Museum, Oxford
56 Petrie Museum, University College London (UC.28614B')
57 The Byzantine Collection (29.1), © 1992 Dumbarton Oaks, Trustees of Harvard University
58 WAG (T.8549)
59 WAG (T.8362)
60 WAG (T.8383)
61 Manchester Museum, University of Manchester (252.1968), photo Geoff Thompson
62 BM (EA 43049)
63 WAG (T.8441a)
64 © Detroit Institute of Arts (46.75)
65 Manchester Museum, University of Manchester (395.1968)
66 National Museum, Copenhagen, photo Lennart Larsen
67 Textile Museum, Neumünster (699)
68 Photo courtesy WAG; BM (WAA 124095)
69 V&A (8579–1863)
70 Musée Historique des Tissus, Lyons (26812/10)
71 Basilica San Ambrogio, Milan
72 TM (73.366)
73 WAG (T.10016)
74 Musée Historique de Lorrain, Nancy (95-1584), photo © Gilbert Mangin
75 Kunsthistorisches Museum, Vienna (KK21)
76 Cathedral Treasury, Sens
77 Schloss Köpenick, Berlin
78 Musée Historique des Tissus, Lyons
79 St Servatius, Maastricht
80 Munster Treasury, Aachen
81 Diocesan Museum, Bamberg
82 Diocesan Museum, Mainz
83 TM (3.219), Acquired by George Hewitt Myers
84 Museum of Fine Arts, Boston (28.13), Gift of Mrs Walter Scott Fitz
85 TM (3.312), Acquired by George Hewitt Myers
86 Royal Ontario Museum, Toronto (962.00.1)
87 Livrustkammaren, Hallwylska Museet, Stockholm (3414)
88 Museum of Applied Arts, Budapest (52.2801)
89 TM (3.94), Acquired by George Hewitt Myers
90 WAG (T.10941)
91 TM (1.70)
92 Topkapi Palace Museum, Istanbul
93 Topkapi Palace Museum, Istanbul
94 Wawel State Art Collection, Krakow (3981)
95 Wawel State Art Collection, Krakow (896)
96 WAG (T.9008)
97 WAG (T.9043)
98 WAG (T.9029)
99 WAG (T.9248)
100 WAG (T.34.1976)

101 V&A (IS.1827-1883; IS.2107; IS.2108; IS.2113)
102 WAG (T.21.1977)
103 BM (IS.2081; IS.9173; IS.2056; IS.2069; IS.5768), photo Daniel McGrath
104 BM (Eth.1966.As.1.65)
105 BM (Eth.1966.As.1.69)
106 BM (Eth.1971.As.10.1; Eth.1968.As.4.19)
107 BM (Eth.1970.As.15.5)
108 BM (Eth.N.1981.As.23.2)
109 BM (Eth.1971.As.1.6)
110 V&A (IM.160-1929)
111 Brooklyn Museum (14.719-2), Special Fund
112 Brooklyn Museum (14.719-6), Special Fund
113 V&A (IS.8358c)
114 V&A (IS.70-1954)
115 V&A (IS.50-1967)
116 Dept of Arts & Libraries, Renfrew District Council (Paisley Museum 43B/1942)
117 V&A (IS.7825)
118 V&A (IS.60-1966)
119 V&A (IS.6105)
120 BM (Eth.N.1984.As.17.1)
121 V&A (1377-1852)
122 BM (Eth.1933.7-15.324)
123 BM (Eth.1933.7-15.317)
124 BM (Eth.1970.As.21.23a)
125 BM (Eth.As.1934.A723.16)
126 BM (Eth.As.1948.A10.34a)
127 TM (R16.1.3)
128 Museum für Islamische Kunst, Staatliche Museen zu Berlin (1.4)
129 National Portrait Gallery, London
130 MMA (17.120.137), Mr & Mrs Isaac D. Fletcher Collection, Bequest of Isaac D. Fletcher, 1917
131 Saint Louis Art Museum (79.1929), Gift of James F. Ballard
132 Photo courtesy Yanni Petsopoulos
133 V&A (272-1893), photo Daniel McGrath
134 MMA (14.40.721), Bequest of Benjamin Altman, 1914
135 Musée des Arts Décoratifs, Paris (38051)
136 Corcoran Gallery of Art, Washington, DC (26.278), William A. Clark Collection
137 Residenz, Munich (W.C.3)
138 WAG (T.85.1975)
139 Glasgow Museums, Burrell Collection (9/38)
140 V&A (T.264-1927)
141 Keir Collection, Richmond (60)
142 Musée Historique des Tissus, Lyons (25.095)
143 TM (R37.1.5)
144 V&A (854-1876)
145 V&A (T.147-1911)
146 Photo Patricia L. Baker
147 MMA (22.100.35), Gift of James F. Ballard, 1922
148 Jingzhou Museum, Hubei
149 Hunan Museum, Changsha
150 Xinjiang Museum, Urumqi
151 Xinjiang Museum, Urumqi
152 Office of the Shōsō-in Treasure House, Nara
153 V&A (Ch.00342; Ch.i.0022), Stein Loan, photo Ian Thomas
154 National Palace Museum, Taipei, Taiwan
155 Peoples' Republic of China
156 Royal Ontario Museum, Toronto

(956.67.2)
157 V&A (FE.41-1985)
158 WAG (T.8837; T.52.1977; T.130.1977)
159 V&A (T.121-1933)
160 Sotheby's, London
161 V&A (T.84-1927)
162 V&A (T.362-1865)
163 Tokugawa Art Museum, Tokyo
164 National Museum of Japanese History
165 V&A (FE.32-1982)
166 BM (JA 1940.11-1.047, 1&2)
167 National Museum of Japanese History
168 V&A (T.325-1960)
169 V&A (Circ. 169-1927)
170 V&A (T.18-1963)
171 V&A (FE.421-1992), photo Ian Thomas
172 Comme des Garçons, Paris, photo Peter Lindbergh
173 Pitt Rivers Museum, Oxford (1899.41.1)
174 TM (1985.7.1), Ruth Lincoln Fisher Fund
175 BM (Eth.As.1936.10-6.2)
176 BM (Eth.As.1950.3.17)
177 Photo Susan Conway (*Thai Textiles*, London, 1992)
178 BM (Eth.As.1910.57)
179 TM (1985.31.4), Ruth Lincoln Fisher Fund
180 BM (Eth.As.1962.2.1)
181 Dept of Anthropology, Smithsonian Institution, Washington, DC (286123)
182 BM (Eth.As.1905.4.10)
183 TM (1990.33.1.)
184 TM (1985.57.8), Gift of Alice Bradley Sheldon, Collector Mary Hastings Bradley
185 BM (Eth.As.1980.8.1)
186 WAG (T.3.1984)
187 Kestner Museum, Hannover (3875)
188 Kunsthistorisches Museum, Vienna
189 V&A (778-1893)
190 V&A (1265-1864)
191 V&A (1304-1864)
192 Keir Collection, Richmond (31)
193 Collection of Mr Humphrey Butler Bowdon, on loan to V&A
194 The Trustees of Stonyhurst College
195 V&A (402-1907)
196 Trustees of the Wallace Collection, London
197 WAG (T.11586)
198 WAG (T.8331)
199 WAG (T.12710)
200 WAG (T.10119; T.10122)
201 Temple Newsam House, Leeds City Art Galleries
202 Musée Historique des Tissus, Lyons (29782)
203 Keir Collection, Richmond (17)
204 Abegg-Stiftung, Riggisberg (669)
205 Musée Historique des Tissus, Lyons (29069)
206 Keir Collection, Richmond (32)
207 Harris Collection, Courtauld Institute of Art, London, photo J. Herald
208 Musée Historique des Tissus, Lyons (33845)
209 Musée Historique des Tissus, Lyons (1456)
210 V&A (T.221-1987)
211 Musée Historique des Tissus, Lyons (25427)

Index